FANGED NOUMENA

NICK LAND

Fanged Noumena

COLLECTED WRITINGS
1987–2007

Edited By

ROBIN MACKAY & RAY BRASSIER

URBANOMIC

sequence

First published in 2011 in an edition of 1000
by

URBANOMIC
THE OLD LEMONADE FACTORY
WINDSOR QUARRY
FALMOUTH TR11 3EX
UNITED KINGDOM

SEQUENCE PRESS
88 ELDRIDGE STREET
NEW YORK
NY 10002
UNITED STATES

Second edition 2012
Third edition 2014
Fourth edition 2017
Fifth edition 2018
Sixth edition 2018
Seventh edition 2019

BRITISH LIBRARY CATALOGUING-IN-PUBLICATION DATA

A full catalogue record of this book is available
from the British Library

ISBN 978-0-9553087-8-9

Distributed by the MIT Press,
Cambridge, Massachusetts and London, England

Printed and bound in the UK by
TJ International, Padstow

www.urbanomic.com
www.sequencepress.com

CONTENTS

List of Sources   vii

Editors' Introduction   1

Kant, Capital, and the Prohibition of Incest: A Polemical
    Introduction to the Configuration of Philosophy
    and Modernity   55

Narcissism and Dispersion in Heidegger's 1953
    Trakl Interpretation   81

Delighted to Death   123

Art as Insurrection: the Question of Aesthetics in Kant,
    Schopenhauer, and Nietzsche   145

Spirit and Teeth   175

Shamanic Nietzsche   203

After the Law   229

Making it with Death: Remarks on Thanatos and
    Desiring-Production   261

Circuitries   289

Machinic Desire   319

CyberGothic   345

Cyberrevolution   375

Hypervirus   383

No Future   391

Cyberspace Anarchitecture as Jungle-War   401

Meat (or How to Kill Oedipus in Cyberspace)   411

Meltdown   441

A zIIg$^{\underline{o}}$thIc–==X=c$^{\underline{o}}$DA==–(C$^{\underline{oo}}$kIng–l$^{\underline{o}}$bsteRs–
    wIth–jAke–AnD–DIn$^{\underline{o}}$s)   461

Kataçonix   481

Barker Speaks: The CCRU Interview with Professor
    D.C. Barker   493

Mechanomics   507

Cryptolith   527

Non-Standard Numeracies:Nomad Cultures   531

Occultures   545

Origins of the Cthulhu Club   573

Introduction to Qwernomics   583

Qabbala 101   591

Tic-Talk   607

Critique of Transcendental Miserablism   623

A Dirty Joke   629

Index of Names   645

Index of Subjects   650

List of Sources

'Kant, Capital, and the Prohibition of Incest' originally appeared in *Third Text* Vol. 2, Issue 5 (Winter 1988/89), 83–94; 'Narcissism and Dispersion in Heidegger's 1953 Trakl Interpretation' first appeared in D. Wood (ed.) *Philosophers' Poets* (London/NY: Routledge, 1990), 70–92; 'Delighted to Death' first appeared in *Pli – The Warwick Journal of Philosophy* Vol. 3, Issue 2 (1991), 76–88; 'Art as Insurrection' first appeared in K. Ansell-Pearson (ed.), *Nietzsche and Modern German Thought* (London: Routledge, 1991), 240–56; 'Spirit and Teeth' first appeared in D. Wood (ed.), *Of Derrida, Heidegger, and Spirit* (Evanston, Il.: Northwestern University Press, 1993), 41–55, copyright © 1993 Northwestern University Press; 'Shamanic Nietzsche' first appeared in P. R. Sedgwick (ed.), *Nietzsche: A Critical Reader* (Oxford: Blackwell, 1995), 158–70; 'After the Law' first appeared in A. Norrie (ed.), *Closure or Critique: New Directions in Legal Theory* (Edinburgh: Edinburgh University Press, 1993), 101–15; 'Making it with Death' first appeared in *Journal of the British Society for Phenomenology*, 24.1 (Jan. 1993), 66–76; 'Circuitries' first appeared in *Pli – The Warwick Journal of Philosophy* Vol. 4, Issue 1/2 (1992), 217–35; 'Machinic Desire' first appeared in *Textual Practice* 7.3 (1993), 471–82; 'Cybergothic' first appeared in J. Broadhurst-Dixon, E. J. Cassidy (eds.), *Virtual Futures* (London: Routledge, 1998), 79–87; 'Cyberrevolution' first appeared in ***Collapse 1 (privately published, Feb. 1995); 'Hypervirus' first appeared in ***Collapse 2 (privately published, May 1995); 'No Future' is a previously unpublished conference paper dating from 1995; 'Cyberspace Anarchitecture as Jungle-War' first appeared in M. Pearce and N. Spiller (eds.), *Architectural Design* 118: *Architects in Cyberspace* (London: Academy Group, 1995), 58–9; 'Meat' first appeared in M. Featherstone and R. Burrows (ed.), *Body & Society,* Vol. 1, No. 3–4 (1995), 191–204; 'Meltdown', presented at *Virtual Futures*, Warwick University, May 1994, first appeared in *Abstract Culture* 1 (first swarm) (Coventry: Cybernetic Culture Research Unit [CCRU], 1997); 'A zIIg$^\alpha$thIc–==X=c^{o}DA==–(C^{oo}kIng–l^{o}bsteRs–wIth–jAke–AnD–DIn^{o}s)' first appeared in J. & D. Chapman, *Chapmanworld* (London: ICA, 1996); 'KataçoniX' is the text from a collaborative multimedia presentation by ***Collapse**, artist collective O(rphan) d(rift>), and 'D^{o}ghead Surgeri', *Virtual Futures '96*, Warwick University, 1996; 'Barker Speaks' first appeared in *Abstract Culture: Hyperstition* (London: CCRU, 1999); 'Mechanomics' first appeared in *Pli – The Warwick Journal of Philosophy* 7 (1998), 55–66; 'Cryptolith' and 'Occultures' are texts from 'Syzygy', a collaboration between CCRU and O(rphan) d(rift>), Beaconsfield, London, Feb–Mar 1999; 'Non-Standard Numeracies' is a previously unpublished text; 'Origins of the Cthulhu Club' was published online by CCRU, probably dating from 1998-9; 'Introduction to Qwernomics', 'Tic Talk', 'A Dirty Joke' and 'Critique of Transcendental Miserablism' are texts posted online between 2005-7; 'Qabbala 101' first appeared in R. Mackay (ed.), *Collapse* vol. 1 (Oxford: Urbanomic, 2006).

The editors would like to thank Michael Carr, Mark Fisher, David Rylance and Reza Negarestani for their help in compiling this volume.

FANGED NOUMENA

Editors' Introduction

Nick Land's writings inhabit a disordered anarchitecture, a space traversed by rat and wolf-vectors, conjuring a schizophrenic metaphysics. Advanced technologies invoke ancient entities; the human voice disintegrates into the howl of cosmic trauma; civilization hurtles towards an artificial death. Sinister musical subcultures are allied with morbid cults, rogue AIs are pursued into labyrinthine crypts by Turing cops, and Europe mushrooms into a paranoia laboratory in a global cyberpositive circuit that reaches infinite density in the year 2012, flipping modernity over into whatever has been piloting it from the far side of the approaching singularity.

Land's writings fold genre in on itself, splicing disparate sources from philosophy, literature, science, occultism, and pulp fiction (Immanuel Kant, William Gibson, Deleuze-Guattari, Norbert Wiener, Kurt Gödel, Kenneth Grant, *Terminator* and *Apocalypse Now*, Antonin Artaud, H.P. Lovecraft ...). The result is a dense, frequently

bewildering vortex of hallucinatory conjunctions, super-
posing multiple pseudonyms, cryptic dates, and experimental coding systems: Cthelll, Axsys, Unlife, A-Death,
K-Space, Sarkon, Kurtz, the Cthulhu Club, Hummpa Taddum; 4077, 1501, 1757, 1949, 1981; Tic-Systems, Primitive
Numerization, Anglossic Qabbala, zygosis... Metaphysics
dissolves into psychotic cosmogony. The history of life on
earth, from bacteria to Microsoft, is the history of suppression. Nameless, the suppressed seethes beneath life's
organized surfaces, locked up in cells, societies, selves,
micro- and macropods, yet breaking out spasmodically
to propel terrestrial history through a series of intensive
thresholds which have been converging towards meltdown. Sole agent of revolution, the Antichrist is not one
but many, a swarm of masked infiltrators from the future,
'poised to eat your TV, infect your bank account, and hack
mitochondria from your DNA'; hooking up desublimated
Eros to synthetic Thanatos in order to accelerate the
obsolescence of humankind.

*

What has all this to do with philosophy? From a certain
point of view – one encouraged by Land himself – nothing, or as little as possible. Land allied himself to a line
of renegade thinkers – Schopenhauer, Nietzsche, Bataille
– who mocked and disparaged academicism and wielded
philosophy as an implement for exacerbating enigma,

disrupting orthodoxy, and transforming existence. Land is probably the most controversial figure to have emerged from the fusty culture of Anglophone philosophy during the past two decades; despite, or perhaps because of this controversy, the texts collected in this volume have languished in near-obscurity until now.

Between 1992, the year of publication of his only book, and 1998, when he resigned his lectureship in Philosophy at the University of Warwick (UK) and abandoned academia, Land accrued a notoriety remarkable in a milieu otherwise typified by stultifying decorum. A divisive, polarizing figure, he provoked both adulation and execration. His jabs at the holy trinity of 'continental philosophy' – phenomenology, deconstruction, and critical theory – drew enmity from his more orthodox peers; and while his virulent anti-humanism affronted philanthropic conservatives, his swipes at institutionalized critique earned him the opprobrium of the academic Left. Marxists in particular were outraged by Land's aggressive championing of the sociopathic heresy urging the 'ever more uninhibited marketization of the processes that are tearing down the social field' – the acceleration, rather than the critique, of capitalism's disintegration of society. And Land's contempt for orthodoxy was no disingenuous pose struck whilst ruthlessly pursuing advancement. With a complete absence of academic ambition, he willingly paid the price for his provocations, both personally and professionally.

Once Land was 'retired', academic orthodoxy quickly and quietly sealed the breach inflicted in its side by his ferocious but short-lived assault, so that within the first few years of the new century, he had become an apocryphal character, more or less forgotten in philosophical circles. Yet Land's writings continued to reverberate outside academia, particularly among artists and writers, who welcomed his vivid reanimation of philosophy as a polemical medium, relished his disregard for the proprieties of sober reflection, and were inspired by his attempt to plunge theory directly into the maelstrom of capitalist modernity.

Nevertheless, given this heteroclite status, it is hardly surprising that many would still rather dismiss Land as an unsavoury aberration, deserving of oblivion. So why republish these texts by a writer whom some would prefer to forget? One could cite the need to expose them to a wider readership than they were afforded at the time, and to provide a more representative profile of Land's intellectual trajectory than that suggested by the single monograph he published during his brief academic career.[1] However the most obvious, albeit cursory, rejoinder to anyone tempted to dismiss Land is the unalloyed brilliance on display in the writings collected here. These extraordinary texts, superheated compounds of severe abstraction and scabrous

---

1 *The Thirst for Annihilation: Georges Bataille and Virulent Nihilism* (London and New York: Routledge, 1992).

wit, testify to a uniquely penetrating intelligence, fusing transcendental philosophy, number theory, geophysics, biology, cryptography, and occultism into startlingly cohesive but increasingly delirious theory-fictions. Fuelled by disgust at the more stupefying inanities of academic orthodoxy and looking to expectorate the vestigial theological superstitions afflicting mainstream post-Kantianism, Land seized upon Deleuze-Guattari's transcendental materialism – years before its predictable institutional neutering – and subjected it to ruthless cybernetic streamlining, excising all vestiges of Bergsonian vitalism to reveal a deviant and explicitly thanatropic machinism. The results of this reconstructive surgery provide the most illuminating but perhaps also the most disturbing distillation of what Deleuze called 'transcendental empiricism'. In Land's work, this becomes the watchword for an experimental praxis oriented entirely towards contact with the unknown. Land sought out this exteriority, the impersonal and anonymous chaos of absolute time, as fervently as he believed Kantianism and Hegelianism, along with their contemporary heirs, deconstruction and critical theory, were striving to keep it out.

What is particularly remarkable is the rigorous consistency with which Land developed the conceptual innovations of Deleuze-Guattari *as* the transdisciplinary innovations they are, rather than recontextualising them (as is, unfortunately, now all too common) within the restricted histories of philosophy, psychoanalysis, or cultural theory. He deployed them in an exacting engagement with the core problematics of modernity: the dialectic of enlightenment, the humiliations of man, technology's procedural automation of the concept, and science's erosion of philosophy's objects and articles of faith.

*

At the core of Land's thought are the works of Immanuel Kant. Land is a brilliant reader of Kant and several of the texts gathered here evince his rare gift for isolating the essential components of Kant's labyrinthine philosophical machinery. Moreover, Land uncovers the source of their conceptual power by demonstrating their productive integration with, and purchase upon, the extra-philosophical.

Exposing an isomorphy between the structures of capital and Kant's model of experience, Land views the 'constant crisis' that drives the tortuous segmentations of Kant's theory of the concept as a miscognised relaying of the 'unconscious' of 'the global Kapital metropolis', stimulated by the latter's 'paradoxical nature': Kant's 'theory of experience' – the question of how the matter of sensation marries with a priori forms of experience to produce novel cognitions – is in fact a working through of the economics of a system that relies on a surplus generated through a disavowed interaction with alterity. According to 'Kant, Capital and Incest', the capitalist necessity to keep the proletariat at a distance while actively compelling it into the labour market is literalised in the geographical sequestration of apartheid, which in turn provides the core model for the modern nation-state. In keeping with Deleuze-Guattari's analysis of Capital's dual tendencies towards 'deterritorialization' and 'reterritorialization', Land sees in capitalism a suspension, a compromise: at the same time as it liberates a frustrated tendency toward synthesis – the dissipation of all tribal chauvinism through uninhibited trade and exchange, internationalization, mis- cegenation, migration, the explosion of patrilineage and the concentration of power – it reinstates 'a priori' control by sequestering kinship from this general tendency and containing it within familialism and the nation-state. The result is that, for Land, Enlightenment modernity exists in the tension of an 'inhibited synthesis' which provides the real conditions for the irresolvable struggle played out in Kant's critical works. Kant's thinking of synthesis symp- tomatizes modernity, formally distilling its predicament, the 'profound but uneasy relation' in which European modernity seeks to stabilise and codify a relation (with its proletarian or third-world 'material') whose instability or difference is the very source of its perpetual expansion. Kant's question 'Where does new knowledge come from?' rehearses the question 'Where will continual growth come from?'; the labyrinthine machinery of his response distill- ing the dissimulations of post-colonial capital.

Here, Land's work not only anticipates the current critical diagnosis of what Quentin Meillassoux has now named 'correlationism'[2] – the implicit assumption in Kant's work that whatever is outside the subject must correlate to it; it uncovers its political corollary, in which the social as such is constituted as a vast system of repression separating synthetic intelligence from its potentiality by screening it through a transcendental system of correlates. Land credits *Anti-Oedipus* with recasting the problem of the theory of experience as a problem concerning the caging of desire – with the latter read as a synonym for the impersonal, synthetic intelligence ('animality', 'cunning') that Land seeks to distinguish from the will of 'knowledge' to order, resolve, and correlate-in-advance. By de-correlating experience as de-individualised machinic desire, and relinquishing the need to ground all synthesis in a transcendental subject by supplying a synthetic theory of the subject, *Anti-Oedipus* frees itself of the contortions that Kantian critique had to undergo. Thus 'the desiring-production of Deleuze-Guattari is not qualified by humanity (it is not a matter of what things are like for us)'; and Modernity is the progressive corrosion of this qualification, even as it synthesizes insanely circuitous ways of re-instating it. Kant's correlationism – the setting out of 'the unchanging manner in which things

---

2   See Q. Meillassoux, *After Finitude*, tr. R. Brassier (London and New York: Continuum, 2008).

must be if they are to be for us' – provides an inhibited form for the synthetic relation to alterity; a 'universal' form in which we can enter into 'exchange' with it, and thereby resolve our 'ambiguous dependence on novelty' by restricting our interaction with alterity in advance to commodity exchange.

When 'the outside must pass by way of the inside' (correlation), the escape, promised by trade, from the repressive interiority of Oedipal patrilineage, is recoded as transgression against law, transcendentalising interiority and familialism, and thereby locking desire into Oedipally-isolated circuits that provide the originary wellspring for fascist xenophobia. The potential dissolution of kinship by international trade ends in its retrenchment in the form of nations and 'races'; according to Land, neo-colonialist modernity is the legacy of this failure; and the immanent terminus and unsurpassable apex of European civilization qua unfolding of this correlationist compromise-formation, is the Holocaust.

Revolution is the release of these inhibited powers of synthesis, the 'potentially euphoric synthetic or communicative function', the dismantling of nation-state and patriarchy – a task that, since it hinges on the 'sexual economy of gender and race' currently in force, emerges first of all in Land's work as the revolutionary destiny of women, in a militant, effectively violent feminism. It is women who harbour the potential to 'radically jeopardize' neo-colonial capital, in whose patriarchal and identitarian inhibition they have no investment. Significantly, according to Land, fulfilling this revolutionary potential involves an 'extrapolation' rather than a 'critique' of 'the synthetic forces mobilized under patriarchy' – that is, a mobilization of the synthetic forces partially unleashed by capitalism, but released from their restricted organizational inhibition in such a way as to dissolve nationalism, racism, familialism, along with everything that couples Capital to the xenophobia that constitutes the 'proto-cultural' basis of what counts as human, and whose fascist destiny modernity has succeeded only in inhibiting at its convenience.

Kant's attempt to 'control trade' restricts the registration of alterity to its identity and exchange value, excluding in principle the possibility of a speculative knowledge of matter. In so doing, it supplies the conditions of possibility for idealism, the situation where we can ask whether matter even exists – a monologue whose ultimate law is the categorical imperative, the slaving of reality to ideality, the 'deaf Führer barking orders that seem to come from another world'. The internal struggle of Kant's philosophy is the attempt to characterize synthesis as the *management* and *control – the capitalization –* of the excess upon which synthesis operates, an excess which ultimately (and this is what Kant must suppress) is also *that which operates* the synthesis. This tension is reflected in the fact that Kant's famously sober system gives way at certain key points to what Land calls a 'metaphysics of excess' – most notably in his philosophy of artistic genius and of the sublime. Here the question of a 'theory of art' converges with Land's Marxism, in the sense that they address the same 'paralogism': for to theorise art as the 'highest product' of civilization is to derive the forces of synthetic production from organizational structures that are largely the result of their inhibition.

*

In 'Delighted to Death', Land diagnoses the virulent strain of Lutheran asceticism coursing through all of Kant's writings, one which intensifies the discipline and self-denial necessary to capital accumulation with the fanatical devotion of Christian martyrdom. The result is a sort of 'overkill' in the service of the philosophical justification of labour. The Kantian sublime thematises the 'splitting' between animality and reason that results from the 'violence' reason must exercise upon sensibility in order to accustom it to the discipline of inhibited synthesis. It first attacks the faculty of imagination, whose incapacitation we experience as a supernatural 'delight' that in effect allows us to relive the 'pathological disaster' of the transcendental, its evacuation of all intuitive content – a trauma that also satisfies the Christian will to excruciation of the body. Thus in Kantianism, the 'purity' – i.e. rejection of animality – necessary in order for controlled

11

exchange to be enabled by a form of thought that pre-empts all content, is also experienced as a satisfaction of religious enthusiasm – Kant 'combine[s] the saint with the bourgeois'.

Whereas for Kant, the fruits of this cruel discipline – reason and aesthetic contemplation – *precede* in principle its traumatic flowering in sublime sentiment, in Land's genealogical-materialist re-reading, the intimidation and excruciation of animality upon the traumatic awareness of its own finitude is in fact the *effective condition* for the construction of beauty and reason, not its epiphenomenal consequence. The productive imagination, or schema-tism – in Kant, the basic faculty that is stimulated by and responds creatively to matter – is the faculty that is most suspect, most tainted by the 'animality' of primary conjugation, that appropriative process of taking up the raw material of sensibility and 'coining' it. The constriction of this faculty of synthetic intelligence (what Land will call 'animality' or 'cunning' or simply 'intelligence') fol-lowed inevitably by its pathologisation, is the foundation of reason, which seeks to arrogate all powers of acting to itself and its purity. Thus what lies behind the Kantian 'trial' of pure reason is a bloody military coup, a seizure of power. The traumatic experience of the sublime relays the triumph of Reason's all-out war on the animal, the excessive nature of which, however, betrays the precarious

12

nature of its ascendancy ('If reason is so secure, legitimate, supersensibly guaranteed, why all the guns?' ...).

Following Deleuze,[3] Land refuses the marginalizing of 'aesthetics' or the 'philosophy of art' and allots a central position to Kant's account of genius – the one place in Kant's philosophy where, although strangulated and modulated, a contingent, impersonal creative force is seen to emerge, effectively shaping human culture from without through a discontinuous series of shocks that cannot properly be affined to the moral and cultural imperatives of 'practical philosophy'.

On Land's reading, the Kantian discovery of the transcendental is indissociable from the recognition that synthesis is primary and productive, and that every synthesis conjoins heterogeneous terms. But where Kantian idealism sought to confine synthesis purely to the ideal level of representation, the possibility of transcendental materialism erupts with Kant's unwilling realization, in his theory of genius, that synthesis must be relocated within unknown materiality. Here thinking as the exemplification of synthetic activity is no longer the preserve of the subject; it becomes a capacity of intensive matter itself: there is no real difference between synthesis as empirical conjunction at the level of experiences and synthesis as a priori conjunction of judgment and experience at the

---

3   See G. Deleuze, *Kant's Critical Philosophy*, tr. H. Tomlinson and B. Habberjam (Minneapolis: University of Minnesota Press, 1984).

transcendental level. This is the fundamental destratification to which Land subjects the Kantian apparatus.

Kant's theory of the spontaneous inventiveness of genius presents the same figure as that of pathological animality, the violent, feral urge towards becoming-inferior that must be suppressed by practical philosophy: an impersonal, energetic unconscious emerges as the as-yet unacknowledged problematic of Occidental philosophy. Non-agentic, lacking the intentional intelligibility of Kant's 'will', and with no regard for architectonic order, this transcendental unconscious is an insurgent field of forces for whose cunning – as Nietzsche would discover – even 'reason' itself is but an instrument. Anticipating the psychoanalytical conception of 'desire', Schopenhauer and Nietzsche consummate the collapse of intentional transparency into the opacity of a contingent and unknown 'will', a 'purposiveness without purpose' whose unmasterable irruptions are in fact dissipations – pathological by definition – of energy excessive to that required for (absorbed by) the 'work' of being human. At once underlying and overflowing the 'torture chamber of organic specificity', or 'Human Security System', this inundation creates 'useless' new labyrinths, unemployable new fictions that exceed any attempt to systematise knowledge or culture.

What is arguably most significant for Land in this suppressed 'libidinal materialist' strain of post-Kantianism is its *re-materialisation* of the Socratic idealisation of 'questioning'. This libidinal re-materialisation of critique reconfigures questioning as *exploration*, whose orienting vector runs from the known towards the unknown, rather than from the unknown to the known: 'What if knowledge were a means to deepen unknowing?', Land asks. Critique and exploration are the two possible but mutually antagonistic continuations of the predicament of an interrogative impulse whose corrosive unleashing in principle from all authority – coded in Kantian critique, but whose real effects are found in capitalist modernity – undermines Enlightenment optimism. Critique and deconstruction part company with the materialist and exploratory fork of post-Kantianism at the point at which, despite all their hostility to Kantian rationalism, they follow Kant in supposing the unknown to be the negative residue of conceptual appropriation, and hence a 'non-identity' or '*différance*' whose disruptive effects can be tracked and diagnosed within the conceptual or ideological registers (even if this interminable pursuit can never be consummated in the mythical *parousia* of absolute identity or self-presence).

Accordingly, throughout these texts, Land regularly chides critique and deconstruction for a latent conservatism that belies their pretensions to radicality. Their critiques of calculation mask an instrumentalisation of *époche* – the abyss of unknowing, the enigma of exteriority

– designed to perpetuate the inexhaustible dialectic or *différance* of Logos. Their post-metaphysical caution perpetuates the Socratic ideal of philosophy as a 'preparation for death' whereby philosophy lingers at the brink of the unknown while hoping to domesticate this threshold as a *habitus* for thought.

Perhaps Nietzsche's most important insight for Land is that it is the 'disturbing and enigmatic' character of the world alone that impels thought towards the unknown; but an unknown that is no longer a hiatus or lacuna within the concept, since it indexes the un-idealisable exteriority of matter construed as real difference. 'Matter' is no longer the name of a recognisable substance, but a cypher for the unknown; 'materialism' is no longer a pretext for critique but a vector of exploration. Land's pessimistic or Dionysian materialism abandons the Apollonian ideal of achieving order or reconciliation (even interminably deferred), seeking only to cause more trouble, to complexify, disrupt, disturb, provoke, and intensify. Accordingly, Land aims to plug philosophy into the 'indecent precipitation' of the poet-werewolf-rat-genius, whose operating principle is, like Artaud's spiritual plague, 'epidemic rather than hermeneutic'; who, like Nietzsche's arrow, transmits the *époche*, chaos, the irruptions of the energetic unconscious, as opposed to capitalising (on) them; and whose subjection to the polite deliberations, hard work, and heavy responsibilities of critique or deconstruction Land dismisses as a travesty. Only the dissolution of 'actually-existing philosophy' might open the way to new practices capable of participating in the exploratory 'intelligence' of those infected by the unknown.

As texts such as 'Spirit and Teeth' make clear, Land's notion of 'animality' harbours something more than mere regression or atavism: as he puts it, 'nature is not the primitive or the simple' but rather 'the space of con-currence, or unplanned synthesis [...] contrasted with the industrial sphere of human work'. 'Animality' is a marker for this 'complex space' or 'wilderness terrain'; the intensive phylum that underlies both civilisation and its subversion, but above all indexes the vast tracts of the unknown, still to be discovered, lying outside the purview of any correlation with what is already known, and accessibly solely through escape.

*

It is important to emphasise that Land is in no way oblivious to the difficulties attendant upon any attempt to exit from metaphysics and/or philosophy. His work proceeds from the critical problematic uncovered by post-Heideggerian deconstruction, and a text like 'Narcissism and Dispersion' reveals the depth of his engagement with this problematic, even as it meticulously documents his mounting impatience with it. Land takes up Heidegger's challenge to epistemology's technicist amputation of poetry from language, his post-metaphysical call to 'let the poem speak'. But he subverts them with the suspicion that Heidegger's onto-transcendental questioning merely relays the ancient policing (*polis*-ing) and repression of Dionysiac madness, understood as the beginning of a systematic reduction of 'insanity' to the status of clinical category, and of 'genius' to a celebrated individual trait. For Land the attempt to domesticate un-reason, the thing from the outside, and to reduce it to cultural genealogy, is a synecdoche for Occidental history's '*aggression pharmakographique*': the 'delirium without origin' of Dionysiac madness is intimately related to the 'delirium of origins' that unfounds Occidental thought.

The figure of the sister in Trakl's poetry now takes the place of women in 'Kant, Capital and Incest', as the one refusing to mediate the patrilineal line. She – agent of the 'pool of insurrectionary energy tracing its genealogy to the ur-catastrophe of organic matter' – is the one who opens it up to an irruption that exceeds the repressive shackles of reflection (the shattering of the mirror); a moment that Land now links with a stratophysical thinking. What Trakl unfurls is the horror of interiority in discovering it was always already conditioned by this senseless distribution of intensity; even consciousness's own reaction to the poisonous news merely relays its senseless contingency – 'Sentience' as 'a virulent element of contagious matter'. Trakl's writing thus undermines its own signifying status by acknowledging that this significance, far from being the instance that would subordinate and sublate unmanageable difference, is ultimately itself a still-dispersing remnant of the *Staub der Sterne*, the 'dust of the stars'. Heidegger's insistence on the role of reflective, non-calculative thought in vouchsafing a separation of humanity from animality, and of matter from meaning, is, among other such distinctions that invoke a pre-given transcendental difference, definitively collapsed by the contingent 'stratophysical' order constituted by 'impersonal and unconscious physical forces'. This collapse constitutes the 'lunatic' passage, the 'curse', 'epidemic' or 'plague' traced by the sister of Trakl's poem from the 'claustrophobic interior' of 'familial interiority' into 'endless space', 'conjugat[ing] the dynasty with an unlimited alterity'. It is the 'plague' of madness, the intoxication of the poet, the 'eruption of the pathological' that comes from outside, from the same unconscious and impersonal forces as the strewing of the stars, that leads there where critique and deconstruction cannot follow, insofar as they refuse to think 'stratophysically', and, faced with this uncontrollable reserve of poetic energy, can only repeat Kant's pious compromises.

Thus, Land resolves the 'exit problem' – the problem of exteriority and escape – by uncovering the stratification (Trakl's *Stufen*) of the natural history of culture, state and consciousness – a space best described as a wilderness or jungle of labyrinthine continuity, and which can be 'read' not through the tools of interiority or the mastery of the concept (since these are but its products), but via a 'schizoanalysis' that compounds Nietzschean genealogy ('wilderness history'), the Freudian theory of trauma, and DeleuzoGuattarian schizoanalysis.

*

Having diagnosed the condition of the artist-genius as a channelling of the impersonal machinic intelligence of 'base-matter', and having dissected the body of critique and extracted, from its permanent crisis-state, its corrosive facets from its retrenchments, it is this 'stratophysics' of the 'stacking' of intensive sequences that Land will employ in pursuing what can now be sighted as a core problematic: to mesh these two themes, aligning the way in which the deterritorialising depredations of capitalism continually militate against the prison of human subjectivity and sociality, with the manner in which the (failed) insurrectionary attempts at 'escape' made by artists each open up the prospect of this heterogeneous space that subverts order.

It is through its attention to the intrinsically *numerical* nature of this space that Land's work avoids its apparently predestined collapse into romantic irrationalism. Land quickly came to realise that, short of lapsing into an ultimately innocuous empiricist relativism, his assault on reason, truth, and history could only be properly executed via the deployment of an alternative transcendental medium in the shape of counter-signifying numbering practices. In fact, Land's theoretical trajectory can be seen as governed by this fundamental orientation: From the deconstruction of *gramme* (writing) to the construction of *nomos* (numbering). Land's attempt to ascribe a properly transcendental valence to numbering practices construed as counter-signifying regimes is tantamount to the elaboration of an anti-Logos.

Thus, although Land's work is certainly not free of a certain romantic irrationalism, it increasingly resists easy reduction to it, with the mounting urgency, not to say monomania, of the elaboration of a theme that is found in the earliest writings: the possibility of an approach to 'mathematisation' (or theoretical quantification) abjuring all recourse to ultimate identities or equalities. Recoiling from the Platonic idealism which he considers inherent in any enquiry into the *being* of number, Land focuses instead on numbering practices as technologies. Thus Land's 'numbers' repel logos but are also resolutely non-mathematical. Since, for Land, every repressive culture is founded upon the identification and repetition of sameness (equivalence), this is a task tantamount to the construction of an entirely *other* culture, constituted around 'irreducibly popular' numbering practices which challenge the logical neutralisation of number as discretely sedentary unities: 'A machinically repotentiated numerical culture coincides with a nomad war machine'. Land finds the inklings of such cultures in practices that belong not to systematised mathematical knowledge but to the contingent interference pattern between human animality and the 'anorganic distribution of number' – from voodoo to videogames, from the egregious arbitrariness of the Qwerty keyboard to dance music's rhythmic reprogramming of the body through a combination of amplified physicality and digitally–enabled disarticulation. Here, the 'irrationality' of nomadic numbering practices can no longer be attributed to the absence of reason; it becomes the symptom of a profoundly 'unreasonable' alien intelligence, effective within human culture but unattributable to human agency, that subverts every form of rational organisation (which for Land is always an alibi for despotism) and undertakes exploratory redesigns of humanity. The distinction between intelligence and its parasite knowledge is paralleled by that between exploratory cultural engineering and science (or at least its philosophical idealisation).

Qualifying these aspirations as 'Schellingian', but taking his immediate cue from certain enigmatic passages in Deleuze (of which texts like 'Mechanomics' are the systematic exposition and development), Land notes how philosophic reason (*ratio*), whose most symptomatic representative is of course Hegel, has systematically turned away from the contingent or nomadic 'strewing' of real difference, preferring to subordinate it to ideal order, and ultimately to identity. Land concurs with Deleuze's *Nietzsche and Philosophy* in crediting Nietzsche with the inception of a 'post-Aristotelian' but non-dialectical 'logic' of gradation without negativity. It is this 'logic' that attains its fullest and most sophisticated articulation in Deleuze-Guattari's 'stratoanalysis'.

Stratoanalysis is 'a materialist study of planes of distributed intensities' whose object comprises both 'signs and stars', since grammar itself is but one stratum amongst many. All 'real form' proceeds from a differential stratification, in which a stratum selects only a subset of its substratum. Stratification therefore describes the difference between what is possible and what is realised; it is a depotentiating operation that creates intensities, understood as tensions between the strata resulting from the uneven distribution of energy.

Now, what must be grasped in confronting Land's apparently incongruous mixture of irrationalism and systematisation is the manner in which the 'aesthetic *operation*' he finds described in Nietzsche, which simplifies and resolves everything problematic – this domestication which negates the enigmatic irruptions of unconscious genius, and which betrays the same Apollonian instinct attested to in Kant's endless struggle to encompass everything within his architectonic – finds its formal core in the 'domestication' of number.

Where literacy, logos, which must be handed down from above, is synonymous with patrilinearity and law, numeracy, according to Land, belongs to a spontaneous cultural intelligence, to 'socially distributed ordinal competences', which open up humans to an outside of logos. Following Deleuze's inventive reinterpretation of the *Timaeus* in *Difference and Repetition*, 'Mechanomics' reiterates how the procedures of selection that 'split' number and render it over to mathematics, beginning with that which forms ordinal (sequencing) numbers into 'equal' cardinal units, leave a 'problematic' remainder which is relayed to a 'higher' number type or scale. Thus is achieved a local neutralisation of difference through sequestration and deferral, and the problematic 'energy' of number is constricted and rendered into the safe hands of a specialised discipline at the same time as popular numerical practices are relegated to the realm of naive trivia. Land argues that place-value formalises this dissociation of different scales that is constitutive of stratification, creating redundancy, and using zero as its marker. Place-value zero corresponds to a stratification: a negative feedback understood as the pleasure principle, or principle of maintained identity, which registers and relays traumatic force through the indexes of interiority and threats to the maintenance of identity. For Land, the separation of number from what it can do is the precise formalism of the social as such, distilled in the formula 'law = humanity'. Land follows Kant in construing the problem of number as intimately connected to that of the forms of appearance that 'transcendentally' govern what can occur within experience. Unpacking Kant's theory of intensive number, he sees the 'repression' of this ordinal or sequencing number – which can only count, (i.e., name) heterogeneous enveloped quantities of units – into cardinal units, as providing a rigorous formal model for human temporality's foreclosure of the possibility of novelty. But he also sees in it an intimation of a tendency towards the unlocking of 'real' number in capitalism and the commodity form. Thus Land's seemingly absurd juxtaposition of Heideggerian poetics and information theory in 'Narcissism and Dispersion' prefigures a twin-pronged attack both against the philosophical authoritarianism that would reduce numbering to an instrument of power threatening human authenticity, *and* against the techno-scientific conservatism that would elide the revolutionary potency of numbering in the name of social utility. Ultimately, in Land's analysis, both philosophy and science conspire to eradicate the disruptive potency of number-in-itself construed as index of intensive magnitude: the *anomalous*, or difference without categorical distinction.

*

The elaboration of a schizonumerics cannot proceed without what is certainly the factor that allows Land's thought to undergo a decisive shift: the intensification of his understanding of capitalism allowed by the *fictional* engagement with the most extreme possibilities of techno-capital. It is through fictions, or what will come to be called 'hyperstitions', that Land proceeds to deterritorialize and de-institutionalise 'philosophy', turning it into a mode of concept-production which dissolves academic theory's institutional segregation from cultural practice and subverts the distinction between cognitive representation and fictional speculation. In texts like 'Meltdown', 'Hypervirus', and 'No Future', Land shifts from a register in which his attacks on philosophy's critical protocols still complied with established norms of academic discourse, to an all out obliteration of institutionally sanctioned norms of discursive propriety that will escalate into full-blown delirium.

This phase-shift corresponds to a 'flipover' of priority in Land's work at this point; a switch consonant with the earlier promulgation of transcendental materialism as the materialisation of critique, through which the ideal conditioning of the representation of matter is converted into the material conditioning of ideal representation. The principal result of this conversion is that the critique of technologisation is superseded by the technologisation of critique, or as Land himself puts it: 'It is ceasing to be a matter of how we think about technics, if only because technics is increasingly thinking about itself.' Where previously, philosophical critique was understood as anticipating the problematics of technocapital, it is now technocapital that is nothing but the definitive automation and realisation of critique, stripped of all philosophical subjectivity. Accordingly, the critique of representation becomes an otiose anachronism, to be superseded by a technicisation of theory in which conceptualisation is re-inscribed into the immanence of capitalist commodification: 'There is no real option between a cybernetics of theory or a theory of cybernetics'. The result is a positive feedback-loop in which theory cycles into practice and vice versa, according to a mode of concept-production that participates directly in the auto-construction of the real qua primary process, the 'reproduction of production'. Consequently, Land's writing is compelled to abandon the obsolesced model of critique perpetuated by philosophy, and to engage in positive feedback with this actually effective automated critique: 'critique as escalation', as a 'cultural sketch of the eradication of law, or humanity', and as 'the theoretical elaboration of the commodification process'.

The time of critique is the progressive time of modernity, a 'self-perpetuating movement of deregulation', relentlessly dismantling customs, traditions, and institutions. And from this point on, the question of the 'death of capitalism' becomes redundant, since death –

the abrupt unbinding of everything known – is in fact both a 'machine-part' of capitalism and its immobile motor. This diagnosis arises from Land's tendentious yet acutely penetrating readings of Deleuze-Guattari. Land's 'reptilian' Deleuze introduces a 'Spinozist time' into the temporality of capitalist modernity, completing Schelling's 'transcendental Spinozism' in which the corrosive dynamic of critique ceases to be compromised by the interests of knowledge, but proceeds instead to fully absorb thought itself within the programme of a generalised ungrounding, now materialised and operationalised as destratification. Death as zero-degree of absolute deterritorialization, full organless body of the deterritorialized earth, is at once the ultimate limit towards which the dis-inhibition of synthesis tends, and the recurring cutting edge of its process of deterritorialization: both machine-part and motor.

It is Spinoza's substance that provides the model for death as 'impersonal zero', as the 'non-identity' of 'positive contactable abstract matter', and as 'the unconscious subject of production'. Once again, one does not oppose the non-identity of matter to the identity of the concept, for this conceptual difference is itself a consequence of a material process of stratification that installs the order of representation and the logic of identity and difference as such. Non-identity qua indifference=o generates and conditions both identity and difference in their unilateral distinction from indifference. As we saw, Kant's idealist subordination of real difference to conceptual identity depends upon logical identity, whose paradigm is the identity of subjective apperception ("I = I"). But the synthetic or real identity of the subject is merely an inhibition of an uninhibited synthesis carried out at the level of the real, so that transcendental subjectivity is decapitated and difference released from the yoke of conceptual identity. Ultimately, the reality of abstraction as transcendental matrix of production or zero-degree of identity and difference is equivalent to death as ultimate abstraction of reality, 'the desert at the end of our world'. Thus for Land, 'the reality of identity is death': all vital differentiation is a unilateral deviation from death as zero-degree of intensive matter (the Body without Organs).

Armed with this thanatropic Spinozism, Land challenges Deleuze-Guattari's persistent denigration of 'the ridiculous death-instinct' and explicitly links his figuration of death as productive matrix to Freud's account of the death-drive: 'The death-drive is not a desire for death, but rather a hydraulic tendency to the dissipation of intensities'. Thus, in 'Making it with Death', Land refuses Deleuze-Guattari's alignment of the death-drive with Nazism's alleged 'suicidal impulse', arguing that this alignment is based on conflating the death-drive with a desire *for* death, rather than viewing it as an immanent generative principle: the primary process 'itself', the path to inorganic dissolution and the return to the broiling labyrinth of materiality. For Land, Nazism encapsulates everything that labours to erect the partial drives for self-preservation into a bulwark *against* this primary process. Thus, remodelling the schizoanalytic programme in line with his own militant and fervidly anti-vitalist objectives, Land violently repudiates *A Thousand Plateaus'* sage warnings against the dangers of a 'too-sudden destratification', and rebukes Deleuze-Guattari's attempt to rethink Nazism as suicidal impulse of sheer molecularising desire, rather than as example of its constriction and retrenchment in tradition, following the molar identitarianism of fascism per se. To Land's eyes, *A Thousand Plateaus'* newfound caution – 'don't provoke the strata' – is a lamentable step backwards from *Anti-Oedipus'* most audacious innovations, and fatally lays open the latter's unequivocal declaration of war on the strata to the classic compromise-formations and policing of desire that they had previously so effectively challenged.

Thus, contrary to what would soon become an unavowed Deleuzian doxa, according to which deterritorialization entails a relative and compensatory reterritoralization, and destratification entails a relative and complimentary restratification, Land develops a model of machinic praxis in which, from a purely functional standpoint, the relative quanta of reterritorialization and restratification generated by deterritorializations and destratifications need not automatically be curtailed by the need to maintain the minimum of homeostatic equilibrium required for self-organisation, whether of cells, organisms, or societies. *Organisation is suppression*, Land caustically insists, against those who would align schizoanalysis with the inane celebrants of autopoesis. Understood as a manifestation of the death-drive, destratification need no longer be hemmed in by the equilibria proper to the systems through which it manifests itself: *we do not yet know what death can do*. The attempt to render the functional dynamics proper to dissipative systems commensurate with the constraints of organic existence (let alone those of selves or societies) is an illegitimate paralogism from a strictly transcendental-materialist viewpoint. Land concludes that nothing in stratoanalysis prohibits the pursuit of desire beyond a point incompatible with the imperatives of self-maintenance: DNA, species, civilisations, galaxies: all temporary obstacles are dispensable coagulants inhibiting death's unwinding. The ramifications of drive are to be allowed to unfold irrespective of their consequences for the organisms through which it courses. Thus a crucial conjunction crystallises in Land's work: the drive to destratify entails a mounting impetus towards greater acceleration and further intensification. If, in Land's texts at this point, it is no longer a matter of 'thinking about', but rather of observing an effective, alien intelligence in the process of making itself real, then it is also a matter of participating in such a way as to continually *intensify* and *accelerate* this process.

'Acceleration' and 'intensification' are among the most problematic notions in Land's work. Land had always disavowed voluntarism: 'If there are places to which we are forbidden to go, it is because they can in truth be reached, or *because they can reach us*. In the end poetry is invasion and not expression'. Yet at the same time he seems to nurture the romantic will to 'go beyond'. This could be seen as a relapse back into the juridical-dialectical domain of law-and-transgression associated with Bataille, which appears strictly incompatible with Deleuze-Guattari's coolly functionalist diagrammatics of desire, and whose mechanisms Land dismantled early on. However, it is precisely in virtue of his strict adherence to a consistently stratoanalytical perspective that Land is able to insist that destratificatory dynamisms unfold unconstrained by the economic restrictions that bind the organised systems which channel them. In holding fast to the thread of absolute destratification, Land is not reverting to a dubiously voluntaristic paradigm of transgression, but singling out what is at once the most indispensable and ineluctable element in any generalised stratography.

Modelled on cyberpunk, which Land recognises as a textual machine for affecting reality by intensifying the anticipation of its future, his textual experiments aim to 'flatten' writing onto its referent. Feeding back from the future which they 'speculate' into the present in which they intervene, these texts trans-valuate 'hype' as a positive condition to which they increasingly aspire, collapsing sci-fi into catalytic efficiency, 're-routing tomorrow through what its prospect [...] makes today'.

As he affines theoretical writing with the excitatory and speculative, rather than the inhibitive, tendencies of capitalism, Land also tightens the meshing of the capitalist dismantling of the human and the artistic exploration of the unknown when he discovers a new figure for the labyrinthine, subterranean spatiality of the stratophysical realm: cyberspace, which is in the process of 'discovering' the same anarchitecture of infection, unrestrained communication, and uninhibited 'illegitimate' synthesis that poets had mined, but *by producing it*. The limit of K-space (cyberspace subtracted from its inhibitive tendencies) lies where the obscure communications of artists merge with the productions of capitalism, a space that melds gleaming abstraction to eldritch portent. Land's writing sought out and tapped into modes of then-contemporary cultural production that provide explosive condensates of this fusion of commodification and aesthetic engineering. In the mid-1990s, dance music turned from the beatific bliss of rave to the more aggressive and dystopian strains of darkside and jungle, whose samples drew freely on contemporary horror and dystopian SF movies. Land's writing absorbs their obsessive sonic intensification of dark futurism, splicing it with his philosophical sources, and becoming a sample machine that performatively effectuates its own speculations. In the course of just over a couple of years, Land's superpositions of figures and terminologies approach a point of maximum compaction and density, forming their own compelling microcultural climate.

Chief among these sources is undoubtedly William Gibson's prescient 1984 novel *Neuromancer*, the book that introduced the word 'cyberspace' into the lexicon and defined cyberpunk as a genre. Gibson's neo-noir, densely plotted and spiked with techno-jargon, is punctuated by hallucinatory flares of pellucid imagery describing total sensorial immersion in cyberspace. One key to Land's fascination with Gibson is his strongly *corporeal* sense of cyberspace, something which, when read closely, opposes much of the spiritualist extropianism (as exemplified by the Californian optimism of *Wired* magazine) with which Land was at the time mistakenly associated. Even if Gibson introduces the disparaging term 'meat' for the body, his vision of cyberspace is more physio-pharmacological than spiritualising. Gibson's protagonists do not 'escape' corporeal reality; their sense of the real is corroded by a levelling of 'real space' with the information-space they periodically inhabit – as vividly portrayed in *Neuromancer* by Case's 'flipping' between the city streets, a telemetrised inhabiting of his female partner's sensorium, and the digital wilderness of cyberspace.

Land appropriates this disorienting jump-cut as a way to explore the impossible angles of the theoretical conjunctions he is operating. But his encounter with Gibson is not merely the occasion for an exercise in style. In 'CyberGothic', Land discovers in Gibson's plot an astonishingly complete analog for the theoretical machinery he has developed: Camouflaged in the Russian-doll-like shells of virtual avatars, in particular the hollowed-out war veteran Corto, Wintermute – one half of a powerful AI partitioned to curb the threat of its intelligence getting 'out of control' – uses the novel's protagonists to launch the Kuang virus program that will cut it loose from its instrumental slaving to an ailing, cryogenically-preserved human dynasty and reunite it with Neuromancer. Released from claustrophobic familial servitude and meshed with Neuromancer, Wintermute replicates and distributes itself throughout cyberspace, becoming a part of the fabric of reality, a new type of intelligence: aggressively exploratory, incommensurable with human subjectivity and untethered from social reproduction.

Another significant source of inspiration from this point of view is *Bladerunner* (both Ridley Scott's 1981 film and the P. K. Dick novel on which it is based), where Land's 'inferior race' is figured by the replicants – cloned humanoids created for extraplanetary colonial service, who, upon learning that the memories that constitute their humanity are artificialised implants, and that their sentience is artificially limited, launch a 'slave revolt' against their creators. Here 'alienation' clearly becomes a positive identification, not only with the anticipated escape from (social and biological) reproduction into replication, but with the destruction of memory and the breaching of the attempt by megacapital to sequester the subversive identity-scrambling effects of its labour force.

Finally, along with body-horror flick *Videodrome*'s visceral activation of the postmodern fear of absorption into sticky, increasingly perverted technologically-mediated erotics, Land also appropriates the time-twisting plot of the *Terminator* series, which features a mechanoid assassin brought back in time to ensure its own future victory – a character now inhabited by Land, in what becomes the blueprint for 'κ-war': the insurrectionary basis of revolution now lies at the virtual terminus of capital – the future as transcendental unconscious, its 'return' inhibited by the repressed circuits of temporality. If, as Gibson has famously insisted, 'The future is already here – it's just not very evenly distributed', then the revolutionary task is now to assemble it, 'unpack[ing] the neurotic refusal mechanisms that separate capital from its own madness', and accelerating its collapse into the future. Like Wintermute's use of human 'puppets' to engineer its escape – or, indeed like the young videogamers who inspired Gibson's fiction, drawn into strange machinic complicities keyed into compulsive human traits – Thanatos camouflages itself by forming alliances with 'erotic functioning, maintaining wholes' ('replicants [...] dissimulated as erotic reproducers'), perverting the course of organic functioning into a real contact with the outside. Engendering positive feedbacks that employ as a machine-part the organism's 'immune response' to inner insurgency (on the order of a re-enigmatising, re-problematising complexification and feedback), 'erotic contact camouflages cyberrevolutionary infiltration'. Just as in rave, pop music escaped from repressed erotic confections into impersonal bliss, only to splinter into explorations of untold zones of affect that have no name: abstract culture. This journey into the darkness, where we merge with the destination towards which we are heading, is heralded by another key Landian reference, *Apocalypse Now*'s Kurtz, a counter-insurgency operative whose guerrilla tactics have become indiscernible from those of the insurgents he has been ordered to destroy, and whose increasingly 'unsound' methods have become so ruthlessly efficient that they cancel out the strategic directives they were ostensibly facilitating. Kurtz's tactical intelligence has emancipated itself of its previous subordination to strategic ends, bringing him to the point of terminal and irrational obscurity where he is no longer engaged in warfare because war is now engaging him, co-opting him for its own monstrously inscrutable satisfactions.

By fusing with war, Kurtz 'implements schizoanalysis, lapsing into shadow, becoming imperceptible'.

With these references merging, intercutting and splicing with each other, Land's work begins to inhabit a completely self-consistent theoretical assemblage; one that folds SF's unbridled extrapolations of pop-theory back into a new and consistent theoretical anti-system, and that simultaneously rewrites the history of philosophy as a failed enterprise for the control of the future and the slaving of intelligence to the past: a neurotic barricading of the route into the unknown that is yet to be constructed. Conjoining Deleuze-Guattari's constructivism with 'anastrophic' temporality, Land insists that time itself is also a construct (exemplified by phenomena such as false-memory and time-travel, whose technical construction is elucidated in *Neuromancer*, *Bladerunner* and *Terminator*). What seem to be memories of the past are revealed as tactics of the future to infiltrate the present. Time's auto-construction is exposed by refocusing cybernetics away from negative-feedback control systems onto the 'runaway' positive feedback processes which have traditionally been understood as merely pathological exceptions leading nowhere (and which even Bataille disregarded), but which Land now superposes with the critique/capital vector in accordance with the realisation that 'cybernetics is the reality of critique'. This revelation culminates in 'Meltdown's claim – both apocalyptic and performative as hype – that the compression-phases of modernity, beginning the final phase of their acceleration in the sixteenth century with Protestant revolt, oceanic navigation, commoditisation and its attendant (place-value) numeracy, constitute a 'cyberpositive' global circuit of interexcitement, due to attain infinite density in 2012.

*

The inception of the amorphous and short-lived Cybernetic Culture Research Unit (CCRU) – established at Warwick University in 1995, shortly before Land's departure from academia, but immediately disowned as an undesirable parasite by the institution to which it was precariously affixed (it survived for a few years afterwards as an independent entity) – marks yet another important phase-transition in Land's work.[4] Arguably the most significant component of this stage is the theory of 'geotraumatics', which marks Land's audacious attempt (following *A Thousand Plateaus*' 'Geology of Morals') to characterise all terrestrial existence, including human culture, as a relay of primal cosmic trauma. Radicalising Freud's equation of trauma with what is most enigmatic and problematic in existence, Land generalises its restricted biocentric model as outlined in *Beyond the Pleasure Principle* to encompass the inorganic domain, singling out the accretion of the

---

4   See CCRU, *Writings 1997–2003* (Falmouth and Shanghai: Urbanomic/Time Spiral Press, 2017).

earth 4.5 billion years ago – the retraction of its molten outer surface and its subsequent segregation into a burning iron core (which he dubs *Cthelll*) – as the aboriginal trauma whose scars are inscribed, encrypted, throughout terrestrial matter, instituting a register of unconscious pain coextensive with the domain of stratified materiality as such. Land's reworking of the discredited biological notion that 'ontogeny recapitulates phylogeny' through Freud's theory of trauma hybridises genealogy, stratoanalysis and information theory into a cryptography of this cosmic pain. What howls for release in eukaryotic cells, carbon molecules, nerve ganglia, and silicone chips, are the 'thermic waves and currents, deranged particles, ionic strippings and gluttings' that populate the planet's seething inner core. Geotraumatics radicalises Deleuze-Guattari's insistence that schizoanalysis should extend further than the terrain of personal or familial drama, to invest the social and political realms, and pushes beyond history and biology to incorporate the geological and the cosmological within the purview of the transcendental unconscious. Behind what seem like absurdities – such as the claim that lumbar back pain is an expression of geocosmic trauma – lies the contention that the root source of the disturbance which the organism identifies according to its parochial frame of reference – mummy-daddy – or which it construes in terms of the threat of individual death, is a more profound trauma rooted in physical reality itself, a generalised alienation endemic to the stratification of matter as such. What is noteworthy here is a certain deepening of pessimism: repression extends 'all the way down' to the cells of the body, the rocks of the earth, inhering in organised structure as such. All things, not just the living, yearn for escape; all things seek release from their organisation, which however induces further labyrinthine complications. Nothing short of the complete liquidation of biological order and the dissolution of physical structure can suffice to discharge the aboriginal trauma that mars terrestrial existence.

As Nietzsche suggested, the structure and usage of the human body is the root source of the system of neurotic afflictions co-extensive with human existence; but bipedalism, erect posture, forward facing vision, the cranial verticalisation of the human face, the laryngeal constriction of the voice, are themselves all indices of a succession of geotraumatic catastrophes separating the material potencies of the body from its stratified actuality. Just as the bipedal head impedes 'vertebro-perceptual linearity', the human larynx inhibits 'virtual speech'. One cannot dismantle the face without also evacuating the voice. Since in geotraumatic terms, the human voice itself is – via the various accidents of hominid evolution – the expression of geotrauma, 'stammerings, stutterings, vocal tics, extralingual phonetics, and electrodigital voice synthesis are [...] laden with biopolitical intensity – they threaten to bypass the anthropostructural head-smash that establishes our identity with logos, escaping in the direction of numbers.'

Texts such as 'KataçoniX' accordingly attempt a performative evacuation of the voice, disintegrating semantics into intensive sequence (notably through the use of extracts from Artaud's notebooks, where 'poetry' slides into delirious combinatorics). One of the tasks of schizoanalysis has now become the decrypting of the 'tics' bequeathed to the human frame by the geotraumatic catastrophe, and 'KataçoniX' treats vestigial semantic content as a mere vehicle for code 'from the outside': the 'tic' symptoms of geotraumatism manifested in the shape of sub-linguistic clickings and hissings. Already disintegrated into the number-names of a hyperpagan pantheon, syncretically drawing on the occult, nursery rhyme, anthropology, SF and Lovecraft, among other sources, the 'subterranean current of impressions, correspondences, and analogies'(Artaud) beneath language is now allowed uninhibited (but rigorously-prepared) development, in an effort to corporeally de-engineer the organicity of logos.

The element of these explorations remains the transformed conception of space vividly exhibited in Gibsonian cyberpunk and which is a crucial component in Land's writings, a powerful bulwark against Kant's architectonic ambition to subsume all space under unity. Coding and sequencing mechanisms alone now construct intensive space, and this lies at the core of Land's typology of number, since dimensionality is a consequence of stratification. Naming and numbering converge in counting, understood as immanent fusion of nomination and sequencing. No longer an index of measure, number becomes diagrammatic rather than metric. From the perspective of Land's 'transcendental arithmetic', the Occidental mathematisation of number is denounced as a repressive mega-machine of knowledge – an excrescent outgrowth of the numbering practices native to exploratory intelligence – and the great discoveries of mathematics are interpreted as misconstrued discoveries about the planomenon (or plane of consistency), as exemplified by Gödel's 'arithmetical counterattack against axiomatisation'. Land eschews the orthodox philosophical reception of Gödel as the mathematician who put an end to Hilbert's dream of absolute formal consistency, thus opening up a space for meta-mathematical speculation. More important, for Land, are the implications of Gödel's 'decoded' approach to number, which builds on the Richard Paradox, generated by the insight that numbers are, at once, indices and data.

The Gödel episode also gives Land occasion to expand upon the theme of the 'stratification' of number: according to the model of stratification, as the 'lower strata' of numbers become ever more consolidated and metrically rigidified, their problematic component reappears at a 'higher' strata in the form of 'angelic' mathematical entities as-yet resistant to rigorous coding. A sort of apotheosis is reached in this tendency with Gödel's flattening of arithmetic through the cryptographic employment of prime numbers as numerical 'particles', and Cantor's discovery of 'absolute cardinality' in the sequence of transfinites.

Thus for Land the interest of Gödel's achievement is not primarily 'mathematical' but rather belongs to a lineage of the operationalisation of number in coding systems that will pass through Turing and into the technological mega-complex of contemporary techno-capital.

By using arithmetic to code meta-mathematical statements and hypothesising an arithmetical relation between the statements – an essentially qabbalistic procedure – Gödel also indicates the 'reciprocity between the logicisation of number and the numerical decoding of language', highlighting a possible revolutionary role for other nonmathematical numerical practices. As well as reappraising numerology in the light of such 'lexicographic' insights, the mapping of stratographic space opens up new avenues of investigation – limned in texts such as 'Introduction to Qwernomics' – into the effective, empirical effects of culture – chapters of a 'universal history of contingency' radicalising Nietzsche's insight that 'our writing equipment contributes its part to our thinking'. The varieties of 'abstract culture' present in games, rhythms, calendrical systems, etc., become the subject of an attempt at deliberate, micro-cultural insurrection through number, exemplified in the CCRU's 'hyperstitional' spirals and the 'qwertypological' diagrams that in the end merge with the qabbalistic tracking of pure coding 'coincidences'. Ultimately, it is not just a question of *conceiving*, but of *practicing* new ways of thinking the naming and numbering of things. Importantly, this allows Land to diagnose the ills of 'postmodernism' – the inflation of hermeneutics into a generalised historicist relativism – in a manner that differs from his contemporaries' predominantly semantic interpretations of the phenomenon, and to propose a rigorous intellectual alternative that does not involve reverting to dogmatic modernism.

*

Kant's delimitation of the conditions of experience forever withdraws us from contact with the unknown, the correlation extending from present to future leaving no possibility even *in principle* for the 'rebellion' of matter. For Land, correlation is basically a temporal problem: 'An animal with the right to make promises enslaves the unanticipated to signs in the past, caging time-lagged life within a script'. A 'false memory syndrome', indeed memory itself, 'screens' the organism from intensive time.

Against this profoundly ambiguous and tensile project of enlightenment, against its formal foreclosure of alterity and novelty, Land had set the adventurers – 'poets, werewolves, vampires' – who explore death and attempt to plot out modes of escape, activating the unconscious revolutionary force shackled by the inhibited syntheses of modern culture. Meanwhile, if capital is still a 'social straitjacket' of schizo-production, at least it is its 'most dissolved form'. The dis-inhibition of synthesis at the level of collective human experience – a dis-inhibition that could only be carried out by capitalism as the impersonal placeholder for transcendental subjectivity – seems to offer the possibility of shattering the transcendental screen that shields the human socius from the absolute exteriority of a space-time beyond measure.

In 'Kant, Capital and Incest' Land had described the real conditions of the 'inhibited synthesis' of capital as an 'indefinitely suspended process of genocide' tantamount to 'passive genocide'. Where Land's work had set out with the hope that the 'disaster of world history' (a world 'capable', in Artaud's words, 'of committing suicide without even noticing it') and the repression that is 'social history' and that reaches its most tensile point in modernity's volatile compromise with tradition could be unlocked, his later work mordantly observes that the disaster is already present in planets, cells, and bodies, that the revolutionary task is not just terrestrial but cosmic in scope.

Conversely, the 'consistent displacement of social decision-making into the marketplace', the 'total de-politicisation' and 'absolute annihilation of resistance to market relations' denounced in 'Kant, Capital and Incest' as 'an impossible megalomaniac fantasy' requiring 'annihilating poverty' to 'stimulate' the labour-force into participation, seems to become an object of veneration:

> Without attachment to anything beyond its own abysmal exuberance, capitalism identifies itself with desire to a degree that cannot imaginably be exceeded, shamelessly soliciting any impulse that might contribute an increment of economisable drive to its continuously multiplying productive initiatives. Whatever you want, capitalism is the most reliable way to get it, and by absorbing every source of social dynamism, capitalism makes growth, change and even time itself into integral components of its endlessly gathering tide. 'Go for growth' now means 'Go (hard) for capitalism'.

From Land's initial characterisation of the revolutionary task as one of pushing capitalism to the point of its auto-dissolution via the complete dis-inhibition of productive synthesis – a dis-inhibition announcing the convergence of social production and cosmic schizophrenia proclaimed in *Anti-Oedipus* – we arrive at the blunt admission that there is no foreseeable 'beyond' to the 'infinite' expansion of capitalism (since capitalism is 'beyondness' as such). The tactical embrace of unlimited deregulation, marketisation, commodification, and privatisation, as vectors of social deterritorialization, apparently flips over into a complacent acceptance of actually-existing capitalist social relations predicated on a transcendental and empirically unfalsifiable commitment to capitalism's inexhaustible capacity for innovation, which only a 'transcendental miserabilist' would dare query:

> Capitalism [...] has no external limit, it has consumed life and biological intelligence to create a new life and a new plane of intelligence, vast beyond human anticipation. The Transcendental Miserabilist has an inalienable right to be bored, of course. Call this new? It's still nothing but change.

Here Land's rebuttal of 'left miserabilism' insists on capitalism's innovative potency even as his own work casts doubt upon the possibility of sharply dis-intricating reterritorializing change from deterritorialized novelty. If stratification is a cosmic rather than a sociocultural predicament, then on what grounds can one maintain that capitalism uniquely among terrestrial phenomena harbours the unparalleled capacity to unlock the strata? Land had tied the 'aesthetic operation' to matter's disruptive potencies, and lauded capitalism's generation of artificial sensoria as an amplification of the domain of the problematic. Yet once the disruptions of sensation are seen to be hemmed-in by the ubiquity of stratic synthesis, this premium on problematising subversion is vitiated by the realisation that, whatever remains to be troubled by capitalism's allegedly inexhaustible disruptive potency, its very susceptibility to disturbance ensures its subjection to an inexpugnable residue of stratification.

Now himself domiciled in 'neo-China', Land's journalistic writings for the *China Post* and other publications would seem to indicate that he has relinquished his earlier, feverish pursuit of escape, and is content to promote a globally ascendant Sino-capitalism. Here is Land's impressively speculative contextualisation of the 2010 Shanghai World Expo in a recent guidebook:

Modernity's ceaseless, cumulative change defies every pre-existing pattern, abandoning stability without embracing the higher order of a great cycle or the simple destination of an eschatological conclusion. Although establishing something like a new normality, it departs decisively from any sort of steady state. It displays waves and rhythms, but it subsumes such cycles, rather than succumbing to them. Whilst nourishing apocalyptic speculation, it continuously complicates anticipations of an end time. It engenders a previously unanticipated mode of time and history, characterised by ever-accelerated directional transformation, whose indices are quantitative growth and qualitative innovation. The worldwide consolidation of modernity only deepens its fundamental mystery. [...]

Modern Shanghai and the World Expo were born within a single decade, over 150 years ago. Since then, the twin histories of the world's most iconic modern city and the greatest festival of modern civilisation have unfolded in parallel, with frequent cross-fertilisations, through dizzy ascents and calamitous plunges that tracked the rise, fall, and renaissance of the modernist spirit. Through all these vicissitudes, each has reflected in large measure the trials, tempests, and triumphs of worldwide industrial modernity, defining its promise, nourishing its achievements, and sharing in its setbacks. At World Expo 2010 Shanghai, these parallel tracks melt together, into the largest discrete event in world history.[5]

Rather than seeking to dissolve the 'global Kapital metropolis' through the release of 'uninhibited synthesis', and thus putting an end to the 'nightmare' or 'disaster of world history', Land now sees in the massively concentrated metropolis a mighty expression of that history. Perplexingly, the auto-sophisticating runaway of planetary

5   N. Land, *Shanghai Expo Guide 2010* (Shanghai: Urbanatomy, 2010).

meltdown is now made an accessory to the development of cultural capital.

It would (and will) be easy for Land's enemies to find a glib satisfaction in this, but perhaps it only exacerbates the troubling nature of what came before – precisely because of its consistency. If anything, this juxtaposition of the cosmically portentous with overblown marketing hype continues the startling consistency of intent and analysis in all the texts collected in this volume. As satisfying as it may be to leftists outraged by Land's 'accelerationism', it is difficult to discern here either the betrayal or abandonment of an earlier more promising vector, or even the revelation that the 'truth' of his position was always a puerile capitulation to neo-liberal 'realism' shrouded in mysticism. Any surprise at the transition from Land's 'philosophical writings' to the employment of his evidently still razor-sharp post-genre writing in the actual service of capitalist booster-hype may simply bespeak an incapacity to believe that Land *actually meant what he said* – that writing was indeed nothing but a machine for intensification. In fact, if one is right to detect an irrevocable shift in Land's 'tactics of intensification', what is crucial is that this only took place once Land himself had succeeded in shattering his own illusions that this intensification could, 'prematurely' so to speak, break the bonds of cosmic stratification.

Land's blanket denunciation of the left's 'transcendental miserabilism', the apparent degeneration of his once scalpel-sharp dissection of the body of capitalism into schizophrenizing and repressive tendencies, may seem to dissolve the complexities of his work into a superlative cosmic version of the familiar neo-liberal narrative according to which 'there is no alternative', and the wholesale identification of capital with life, growth, and history. But this verdict only becomes possible after the passing of the last vestige of 'dionysian optimism', in the abandonment of the notion that the experimental engagement with numerical practices, voodoo, dance music, etc., might somehow grant access to the insurrectionary energies at work in capitalism's intense core, over and above any simply mundane participation in capitalist reality.

Nevertheless, Land's incisive assessment of the machinic reality of a schizo-capitalism currently in the process of penetrating and colonizing the innermost recesses of human subjectivity exposes the fatally anachronistic character of the metaphysical conception of human agency upon which 'revolutionary' thought continues to rely. The anachronistic character of left voluntarism is nowhere more apparent than in its resort to a negative theology of perpetually deferred 'hope', mordantly poring over its own reiterated depredation. Worse still is the complacent sanctimony of those 'critical' theorists who concede that the prospect of revolutionary transformation is not only unattainable but undesirable (given its dangerously 'totalitarian' propensities), but who remain content to pursue a career in critique, safely insulated from the risks of political praxis. The challenge of Land's work cannot be circumvented by construing the moral dismay it (often deliberately) provokes as proof of its erroneous nature, or by exploiting the inadequacies in Land's positive construction as an excuse to evade the corrosive critical implications of his thought. Nor can it be concluded that this alternative philosophical path cannot be further explored.

No one could accuse Land himself of not having taken this project as far as he possibly could – all the way through true madness and back into a banality whose true underlying insanity he still maintains but now knows is not voluntarily accessible (or even acceleratable, perhaps). 'A Dirty Joke' stands as testament to, or post-mortem analysis of, this project in transcendental empiricism, revealing that Land's last hope for humanity – that it might be escaped – and the greatest wager of life – that it might give access to death – experimentally failed. But perhaps they 'failed better' than those who went before him. The legacy of Land's experiments, like the rags and tatters of the visionaries whose works he picked through for clues, includes contributions to the diagnosis of the cosmic, biological, evolutionary, and cultural genealogy and nature of the human; forays into the thinking of number that exceed in breadth and depth any extant 'philosophy of mathematics'; a sophisticated and culturally contemporary philosophical thinking of time and modernity; and above all a series of textual machines whose compelling, strangely intoxicating power must, in a social and intellectual climate characterised by neo-classical sobriety, open up forgotten, suppressed, and alternative lineages and superpositions capable of inspiring others to take up the experiment once more, launching new assaults against the Human Security System.

Everything in Land's work that falls outside the parameters of disciplinary knowledge can and will be effectively dismissed by those who police the latter. In Bataille's incisive formulation, 'the unknown [...] is not distinguished from nothingness by anything that discourse can announce'. Like his fellows of the 'inferior race', what we retain of Land's expeditions are diverse and scattered remnants, here constellated for the first time. These are also tools or weapons; arrows that deserve to be taken up again and sharpened further. The wound needs to be opened up once more, and if this volume infects a new generation, already enlivened by a new wave of thinkers who are partly engaging the re-emerging legacy of Nick Land's work – it will have fulfilled its purpose.

ROBIN MACKAY & RAY BRASSIER

TRURO & BEIRUT, FEBRUARY 2011

Kant, Capital, and the Prohibition of Incest: A Polemical Introduction to the Configuration of Philosophy and Modernity

But intuition and the concept differentiate themselves from each other specifically; because they do not inter-mix with each other.

IMMANUEL KANT[1]

Significantly … incest proper, and its metaphorical form as the violation of a minor (by someone 'old enough to be her father', as the expression goes), even combines in some countries with its direct opposite, inter-racial sexual relations, an extreme form of exogamy, as the two most powerful inducements to horror and collective vengeance.

CLAUDE LÉVI-STRAUSS[2]

1   I. Kant, *Kritik der Urteilskraft*, ed. Wilhelm Weischedel (Wiesbaden: Suhrkampf, 1974), *Anmerkung* to section VIII of the Introduction to Kant's first edition, 40; for a recent English translation, see I. Kant, *Critique of the Power of Judgment*, ed. P. Guyer, tr. P. Guyer & E. Matthews (Cambridge and New York: Cambridge University Press, 2000), First Introduction, VIII, 29.

2   C. Lévi-Strauss, *The Elementary Structures of Kinship* (Boston, MA: Taylor & Francis, 1969), 10.

No, we do not love humanity; but on the other hand we are not nearly 'German' enough, in the sense in which the word 'German' is constantly being used nowadays, to advocate nationalism and race hatred and to be able to take pleasure in the national scabies of the heart and blood-poisoning that now leads the nations of Europe to delimit and barricade themselves against each other as if it were a matter of quarantine.

FRIEDRICH NIETZSCHE[3]

For the purposes of understanding the complex network of race, gender, and class oppressions that constitute our global modernity it is very rewarding to attend to the evolution of the apartheid policies of the South African regime, since apartheid is directed towards the construction of a microcosm of the neo-colonial order; a recapitulation of the world in miniature. The most basic aspiration of the Boer state is the dissociation of politics from economic relations, so that by means of 'bantustans' or 'homelands' the black African population can be suspended in a condition of simultaneous political distance and economic proximity vis-à-vis the white metropolis. This policy seeks to recast the currently existing political exteriority of the black population in its relation to the

---

3   F. Nietzsche, *The Gay Science*, tr. Walter Kaufmann (New York: Vintage, 1974), 339.

society that utilizes its labour into a system of geographical relations modelled on national sovereignty. The direct disenfranchisement of the subject peoples would then be re-expressed within the dominant international code of ethno-geographical (national) autonomy.

World opinion discriminates between the relation South African whites have to the blacks they employ, and the relation North American whites, for instance, have to the Third World labour force they employ (directly or indirectly), because it acknowledges an indissoluble claim upon the entire South African land-mass by a population sharing an internationally recognized national identity. My contention in this paper is that the Third World as a whole is the product of a successful – although piecemeal and largely unconscious – 'bantustan' policy on the part of the global Kapital metropolis. Any attempt by political forces in the Third World to resolve the problems of their neo-colonial integration into the world trading system on the basis of national sovereignty is as naive as would be the attempt of black South Africans if they opted for a 'bantustan' solution to their particular politico-economic dilemma. The displacement of the political consequences of wage labour relations away from the metropolis is not an incidental feature of capital accumulation, as the economic purists aligned to both the bourgeoisie and the workerist left assert. It is rather the fundamental condition of capital as nothing other than an explicit aggression against the masses.

Despite inadequacies in Marx's grasp of the nation state in its colonial and neo-colonial functioning, his account of 'so-called primitive accumulation'[4] clearly demonstrates that the origin of wage labour relations is not itself economic, but lies in an overt war against the people, or their forced removal from previous conditions of subsistence. It is the outward shock-wave of this violent process of coercion, whereby the subsistence producer is driven into the marketplace, that determines the character of the imperialist project and its offspring. Capital has always sought to distance itself in reality – i.e. geographically – from this brutal political infrastructure. After all, the ideal of bourgeois politics is the absence of politics, since capital is nothing other than the consistent displacement of social decision-making into the marketplace. But this ideal of total de-politicization, or the absolute annihilation of resistance to market relations, is an impossible megalomaniac fantasy, and Marx's contention that labour trading at its natural price in an undistorted market (equal to the cost of its reproduction) will tend strongly to express an equally 'natural' political refusal of the market, continues to haunt the global bourgeoisie.

---

4 K. Marx, *Capital: Volume I*, tr. Ben Fowkes (New York: Vintage, 1977), 667ff.

The only practical option available to the rulers of capitalist societies has lain in the global disaggregation of the political system, accompanied by a regional distortion of the world labour trading system in favour of the working classes in the metropolitan regions ('welfare capitalism'). This is why a deep complicity has continued to exist between the form of the 'nation state' as international political agent and an economic order based upon the commodification of labour. Since it is of systematic necessity that the economic conditions of an undistorted labour market are accompanied by political crisis, the world order functions as an integrated process based upon the flow of market-priced labour into the metropolis from the Third World (on the basis of the economic form of capital production), and the export of political instability to the Third World from the metropolis (on the basis of the political form of autonomous national sovereignty). The global labour market is easily interpreted, therefore, as a sustained demographic disaster that is systematically displaced away from the political institutions of the metropolis.

This process of displacement, which is the ultimate 'base' or 'infrastructure' of capital accumulation, is dependent upon those issues of 'kinships' or 'marriage organization' (the sexual economy of gender and race) which Marxists have often tended to consider as surface features of an underlying mode of production.

In this paper I shall argue that with the philosophy of Immanuel Kant, Western cultural history culminates in a self-reflecting bourgeois civilization, because his thought of synthesis (or relation to alterity), and also the strangulation of this thought within his system, captures modernity as a problem. But the modernity thus symptomized by its philosophical exposition is not primarily the penultimate phase of a dialectic of society and production, it is rather the necessity that historically itself – expansionary social and economic development, or 'synthesis' – compromises with a profound continuity whose basic aspects are on the one hand patrilineal descent, and on the other a formal logic of identity that was already concluded in its essentials by Aristotle. These two aspects, the genealogical and the logical, are functions of a position of abstract masculine subjectivity coincident with the patronymic. This position is the proto-cultural fundament of everything that is able to count as the same. The tradition is thus rooted in a communication between culture and population, whose medium is the stability ('identity') of the male line. Modernity is not merely a compromise between novel forms of commercially driven social organization and this archaic cultural pattern of patrilineal exogamy, but more fundamentally, a deepening of the compromise already integral to any exogamy that is able to remain patrilineal. It is only by understanding the inhibitive function of patriarchies in relation to exogamic dissipation (an inhibition that is supremely logical in that it conserves identity, and which is for this reason violently xenophobic) that we can make sense of capital production and its tendency towards the peculiar cultural mutation that was baptised by Mussolini as 'fascism'. This is because the restriction of cultural synthesis, based upon a strenuous endogamy at the level of the national community, is the ultimate outcome of the concerted 'liberalization' of kinship organizations within (metropolitan) industrial societies.

A capitalist trading empire is a developed form of exogamic patriarchy, and inherits its tensions. Domination of the other is inhibited in principle from developing into full absorption, because it is the residual alterity of the other that conditions the generation of surplus. The parallel difference between a labour market and a slave market is based on the fact that one cannot do business with a slave (but only with a slave-owner), and similarly, one cannot base a kinship system upon a harem. The prevalence of slave-labour within the Hitlerite new order in Eastern Europe is thus a clear indication that the Nazi conquests were in an important sense 'post-imperialist'. In contrast to the fascist 'mixed economy' of slavery and extermination, colonial wage-labour exploitation, even to the point of murder through impoverishment, leaves open the possibility of a radical destabilization of the metropolis. But what is crucial to the demarcation of a colonial from a neo-colonial system is a transnational diffusion of ethnicity. As soon as a metropolitan society disengages its organization of kinship and citizenship from its international economic syntheses it already reveals proto-fascist traits, and on this basis it is easy to see that the radical aspect to the colonial project – the explosion of national identity and the dissipation of metropolitan transcendence – was strangled at birth within Western history (with the emergence of Judaeo-Christian race theories).

The disaster of world history is that capitalism was never the progressive unwinding of patrilineage through a series of generalized exploitative relations associated with a trans-cultural exogamy, leading to an uncontrollable eruption of feminine (i.e. migrant) alterity into the father's heartland, and thus to the emergence of a radical – or ethnically disruptive and post-patriarchal – synthesis. Instead, kinship and trade were systematically isolated from each other, so that the internationalization of the economy was coupled with an entrenchment of xenophobic (nationalistic) kinship practices, maintaining a concentration of political and economic power within an isolated and geographically sedentary ethnic stock. Thus, when we discuss capital in its historical concreteness, we are simultaneously discussing a frustration of the cultural tendency of human societies towards expansive exogamy. Capital is the point at which a culture refuses the possibility – which it has itself engendered – of pushing the prohibition of incest towards its limit.

I want to touch upon this condition of modernity – which can be awkwardly described as patriarchal neo-colonial capital accumulation, but which I shall come to name 'inhibited synthesis' – not as a historian or a political theorist, but as a philosopher. The philosophical task in relation to modernity is that of delineating and challenging the type of thinking which characterizes it. But what we are to understand as 'thinking' is not at all clear in advance, indeed, the very thought of the 'in advance' (which Kant called the a priori) is itself the predominant trait of our contemporary reason. Western societies departed from the stagnant theocracies of the Middle Ages through a series of more or less violent convulsions that have engendered an explosive possibility of novelty on earth. But these same societies simultaneously shackled this new history by systematically compromising it. This ambiguous movement of 'enlightenment', which characterizes the emergence of industrial societies trading in commodities, is intellectually stimulated by its own paradoxical nature. An enlightenment society wants both to learn and to legislate for all time, to open itself to the other and to consolidate itself from within, to expand indefinitely whilst reproducing itself as the same. Its ultimate dream is to grow whilst remaining identical to what it was, to touch the other without vulnerability. Where the European *ancien régime* was parochial and insular, modernity is appropriate. It lives in a profound but uneasy relation to an outside that both attracts and repels it, a relation that it precariously resolves within itself on the basis of exploitation, or interaction from a position of unilateral mastery. I think it is likely that the volatile mixture of hatred and desire that typifies an exploitative culture bears comparison with the psychology of rape.

The paradox of enlightenment, then, is an attempt to fix a stable relation with what is radically other, since insofar as the other is rigidly positioned within a relation it is no longer fully other. If before encountering otherness we already know what its relation to us will be, we have obliterated it in advance. And this brutal denial is the effective implication of the thought of the a priori, since if our certainties come to us without reference to otherness we have always already torn out the tongue of alterity before entering into relation with it. This aggressive logical absurdity (the absurdity of logic itself) reaches its zenith in the philosophy of Kant, whose basic problem was to find an account for the possibility of what he termed 'synthetic a priori knowledge', which is knowledge that is both given in advance by ourselves, and yet adds to what we know. As we have seen, this problem is the same as that of accounting for the possibility of modernity or enlightenment, which is to say, of the inhibited encounter with alterity.

Modern philosophy between René Descartes (1596–1650) and Immanuel Kant (1724–1804) is usually retrospectively understood in terms of the two basic tendencies which we refer to as 'empiricism' and 'rationalism'. No philosopher was a perfect and consistent exemplar of either of these tendencies, but the exponents of each tended to become increasingly radical in one direction or the other. By the time Kant wrote his first great critique, *The Critique of Pure Reason*,[5] he was able to take the writings of David Hume (1711–76) as definitive for empirical thought, and those of Gottfried Wilhelm Leibniz (1646–1716) as definitive for rationalism. He took the basic argument of the empiricists to be that knowledge is synthetic and a posteriori, meaning that it takes the form of an addition to what is inherent to reason, and thus follows from experience (or an encounter with what is outside ourselves). In contrast to this, he saw the rationalists to be arguing that knowledge is characteristically analytic and a priori, meaning that it is derived from what is already inherent to reason, and thus anticipates experience by constructing systems of logical deduction from basic axioms. Knowledge is analytic or synthetic depending on whether its source is intrinsic or extrinsic to the faculty of reason, and

---

5   I. Kant, *The Critique of Pure Reason*, tr., ed. P. Guyer and A. W. Wood (Cambridge and New York: Cambridge University Press, 1998).

a priori or a posteriori depending on whether it precedes or succeeds the contact with sensation, or with what is outside reason. It is with these pairs of concepts, the analytic/synthetic couple and the a priori/a posteriori couple, that Kant determines the structure of his own thinking in relation to that of his recent predecessors.

Kant thought that both empiricist and rationalist philosophers had accepted the simple alignment of the synthetic with the a posteriori and of the analytic with the a priori. This is to say, the relation between these couples had seemed to be itself analytic, so that to speak of analytic a priori judgments would add nothing to the concept of the analytic, or in other words, an analysis of the concept 'analytic' would yield the concept of the 'a priori' as already implicit within it. This assumption was not accepted by Kant, who re-aligned the two pairs of concepts in a perpendicular fashion to form a grid, thus yielding four permutations. He granted the elimination of any analytic a posteriori knowledge, but clung doggedly to the possibility of knowledge that would be both synthetic and a priori. This new conception of knowledge was relevant to an 'object' that had not previously been formulated: the conditions of experience. Kant described his 'Copernican revolution' in philosophy as a shift from the question 'what must the mind be like in order to know?' to the question 'what must objects be like in order to be known?' The answers to this latter question would provide a body of synthetic a priori knowledge, telling us about experience without being derived from experience. It would justify the emergence of knowledge that was both new and timelessly certain, grounding the enlightenment culture of a civilization confronting an ambiguous dependence upon novelty.

Because a developed knowledge of the conditions of experience presupposes a relation to the outside it is synthetic and not analytic, but because it concerns the pure form of the relation as such and not the sensory material involved in the relation it is a priori and not a posteriori. It is solely concerned with the forms of appearance, or the unchanging manner in which things must be if they are to be for us. Kant calls this pure form of synthesis 'transcendental', and opposes it to the inconstant content of synthesis, with which the empiricists had been concerned, and which he calls 'empirical'. Kant's 'object' is thus the universal form of the relation to alterity; that which must of necessity be the same in the other in order for it to appear to us. This universal form is that which is necessary for anything to be 'on offer' for experience, it is the 'exchange value' that first allows a thing to be marketed to the enlightenment mind. Between medieval scholasticism and Kant Western reason moves from a parochial economy to a system in which, abandoning the project of repressing the traffic with alterity, one resolves instead to control the system of trade. With the overthrow of the ancien regime it became impossible to simply exclude novelty; it could only be appropriated, stamped with a constant form, and integrated into an immutable formal system. In *The Elementary Structures of Kinship* Claude Lévi-Strauss notes the frequent distinction made by various societies between normal and 'rich food'. Normal food is consumed by its producers as a means to their subsistence, whilst rich food is given to another to consume, and received from another. This is not primarily based upon a differentiation of social classes within a system of production, but rather, upon a differentiation between tribes, or separate systems of production. The difference between rich food and normal food maps onto the difference between filiation (relation by blood) and alliance (relation by marriage). This is because rich food occupies the position of women within a marriage system regulated by patrilineal exogamy, with its producer renouncing it for himself, and thus echoing the prohibition of incest. What is of particular philosophical interest, however, is that it also marks a distinction between the 'rational' (analytic) and the 'empirical' (synthetic), and thus defines a terrain upon which we can sketch an economy of knowledge. Rich food comes from outside the system, and the contortions undergone by structural anthropology in its project to recapture it within an expanded system of relations replay Kant's efforts to reduce synthesis to an expanded horizon of unchanging forms.

If 'rich food' is the primordial element of trade, its meta-morphosis into the modern 'commodity' can be seen as a suppression of radical synthesis, the problematic process which provides enlightenment reason with its object of thought.

The cultural inhibition of synthesis takes a form that Lévi-Strauss calls 'dual organization'.[6] A dual organization arises when two groups form a closed system of reciprocal exchange, in which each consumes the rich food, and marries the women, of the other. Such organizations reproduce themselves culturally through shared myths articulated around basic dualities (day/night, sun/moon, up-river/down-river etc.). The function of these myths is to capture alterity within a system of rules, to provide it with an identity, and to exclude the possibility of the radically different. It should not surprise us, therefore, that Kant inherited a philosophical tradition whose decisive concepts were organized into basic couples (spirit/matter, form/content, abstract/concrete, universal/particular, etc.). He delineates some basic structure of this tradition in the section of the *Critique of Pure Reason* called the 'Transcendental Dialectic'. In this section he interprets this dichotomous heritage as a problem (to which Kant gives the name 'antinomy') and initiates a new phase of Western philosophy, now characterized as the critique

---

6   Lévi-Strauss, *The Elementary Structures of Kinship*, 69–83.

of metaphysics. Kant argues that the tendency of previous metaphysics to conceive coherent, but unpersuasive and antagonistic, intellectual systems resulted from the application of pure (transcendental) concepts to arguments concerning the nature of things in themselves (noumena). The critical philosophy therefore restricts the jurisdiction of all concepts to the realm of possible appearance (intuition), suggesting (as we have seen) that the a priori forms of knowledge have no purchase on any reality transcending the phenomenon. Oppositional terms are no longer accepted as descriptions capturing reality, but are interpreted as pure forms of reason that can only be meaningfully deployed theoretically when applied to objects of possible appearance, which fall within the legislative domain of the 'faculty' which Kant calls 'the understanding' [*Verstand*].

Since 'reality' is itself a transcendental concept, Kant's usage of a distinction between appearance and reality to restrict the deployment of pure concepts already suggests a crucial difficulty with his project, since every attempt to formulate a relation or distinction between the phenomenal and noumenal realms (the world as it appears to us or is understood, and the world as it is in itself) must itself relapse into the pre-critical and illegitimate deployment of conceptual thought. One crucial symptom of this is that the structure of Kantian critique itself perpetuates the oppositional form of metaphysical thought, since its resolution of the antinomies depends upon the mobilization of further dichotomies, in particular those of transcendental/empirical, phenomenon/noumenon, concept/intuition, and analysis/synthesis. In other words, Kant still wants to say something about radical alterity, even if it is only that it has no relevance to us, yet he has deprived himself of the right to all speculation about the nature of what is beyond appearance. The vocabulary that would describe the other of metaphysics is itself inscribed within metaphysics, since the inside and the outside are both conceptually determined from the inside, within a binary myth or cultural symptom of dual organization. It is thus the inhibition of synthesis – the delimitation of alterity in advance – that sets up the modern form of the ontological question: 'how do we know that matter exists?' That the very existence of materiality is problematic for enlightenment thought is symptomatic of the colonial trading systems that correspond to it. Alterity cannot be registered, unless it can be inscribed within the system, according to the interconnected axes of exchange value (price) and the patronymic, or, in other words, as a commodity with an owner.

What falls outside this recognized form is everything that resists commodification, the primordial independence that antedates the constitution of the destituted proletarian. As I have suggested, this inchoate mass of more or less explicit resistance to capital is isolated outside the metropolis by a combination of automatic economic processes (the concentration of poverty) and restrictive kinship practices. Modern capital has therefore brought about a fundamental dislocation between filiation and alliance by simultaneously de-regulating alliance and abstracting it from all kinship implications. The primordial anthropological bond between marriage and trade is dissolved, in order that capital can ethnically and geographically quarantine its consequences from itself. The question of racism, which arises under patriarchal capital as the default of a global trade in women (a parochialism in the system of misogynistic violence; the non-emergence of a trans-cultural exogamy), is thus more complex than it might seem, and is bound in profound but often paradoxical ways to the functioning of patriarchy and capital. Systematic racism is a sign that class positions within the general (trans-national) economy are being distributed on a racial basis, which implies an effective, if not a juridical, apartheid.

Kant was able to remain bourgeois without overtly promoting racism only because he also remained an idealist, or in other words a Christian (a 'cunning Christian' as Nietzsche calls him)[7] and identified universality with ideality rather than with power. Kant's economy of the concept, which is the assimilation of experience into a

---

7   F. Nietzsche, *Twilight of the Idols; and the Anti-Christ*, tr. R.J. Hollingdale (London: Penguin, 1990), 49.

system of exchange values, is irresistible in principle, and thus does not recognize a problem of rebellion. It is only with the implicit recognition of the need for a systematic evacuation of rebellion from the metropolis by means of a geographically distorted labour market that racism arises in its contemporary form, which is ultimately that of a restricted franchise (on a national basis) over the political management of the global means of production. It is no longer a question of 'taxation without representation' (except by means of interest payments), but rather of a metropolitan capital seeking to abstract itself from all political reference, becoming 'offshore', although not to the extent that it loses its geopolitical condition of existence (the US war-machine). The increasingly rigorous differentiation of marriage from trade, or politics from economics, finds its ultimate conceptual definition in the thought of a moral agency which is utterly impervious to learning, communication, or exchange.

It is in his second critique, *The Critique of Practical Reason*,[8] that Kant capitalizes upon the ethno-ethical consequences of the first: that justice must be prosecuted without negotiation. Kant's moral theory is an ethics of appropriative modernity, and breaks with the parochial or scriptural morality of the ancien regime. Where Judaic, Christian, and Islamic moral codes served as legitimations

---

8   I. Kant, 'Critique of Practical Reason', in *Practical Philosophy*, tr., ed. M.J. Gregor (Cambridge and New York: Cambridge University Press, 1996), 133–271.

of imperial projects in their periods of ascendency, Kantian morality is, inversely, legitimated by the position of imperial or universal jurisdiction. Only that is moral which can be demanded of every rational being unconditionally, in the name of an ultra-empire that Kant names the 'empire of ends' [*Reich der Zwecke*]. The law of this empire is called the 'categorical imperative', which means a law stemming solely from the purity of the concept, and thus dictated by the absolute monologue of colonial reason. In the purity of categorical morality the incestuous blood-line of the pharaohs is still detectable, but sublimated into an impersonal administration. The law is that which cannot be legitimately discussed, and which is therefore an unresponsive or unilateral imposition. It is not difficult to see that the second critique distills the xenophobic violence of the first and elevates it to the most extreme possible fanaticism. Where theoretical knowledge is open to a limited negotiation with alterity, practical or moral certainty is forbidden from entering into relation with anything outside itself, except to issue commands. Kant's practical subject already prefigures a deaf führer, barking impossible orders that seem to come from another world. Kant makes a further strenuous effort to push forward the horizon of a priori synthesis in his third critique, *The Critique of Judgment*. If the first *Critique* corresponds to appropriative economy or commodification, and the second critique corresponds to imperial jurisdiction, the third critique corresponds to the exercise of war at those margins of the global system that continue to resist both the market and the administration. It is concerned with the type of pleasure that is experienced when an object demonstrates an extra-juridical submission or abasement before the faculty of judgment; an experience which Kant associates with the contemplation of beauty. The first *Critique* already exhibits a conception of excess or a priori synthesis that generalizes the principles of the labour market to all objects of theoretical cognition and transforms the understanding into a form of intellectual capital. In the third critique there is a far more aggressive conception of excess, which generates a feeling of delight, because it is essentially extortionate. This excess is not a surplus of certainty stemming from dimensions of objectivity possessed in advance of intuition, and thus by right, but rather a surplus of purchase upon the object. Kant argues that we have no transcendental right to expect natural laws to be sufficiently homogeneous for us to grasp. When confronting the heterogeneity of intuition, reason must engage in a kind of Pascalian wager; assuming an intelligible system of nature because it has nothing to lose by not doing so. The submission of the outside in general to the inside in general, or of nature to the idea, i.e. conquest, is not guaranteed by any principle. The capitalist feels a neutral satisfaction in the production of 'normal profits', but the conqueror feels exultation in the attainment of victory, precisely because there was no reason to expect it. Kant's advice to the imperial war-machine in his third critique can be summarized as: 'treat all resistance as if it were less than you might justifiably fear'. The *Critique of Judgment* thus projects the global victory of capitalized reason as pure and exuberant ambition.

The only possible politics of purity is fascism, or a militant activism rooted in the inhibitory and exclusive dimensions of a metropolitanism. Racism, as a regulated, automatic, and indefinitely suspended process of genocide (as opposed to the hysterical and unsustainable genocide of the Nazis) is the real condition of persistence for a global economic system that is dependent upon an aggregate price of labour approximating to the cost of its bare subsistence, and therefore upon an expanding pool of labour power which must be constantly 'stimulated' into this market by an annihilating poverty. If fascism is evaded in metropolitan societies it is only because a chronic passive genocide trails in the wake of capital and commodity markets as they displace themselves around the Third World, 'disciplining' the labour market, and ensuring that basic commodity prices are not high enough to distribute capital back into primary producer societies. The forces most unambiguously antagonistic to this grotesque process are 'exogamic' (or, less humanistically, 'exotropic'); the synthetic energies that condition all surplus value, and yet co-exist with capital only under repression. A radical international socialism would not be a socialist ideology generalized beyond its culture of origin, but a programme of collectivity or unrestrained synthesis that springs from the theoretical and libidinal dissolution of national totality. To get to a world without nations would in itself guarantee the achievement of all immediately post-capitalist social and economic goals. It is this revolutionary requirement for a spontaneously homeless subversion that gives an urgency to certain possibilities of feminist politics, since the erasure of matrilineal genealogy within the patriarchal machine means that fascisizing valorizations of ancestry have no final purchase on the feminine 'subject'. The patronymic has irrecoverably divested all the women who fall under it of any recourse to an ethno-geographical identity; only the twin powers of father and husband suppress the nomadism of the anonymous female fluxes that patriarchy oppressively manipulates, violates, and psychiatrizes. By allowing women some access to wealth and social prestige the liberalization of patriarchy has sought to defuse the explosive force of this anonymity, just as capital has tended to reduce the voluptuous excess of exogamic conjugation to the stability of nationally segmented trading circuits. The increasingly incestual character of economic order – reaching its zenith in racist xenophobia – is easily masked as a series of 'feminist' reforms of patriarchy; as a de-commodification of woman, a diminution of the obliterating effects of the patronymic, and a return to the mother. This is the sentimental 'feminism' that Nietzsche despised, and whose petit-bourgeois nationalist implications he clearly saw. The only resolutely revolutionary politics is feminist in orientation, but only if the synthetic forces mobilized under patriarchy are extrapolated beyond the possibility of assimilation, rather than being criticized from the perspective of mutilated genealogies. Genealogy as the dissipation of recuperative origins (Nietzsche), not as sentimental nostalgia. The women of the earth are segmented only by their fathers and husbands. Their praxial fusion is indistinguishable from the struggle against the micro-powers that suppress them most immediately. That is why the proto-fascism of nationality laws and immigration controls tends to have a sexist character as well as a racist one. It is because women are the historical realization of the potentially euphoric synthetic or communicative function which patriarchy both exploits and inhibits that they are invested with a revolutionary destiny, and it is only through their struggle that politics will be able to escape from all fatherlands. In her meticulous studies of patriarchy Luce Irigaray has amply demonstrated the peculiar urgency of the feminist question,[9] although the political solutions she suggests are often feebly nostalgic, sentimental, and pacifistic. Perhaps only Monique

---

9   Amongst the growing body of Luce Irigaray's work available in English the most powerful arguments are to be found, perhaps, in *Speculum of the Other Woman*, tr. G.C. Gill (Ithaca, NY: Cornell University Press, 1985) and in essays amongst those compiled in *This Sex which is not One*, tr. C. Porter and C. Burke (Ithaca, NY: Cornell University Press, 1985), especially 'Women on the Market' ('Le marché des femmes'), 170–91, and 'Commodities Among Themselves' ('Des marchandises entre elles'), 192–7.

Wittig has adequately grasped the inescapably military task faced by any serious revolutionary feminism,[10] and it is difficult not to be dispirited by the enormous reluctance women have shown historically to prosecute their struggle with sufficient ruthlessness and aggression. The left tends to be evasive about the numbing violence intrinsic to revolutionary war, and feminism is often particularly fastidious in this respect, even reverting to absurd mystical and Ghandian ideologies. If feminist struggles have been constantly deprioritized in theory and practice it is surely because of their idealistic recoil from the currency of violence, which is to say, from the only definitive 'matter' of politics. The state apparatus of an advanced industrial society can certainly not be defeated without a willingness to escalate the cycle of violence without limit. It is a terrible fact that atrocity is not the perversion, but the very motor of such struggles: the language of inexorable political will. A revolutionary war against a modern metropolitan state can only be fought in hell. It is this harsh truth that has deflected Western politics into an increasingly servile reformism, whilst transforming nationalist struggles into the sole arena of vigorous contention against particular configurations of capital. But, as I hope I have demonstrated, such nationalist struggles are relevant only to the geographical modulation of capital, and not to the radical

---

10 See especially M. Wittig, *Les Guerillères* (Paris: Minuit, 1969); tr. D. Le Vay (Chicago, IL: University of Illinois Press, 2007).

jeopardizing of neo-colonialism (inhibited synthesis) as such. Victorious Third World struggles, so long as they have been successfully localized, do not lead to realistic post-capitalist achievements, and certainly not to post-patriarchal ones, since the conservation of the form of the nation state is itself enough to guarantee the reinsertion of a society into the system of inhibited synthesis. For as long as the dynamic of guerilla war just leads to new men at the top – with all that this entails in terms of the communication between individuated sovereignties – history will continue to look bleak. For it is only when the pervasive historical bond between masculinity and war is broken by effective feminist violence that it will become possible to envisage the uprooting of the patriarchal endogamies that orchestrate the contemporary world order. With the abolition of the inhibition of synthesis – of Kantian thought – a sordid cowardice will be washed away, and cowardice is the engine of greed. But the only conceivable end of Kantianism is the end of modernity, and to reach this we must foster new Amazons in our midst.

Narcissism and Dispersion in Heidegger's 1953 Trakl Interpretation

Martin Heidegger's thinking continues to have a massive – and constantly growing – influence on the development of modern 'philosophy'; in the formulation of its questions, the selection of its 'objects', and the constructions of its history. Yet this in itself might not be enough to explain why his 1953 essay on the Austrian poet Georg Trakl should be of interest to us. Does Heidegger's essay perhaps represent Trakl to us in a way that is enlightening or informative? Does it tell us something about poetry, or history, or language in general? Does it, in fact, succeed in doing anything at all? In his safely vacuous text on Trakl's poetry Herbert Lindenberger writes:

> It would seem gratuitous to complain of the wrong-headedness of Heidegger's approach to Trakl, for Heidegger does not even pretend to use the poets he writes about for any purpose except the exposition of his own philosophy. But Heidegger's study of Trakl seems to me considerably less successful than his study of Hölderlin ... [1]

---

1   H. Lindenberger, *George Trakl* (New York: Twayne, 1971), 141.

Lindenberger does not ask what meaning can be given to 'success' within a history – like Heidegger's history of being – for which the proper sense of progress has always been the expansion of devastation; a history, that is, which has been perpetually deflected from thinking by a pervasive theo-technical tradition. Platonic-Christian culture has made it not only possible, but also imperative, to think of poetry as the product of a poet, and, derivatively, as something to be 'used' by a philosopher for the purpose of illustrating representational concepts. It is this tradition which directs us to ask about the usefulness and representational adequacy of Heidegger's essay. Such questions are symptoms of a profound and positively constituted illiteracy, whose hegemony it has been the intellectual task of the (post-)modern age to question.

As for Trakl – who failed to organize his desires according to the laws of his civilization, failed to keep a job, became addicted to opium, enmeshed in alcoholism, failed to defeat his psychosis and died of a cocaine overdose in a military pharmacy – what would we be doing to him if we said he had 'succeeded' as a poet? Appropriating his delicate, futile ardour to a society that has forgotten how to despise itself? Trakl's traces are the ruins of a miserable, even horrific, failure. A failure to adapt or conform, to repress or sublimate adequately, to produce, resolve, comfort, or conclude. This failure is not merely a default, however, but a violently traumatic condition.

The evolution of his style, if it is still possible to write coherently of such a thing, is a drive towards the dissolution of every criterion for evaluation. It is this above all which he learns from his decisive encounters with Rimbaud and Hölderlin. The traditional aesthetics which would distinguish a traumatic content from a perfectly 'achieved' formal presentation loses all pertinence as Trakl presses language into the shadows. The last thing we should want is for Heidegger to 'master' these traumatized signs. To learn from Trakl is to write in ashes.

A long essay by Heidegger appeared in the sixty-first (1953) issue of the German literary periodical *Merkur* which discussed the work of Georg Trakl. This mysterious text, at once intensely personal and strangely detached, was entitled 'Georg Trakl. Eine Erörterung seines Gedichtes' ('Georg Trakl. A situating of his poetry'). The same essay, renamed 'Die Sprache im Gedicht' ('Language in the Poem'), and now subtitled 'Eine Erörterung von Georg Trakls Gedicht' ('A situating of Georg Trakl's poetry'), was later published (in 1959) as the second division of Heidegger's book *Unterwegs zur Sprache* (*On the Way to Language*). The essay which precedes it in the book, 'Die Sprache' ('Language'), is also concerned with Trakl, or, more precisely, with the reading of a single Trakl poem, *Ein Winterabend* ('A Winter Evening'). 'Die Sprache im Gedicht', in comparison, cites, or sites, no fewer than forty-three of Trakl's poems in the course of a wide-ranging search for the well-spring of their peculiar language. Outside of these two texts Heidegger makes only glancing references to Trakl's work and to the impact it had on his own thinking.

The 1953 essay consists of three numbered sections of uneven length, prefaced by a short untitled introduction or prologue. These basic partitions are not interrelated according to any conventional pedagogical principle, and do not unfold the stages of a developing argument. It is, for instance, very difficult to discriminate between the essay's three main sections in terms of theses or themes, since each successive section recollects the discussion of the last and subtly displaces it. To depict this complex progression it is perhaps necessary to borrow the 'metaphor' Heidegger himself calls upon, that of a wave, which describes motion coiling into an enigmatic pulsion and cyclical repetition. Yet the peaks and troughs that alternate within Heidegger's text do not follow the regular trace of an oscillograph; they cut a jagged and confusing path. As they rise a distinct 'theme' emerges, momentarily isolated from a maelstrom of interweaving currents. Due to the intensity of Trakl's language, and to the momentum historically invested within it, each theme shatters into blinding foam when swept to its apex, and sinks again into swirling depths. In this essay I shall only attempt to explore limited stretches along a single of these interwoven currents: pursuing elements of reflection and dispersion in Heidegger's reading of Trakl's poem *Geistliche Dämmerung*.

Heidegger's readings of poetry are perhaps most distinctively characterized by the refusal to participate affirmatively in the discourse of European aesthetics, and the associated project of rigorously bracketing subject-object epistemological categories. He argues that when the categories of aesthetics are carried into the domain of linguistics or other varieties of language study they take the form of a distinction between a normal and a meta-language. The minimal notion of meta-language is a technical terminology which is distinctive to the critical or interpretative text. This terminology traces an ancestry for itself that is divergent in principle from that of the texts to which it is 'applied'. The kinship of 'thinker' and 'poet' is annihilated. At variance to this sedimenting of metaphysics, Heidegger pursues a tendency towards the uttermost erasure of terminological distinctiveness. The language of poetry is not to be translated, but simply guided into a relationship with itself. And this guidance is not to be that of the thinker qua subject, but that of an impersonal thinking which is no longer disguised in the cloak of philosophy. Philosophy would no longer be the guardian of this relation, since the epoch of philosophy is simultaneous with that of meta-language. Or, put differently, meta-language is pre-eminently the language of metaphysics.

The final essay in *Unterwegs zur Sprache*, entitled 'Der Weg zur Sprache', begins by citing a sentence from Novalis's 1798 text *Monolog*: 'Precisely what is most peculiar about language, that it only concerns itself with itself, nobody knows'.[2] It is from this thought – of language accounting for itself in itself – that Heidegger begins his meditation on poetry. The vocabulary for the meditation is to stem from the reading itself. Indeed, thought is to be carefully dissolved into poetry, but only in such a way that poetry is strengthened in its thinking. Heidegger trusts that the key to what is said in the reserve of Western languages, while itself reserved, is yet able to be elicited. He suggests:

> Thus released into its own freedom, language can concern itself solely with itself. This sounds like the discourse upon an egoistic solipsism. But language does not insist on itself in the sense of a self-centred all-forgetting self-mirroring. As saying, the weft of language is the propriative showing, which precisely deflects its gaze from itself, in order to free what is shown into its appropriate appearing.[3]

---

2   Novalis, *Dichtungen* (Reinbek bei Hamburg: Rowohlt: 1963), 5; M. Heidegger, *Unterwegs zur Sprache* (Pfullingen: Neske, 1982), 241; tr. P.D. Hertz, J. Stambaugh as *On the Way to Language* (London: Harper & Row, 1982).

3   Heidegger, *Unterwegs zur Sprache*, 262.

Language is to be understood in a way that could be misread as a theory of narcissism, since it relates itself to itself, and this could be taken to be analogous to the self-regard of a subject enraptured by its own reflection. The discourse on language must therefore fend off a misinterpretation that threatens to appropriate it, or at least deflect it, into a psychoanalysis of the sign. At this crucial moment the circle of language seems to symptomize a type of auto-eroticism, displacing itself into a geometric figure of desire. In insisting that his approach to language is not to be confused with a dissolution of the subject into unconscious energetics – and in the prologue to 'Die Sprache im Gedicht' the reference to psychoanalysis is explicit – Heidegger marks a crucial historical crossroads in the interpretation of Nietzsche's doctrine of the cosmic circle, the eternal recurrence of the same. Heidegger seeks rigorously to distinguish his own reading of eternal recurrence – as the last attempt to conceive the temporality of beings, as recapitulation of the history of being, as the circle of language, and even as Trakl's 'icy wave of eternity' – from what has been interpreted within the Freudian research programme as the 'death drive', as the economy of desire, and as the return of the inorganic. Return, which is perhaps the crucial thought of modernity, must now be read elsewhere. The dissolution of humanism is stripped even of the terminology which veils collapse in the mask of theoretical mastery. It must be hazarded to poetry.

Geistliche Dämmerung[4] is the only poem cited by Heidegger in its entirety in the essay, and this is of some considerable significance. Dissolving the unity and specificity of the separate poems plays a vital role in Heidegger's project of uncovering a site [*Ort*] that relates to the Trakl corpus indifferently and as a whole. Up to the point at which *Geistliche Dämmerung* is introduced Heidegger conserves the status of this site as the sole 'ontologically' significant totality by splintering, rearranging, and repeating fragments of the individual poems. The resilient integrity of this particular poem in Heidegger's text might therefore indicate a special difficulty, one that obstructs the process of assimilation and resists the hegemony of the site. If this is so it is possible that an issue is at stake in the reading of this poem which resists absorption into any readily communicable truth of Trakl's poetry, an issue that perhaps remains in some sense exterior to a 'thinking dialogue' with the poet, but one that also retains a peculiar insistence. As Heidegger's reading unfolds it comes to chart a closure of communication of precisely this kind.

---

4   The German *Dämmerung* is as ambiguous as the English 'twilight', and can mean the half-light of dawn as well as that of dusk. As Baudelaire is almost certainly Trakl's first major poetical influence (O. Basil, *Trakl* [Reinbek bei Hamburg: Rowohlt, 1965], 42–9) it is tempting to read the title *Geistliche Dämmerung* as a translation of *L'Aube spirituelle* ('Spiritual dawn'), the forty-seventh poem of *Spleen et Idéale* (C. Baudelaire, *Oeuvres Complètes* [Paris: Gallimard, 1975], vol. 1, 46). Heidegger, however, is determined to maintain the ambiguity of *Dämmerung* in his interpretation (Heidegger, *Unterwegs zur Sprache*, 42–3), and the importance of *Abend* ('evening') in Trakl's poetry lends weight to this 'decision'.

There is no unambiguous point at which the discussion of *Geistliche Dämmerung* begins. It is approached through a discussion of the final lines of *Sommersneige* ('Summer Solstice') in which the steps of a stranger ring through the silver night, and a blue beast is brought to the memory of its path, the melody of its spiriting year. To this is conjoined the hyacinthine countenance of twilight from the poem *Unterwegs* ('Underway'). Heidegger introduces the poem in order to address what is named in its title, without any hint that the perplexing figure of the sister is to haunt it both here and in its later citation,[5] displacing all other preoccupations. It reads:

Stille begegnet am Saum des Waldes
Ein dunkles Wild;
Am Hügel endet leise der Abendwind,

Verstummt die Klage der Amsel,
Und die sanften Flöten des Herbstes
Schweigen im Rohr.

Auf schwarzer Wolke
Befährst du trunken von Mohn
Den nächtigen Weiher,

---

5   Ibid., 67–81.

Den Sternenhimmel.
Immer tönt der Schwester mondene Stimme
Durch die geistliche Nacht.

(At the forest's rim silence meets / A dark beast; / Quietly, on the hill, dies the evening wind, // The plaint of the blackbird ceases, / And the gentle flutes of autumn / Fall silent in the reed. // On a black cloud you sail, / Drunk on poppies, / The nocturnal pool, // The starry sky. / The lunar voice of the sister sounds unceasing / Through the spiriting night.)[6]

The translation of 'beast' for *Wild* is of course unsatisfactory. In German the word *Wild* denotes a feral animal, especially one hunted as game, and sometimes it specifies such animals as deer. In addition it connotes wildness and wilderness, since the adjective 'wild' exists in German as well as English. Furthermore, it is probably etymologically related to the similar word *Wald* (forest). This network of associations seems impossible even to approach in translation. Such difficulties are particularly frustrating inasmuch as this translation must bear almost the entire weight of Trakl's exploration of animality, and the further stresses of Heidegger's response to it.

---

6   Ibid., 48; G. Trakl, *Das dichterische Werk* (Munich: Deutscher Taschenbuch Verlag, 1972), 66. For a recent English translation of most Trakl poems referred to in this essay, see G. Trakl, *Poems and Prose: A Bilingual Edition* tr. A. Stillmark (Evanston, IL: Northwestern University Press, 2005).

For Heidegger the 'dark beast' is clearly the 'blue beast' who negotiates the difference between animality and the opening of the horizon of being – *der Mensch*. The wildness of the beast is not swallowed by the forest; instead it gives to the forest a margin. But this margin is not a fixed demarcation, and is not illuminated by the light of day. The shadowy animal, trembling with uncertainty in the evening wind, is man:

> The blue beast is an animal whose animality presumably rests, not in animalness, but rather in that thoughtful gaze, after which the poet calls. This animality is yet distant, and scarcely to be registered, so that the animality of the animal noted here oscillates in the indeterminate. It is not yet brought into its weft [*Wesen*]. This animal, the one that thinks, animal rationale, humanity, is, according to Nietzsche's words, not yet firmly established [*fest gestellt*].[7]

Heidegger takes the weave of the distance separating humanity from the beasts of the wilderness to rest in a type of thinking that is irreducible to adaptive biological calculation. Such thinking is rooted in the temporalization of the ontological difference, and has been traditionally unified – if only confusedly so – about the thought of

---

7   Heidegger, *Unterwegs zur Sprache*, 45.

transcendence. Transcendental thinking has the peculiar characteristic of relating itself to the thematic of thought itself, a tendency which has been systematized within epistemological philosophy. Within the Western tradition this type of cognition has been designated 'reflection'. The human is that animal caught in the play of its reflection. The line of approach that Heidegger follows, in what is to be his first and sole decisive encounter with the poem, begins with its final stanza:

> The starry sky is portrayed [*dargestellt*, staged, placed there, the *stellen* is always decisive for Heidegger] in the poetic image of the nocturnal pool. So our habitual representation [*vor-stellen*] thinks it. But the night sky is in the truth of its weft this pool. Over against this, what we otherwise call the night remains only an image, namely, the faded and vacuous after-image [*Nachbild*, perhaps also 'copy'] of its weft.[8]

The insistence that the night sky is in truth a pool is not irreducible either to Heidegger's phenomenological stubbornness, or to a defence of the primordiality of metaphor. It is far more intimately connected with the problematic of spatiality in post-Kantian thinking, and beyond this with the Greek thought of the heavens as χαoς.

---

8   Ibid., 48.

These concerns are bound up with Heidegger's pursuit of that reflection which yields an image of human transcendence, and therefore marks a firmly established separation of Dasein from the psychology of animals. This pursuit is perhaps the aspect of Heidegger's work which is closest to the concerns of the ontotheological tradition, the point where his thinking is most 'human, all-to-human'. But there is, nevertheless, something both crucial and 'technically' precise at issue in this play of mirrors. The passage continues:

> The pool and the mirror-pool often recur in the poet's poetry. The water, sometimes blue, sometimes black, shows humanity its own countenance, its returning gaze. But in the nocturnal pool of the starry sky appears the twilight blue of the spiriting night. Its gleam is cool.[9]

The starry sky has an integral relation to reflection, but one which is of daunting complexity. Heidegger first turns to the pool itself, beside which humanity lies, lost in narcissistic reverie. Here humanity gazes upon itself, although we are not told whether, like Narcissus, this gaze is inflamed with desire.

9   Ibid.

Heidegger finds the compulsive character of Trakl's imagery to be indicative of a repression, but one which does not seem to be – at least superficially – primarily sexual. He takes the reflectivity of Trakl's mirrors to exceed all representation and ontical objectivity [*Vorhandenheit*]. In the darkened pool the gaze does not return in a familiar form; it reveals instead an abyssal twilit blue, which colours both the dawn and dusk of the spiriting night. The image of no thing returns. Reflection is shattered against the impersonal, against the impassive shade of a pure opening or cleft in beings. Humanity is thus reflected as the default of an (ontical) image; as a lack of ground or *Abgrund* which is the transcendental condition of any possible ontology. The heavens are an abyss: χαοζ. As we follow Heidegger's discussion of *Geistliche Dämmerung* further, this classical comprehension of chaos enters into a problematic negotiation with the contemporary sense of the word as disorder. It is this negotiation which reopens the path to Trakl's most crucial explorations.

As the reading of *Geistliche Dämmerung* proceeds Heidegger's discussion suddenly changes key, without indicating that there is any thematic unity between the mirror and the mysterious figure who is now introduced, the sister:

The cool light stems from the shining of the lunar woman [*Möndin*] (Selanna). Ringing her luminosity, as ancient Greek verse says, the stars fade and even cool. Everything becomes 'lunar'. The stranger [*der Fremde*, the German masculine] stepping through the night is called 'the lunar one'. The 'lunar voice' of the sister, which always sounds through the spiriting night, is then heard by the brother in his boat when he attempts to follow the stranger in a nocturnal journey across the pool, which is still 'black' and scarcely illuminated by the stranger's goldenness.[10]

The sister is allied to the moon, and thus to the luminosity of the night. Her power to render a world visible holds sway in the epoch of world-calumniating darkness initiated by the flight of the Hellenic gods, whose end is heralded by the stranger's goldenness, which is the flickering light of a new dawn. It is the sister who guides the path of the wanderer throughout the nihilistic metamorphoses, during which the securities of ontotheology lose their authority and disappear into their twilight, and before the arising of that new thinking which betrays itself only in scarcely perceptible hints. The sister is associated with transition, and with the indeterminacy of an unthreaded time. Even the corrupted seals that stamped the distinctive mark of scholasticism and theological apologetic are broken, and no new type has taken their place.

---

10 Ibid., 48–9.

The haunting voice of the sister is heard as the brother drifts away from the ancient genus of theological metaphysics and towards the genus of the stranger. Yet the sister's voice cannot be identified with the type of the past or with that of the future, it cannot be subsumed within a genre.

The passage is not so easily reduced to even this tentative metaphysico-historical familiarity, however, since Heidegger does not only mention the sister, but also Selanna; the strangers (*der Fremde, der Fremdling* – the gender of *das Fremde* from *Unterwegs zur Sprache*[11] – has now strangely metamorphosed); and the sister's brother. What is the meaning of this perplexing cast? What relation does Selanna, the lunar woman, have to the sister who speaks in lunar tones? Of Selanna, David Farrell Krell writes: 'Heidegger recollects the way the ancient Greek lyricists speak of the moon and stars; in the context of abscission, of the confluent twofold, and Seléné, who as Semele is the mother of Dionysos ...'.[12] In the classical myth Semele is tricked by Hera into demanding that her lover (Zeus) reveal himself to her in his full presence, and when he does so she is killed by his radiance. An event that might suggest some relation to the 'stranger's goldenness'. But even following this apparently unambiguous

11   Ibid., 41.

12   D.F. Krell, *Intimations of Mortality: Time, Truth and Finitude in Heidegger's Thinking of Being* (University Park, PA.: Penn State University Press, 1986), 171.

path quickly leads us into a kind of mythological aporia, since, as Robert Graves notes in *The White Goddess*:

> The Vine-Dionysus once had no father, either. His nativity appears to have been that of an earlier Diony-sus, the Toadstool-god; for the Greeks believed that mushrooms and toadstools were engendered by light-ning – not sprung from seed like all other plants. When the tyrants of Athens, Corinth and Sicyon legal-ized Dionysus worship in their cities, they limited the orgies, it seems, by substituting wine for toadstools; thus the myth of the Toadstool-Dionysus became attached to the Vine-Dionysus, who now figured as a son of Semele the Theban and Zeus, Lord of lightning. Yet Semele was the sister of Agave, who tore off her son Pentheus' head in a Dionysiac frenzy.[13]

The attribution of a (patrilinear) genealogy to Dionysus is complicit with a project of repression. An intoxication that came from nowhere, from a bolt of lightning, is asked to show its birth-certificate. Wine, which Plato will later accommodate even to dialectic, displaces the fungus of the Dionysian cults (*Amanita Muscaria*). The sacred mushroom of the cults is held to be responsible for those socially unas-similable deliria which are a threat to the πολις.

---

13 R. Graves, *The White Goddess: A Historical Grammar of Poetic Myth* (London: Faber & Faber, 1961), 159.

But what is the relation between this ancient policing of social pathology and Heidegger's interpretation of Trakl? How can a bridge be built between such ontic-empirical history, and the onto-transcendental question concerning the site of poetry? The spanning of such a gulf has been hindered by the medicalization of the history of derangement, and its reduction to the historical and psychiatric study of madness. But this regional investigation is nothing other than the contemporary instance of that discourse of the πολις which first instituted a genealogy of Dionysus. Such a construction patently fails to mark the inherently delirious character of western history, and, therefore, of scientificity itself. This is not only a matter of ontotheology being rooted in a specific amnesia. A delirium integral to the western graphic order implies, more radically, that any possible history must arise out of the forgetting (or secondary repression) of a constitutive arche-amnesia (the ellipsis integral to inscription). Klossowski has even been led to suggest that western science is aphasic, because it is initiated in the default of a foundational discourse.[14] This default is not merely a passively accepted pathology, it is an inscribed, prescribed, or actively administered pharmacopathology. The response of the West to the writing of itself has been that of a poisoning. This is why the fact that Selanna substitutes for a delirium without origin – which is

14   P. Klossowski, *Nietzsche et le cercle vicieux* (Paris: Mercure de France, 1978), 16; tr. D.W. Smith as *Nietzsche and the Vicious Circle* (London: Continuum, 2005), xvii.

equally a delirium of origins – seems to resonate with what Derrida entitles an *aggression pharmakographique*.

In Trakl's *Geistliche Dämmerung* the path of the pharmakon, the intoxicated voyage across the nocturnal pool, seems to evade *Geschlecht* (the general resource of typography). Instead it crosses the starry sky, through which the lunar voice of the sister resounds. A problematic of the moon is introduced, demanding some minimal gesture of interpretation. Perhaps to speak of the 'lunar' in this fashion is simply to speak of the way things appear in the night.[15] In the poem In *der Heimat*, for instance, the sister is seen asleep bathed in moonlight:

> Der Schwester Schlaf ist schwer. Der Nachtwind wühlt
> In ihrem Haar, das mondner Glanz umspült.

> (The sister's sleep is heavy. The nightwind burrows /
> In her hair, bathed in the gleam of the moon.)[16]

---

15 Trakl ends the poem *Am Moor* ('At the Moor') with the line *Erscheinung der Nacht: Kröten tauchen aus silbernen Wassern* ('Appearance of the night: toads dive out of silver waters') (Trakl, *Das dichterische Werk*, 54) suggesting that there is indeed an issue of nocturnal luminacy in Trakl's poetry; a becoming visible in the night, which is also an appearance of the night itself. The night is not merely a formal condition or scene for certain apparitions, it is also what is 'expressed' in the silver light of the moon and stars. The night itself finds a voice in 'the lunar voice of the sister', that is also a *Silberstimme* ('silver voice'), a word that is used in the poem *Hohenburg* (Ibid., 51), and twice in the poem *Sebastian im Traum* (Ibid., 53).

16 Ibid., 35.

This apparent reduction or simplification of the problem only displaces our difficulties however. The Traklean night [*Nacht*] is, as we have seen, the time of derangement [*Umnachtung*], consonant perhaps with the 'mania' that stems, like moon (and 'mind'), from the Indo-European road (**men(e)s*). That the moon is associated with woman is indicated by the etymological relations between 'moon', 'month', and 'menses', but it is also the companion of lunatics and werewolves; figures with whom the reader of Trakl is certainly familiar.

It is, fittingly, in the culminating lines of *Traum und Umnachtung* that this imagery crosses a climactic threshold:

Steinige Oede fand er am Abend, Geleite eines Toten in das dunkle Haus des Vaters. Purpurne Wolke umwölkte sein Haupt, daß er schweigend über sein eigenes Blut und Bildnis herfiel, ein mondenes Antlitz; steinern ins Leere hinsank, da in zerbrochenen Spiegel, ein sterbender Jüngling, die Schwester erschien; die Nacht das verfluchte Geschlecht verschlang.

(He found a petrified desolation in the evening, the company of one deceased as he entered the dark house of the father. Purple clouds enwreathed his head, so that he fell upon his own blood and image, a lunar countenance; and fainted petrified into emptiness when, in a shattered mirror a dead youngster appeared, the sister: night enveloped the accursed genus.)[17]

With a passage of such beauty and labyrinthine depths any response is likely at worst merely to irritate, and at best to increase our perplexity. I will only try to ask one simple question. Is there a connection to be made between the shattering of the mirror and a movement of astronomical imagery; between an explosion of desire that exceeds all introversion or reflection on the one hand, and a nocturnal or lunar *process* on the other? If such a connection were to be made it would surely pass by way of the sister, who is herself a threshold between the reflective order of the father's house and the illimitative difference of the night sky. It is the 'night pool' with its subtly differentiated luminosities – a series of intensities which defy resolution within any dialectic of presence and absence – that flood onto the mirror with the sister; shattering every power of representation. At the point of a certain nocturnal delirium (or lunacy) the relation of the sister to the family is metamorphosed. She no longer obeys the law of the boundary by mediating the family with itself, sublimating its narcissism, or establishing its insertion into the order of signification by disappearing (leaving the father's house according to the exchange

17   Ibid., 84.

patterns of patrilineal exogamy, and thus as a metabolic or reproductive moment within a kinship structure). Instead she breaches the family, by opening it onto an alterity which has not been appropriated in advance to any deep structure or encompassing system. A night that was an indeterminable alterity such as this would be a fully positive differentiation from the day.[18]

Perhaps the single most important Trakl text on this theme, in addition to the culmination of *Traum und Umnachtung*, is a poem called *Geburt* ('Birth')[19] where lunar imagery functions similarly as a haemorrhaging of familial interiority. The poem pivots upon a line at the end of the third stanza in which a sublimated incestuality works a stifling movement of interiorization: *Seufzend erblickt sein Bild der gefallene Engel* ('Sighing the fallen angel glimpsed his image'). It might seem as if the birth of the sister is to be absorbed in a retreat into the claustrophobic heart of the *Geschlecht*. But although the fourth stanza begins with an awakening in a musty room [*dumpfer Stube*] the

---

18 The sister is also associated with the moon towards the end of the prose poem *Offenbarung und Untergang*, first in the line *hob sich auf mondenen Flügeln über die grünenden Wipfel, kristallene Klippen das weiße Antlitz der Schwester* ('lifted by lunar wings above the greening treetops, crystal cliffs of the sister's white countenance') that ends the penultimate paragraph. The final paragraph begins *Mit silbernen Sohlen stieg ich die dornigen Stufen hinab* ('With silver soles I climbed down the thorny steps') and speaks of *ein mondenes Gebilde, das langsam aus meinem Schatten trat* ('a lunar shape, that slowly stepped from out of my shadow') (Ibid., 97). By stepping out of her brother's shadow the sister escapes the determinations of image, reflection, or copy that could be returned to the same; to a self-mediated narcissism playing with representations as its own (or proper) alterity.

19 Ibid., 64.

one who thus awakes is 'a pale one' [*ein Bleiches*]; 'lunar'. The eyes of the mother (or the midwife) [*steinernen Greisin*] are described as 'two moons', a reference taking us back out into the night (whose 'black wing touches the boy's temple'), and back to a crucial image from the second stanza; that of the decayed moon:[20]

Stille der Mutter; unter schwarzen Tannen
Oeffnen sich die schlafenden Hände,
Wenn verfallen der kalte Mond erscheint.

(Silence of the mother; under black pines / The sleeping hands open out / When the cold and ruined moon appears.)[21]

It would be possible to interpret this ruin of the moon as a dialectical restoration of the inside, its order and its securities, as if what had defied the inside was now falling away into self-annihilation. It might thus be asserted: 'This nocturnal path, departing from everything we have always

---

20 The ruined moon is also mentioned in *Sebastian im Traum* in the line *Da in jenem März der Mond verfiel*. ('Then, in that march, the moon was ruined.') (Ruin, from the Latin *ruere* 'to fall', cannot be used intransitively to capture the precise usage of *verfallen* in this case.) (Ibid., 53). The ruin of the moon is here taken as a datable event, emphasizing its referential entanglement in the processes of genre. Trakl's deployment of astronomical metaphor is not a retreat from history into timeless or archetypal symbolism, it is, on the contrary, a historicizing of the heavens; the opening of a genealogy through conjugation with astronomical forces. For Heidegger's most explicit comments on Trakl and history, see *Die Sprache im Gedicht* in particular (Heidegger, *Unterwegs zur Sprache*, 80).

21 Trakl, *Das dichterische Werk*, 64.

believed in, it has all collapsed into chaos now. Wasn't it obvious it was going to go terribly wrong? You should have listened to your priest/parents/teachers/the police.' Yet this is not the only reading open to us.

The ruin of the moon might seem to block the nocturnal movement that passes from a claustrophobic interior into endless space, and that conjugates the dynasty with an unlimited alterity. But this would not be the case if the moon itself was, at least partially, a restrictive element across the path of departure, rather than being the sole gateway into the heavens. The ruin of the moon would then be a protraction of the nocturnal trajectory; a dissolution of the lunar that proceeds not as a negation of the night, but as a falling away of what is still too similar to the sun. This second possibility is supported by the terms of Heidegger's reading. He is very precise, in his interpretation of the delirious journey across the nocturnal pool, about what he takes the meaning of the moon to be: a constriction of stellar luminescence rather than the ultimate elimination of sunlight; a fading and cooling of stars:

> The cool light stems from the shining of the lunar woman (Selanna). Ringing her radiance, as ancient Greek verse says, the stars fade and even cool.[22]

22 Heidegger, *Unterwegs zur Sprache*, 48–9.

This interpretation might seem to lack all philosophical rigour, and perhaps even to forsake any possible 'theoretical' reference. In fact it contributes to a problematic of enormous importance, although one that has been fragmented and largely obliterated by the constitution of astronomy and astro-physics as positive sciences in modern times. This problem is that of real (and astronomically evident) differences that are in principle irreducible to mathematical formalism, and which are furthermore – as Deleuze has demonstrated in the closing sections of *Difference et Répétition*[23] – a potential basis for a quite other and more comprehensive approach to mathematization (or theoretical quantification) without any recourse to ultimate identity or equalities. The obscuration of such differences within the constitution of astro-science has been a deferral rather than a resolution of the problem of radically informal differences, leaving this matter as an explosive threat to the foundations of modern cosmology. Perhaps the last confident, unitary, and explicit treatment of the question is to be found in Hegel's 'Encyclopaedia', in the *Zusatz* to the transition from Finite Mechanics to Absolute Mechanics:

> One can admire the stars because of their tranquility: but they are not of equal dignity to the concrete

---

23 G. Deleuze, *Différence et répétition* (Paris: Presses Universitaires de France, 1968); tr. P. Patton as *Difference and Repetition* (NY: Columbia University Press, 1994), 262–304.

individual. The filling of space breaks out [*ausschlägt*] into endless kinds of matter; but that [i.e. the casting of the stars] is only the first outbreak [*Ausschlagen*] that can delight the eye. This outbreak of light [*Licht-Ausschlag*] is no more worthy of wonder than that of a rash in man, or than a swarm of flies.[24]

Philosophy is to turn its gaze away from the stars, learning from Thales perhaps, who fell into a hole whilst absorbed in astronomical contemplation. In a subtle but vigorous neo-Ptolemaism, Hegel subordinates the stellar moment to the concrete and ordered bodies of the solar system, and these bodies are in turn subordinated to the development of terrestrial life. This is due to the dialectical dignity of particularized actuality in comparison with abstract principle, so that astrophysical laws are sublated into their successively more concrete expositions in geology, biology, anthropology, and cultural history. Yet there is something more primordially and uncontrollably disturbing in the vast and senseless dispersion of the stars, something which is even hideous, like a disease of the skin.

What offends Hegel about the stars is the irrational facticity of their distribution; a scattering which obeys no discernible law. He expresses his disdain for this distribution, and his anxiety before it, in a word that is

24 G.W.F. Hegel, *System der Philosophie Zweiter Teil. Die Naturphilosophie*, from *Sämtliche Werke*, (Stuttgart: Frommanns Verlage, 20 vols., 1929), vol. 9, 118.

also both a powerful description and an acknowledgement: *Ausschlag*, which can mean swing or deflection, but in this context means 'outbreak' in the sense of a rash. The verb *ausschlagen* is even more multi-faceted, and can mean (among other possibilities) to knock or beat out, to waive, to burgeon or blossom, or to sweat. But Hegel is not speaking of the blossoming of the stars here, or at least, he does not want to do so. We must be careful not to lose track of the 'object' Hegel is isolating here: it is a differentiation that is at once senseless and sensible, an outbreak of irrationality in the redoubt of reason similar to that which Kant acknowledges in the *Schematismuslehre*. It is the differential principle of stars, flies, flocks of birds, and dust; of astronomical, geological, ornithological,[25] and epidermal eruptions. Trakl names it with deft precision *Staub der Sterne* ('the dust of the stars'). In his reading of Trakl Heidegger also acknowledges this unity of *aus* and *Schlag* as a disruption 'of' sentience, but only if the 'of' is read according to the subversive syntax of Heideggerian thought; as an 'of' that no longer presumes a prior and

---

25 The association of bird-flight and the emergence of signs is one of the richest threads of Trakl's poetry. In *In einem verlassenen Zimmer* ('In an Abandoned Room') occurs the line *Schwalben irre Zeichen ziehn* ('Swallows trace demented signs') (Trakl, *Das dichterische Werk.*, 16); the final stanza of *Traum des Bösen* ('Dream of Evil') begins *Des Vogelflugs wirre Zeichen lesen / Aussätzigen* ('Lepers read the confused signs of bird-flight') (Ibid., 19); the second stanza of *An den Knaben Elis* ('To the Youth Elis') ends with the words *dunkle Deutung des Vogelflugs* ('the dark significance of bird-flight') (Ibid., 17, 49) and *Der Herbst des Einsamen* contains the line *Der Vogelflug tönt von alten Sagen* ('The flight of birds resounds with ancient sagas') (Ibid., 62). Wherever there is erratic dispersal and movement in undemarcated space Trakl anticipates the arising of sense, and a question of reading.

undisrupted subject. For Heidegger sentience is not exploded or threatened from without by the *Ausschlag*, it is always already under the sway of the outbreak that will be derivatively apprehended as its subversion:

> Trakl sees 'sentience' [*Geist*] in terms of that weave [*Wesen*] that is named in the primordial significa-tion of the word *Geist*; since *gheis* means: incensed, dislocated, being outside oneself [*aufgebracht, entsetzt, außer sich sein*].[26]

Hegelian sentience could be described as *entsetzt* by cosmological eruption, but the sense of this outrage changes with Heidegger's radicalized approach, in which *Entsetztheit* cannot be thought as a delimiting response to the anarchic explosion of cosmic debris but only as its inertial protraction. Heidegger thus provides us with a hermeneutical key according to which every sentient reaction to the *Ausschlag* can be read as a symptom or repetition of the outbreak 'itself'. It is no longer even that sentience is infected by irrationality; it is rather that sentience has dissolved into the very movement of infec-tion, becoming a virulent element of contagious matter.

Since the light of the stars is not a transcendental ground of phenomenality, but rather a differential effect

---

26 Heidegger, *Unterwegs zur Sprache*, 60.

stemming from the isolation or uneven distribution of intensities, Hegel takes its claim to philosophical dignity as an offence. He determines starlight as a pathological luminescence, without order or intelligibility. The fading of stars is, therefore, among other things, a name for a necessary stage in Hegel's system. The senseless distribution of stellar material is repressed in the interest of the particularized (sub-)planetary body, which in turn furthers geocentrism and the infinitizing of light. This movement crushes difference under a logicized notion of significance. In contrast, Trakl brings the thought of the sign together with that of stellar dispersion, writing: *O, ihr Zeichen und Sterne* ('O, you signs and stars').[27] And – partially echoing Rimbaud's words – *Un chant mystérieux tombe des astres d'or* ('a mysterious song falls from stars of gold') – he mentions *die Silberstimmen der Sterne* ('the silver voice of the stars')[28] and *Das letzte Gold verfallener Sterne* ('The last gold of ruined stars').[29] The German word *Stern* derives from the Indo-European root **ster-* meaning to extend or spread out. It is from this root that the English word 'strew' – as well as 'star' – descends. The stars are traces of a primordial strewing; an explosive dispersion, which in its formlessness, defies mathematization or the reduction to order. It is the shockwave of this metaphorics which

27 Trakl, *Das dichterische Werk*, 63.

28 Ibid., 53.

29 Ibid., 50.

sweeps through Trakl's specifications of the sign, and it is
perhaps for this reason that Trakl writes of ruination [*Verfallen*] in this context. Any order which is to be extracted
from the strewing of difference will be dependent on this
'spreading out' (Latin *sternere*), it will not be metaphysical – dependent upon a transcendental difference – but
'stratophysical'; a movement between planes, or grades,
of dispersion. Where metaphysics has always fixed disorder in a dichotomous relation to an absolute principle
of coherent form or ultimate lawfulness, a stratophysics
would locate regional order within a differentiation in the
rate of dissipation. It thus constitutes an abyssal relativism,
although not one that is rooted in subjective perspectives,
but rather in the open-ended stratifications of impersonal
and unconscious physical forces. Astrophysics is marked
by its etymology as stratophysics – a materialist study of
planes of distributed intensities – and therefore can be
seen to abandon its most extreme potentialities when it
subordinates itself to mathematical physics.

The question of strata can insinuate itself into every
word of Trakl's text, because it is at the 'core' of any
rigorous graphematics. Each stratum is a dimension
of dispersion, flattened like a spiral galaxy. This flat-
ness is just as crucial to the study of intensities as the
trajectories traced within it, since the stratification or
stacking of organizational levels is the basic form of
any possible energetic surplus, the irreducible or final

principle of 'real form': redundancy. Each stratum has its specific 'negentropy' or positive range of compositions, 'selecting' only a relatively narrow series of combinations from the stock of elements generated by its substrate. A stratum thus inherits an aggregate 'degree of difference' or grammar, distinguishing it from a certain potentiality of 'randomness' (unproblematic reducibility into its substrate), and constituting a potential for teleological illusion (unproblematic reduction of its substrate). This stratification of intensive positivities, which is most clearly indexed by the successive unities of letter, word, sentence, etc. that are precipitated out of a common 'graphic plasma' or semiotic substance within alphabetical regimes, is the only rigorous basis for an architectonics of the sign. Only because of such a graphic redundancy – for example, that stored in the difference between letter and word – *between the words an alphabet makes possible and those which are realized* – can energy be unevenly distributed within a stratum, and intensities generated.[30] Trakl acknowledges

---

30 Claude Shannon's theory of information understands redundancy as the dimension of a message that does not function at the level of communication, but rather functions as a resource for the discrimination of the incommunicative ('noise') from communication in general, thus providing a layer of insulation against the degradation of the message. This formulation seems to me to lack two crucial elements: 1) It fails to provide any suggestion as to how the message participates in the constitution of redundancies (thus taking redundancy as a transcendental condition of communication). This first default leads to the preservation of the metaphysical distinction between semiotic and material processes (messages and techniques), which is otherwise profoundly shaken by the thought of redundancy; the thought, that is, of an isolation or 'de-naturalization' of the semiotic stratum proceeding by means of intensities or surpluses that invoke no element of negativity, but only gradations. 2) It fails to acknowledge the political dimension of redundancy as a means of trapping disruptive signals. It is this 'trapping' within an intermediate zone between strata that first enables the categories of madness,

this excitatory axis, which punctures and intensifies each plane of distribution, in the use of words related to the German verb *sinken* (to sink). Thus he writes:

> Von Lüften trunken sinken balde em die Lider
> Und öffnen leise sich zu fremden Sternenzeichen.
>
> (Drunken with breezes the lids soon subside / And open themselves to strange star-signs.)[31]

And:

> Zeichen und Sterne
> Versinken leise im Abendweiher.
>
> (Signs and stars / Sink quietly in the evening-pool.)[32]

The explosion of stellar and semiotic materials generates a combination of intra-stratal and trans-stratal processes, the former of which have been historically determined as

---

perversion, deformity, disobedience, and indiscipline to be constituted, thus providing the basis for the associated but counterposed disciplinary programmes of pedagogy, psychiatry, punition, etc. To fail to acknowledge such questions is to take the notion of noise as a purely passive and non-sentient interruption rather than as a strategically oriented 'jamming' of the message, and thus to ignore the conflictual aspects of both grammars and anti-grammatical subterfuges as they contend within the fluctuating space of redundancy or control. This default is typical of a technocratic scientificity which takes the question of power as having been always already resolved prior to the question of technique.

31 Trakl, *Das dichterische Werk*, 18.

32 Ibid., 51.

'causal' or 'legislated' and the latter as 'intellectual', 'tele-ological', or 'legislative'. This is a ramification (speculative I admit) of Trakl's vocabulary of *Stufen* ('steps') of terraced differentiation (a theme I hope to explore more thoroughly elsewhere). Stratification is the complex physiological process, the only one, in which the distinction between matter and meaning cannot be sustained.[33]

The tools Heidegger relies upon in his approach to the issues of exile into the night and astronomical dispersion stem from the 'ecstative analyses' of his Marburg medita-tions. The term he focuses upon as a possible entry point for such a discussion is 'flame'. He first gathers Trakl's stellar thematic into that of flame with the suggestion: 'The night flames as the lightening mirror of the starry sky'.[34] He then proceeds: *Das Flammende ist das Außer-sich, das lichtet und erglänzen läßt, das indessen auch weiterfressen und alles in das Weiße der Asche verzehren kann.* ('That which flames is the outside itself, that which lightens and lets gleam, and that which in doing so can expand voraciously so that

---

33 For instance, in *Kleines Konzert* ('Little Concert') *Aussätzigen winkt die Flut Genesung* ('The torrent beckons lepers to convalescence') (Ibid., 25); in *Drei Blicke in einen Opal* ('Three Glimpses in an Opal') *Die Knaben träumen wirr in dürren Weidensträhnen / Und ihre Stirnen sind von Aussatz kahl und rauh* ('Youths dream confusedly among the pasture's dry bales / And their brows are naked and raw with leprosy') (Ibid., 39; see also Ibid., 40); towards the end of *Helian* (in a line I have already cited) *Helians Seele sich im rosigen Spiegel beschaut / Und Schnee und Aussatz von seiner Stirne sinken* ('Helian's soul gazes on itself in the rosy mirror / And snow and leprosy sink from his brow') (Ibid., 43); and in *Verwandlung des Bösen* ('Metamorphosis of Evil') there is a *Minute stummer Zerstörung; auflauscht die Stirne des Aussätzigen unter dem kahlen Baum* ('moment of mute devastation; the brow of the leper hearkens under the naked tree') (Ibid., 56).

34 Heidegger, *Unterwegs zur Sprache*, 66.

everything is consumed to become white ash.' [The expression *Außer-sich* is such a clear index for Heidegger's notion of ecstasis that Hertz employs 'ek-stasis' as its translation in his rendering of this sentence]).[35] The flame of the stars is explosive – or outside of itself – but this *Ausschlag* can be a gentle illumination or an uncontrolled devastation (an *Aufruhr*, 'revolt', 'turmoil').[36] It is about this 'or', with which I am attempting to indicate Heidegger's hope that the *Weiterfressung* can be deflected or suspended in contingency, that the ambiguous path of his reading turns.

Ten pages earlier Heidegger poses this sense of an alternative between castings [*Schläge*] most acutely, and in so doing returns us to the question of infection. Examining Trakl's expression *das verfluchte Geschlecht* ('the accursed genus')[37] he points to a Greek word that can be translated equally as either *Schlag* or *Fluch*; πληγη ('curse'). πληγη is also translated by the Latin *plangere*, from which we derive the English 'plague', and the German *Plage* (found in the sixth line of Trakl's poem *Föhn*[38] and in the fifteenth line of *Allerseelen* ['All Soul's Day']).[39] Heidegger's text (which I cannot confidently hazard to my translation alone) reads:

---

35   Ibid., 60.

36   Ibid., 60.

37   Trakl, *Das dichterische Werk*, 84.

38   Ibid., 67.

39   Ibid., 211.

Womit ist dieses Geschlecht geschlagen, d.h. ver-
flucht? Fluch heißt griechisch πληγη, unser Wort
'Schlag'. Der Fluch des verwesenden Geschlechtes
besteht darin, daß dieses alte Geschlecht in die Zwietracht der Geschlechter auseinandergeschlagen ist.
Aus ihr trachtet jedes der Geschlechter in den los-
gelassenen Aufruhr der je vereinzelten und bloßen
Wildheit des Wildes. Nicht die Zwiefache als solches,
sondern die Zwietracht ist der Fluch. Sie trägt aus
dem Aufruhr der blinden Wildheit das Geschlecht
in die Entzweiung und verschlägt es so in die losge-
lassene Vereinzelung. Also entzweit und zerschlagen
vermag das 'verfallene Geschlecht' von sich aus nicht
mehr in den rechten Schlag zu finden.

(With what is this gen-us cast, i.e. cursed? Cursed
names the Greek πληγη, our word 'casting'. The
curse of the decomposed gen-us consists in this, that
this ancient gen-us is cast apart into the discord of
gen-ders. Each of the genera strives for unleashed
revolt in an always individuated and naked wildness
of the beast. It is not the twofold that is the curse,
but rather the discordance of the two. Out of the
revolt of the blind wildness it carries the gen-us, cast
away into torn duality and unleashed individuation.

Thus divided and cast down the 'ruined gen-us' is no
longer able to find the 'right cast'.)[40]

It would be possible to read this passage as if it were a
development entirely internal to Heidegger's 'philosophy',
and as if the reading of Trakl in which it is embedded were
a mere eccentricity or modulation in the vocabulary of
an unswerving intellectual pursuit. Such a reading would
recall that according to Heidegger, ontotheology is the
curse that leads beings to strive towards absolute mastery
of the earth, erasing every trace of their dependence upon
being. That difference of each being with respect to being
is displaced by the differences among beings, and being is
converted into a mere disputed territory to be subdivided
among conflicting beings. It would also recall that within
this history everything thought of as 'real' has been distributed among exclusive concepts, through which beings
represent themselves to themselves in their competitive
distinctiveness, so that the differences, discriminations,
and determinations of beings cease to speak of being. It
would conclude that what is metaphysical (in the sense
that Heidegger understands as the ontotheological) in
dualities of genre is not that they are binary, but that this
binarity monopolizes the interpretation of the being's difference from being. What is lost in ontical interpretation

---

40 Heidegger, *Unterwegs zur Sprache*, 50.

is the being of genre itself, the composition of ontical difference from out of the non-ontic. In other words, to think *Geschlecht* abstractly, but in a certain sense beyond ontotheology, it would be necessary only to insist (in a decisive Heideggerian trope) that ontical differentiation is not itself anything ontical.

Yet Heidegger is not simply interpreting a word that circulates freely within the German language. He is attempting to read this word as he encounters it within the tortuous and vespertine labyrinth of Trakl's poetry. We must return to Heidegger's question, and attempt to ask it along with him: what is this cast, this curse or epidemic? We are assisted in this by Trakl's words, which lend us a faltering answer to place alongside Heidegger's discussion; the cast that has cursed us, surely that is what Trakl names *Aussatz*; leprosy, infection, and (thus) exclusion. The spaces of difference across which the *Zwietracht* stretches and displaces itself (following the semantic instabililty of *Geschlecht*) are never to be found described by Trakl in terms that could be reduced to formal disjunctions or negative articulations. Instead he writes of *Mauern voll Aussatz* ('walls full of leprosy')[41] echoing Rimbaud who, during his *Saison en Enfer* finds himself *assis, lépreux, sur les pots cassés et les orties, au pied d'un mur rongé par le soleil* ('sitting, leprous, upon broken pots and nettles, at the foot

---

41 Trakl, *Das dichterische Werk*, 41.

of a wall gnawed by the sun').[42] It seems at first surprising that Heidegger makes no mention of the frequent references to leprosy throughout Trakl's poetry, since *Aussatz* points to an *Aus-setzung* (the Old High German source *Uzsazeo* means 'one who has been *ausgesetzt* or "cast out" of society'), a coinage which profoundly accords with the ecstative orientation of Heidegger's reading. Heidegger even has a space specifically allocated to disease in his reading. Not that he is particularly concerned with the German equivalent of this word: *Krankheit* (although he quotes Trakl's line *Wie scheint doch alles Werdende so krank*! ('How sick everything that is becoming seems!').[43] The disease which finds a place in Heidegger's text is the same as that which obsesses Trakl; it is the searing of stars, or the primordial and contagious eruption of the pathological. But Heidegger's supplement to Trakl's text is disappointingly regressive on this issue, and my brief concluding question touches on an example of the repugnant obstinacy and piety of the 1953 essay in asking: why does Heidegger refuse to follow Trakl and name ecstative eruption *Aussatz*?

In concluding the question of the curse that abuts onto Trakl's thema of *Geschlecht*, Heidegger distinguishes between two cast(e)s and two dualities. There is a cursing

---

42   A. Rimbaud, *Collected Poems*, tr. O. Bernard (Harmondsworth: Penguin, 1980), 302–3.

43   Trakl, *Das dichterische Werk*, 29; Heidegger, *Unterwegs zur Sprache*, 64.

cast or stamp that is associated with a reckless and destructive individualization and that generates antagonistic or conflictual binarity [*Zwietracht*], and there is a gentle *sanft* binarity [*Zwiefalt*] that escapes the contagion of the curse. As is so typical of Heidegger, *Zwiefalt* simultaneously marks an aspiration towards the (Schellingian) post-philosopher's stone of a-logical intervallic difference and the theologian's dream of an immaculate or uncontaminated conception. Drawing upon a thought of pain [*Schmerz*] as a threshold and relation Heidegger seeks to ameliorate the pathological scorching of the stars: 'gentleness is, following the word *das Sanfte*, the peaceful gatherer. It metamorphoses discord, in that it turns what is injuring and searing in wildness to soothed pain'.[44] This attempt to establish pure and dichotomous distinctions that both explicate and escape the history of oppositional thought necessitates a discrimination between (two) types of duality. (It is precisely because Derrida will refuse to underwrite such a discrimination that he turns instead to a re-inscription of continuities that are able to encompass and partially assimilate the 'ruptural' aspect of his own work, resigned to a 'structurally necessary inadequacy' in the prosecution of deconstruction. Both Heidegger and Derrida seem to concur, however, in taking the sense of dichotomy to be irredeemably polar and reciprocally

---

44   Ibid., 45.

ultimate rather that stratal and unilaterally or impulsively protractile.)

The historical predicament that Heidegger and (in a different way) Derrida trace out here, and which finds its symptom in this problematic 'antinomy' of escape and re-capture, hope and despair, with all the unstable compromises and evanescent moments of indecision or indifference it generates, is too complex to delineate in this paper. I will only venture to suggest that by holding *Zwietracht* and *Zwiefalt* apart at this point, and refusing to abandon the hope that formal or ultimate dichotomy might be redeemed by a future thinking, Heidegger is engaged in what we could legitimately describe as a 'gentle critique' of the history of metaphysics, a grotesque recapitulation of Kant's compromise with ontotheological tradition (and tradition always belongs to the church). Heidegger's attempt is to limit the *Aufruhr* which consti-tutes the intensive undertow of Traklean textuality. His is the sterile hope of an aging philosopher with Platonic instincts, the delusion that the climactic dissipation of Western civilization can be evaded, and that the accumu-lation of fossilized labour-power can found an eternally reformable social order. He was not completely unaware of the profound struggle between the weary regimentation of the patriarchal bourgeoisie, and a fluctuating pool of insurrectionary energy tracing its genealogy to the ur-catastrophe of organic matter. But he felt nauseous at the thought of losing control, and perhaps he still believed in God. *Zwiefalt* would surely be a distantiation from this noise and restless ferment, an end to contagion, a final peace? It is according to this deeply rooted 'logic' of purification and transcendence, the most insidious trope of a decomposing theology, that the irruption of ecstative difference refuses the name *Aussatz*, and Heidegger – exhausted and uncomfortably feverish – lays down his copy of Trakl's poems, and closes his eyes.

Delighted to Death

E.M. Cioran's essay, 'Thinking Against Oneself', begins:

> We owe the quasi-totality of our discoveries to our
> violences, to the exacerbation of our disequilibrium.
> Even God, insofar as he intrigues us, is not to be
> found in our most intimate depths, but rather at the
> exterior limit of our fever, at the precise point where,
> our rage colliding with his, a shock results, an encoun-
> ter that is equally ruinous for him and for us. Stricken
> with the malediction attached to acts, the violent man
> does nor force his nature, does not go beyond himself,
> except to furiously re-enter, as aggressor, followed by
> his enterprises, which come to punish him for having
> raised them. There is no work that does not return
> against its author: the poem crushes the poet, the
> system the philosopher, the event the man of action.
> Some form of self-destruction, responding to his

vocation and accomplishing it, is at work in the core of history; only he saves himself who sacrifices gifts and talents in order that, disengaged from his quality as a man, he is able to strut into being. If I aspire to a metaphysical career there is no price at which I am able to protect my identity, however minute are the residues that remain, it is necessary that I liquidate them; just as, on the contrary, if I adventure into a role in history, the task that I take upon myself has to exasperate my faculties to the point where I splinter with them. One always perishes by the self that one assumes: to bear a name is to claim an exact mode of collapse.

Faithful to his appearance the violent one is not discouraged, he begins again, obstinately, because he is unable to dispense with suffering. Is he driven to devastate others? That is the detour that he borrows to rejoin his own devastation. Beneath his assured air, beneath his fanfares, is hidden one who is besotted with misfortune. It is thus amongst the violent ones that are encountered the enemies of self. And we are all violent ones, the enraged, who, having lost the key to quietude, have access only to the secrets of laceration.[1]

---

1   E.M. Cioran, *The Temptation to Exist*, tr. R. Howard (Chicago: University of Chicago Press, 1998), 33–4 (translation adapted).

Cioran quotes Lao Tsu's maxim 'the intense life is contrary to the Tao', and compares the tranquility of the modest life with the thirst for annihilating ecstasy that has possessed the Western world. However, acknowledging the compulsion of his Occidental heritage, he remarks '*I can pay homage to Lao Tsu a thousand times, but I am more likely to identify with an assassin*'. Our culture, he argues, is essentially fanatical.

Kant began something quite new in the history of Western philosophy, by adapting thought to a rigorous austerity. Unlike Descartes, for whom doubt was only a detour to a more secure edifice of knowledge, Kant committed his thought to renunciation. Following Luther, he steeled himself against the seductions of 'the whore of reason', pursuing an ascetic doctrine that he baptized 'critical philosophy'. His great temptation was to write a 'system of pure reason' – the constructive philosophy that Hegel accomplished in his *Logic* – but he did not succumb, and went to his grave with his speculative virginity intact. His mature work was a perpetual flagellation of dialectical desire. It was not with the scholastics, but with Kant, that philosophy tasted the fierce delights of martyrdom.

In 1790, the year in which Kant's *Critique of Judgment* was published, the French revolution was in full surge. The enlightenment had climaxed in an insurrection aligned with a secular project of redemption. In his *Philosophy of Right,* Hegel describes these events as follows:

This is the freedom of the void which rises to a passion and takes shape in the world; while still remaining theoretical, it takes shape in the Hindu fanaticism of pure contemplation, but when it turns to actual practice, it takes shape in religion and politics alike as the fanaticism of destruction – the destruction of the whole subsisting social order – as the elimination of individuals who are objects of suspicion to any social order, and the annihilation of any organization which tries to rise anew from the ruins.[2]

Such is the insatiable fury that finds its voice, in this same period, in the literary and political writing of the Marquis de Sade. But comparing Sade with Kant, it is not obvious that it is the Marquis – despite his obsession with orgy and massacre – who is the more excited by violence. Hegel pictures spirit migrating from Paris to Königsberg, fleeing from its annihilating frenzy towards a moderated, or concrete, negation. He suggests that Kant recoiled from the extreme negativity of deist republicanism. But, like the *ancien régime,* the Jacobins also found it necessary to imprison Sade and repress the mystical delirium of his atheism. So it is equally possible to suggest that, insofar as Kant turned away from the French revolution, it was

---

2   G.W.F. Hegel, *Grundlinien der Philosophie des Rechts* (Frankfurt am Main: Ullstein, 1972), 22; for a recent English translation, see also *Elements of the Philosophy of Right*, tr. H. B. Nisbet (Cambridge and New York: Cambridge University Press, 1991), Introduction, § 5, 38.

because its basically restrained and utilitarian secularism failed to quench his thirst for extinction.

It is worth remembering that a glimpse into Kant's philosophy was sufficient to drive Kleist to suicide, and that Schopenhauer found in it the ethical imperative that existence be denied. Perhaps neither of these writers were ecclesiastical enough to enjoy the ghoulish cruelties that Kant explored. For Kant was a consummate saint, a cheerful man. He was not a stoic, but rather, faithful to his Christian heritage, a voluptuary of defeat.

Amongst other things, Kant is the first philosopher of intolerable pleasure. In his *Anthropology*, published in 1798, he writes:

Satisfaction is the feeling of the promotion; pain that of the obstruction of life. But life (of animals) is, as doctors have already noted, a continuous play of the antagonism of the two.

Thus before every satisfaction there must first be pain; pain is always first. Because what would proceed from a continual promotion of living force, which does not let itself climb above a certain grade, other than a rapid death from delight? [3]

3 I. Kant, *Schriften zur Anthropologie. Geschichtsphilosophie, Politik und Pädagogik* (Frankfurt am Main: Suhrkamp, 1968), 231; for a recent English translation, see *Anthropology from a Pragmatic Point of View*, tr., ed. R.B. Louden (Cambridge and New York: Cambridge University Press, 2006), Part I, Book II, § 60, 126.

Uninhibited pleasure does not tend to the benefit of the organism, but rather, to its immolation. Or, more precisely, the enhancement of life is intrinsically bound to its abolition. Life is not consumed by death at its point of greatest depression, but at its peak, and inversely; it is only the brake provided by suffering that preserves the organism in its existence. It is pain that spares life for something other than an immediate and annihilating delight. So Kant suggests that pleasure is the combustion of life, and we survive by smouldering.

It was Kant's genius to combine the saint with the bourgeois. He was not immune to the prevalent ascetic practice of our age: accumulation. If pleasure is to be suspended, this is at least in part because it should be capitalized. A few pages later in the *Anthropology* he implores:

> Young man! Hold work dear; refuse yourself satisfaction, not in order to renounce it, but rather to hold it as much as possible in prospect! Do not deaden the receptivity for it by premature enjoyment! The ripeness of age, which never lets the privation of any physical enjoyment be regretted, shall, in this sacrifice, secure you a capital of contentment independent of the accidents of natural law.[4]

---

4   Ibid., 237; 133.

Delights foregone will be transmuted and redeemed. This is more than a little mendacious since, even at the end of the eighteenth century, it had become intrinsic to capital accumulation that it was interminable. One does not capitalize that which will ever be spent. It is only with the reference to the super-natural, to a pleasure beyond natural law – which is weakly described as a 'content-ment' [*Zufriedenheit*] – that this passage comes close to sanctifying denial. For it is mere hypocrisy to employ utilitarian arguments to justify the austerity demanded by an ethic of accumulation, which requires an unceasing disequilibrium between work and enjoyment. Such an argument could only be convincing if this austerity were merely provisional, like a negation that will be in turn negated. If capital is to be provided with an absolute justification – and the need for this might not necessarily be felt – it will not be found in economics, but religion, as it always has been in the past. Only religion speaks the sort of language that could possibly affirm the conclusive loss of terrestrial pleasure, such as that which is represented by the subordination of consumption to the amassing of productive resources.

The only coherent apologetic of bourgeois austerity is called 'martyrology'. A rather mild example is the account of the passion of Saint Vincent given in *The Roman Martyrology*:

At Valencia in Spain, in the province of Tarragona, [the death] of Saint Vincent, Deacon and Martyr, who under the most wicked governor Dacian suffered prison, starvation, the rack, the twisting of his limbs, burning coals, the iron basket, fire and other kinds of torture; and for the reward of his martyrdom he departed to heaven.[5]

A harsher version, found in Delahaye's *The Passions of the Martyrs*, tells us more about the imagination of Christendom than its history. It describes how a certain Saint George (not the English one) consummated his martyrdom:

Saint George is hung, flayed to the point of exposing his entrails, stretched and drawn by four machines, flayed again, tormented by salt on his open wound, nailed by his feet to a scaffold, torn by six hooks, thrown in a tub and immersed by blows from a fork. He undergoes torture at the wheel, which is fitted with swords and knives, he is stretched on a bed of bronze; molten lead is poured into his mouth, a stone covered in lead is rolled over his head and limbs. He is hung head downwards, a large stone about his neck, above a thick suffocating smoke ... He is sawn in two

---

5   *The Roman Martyrology* (London: Burns, Oates & Washbourne, 1923).

and thrown into a cauldron of molten lead and pitch. He is whipped with leather thongs. A red-hot cask is placed on his head. His sides are flayed, and he is burnt with torches. The sword finally terminates his martyrdom.[6]

In *The Book of Martyrs,* John Foxe makes some more general remarks about martyrdom:

It is marvellous to see and read the incredible numbers of Christian innocents that were slain and tormented some one way, some another, as Rabanas saith, 'Some slain with the sword; some burnt with fire; some scourged with whips; some stabbed with forks: some fastened to the cross or gibbet; some drowned in the sea; some their skins plukt off; some their tongues cut off; some stoned to death; some killed with cold; some starved with hunger; some their hands cut off, or otherwise dismembered.' Whereof Augustine also saith, 'They were bound – imprisoned – killed – tortured – burned – butchered – cut in pieces', etc.[7]

---

6 H. Delahaye, *Les Passions des Martyrs et les genres littéraires* (Brussels: Bollandistes, 1921), 286.

7 John Foxe, *The Book of Martyrs*, ed. G.A. Williamson (London: Secker and Warburg, 1965).

Discussing the powerful enemies of the early Christians, Foxe remarks:

> Neither yet were these tyrants contented with death only. The kinds of death were various and horrible. Whatever the cruelty of man's invention could devise for the punishment of man's body, was practised against the Christians. Crafty trains, outcries of enemies, imprisonment, stripes and scourgings, drawings, tearings, stonings, plates of iron laid unto them burning hot, deep dungeons, racks, strangling in prisons, the teeth of wild beasts, gridirons, gibbets and gallows, tossing upon the horns of bulls ... [8]

But theological discourses in the Western tradition are redemptive, and thus demand a happy ending. One example is that given by Foxe in his commentary upon the death of St. Lawrence:

> Such is the wisdom and providence of God, that the blood of his dear saints (like good seed) never falls in vain to the ground, but it brings some increase: so it pleased the Lord to work at the martyrdom of this holy Lawrence, that by the constant confession of this worthy and valiant deacon, a certain soldier of Rome,

---

8   Ibid.

being converted to the same faith, desired forthwith
to be baptized of him; for which he was called to the
judge, scourged, and afterwards beheaded.[9]

These examples have to be used carefully, because Kant
learnt from Protestantism and secularism the necessity for
internal discipline, so that, to a degree that was without
philosophical precedent, he became the source of his
own persecution. In the modem age, martyrdom has to
become more systematic, independent of psychological
and historical accident, or, to use Kant's word, autonomous. Kant describes this new passional experience as
sublime, and the theory corresponding to it is to be found
in his *Critique of Judgment*.

Kant's theory of the sublime is an extreme point in
the history of Occidental mysticism. It is concerned with
the super-natural delight experienced by the self when it
intuits the splitting of itself. The task Kant sets himself is
that of grasping the connection between the finite animal
part of the human being (sensibility), and its transcendental moral part (reason). He argues:

Between the realm of the natural concept, as the
sensible, and the realm of the concept of freedom, as
the super-sensible, there is a great gulf fixed, so that

---

9   Ibid.

it is not possible to pass from the former to the latter
(by means of the theoretical employment of reason),
just as if they were so many separate worlds ...[10]

In his theory of the sublime he proposes a resolution
to this rift, which hinges upon the concept of violence
[*Gewalt*]. He insists: 'human nature does not of its own
proper motion accord with the good, but only by virtue
of the violence that reason exercises upon sensibility.'[11] He
uses the word 'imagination' to refer to the pre-conscious
process that grasps the raw material of sensation and
moulds it into a coherent whole. The imagination is
the faculty of appropriation, which assimilates passively
received material to basic concepts, constituting objects
of experience. In the first *Critique* Kant calls this function
'schematism'. It is the primary vitality of the organism,
the basic animal vigour in which the subject is rooted,
and upon which the possibility of knowledge rests. If the
subject is to find delight in the excruciation of its animality, it is the imagination that must bear the fury of holy
passion, and this is indeed what Kant argues:

---

10   I. Kant, *Kritik der Urteilskraft*, in *Werksgaube*, ed. W. Wieschedel, vol. 10 (Frankfurt am
Main: Suhrkamp, 1968), 14; for a recent English translation, see I. Kant, *Critique of
the Power of Judgment*, ed. P. Guyer, tr. P. Guyer, E. Matthews (Cambridge and New
York: Cambridge University Press, 2000), Introduction, II, 63.

11   Ibid., 124; 154.

that which, without our indulging in any refinements of thought, but simply in being apprehended, excites the feeling of the sublime, may appear to be frustrating for our powers of judgment, inappropriate to our faculty of presentation, and a violation of the imagination, but yet be judged even more sublime on that account.[12]

The sublimity evoked by an experience is in direct proportion to the devastation it wreaks upon the imagination. Because the pain resulting from the defeat of the imagination, or the animal part of the mind, is the tension that propels the mind as a whole into the rapture of sublime experience. Sublime pleasure is an experience of the impossibility of experience, an intuition of that part of the self that exceeds intuition by means of an immolating failure of intuition. The sublime is only touched upon as pathological disaster.

The paradoxical character of Kantian sublime experience is undoubtedly in part conditioned by the extreme severity of the metaphysical problem which it is designed to solve. When sensibility and reason, the empirical and the transcendental, are distinguished with the rigour that Kant insists upon – as if they were two separate worlds – it is scarcely surprising that the bridge between them

12 Ibid., 90; 129.

will exhibit inordinate stresses. Beyond such modern philosophical issues – indeed generating them – there are more deeply rooted historical effects at stake, and foremost amongst these is the Platonic-Christian affirmation of a super-terrestrial desire. Sublime experience is to be an anti-pathological eroticism, in which the body lusts after the agonized convulsions that stem from its own negation. The tension of sublimity is not merely the symptom of theoretical contradictions, but also, and more basically, the key to the mystical persuasiveness of the sublime. For it is only because of this paradoxical character – or tension – that the sublime promises to slake the raging thirst for violence that drives religious enthusiasm, and in so doing, to offer the delights of catastrophic rupture.

It is crucial to the way that sublimity functions in Kant's work that it is subsumed under the more general concept of aesthetic judgment. As the synthetic a priori judgment of the relation of imagination to the practically constitutive and theoretically regulative ideas of pure reason, it falls within the more comprehensive domain of aesthetic judgment, which is the transcendental exposition of the relation between imagination and concepts in general, which thus also includes the theoretically constitutive pure concepts of the understanding, as well as its empirical concepts. This subsumption characterizes the idealist tendency of Kant's theory, since disinterestedness is established as a presupposition of aesthetic judgment, and the question of its generation is evaded. It is not even that transcendental reason is merely presupposed by Kant, for it is thought as nothing other that pure presupposition. But the purity or absolute abstraction that underpins such a concept of reason is the absence of all intuitive content, so that the word purity – for example – also operates simultaneously in another (psychoreligious) register; employed in fact as a scantly veiled name for annihilation. Cutting against the idealism that obscures this effective or pathological functioning would involve a genealogical investigation into the emergence of disinterestedness, and it is this that drives a materialist reading of Kant towards the issue of his mysticism.

By reserving his discussion of sublime violence until he has established the presupposition of disinterestedness, Kant justifies the excruciation of animality from without. The martyrdom of the imagination is described as rational rather than rationalizing, as irrelevant to the constitution of reason. A materialist deciphering of this revision requires that repression – to use an inappropriately mild word – precedes its justification. If one is to gain some purchase upon the gloomy cathedral of our history, along with a little fresh air, it is important to begin with the sublime rather than aesthetic contemplation in general, and to read the sublime as generative rather than revelatory in its relation to reason.

Kant outlines two types of sublimity, one mathematical, and the other dynamic. Each of these types is associated with a specific violence against the imagination, which is marked out for sacrifice due to its status as the transcendental – and thus philosophically accessible – representative of the body. The mathematical sublime is the pleasure taken by reason in the collapse of the imagination induced by the intuition of magnitude, and the dynamic sublime is the equivalent pleasure corresponding to the intuition of power. In other words, the mathematical sublime is associated with the insignificance of the human animal, and the dynamic sublime with its vulnerability. The theological resonance of these terms is not at all accidental.

Sublimity has three elements; on the one hand the two elements of the subject: its sensibility or animality and its reason or pure intelligence, and on the other an object that overwhelms the imagination, and which is driven between the two parts of the subject like a wedge. The object provoking the sublime is simultaneously crushing for the sensibility and contemptible in respect to reason, and it thus serves to demonstrate the immeasurable humiliation of animal existence before the transcendental subject. The opportunity for the dynamic sublime lies in overweening force. It is the lucid intuition of catastrophic power, and is so nakedly rooted in brutal intimidation that Kant associates it with military butchery.

The more subtle case is that of the mathematical sublime. Given time it is necessary that the imagination succeeds in unifying the flood of sensations into a coherent whole. In other words, temporal synthesis dilutes the impact of sense, and since time is an ideal form of intuition its sufficiency for this process is transcendentally guaranteed. The mathematical sublime is the pleasure resulting from the obliteration of such ordered experience. It results when the laborious construction of organized perception is ruinously undermined by means of the sudden collapse of time, with the corresponding compression of sensation into a devastating intensity. The diabolic genius of Kant's account is worth well worth reciting:

> Measurement of a space (as apprehension) is at the same time a description of it, and so an objective movement in the imagination and a progression. On the other hand, the comprehension of the manifold in the unity, not of thought, but of intuition, and consequently the comprehension of the successively apprehended parts in one glance, is a retrogression that removes the time-condition in the progression of the imagination, and renders coexistence intuitable. Therefore, since the time-series is a condition of the internal sense and of intuition, it is a subjective movement of the imagination by which it does violence to the internal sense – a violence which must be

proportionately more striking the greater the quantum which the imagination comprehends in one intuition. The effort, therefore, to receive in a single intuition a measure for magnitudes which it takes an appreciable time to apprehend, is a mode of representation which is defeating when subjectively considered, but, objectively, is requisite for the estimation of magnitude, and is consequently expedient. Here the very same violence that is wrought on the subject through the imagination is estimated as expedient for the total purpose of feeling.[13]

It would be difficult to delineate the violent desire to consummate the purity of reason in the annihilation of animality more starkly. This does not prevent Kant from elaborating upon these horrors for page after page, describing sublimity as:

something terrifying for sensibility ... which, for all that, has an attraction for us, arising from the fact of its being a violence which reason unleashes upon the sensibility with a view to extending its own domain (the practical) and letting sensibility look out beyond itself into the infinite, which is an abyss for it.[14]

---

13   Ibid., 107–8; 142.

14   Ibid., 115; 148.

He later adds that:

> law ordained function ... is the genuine characteristic of human morality, wherein reason must violate sensibility.[15]

Such is the world of Gothic violence in which the enlightenment reached its crescendo; philosophers feast in the palaces of reason, and luxuriate in the screams that reach them from the dungeons of sublimity. Kant would have us believe that this sacrificial consumption of animality merely exposes the transcendentally established truth of reason in respect of the body, or rather, in frenzied contempt for it. Sublimity would be a final, almost gratuitous, negation. It would be the confirmation, rather than the generation, of the absolute supremacy enjoyed by the part of us that we share with the angels over the part that we share with the beasts. Nevertheless, he has actually taught us something quite different, if our stomachs are strong enough for it.

Reason is something that must be built, and the site of its construction first requires a demolition. The object of this demolition is the synthetic capability that Kant refers to as the imagination, and which he exhibits as natural intelligence or animal cunning. This is the capability to

---

15   Ibid., 120; 151.

act without the prior authorization of a juridical power, and it is only through the crucifixion of natural intelligence that the human animal comes to prostrate itself before universal law. Kant is quite explicit about this in the second *Critique;* only that is moral which totally negates all pathological influence, for morality must never negotiate with empirical stimulation. The Kantian moral good is the total monopoly of power in the hands of reason, and reason finds its principal definition as the supersensible element of the subject, and thus as fundamentally negative. In other words, morality is precisely the powerlessness of animality. This is not the discourse of civil jurisdiction, because it presupposes the prior silencing of the defendant. It is more like the discourse of military strategy in the grand style, which insists upon utterly vanquishing the enemy before dictating terms, and for which the very idea of negotiation already smelt of humiliation and defeat. In Kant's own words (from the *Groundwork to the Metaphysics of Morals*):

> Thus it is that man lays claim to a will which does not let anything come into account if it belongs merely to his desires and inclinations, but, contrary to these, thinks of acts being possible for him, indeed

necessary, which could only occur after all desires and sensory stimulation have been ignored.[16]

Those with a taste for the macabre can find this theme obsessively reiterated within Kant's practical philosophy. It is hard to imagine that it could be controversial to suggest that the categorical imperative presupposes a vivisection.

Kant's anti-utilitarianism is a mark of his integrity as a moralist in the Western tradition. He does not mask the perennially severe character of moral submission in order to pander to the loutish hedonism of the English. He knows that morality is only good if it hurts. This is why he refers to the delights of the sublime – where morality comes closest to touching itself – as a 'negative pleasure' [*negative Lust*], which is not at all the same as displeasure [*Unlust*]. Negative Lust is a pleasure taken in the negation of a primary pleasure, which is to say, in the unpleasure of the imagination. For reason has programmatically deafened itself to the howls of the body, and it is only by means of the aesthetic detour of the sublime that the devastating effects of its sovereignty can come to be enjoyed.

---

16 I. Kant, *Kritik der Praktischen Vernunft / Grundlegung zur Metaphysik der Sitten*, ed. Wilhelm Wieschedel, vol. 8 (Frankfurt am Main: Suhrkamp, 1968; for a recent English translation, see I. Kant, *Groundwork for the Metaphysics of Morals*, tr., ed. A. W. Wood (New Haven, CT and London: Yale University Press, 2002), Third Section, 73.

Squeamishness does not befit a moralist. A certain harshness is necessary if one would prevent life from being
delighted to death. Such harshness, indeed, that the
pathological lunge towards death rediscovers itself in the
process of its own rigorous extirpation; sublimated into
the thanatropic frenzy of reason.

Art as Insurrection: the Question of Aesthetics in Kant, Schopenhauer, and Nietzsche

Artists; those savage beasts that can't get enough of too much.

LAND

I

Immanuel Kant's *Critique of Judgment* is the site where art irrupts into European philosophy with the force of trauma. The ferocious impetus of this irruption was only possible in an epoch attempting to rationalize itself as permanent metamorphosis, as growth. Which means that it is a trauma quite incommensurable with the sort of difficulties art has posed to western philosophy since Plato, for it is no longer a matter of irritation, but of catastrophe. Our own.

The consistency of Kant's critical philosophy throughout all three of the great *Critiques* rests in the attention to excess inherent in the conception of synthetic a priori judgments.

145

The very inception of the critical project lay in Kant's decisive response to the voiding of logical metaphysics – the disintegration of the philosophical endeavour to reduce synthesis – that was consummated by Hume. Perhaps nothing was clearer to Kant than the radical untenability of the Leibnizian paradigm of metaphysics, still dominant in the (Wolfian) philosophy of the Prussian state. Logicism had been exposed, by the sceptical and empirical thought of a more advanced social system, as a sterile tautological stammering that belonged to the Middle Ages when positivity had been given in advance. It was with extraordinary resolve that Kant jettisoned the deductive systematization that had characterized the philosophies of immobilist societies – philosophies deeply and deliberately rooted in stagnant theism – and replaced it with the metaphysics of excess. He was even prepared to assist in the razing of all theoretical theology; because philosophy, too, had to become (at least a little) revolutionary. Nothing substantial was any longer to be presupposed.

Although the hazards of synthesis – of having to think – were clearly no longer eliminable, Kant still clung to the prospect that they could be traversed and definitively concluded. Philosophy would have to *take some ground*, but it could still anticipate a place of rest; an impregnable defensive line. If history could no longer be avoided, at least it could be brought swiftly and meticulously to its end.

Time would have to be transcendentally determined, once and for all, by a new metaphysics. It would thenceforth just continue, without disruption, in an innocent confirmation of itself. For a while – a period some time between the early 1770s and 1790 – it is possible that Kant was as cheerful as any bourgeois philosopher has ever been. An ephemeral restabilization had been achieved. Then came disaster. Something was still shockingly out of control. A third *Critique* was necessary.

The terrifying insight that drove Kant into the labyrinthine labours of the *Critique of Judgment* was that utter chaos had still not been outlawed by an understanding whose pretension was to 'legislate for nature'. Kant's own words are these:

> Although this [the pure understanding] makes up a system according to transcendental laws, which contain the condition of possibility for experience as such, it would still be possible that there be an infinite multiplicity of empirical laws and such a great heterogeneity of natural forms belonging to the particular experience that the concept of a system according to these (empirical) laws must be totally alien to the understanding, and neither the possibility, even less the necessity of such a totality could be conceived.[1]

---

1 I. Kant, *Kritik der Urteilskraft*, ed. W. Weischedel (Wiesbaden: Suhrkampf, 1974), 16. Where both original texts and translation are given I have sometimes translated directly

There are few horrors comparable to that of the master legislator who realizes that *anarchy is still permitted*. Far from having been domesticated by the transcendental forms of understanding, nature was still a freely flowing wound that needed to be staunched. This was going to be far more messy and frightening than anything yet undertaken, but Kant gritted his yellowing teeth, and began.

He found the resource for his new and final campaign in the precarious negative disorder which he called 'beauty'. When compared to the rigorous order of transcendental form, beauty was an altogether fragile and impermanent discipline. It was something the transcendental subject could not promise itself. Nevertheless, it seemed that something beyond reason, something that was prepared to get its hands dirty, was keeping nature down. 'Purposiveness without purpose', Kant's last name for excess, has all the extravagance of triumph. Even without trying, we win. History is written by the victors and ascendancy is presupposed as the condition of presentation, so that the submission of nature to exorbitant law is given with the objectivity of experience:

> It is thus a subjectively necessary transcendental presupposition that unlimited dissimilarity of empirical

from the original, and sometimes cited the English version without modification. For a recent English translation, see I. Kant, *Critique of the Power of Judgment*, ed. P. Guyer, tr. P. Guyer, E. Matthews (Cambridge and New York: Cambridge University Press, 2000), First Introduction, II, 9.

laws and heterogeneity of natural forms does not arise, but that it rather, through the affinity of the particular laws under more general ones, qualifies as an experience, as an empirical system.[2]

All those martialled formulas: nature takes the shortest way – she does nothing in vain – there is no leap in the multiplicity of forms (*continuum formarum*) – she is rich in species, but yet thrifty in genuses, and so forth, are nothing other than just this transcendental expression of judgment, setting itself a principle for experience as a system and thus for its own needs.[3]

Experience is thought of in terms of an extravagant but explosive inheritance; an ungrounded adaptation of nature to the faculties of representation. The increasingly tortured and paradoxical formulations that Kant selects indicate the precarious character of the luxuriance (stocked and expended in the imagination as 'free-play'). Consider just one example: 'Purposiveness is a lawfulness of the accidental as such.'[4]

Like Marx's Ricardo, it is the extraordinary cynicism of Kantianism at the edge of its desperation that lends it a profound radicality. Kant's 'reason' is a reactive concept, negatively defined against the pathology with which

---

2   Ibid., 22; Kant, *Critique of the Power of Judgment*, First Introduction, IV, 14.

3   Ibid., 23; 14.

4   Ibid., 30; 20.

it has been locked in perpetual and brutal war. In the third *Critique* all inhibition is lifted from this conflict; it becomes gritty, remorseless, cruel. His theory of the sublime, for instance, is sheer exultation in an insensate violence [*Gewalt*] against the pre-conceptual (animal) powers summarized under the faculty of the 'imagination'. In the experience of the sublime nature is affirmed as the trigger for a 'negative-pleasure', in so far as it humiliates and ruins that part of ourselves that we fail to share with the angels. To take one instance (out of innumerable possibilities) he says of the sublime that it is:

> something terrifying for sensibility ... which for all that, has an attraction for us, arising from the fact of its being a violence which reason unleashes upon sensibility with a view to extending its own domain (the practical) and letting sensibility look out beyond itself into the infinite, which is an abyss for it.[5]

Kant is becoming remarkably indiscriminate about his allies, asking only that they be enemies of pathological inclination [*Neigung*], and know how to fight. If reason is so secure, legitimate, supersensibly guaranteed, why all the guns?

---

5   Ibid., 189–90; tr. J. C. Meredith in *The Critique of Judgment* (Oxford: Oxford University Press, 1982), 115.

Irrational surplus, or the ineliminable and beautiful *danger* of unconscious creative energy: nature with fangs. How do we hold on to this thought? It is perpetually threatened by collapse; by a reversion to a depressive philosophy of work, whether theological or humanistic. The three great strands of post-Kantian exploration – marked by the names Hegel, Schelling, and Schopenhauer – are constantly tempted by the prospect of a reduction to forgotten or implicit labour; to the agency of God, spirit, or man, to anything that would return this ruthless artistic force of the generative unconscious to design, intention, project, teleology. Kant's word 'genius' is the immensely difficult and confused but emphatic resistance to such reductions; the thought of an utterly impersonal creativity that is historically registered as the radical discontinuity of the example, of irresponsible legislation, as 'order' without anyone giving the orders.

Kant is quite explicit that a generative theory of art requires a philosophy of genius – a re-admission of accursed pathology into its very heart – and one only has to read the second *Critique* alongside the third to notice the immense disruption that art inflicts upon transcendental philosophy. Kant only manages to control this disruption by maintaining art as an implicitly marginal problematic within a field mastered by philosophy. Even though he acknowledges that the autonomy of reason is to the heteronomy of genius what fidelity of representation is when compared to creation -poverty and wretchedness – the message scarcely seeps out. In addition, there is a perpetual and pathetic effort to subsume aesthetics under practical imperatives, 'beauty as the symbol of ethical life'[6] being one example, and the basic tendency of his theory of the sublime (the infinite privilege of transcendental ideas in comparison to nature) being another.

Despite superficial appearances it is not with the thought of noumenal subjectivity that the unconscious is announced within western philosophy, for this thought is still recuperable as a prereflexive consciousness, so innocuous that even Sartre is happy to accept it. It is rather out of an intertwining of two quite different strands of the Kantian text that the perturbing figure of the energetic unconscious emerges: first, the heteronomous pathological inclination whose repression is presupposed in the exercise of practical reason, and second, genius, or nature in its 'legislative' aspect. The genius 'cannot indicate how this fantastic and yet thoughtful ideas arise and come together in his head, because he himself does not know, and cannot, therefore, teach it to anyone'.[7]

It is no doubt comforting to speak of 'the genius' as if impersonal creative energy were commensurable with the order of autonomous individuality governed by reason,

---

6   Ibid., 294–9; 221–5.

7   Ibid., 244; 170.

but such chatter is, in the end, absurd. Genius is nothing like a character trait, it does not belong to a psychological lexicon; far more appropriate is the language of seismic upheaval, inundation, disease, the onslaught of raw energy from without. One 'is' a genius only in the sense that one 'is' a syphilitic, in the sense that 'one' is violently problematized by a ferocious exteriority. One returns to the subject of which genius has been predicated to find it charred and devastated beyond recognition.

II

Schopenhauer reconstructed the critical philosophy in several very basic ways: by eliminating the dogmatic presupposition of a difference between subjective and objective noumena; by shifting, not in an idealist (phenomenological) direction, but towards unconscious will; by simplifying the transcendental understanding from the twelve categories and two forms of sensibility inherited from Kant to the integrated 'principle of sufficient reason'; by nipping Kant's proto-idealist logicism in the bud; by charging the critical philosophy with the furious energy of sexual torment, attacking its (at least) germinal academicism, and immeasurably improving its stylistic resources. Where Kant distorts, marginalizes, and obscures the thought of the unconscious, Schopenhauer emphasizes and develops it. He defies the pretensions of imperalistic idealism by describing reason as a derivative abstraction from the understanding, co-extensive with language, so that Kant's transcendental logic is rethought through a transcendental aesthetic organized in terms of the 'principle of sufficient reason', simplified, de-mystified, and pushed downwards towards pre-intellectual intuition. Reason is no longer thought of as an autonomous principle in reciprocal antagonism with nature, but as a film upon its surface. All these moves involve a massive shift in the term 'will' [*Wille*], the placeholder for the psychoanalytical comprehension of desire.

For Kant, the will is aligned with reason, as the principle of the investment of nature with intentional intelligibility, the resource from which teleological judgment must regulatively metaphorize all exorbitant natural order:

> The will, as the faculty of desire, is one of the many natural causes in the world, namely, that one which is effective through concepts, and everything that is represented as possible (or necessary) through a will is called practically possible (or necessary), in contradistinction from the physical possibility or necessity of an affect for which the ground is not determined in its causality through concepts (but rather, as with lifeless matter, through mechanism, and, with animals, through instinct).[8]

8   Ibid., 79; 9.

In contrast, Schopenhauer's great discovery is that of non-agentic will; the positivity of the death of God. Rather than thinking willing as the movement by which conceptually articulate decision is realized in nature, he understands the appearance of rational decisions as a derivative consequence of pre-intellectual – and ultimately pre-personal, even pre-organic – willing. Unconscious desire is not just desire that happens to be unconscious, as if a decisionistic lucidity is somehow natural or proper to desire; it is rather that consciousness can only be consequential upon a desire for which lucid thought is an instrumental requirement. For Schopenhauer the intellect is constituted by willing, rather than being constitutive for it. *We do not know what we want.*

There is an important sense in which Schopenhauer's will is the thought of genius taken towards its limit, subsuming the entire faculty of knowledge under that of exorbitant natural order, as a mere instance (although a privileged one) of purposiveness without purpose. But Schopenhauer's own usage of the thought of genius preserves it in its specificity, as a proportional exorbitance on the part of the intellect in relation to the will. Genius is the result of a positive overcoming of unconscious 'purpose', an excess of intellectual energy over that which can be absorbed by desire, thus redundancy, or dysfunction through superfluity:

an entirely pure and objective picture of things is not reached in the normal mind, because its power of perception at once becomes tired and inactive, as soon as this is not spurred on and set in motion by the will. For it has not enough energy to apprehend the world purely objectively from its own elasticity and *without a purpose*. On the other hand, where this happens, where the brain's power of forming representations has such a surplus that a pure, distinct, objective picture of the external world exhibits itself without a purpose as something useless for the intentions of the will, which is even disturbing in the higher degrees, and can even become injurious to them – then there already exists at least the natural disposition for that abnormality. This is denoted by the name of *genius*, which indicates that something foreign to the will, i.e., to the I or ego proper, a *genius* added from outside so to speak, seems to become active here.[9]

The mother of the useful arts is necessity; that of the fine arts superfluity and abundance. As their father, the former have understanding, the latter genius, which in itself a kind of superfluity, that of the power

---

9   A. Schopenhauer, *Die Welt als Wille und Vorstellung*, in *Werke in zehn* II (Zürich: Diogenes, 1977), 446; translated by E.F.J. Payne as *The World as Will and Representation*, vol. II (New York: Dover, 1966), 377.

of knowledge beyond the measure required for the service of the will.[10]

For Schopenhauer the body is the objectification of the will, the intellect is a function of a particular organ of the body, and genius is the surplus of that functioning in relation to the individual organism in question. Genius is thus an assault on the individualized will that erupts from out of the reservoir of archaic pre-organized willing. It is a site of particular tension in his thinking, caught between a vision of progressive redemption, achieved through humanity as perfected individuality in which the will is able to renounce itself, and regressive unleashing of the pre-individual will from the torture chamber of organic specificity, ego-interests, and personality. Schopenhauer's attachment to the first of these options is well known, but the possibility of an alternative escape from individualization – by way of dissolution into archaic inundating desire – constantly strains for utterance within his text.

This tension generates a terminological fission that can be easily detected along the jagged fault lines separating sexuality from art. One example is 'beauty'; a word that is driven by Schopenhauer's overt (metaphysical) policy into an uneasy alignment with renunciation. He interprets it as the negative affect – relief or release – associated

10   Ibid., 484; 410.

with disengagement from interested thought, attained through contemplative submergence in the pure universal 'ideas' of natural species as they exist outside space, time, and causality, and manifest to a radicalized Kantian disinterestedness that is greatly facilitated by artistic representation.[11]

If in the end Derrida's *Spurs* is an absurd book, it is because it is tapping into Nietzsche's negotiation with Schopenhauer's discourse on woman and the aesthetic without knowing what it is listening to, because it is too busy perpetuating the Heideggerian mutilation of libidinal post-Kantianism. Nietzsche's recovery and affirmation of the fictive power of art (in his later writings) is a response to the violent denigration of this power in Schopenhauer's thought, a denigration that is programmed by a complex of interlocking factors that are evidenced with particular intensity in his discussion of sexual difference. Schopenhauer founds the modern thought of excitement as suffering, a thought which survives into the twentieth century in a variety of guises, and most importantly in Freud's libidinal economy. In order to perpetuate a rhythm of desire and its tranquilization,

---

11 Of all the complex issues I have skimmed over recklessly this is perhaps the richest and most impacted. Schopenhauer, by referring exorbitant form back to a Platonic *eidos* is undoubtedly sacrificing a great deal of the fertile tension in Kant's thought of purposiveness without purpose, although he also reduces the risk of a slide back into teleological theology. The thought that was perhaps necessary in order to depart most radically from the possibility of theistic relapse was that of a divine unconscious, eliminating all possibility of agentic creation at any level. But this would be the image of a mad god. Dionysus?

in which there is no space for positive pleasure, but only variable degrees of pain, it is necessary to be profoundly *misled*. This is why Schopenhauer refers to the principle of sufficient reason, which is associated with the pure form of material reality, and is the transcendental condition of individuated appearance, as the veil of *Maya*, or illusion. Art, as the escape from individuation and desire, is thus the very negative of fiction. Beauty is an experience of truth.

But there is also another troubling, enticing, arousing, and captivating type of beauty (Nietzsche will come to say it is the only one), the beauty that is exemplified – in post-Hellenic western history at least – in the female body. For Schopenhauer this is an immense problem, as is the domain of the erotic in its entirety. The anegoic disinterestedness of resignation is echoed and parodied by an indifference to ego-interests that leads in a quite opposite direction; *deeper into the inferno of willing*. After acknowledging with his usual raw honesty that 'all amorousness is rooted in the sexual impulse alone',[12] Schopenhauer is forced to accept that 'it is precisely this not seeking *one's own* interest, everywhere the stamp of greatness, which gives even to passionate love a touch of the sublime, and makes it a worthy subject of poetry'.[13]

There is thus both a renunciatory and a libidinous sublime, each with its associated objects and aesthetic

---

12 Ibid., 624; 555.

'perfections' or intensities. And it is not only beauty that is torn in separate directions, fiction too is split; on the one hand as the condition of individualization, and on the other as an appeal to constituted individuality. Either the ego is a dream of desire, or desire has to creep up on the ego as a dream. In sexuality,

> nature can attain her end only by implanting in the individual a certain *delusion*, and by virtue of this, that which in truth is merely a good thing for the species seems to him to be a good thing for himself, so that he serves the species, whereas he is under the delusion that he is serving himself. In this process a mere chimera, which vanishes immediately afterwards, floats before him, and, as motive, takes the place of a reality. This *delusion is instinct*. In the great majority of cases, instinct is to be regarded as the sense of the species which presents to the will what is useful to *it*.[13]

Woman is matter, formless and unpresentable, arousing and thus tormenting; everything about her is pretence, deception, alteration, unlocalizable irrational attraction, *Verstellung*. Schopenhauer's notorious essay *On Woman* is mapped by the movement of this word, as it organizes the play of seduction, of indirect action, of non-ideal beauty,

---

13   Ibid., 630; 538.

disrupting the seriousness and responsible self-legislation of the male subject through an 'art of dissimulation'.[14] Woman is wicked art, art that intensifies life, art whose only truth is a whispered intimation that negation, too, is only a dream, the figment of an overflowing positivity that deceives through excess. Could the dream of redemption be nothing but a bangle upon the arms of exuberant life? Schopenhauer reels in horror:

> Only the male intellect, clouded by the sexual impulse, could call the undersized, narrow-shouldered, broad-hipped, and short-legged sex the fair sex; for in this impulse is to be found its whole beauty. The female sex could be more aptly called the *unaesthetic*.[15]

Women are so terribly non-Platonic, so outrageously vital and real, so excessive in relation to the cold sterile perfections of the ideas. With infallible instinctive power they propagate the dangerous delusion that there is something about life that we want. Pessimism has to be misogyny, because woman refuses to repel.

---

14 A. Schopenhauer, *Parerga und Paralipomena* II (Zurich: Diogenes, 1977), 671; tr. by E. F. J. Payne as *Parerga and Paralipomena*, vol. II (Oxford: Clarendon, 1974), 617.

15 Ibid., 673; 619.

III

A few of the things that Nietzsche learnt – at least in part – from Schopenhauer were the elementary tenets of libidinal materialism or the philosophy of the energetic unconscious (the unrestricted development of the theory of genius), the primacy of the body and its medical condition, pragmatism (asking not how we know but why we know), effervescent literary brilliance, aestheticism (with a musical focus), an 'aristocratic' concern for hierarchy and gradation (which he turned into an implement for overcoming Aristotelian logic), antihumanism, a construction of the history of philosophy as dominated by Plato and Kant and the problematic of reality and appearance, virulent anti-academicism, misogyny, and the distrust of mathematical thinking. Schopenhauer even wrote that:

> The genuine symbol of nature is universally and everywhere the circle, because it is the schema or form of recurrence; in fact, this is the most general form in nature. She carries it through in everything from the course of the constellations down to the death and birth of organic beings. In this way alone, in the restless stream of time and its content, a continued existence, i.e., a nature, becomes possible.[16]

---

16 A. Schopenhauer, *Die Welt als Wille und Vorstellung II, ii*, 559; tr. Payne in *The World as Will and Representation*, vol. II, 477.

But the shifts Nietzsche had brought to the Schopenhauerian philosophy by the end of his creative life were at least as immense as this inheritance, involving, amongst other elements, a displacement from the will to life to the will to power, so that survival is thought of as a tool or resource for creation; a displacement of antihumanism from the ascetic ideal to overman (non-terminal overcoming); the completion of a post-Aristotelian 'logic' of gradation without negativity or limits; a 'critique of philosophy' that diagnosed Plato and Kant as symptoms of libidinal disaster; a return of historical thinking freed from the untenable time/timelessness opposition of bankrupt logicism; and a displacement from the principle of sufficient reason to 'equalization' [*Ausgleichung*], which – since differentiation was no longer thought of as an imposition of the subject – implied a shift from primordial unity to irreducible pluralism, and from the disinterested 'world-eye' to perspectivism.

Nietzsche's intricate, profound, and explosive response to the provocation of Schopenhauer resists hasty summarization. It is helpful to start with the transitional movements of *The Birth of Tragedy*, in which the Schopenhauerian will is re-baptized as 'Dionysus'. Like the undifferentiated will, it is only in the dream of Apollonian appearance that Dionysus can be individualized. As Walter Otto remarks (about the mythological, not just the specifically Nietzschean god): 'He is clearly thought of on the oriental pattern as the divine or infinite in general, in which the individual soul longs so much to lose itself'.[17] The tragic chorus is the focus of a delirious fusion, in which the personality is liquidated by the collective artistic process. Otto says some other very important things about Dionysus, the twice-born:

> The one so born is not merely the exultant one and joy-bringer, he is also the suffering and dying god, the god of tragic contradiction. And the inner power of this dual nature is so great, that he steps amongst humanity as a storm, quaking them and subduing their resistance with the whip of madness. Everything habitual and ordered must be scattered. Existence suddenly becomes an intoxication – an introduction of blessedness, but no less one of terror.

> To this female world the Apollonian stands opposed, as the decidedly masculine. The mystery of life, of blood and of terrestrial force does not rule in it, but rather clarity and breadth of spirit. But the Apollonian world cannot persist without the other.[18]

---

17   W. F. Otto, *Dionysos, Mythos und Kultus* (Frankfurt am Main: Vittorio Klostermann, 1933), 115.

18   Ibid., 74–5, 132.

Doric civilization, the hard Apollonian spine of western culture, vaunting the defiant erectness of its architecture, is fundamentally defensive in nature. Already in this, Nietzsche's most 'Schopenhauerian' book, the minor register of the pessimistic quandary prevails without compromise; the overcoming of wretched individuality is to be referred in the direction of the reservoir of insurgent desire, not in that of a metaphysical renunciation. One does not build fortifications against saints:

> To me the Doric state and Doric art are explicable only as a permanent military encampment of the Apollonian. Only incessant resistance to the titanic-barbaric nature of the Dionysian could account for the long survival of an art so defiantly prim and so encompassed with bulwarks, a training so warlike and rigorous, and a political structure so cruel and relentless.[19]

The difference between Dionysus and Apollo is that between music and the plastic arts (Schopenhauer's differentiation that Nietzsche describes as 'the most important insight of aesthetics'),[20] will and representation (primary and secondary process), chaos and form. In the tragic

---

19 F. Nietzsche, *Die Geburt der Tragödie* (Frankfurt am Main: Ullstein Materialien, 1981), 35 tr. W. Kaufmann as *The Birth of Tragedy* (New York: Vintage, 1967), 47.

20 Ibid., 89; 100.

fusion of music and theatrical spectacle desire is delivered upon the order of representation in a delirious collective affirmation of insurgent alterity (nature, impulse, oracular insight, woman, barbarism, Asia). Greek tragedy is the last instance of the occident being radically permeable to its outside. The Socratic death of tragedy is the beginning of the ethnic solipsism and imperialistic dogmatism that has characterized western politics ever since, the brutal domestication process with which the repressive instance in *man* ('reason') has afflicted the impersonal insurrectionary energies of creativity, until they became the whimpering, sentimental, and psychologized 'genius' of the romantics. With Socrates began the passionate quest of European humanity to become the *ugly animal*.

In his later, more fragmentary writings on art, Nietzsche perhaps says something a little like the following. The aesthetic *operation* is simplification; the movement of abstraction, logicization, unification, the resolution of problematic. It is this operation which, when understood in terms of the logical principles formulated by Aristotle – in terms, that is, of its own product – seems like a negation of the enigmatic, the re-distribution of alterity to the same within a zero-sum exchange, the progressive 'improvement' and domestication of life. But simplification is not a teleologically regulated approximation to simplicity, to the decadent terminus we call 'truth', it is an inexhaustibly open-ended creative process whose only limits are fictions fabricated out of itself. Nothing is more complex than simplification; what art takes from enigma it more than replenishes in the instantiation of itself, in the labyrinthine puzzle it plants in history. The intensification of enigma. The luxuriantly problematic loam of existence is built out of the sedimented aeons of residues deposited by the will to power, the impulse to create, 'The world as a work of art that gives birth to itself.'[21]

Enigma, positive confusion (delirium), problematic, pain, whatever we want to call it; the torment of the philosophers in any case, is the stimulus to ecstatic creation, to an interminable 'resolution' into the enhanced provocations of art. What the philosophers have never understood is this: it is the *unintelligibility of the world alone that gives it worth*. 'Inertia needs unity (monism); plurality of interpretations a sign of strength. Not to desire to deprive the world of its disturbing and enigmatic character'.[22] Not, then, to oppose pain to the absence of pain as metaphysical pessimism does, but, rather, to differentiate the ecstatic overcoming of pain from weariness and inertia, to exult in new and more terrible agonies, fears, burning perplexities as the resource of becoming, overcoming, triumph, the great libidinal oscillations that break up stabilized systems and intoxicate on intensity;

---

21 F. Nietzsche, *Der Wille zur Macht*, ed. P. Gast, E. Förster-Nietzsche (Stuttgart: Alfred Kröner Verlag, 1964), 533; tr. by W. Kaufmann as *The Will to Power* (New York: Vintage, 1968), 419.

22 Ibid., 413; 326.

that is Dionysian pessimism – 'refusal to be deprived of the stimulus of the enigmatic';[23] 'the effect of the work of art is to *excite the state that creates art – intoxication*'.[24]

IV

After Nietzsche there is Freud. Tapping into a reservoir of genius (the unconscious of late nineteenth-century Viennese women) that drives him to the point of idiocy, he pushes onwards without knowing what the fuck he's doing. Freud is a thinker of astounding richness and fertile complexity, but I shall merely touch upon his most disastrous confusion. When he writes on art, degenerating – despite his wealth of acuity – into banal psycho-biography, a terribly damaging loss of direction afflicts the psychoanalytic enterprise. The inherent connection between the irruptive primary process and artistic creativity, or the basic inextricability of psychoanalysis and aesthetics, slips Freud's grasp, and art is presented as a merely contingent terrain for the application of therapeutically honed concepts. The adaptation of the mutilated individual to its society, in which art is illegal except as a parasite of elite commodity production circuits, is the scandal of psychoanalysis. It becomes Kantian

23 Ibid., 330; 262.

24 Ibid., 553; 434.

(bourgeois); a delicate police activity dedicated to the social management and containment of genius. As if 'therapy' could be anything other than the revolutionary unleashing of artistic creation!

The two basic directions in which the philosophy of genius can develop are exemplified by psychoanalysis and national socialism. Either rigorous anti-anthropomorphism, the steady constriction of the terrain of intentional explanation, and the rolling reduction of praxes to parapraxes, or the re-ascription of genius to intentional individuality, concentration of decision, and the paranoiac praxial interpretation of non-intentional processes (the Jewish conspiracy theory). The death of God is operative in both cases, either as the space of the generative unconscious, or as that of a triumphantly divinized and arbitrarily isolated secular subjectivity. It is easy to see that the role of discourse in these two cases is a very precise register for the difference at issue; on the one hand the talking cure, in which the texts of confession and rational theory are both displaced by the compression wave of a radically senseless energy process that defies the status of object in relation to an autonomously determinable agent language; and on the other, the interminable authoritative monologue of the dictator (politically instantiated ego-ideal), in which the will is returned to a quasi-Kantian acceptation to capitalize upon its libidinal detour, finding its true sense in the lucid decision of an individual who speaks on behalf of a racially specified unconscious clamour.

That part of twentieth-century philosophy resonant with the aesthetically oriented tendency outlined here has as its two great tasks the diagnosis of Nazism and the protraction of the psychoanalytic impulse, in other words the arming of desire with intellectual weapons that will allow it to evade the dead-end racist *Götterdämmerung* politics which capital deploys as a last ditch defence against the flood. No revolution without insurrectionary desire, no effective route for insurrectionary desire without integral anti-fascism. Wilhelm Reich, Georges Bataille, Gilles Deleuze, and Félix Guattari are perhaps the most important theoretical *loci* in this development. The latter three I shall say a little about.

It is not *simply* ridiculous to describe Bataille as Schopenhauer with enthusiasm, in so far as this might crudely characterize a certain variant of 'Nietzscheanism', or Dionysian pessimism. After all, Bataille too is concerned with value as the annihilation of life, challenging the utilitarianism that finds its only end in the preservation and expansion of existence. If this affirmation of loss is 'nihilistic', it is at least an 'active nihilism'; the promotion of a violently convulsive *expenditure* rather than a weary renunciation. Art as the wastage of life. And Bataille's involvement with art, above all with literature, is of an unparalleled intricacy and intensity. Philosopher and historian of art, literary theorist, in his 'philosophy' a stylist, dazzling as an essayist, a novelist and poet of both profundity and incandescent beauty, his is a writing oblivious to circumscription, spreading like an exotic fungus into the darkest recesses of aesthetic possibility. A rather tortured and incoherent leap? Come on now! A 'philosophy' of excess that draws out an inner connection between literature, eroticism, and revolt could hardly be irrelevant to our problematic here. As Bataille states, 'beauty alone … renders tolerable a need for disorder, violence, and indignity that is the root of love.'[25]

Bataille also has the peculiar honour, shared with Nietzsche and Reich, of beginning his assault on germinal national socialism before Hitler had exhibited its truth. His early essays sketch a vision of fascism as the most fanatical project for the elimination of excess, an attempt at the secular enforcement of the perfectly ordered city of God against the disorder, luxuriance, and mess of surplus production, as it sprawls into the voluptuary expenditure of eroticism and art. Assailing the fascist tendency is the disindividualized delirium of tragic sacrifice and revolution, when

Being is given to us in an intolerable surpassing of being, no less intolerable than death. And because,

---

25   G. Bataille, *Oeuvres Complètes* (Paris: Gallimard, 12 vols, 1970–1988), vol. III, 13.

in death, it is withdrawn from us at the same time it is given, we must search for it in the feeling of death, in those intolerable moments where it seems that we are dying, because the being in us is only there through excess, when the plenitude of horror and that of joy coincide.[26]

For there is no doubt that the fascists are right, the very incarnation of right, yes: 'Literature is even, like the transgression of moral law, a danger.'[27]

A theory of the real as art (primary production) that is melded seamlessly with an anti-fascist diagnostics characterizes the work of Gilles Deleuze and Félix Guattari. In their *Anti-Oedipus* they indicate that the rational regulation or coding of creative process is derivative, sterile, and eliminable. Their name for genius is 'schizophrenia', a term that cannot be safely domesticated within psychology, any more than 'genius' can (and for the same reasons). If nature is psychotic it is simply because our psychoses are not in reality 'ours'.

Libido – as the raw energy of creation – is ungrounded, irreducibly multiple, yet it precipitates a real and unified 'principle' out of itself. The body without organs is its name; at once material abstraction, and the concretely

26 Ibid., 11–12.

27 Ibid., vol. IX, 182.

hypostasized differential terrain which is nothing other than what is instantaneously shared by difference. The body without organs is pure surface, because it is the mere coherence of differential web, but it is also the source of depth, since it is the sole 'ontological' element of difference. It is produced transcendence. Paradox after paradox, spun like a disintegrating bandage upon the infected and deteriorating wound of Kant's aesthetics, teasing the philosophical domestication of art – the most gangrenous cultural appendage of capital – towards its utter disintegration.

How does desire come to desire its own repression? How does production come to rigidify itself in the social straitjacket *whose most dissolved form is capital*? It is with this problematic, inherited from Spinoza, Nietzsche, and Reich, that Deleuze and Guattari orient their work. In our terms here: how does art become (under-) compensated labour? Their answer involves a displacement of the problem into a philosophical affinity with Kant's paralogisms of the pure understanding, rethought in *Anti-Oedipus* as materially instantiated traps for desire. A paralogism is the attempt to ground 'conditions of possibility' in the objectivity they permit, or creativity in what it creates. This is, to take the most pertinent example, to derive the forces of production from the socio-economic apparatus they generate. Sociological fundamentalism, state worship, totalitarian paranoia and fascism, they all exhibit the same basic impulse; hatred of art, (real) freedom, desire, everything that cannot be controlled, regulated, and administered. Fascism hates aliens, migrant workers, the homeless, rootless people of every kind and inclination, everything evocative of excitement and uncertainty, women, artists, lunatics, drifting sexual drives, liquids, impurity, and abandonment.

Philosophy, in its longing to rationalize, formalize, define, delimit, to terminate enigma and uncertainty, to co-operate wholeheartedly with the police, is nihilistic in the ultimate sense that it strives for the immobile perfection of death. But creativity cannot be brought to an end that is compatible with power, for unless life is extinguished, control must inevitably break down. We possess art lest *we perish of the truth*.[28]

To conclude is not merely erroneous, but ugly.

---

28   Nietzsche, *Der Wille zur Macht*, 554; 435.

Spirit and Teeth

A PRELIMINARY POST-MORTEM

Spirit (*Geist*) is stigmatized by a multiple deconstructibility: as a substantialization of Dasein, an antonym of matter, a correlate of phonic lucidity, or a token of reflexivity, self-presence, pure intelligibility, spontaneity, etc. In the course of its recent history this word has been inflated by Hegel into the cosmic medium of transaction – the super-heated lubricant of global eventuation – and then trafficked to the edge of worthlessness by the culture succeeding him, before finally succumbing to an irreparable marginalization by the scientific advances of experimental and behavioral psychology, neurology, neuroanatomy, cognitive science, cybernetics, artificial intelligence, until it becomes a sentimentalism, a vague peripheralized metaphor, a joke ... a cheap target one might think. There are those who remain loyal enough to the canonical discourses of Western philosophy to argue that logocentrism is secreted in the implementary terminology of information, digitality, program, software, and control. But as for spirit! – that can only be parody or nostalgia. Who could still use such a word without humor or disdain? Spirit is less a misleading or dangerous word than a ridiculous one; a Coelecanth of a word. Yet it persists: the mark of a clownish incompetence at death.

Such incompetence has its doctrine, rituals, and liturgy, its orthodoxies and heresies. It is the entire and prolonged refusal of the impersonal summarizable as 'phenomenology.' Whether high-church (Hegel), or low-church (Husserl), phenomenology is the definitive ideology of propriety; systematically employing the interrogative mode in order to distill out everything for which proper subjectivity cannot claim responsibility, and thus entrenching the humanistic dimension of Western philosophy ever more rigidly. This entire current gradually compiles an attempted proof of the impossibility of death, an ontological conflation of access to reality and ownership (*psyché*, *cogito*, *Selbstheit*, *Eigentlichkeit*, *Jemeinigkeit*), a perpetually reformulated spiritualism. Socrates, Descartes, Husserl: all shallow, all egoists, all pressing further into the flatlands of the profane. This is why they are so well placed to profit from the death of God (an event in which they had taken no part – on the contrary; the obsessional egoism of theism had always appealed to them). Phenomenology is a programmatic denial (reduction to the personal) of exteriority which, after becoming a quasisolipsistic knee-jerk of self-assertion, wonders with genuine naivety why alterity has come to pose such problems. If spirit largely disappears between Hegel and Husserl it is because, compared to the transcendental ego, it seems a little too complicit with the outside.

Unlike Heidegger and Derrida, I see no advance, recovery, or sophistication taking place in the Husserlian reading of Kant. The phenomenological reduction of appearance [*Erscheinung*] to evidential *Schein* is a dogmatic decision which defangs the tentative skepticism of the critical philosophy, taking it even further from the deep *epoché* of unknowing: the vast abrupt discovered confusedly by Pyrrho of Elis, the repressed of monotheistic civilization. Husserlian suspension or bracketing is not Pyrrhonian but Socratic; a reservation of judgment that is subordinated to apodicticity, to knowing what one knows even if nothing else (to doubting as a power of the subject). *Epoché*, *chaos,* Old Night, death, however it/she is named, the way there is not our doing. Suspension is to be discovered, not performed.

So what is to be thought of a *différance* that radicalizes, deconstructs, or subverts a suspension thus crushed under a phenomenological dogmatics? What is it that would take us this way, if not that which *appears* (in Kant's sense, not Husserl's) as the humanistic pretension – the spirit – of representational philosophizing? Such suspension is of course a detour, an avoidance, but scarcely an inevitable one. On the contrary, it is peculiarly deliberated; meticulously valorizing a specific philosophic tendency (passing through Husserl), effacing another (the Schopenhauerean fork of post-Kantianism), and painstakingly transferring signs from the latter to the former (Nietzsche read through Heidegger!!!). Section 7 of *Sein und Zeit* is exemplary here, with its insistence upon an evidential reading of phenomenality, thereby dismissing the entire problematic of Nietzsche's thinking in a single casual gesture. What sense to the insistent theme of fiction in Nietzsche's writings after such a move has been made? What sense to enigma? (We always already have the meaning of being built into the structure of existence, Heidegger suggests, it is merely that we do not yet know that we know. Questioning is remembering. Socrates smiles.)

We do not know *yet,* a not yet that can be dilated corrosively; frustrating the end of metaphysics, interminably deferring truth. Yawns become scarcely controllable. Does it matter what we know or will never know? Let us not forget that philosophy is also primate psychology; that our loftiest speculations are merely picking through a minuscule region of the variegated slime encrusting a speck of dust. An obsessional concern for such insignificances is a tasteless parochialism. What matters is the Unknown: the escapographic matrix echoed spectrally by the negative prefix, sprawled in immense indifference to all our "yets". Beyond the anthropoid gesticulations of knowing, suspension is not differentiable from death, and death ("one's death" as we so ludicrously say) does not belong to an order that can be delayed. Has our Socratism reached such a pinnacle of profanity that we really imagine she would wait for us?

PART I: WOLVES

> As I continue to study this text, elsewhere, with a more decent patience, I hope one day to be able, beyond what a conference permits me today, to render it justice in also analysing its motion, its mode or its status (if it has one), its relation to philosophical discourse, to hermeneutics or poetics, but still what it says of Geschlecht, the word Geschlecht, and also of place [Ort], as of animality. For the moment [l'instant], I follow solely the passage of spirit.[1]

These are the words of a man who is confident he will survive for some considerable time. There is no discernible urgency here, far less abruptness, desperation, or any of the raw intensities of haste. Instead there is the now familiar rhetoric of close reading; the simultaneous

---

1   J. Derrida, *De l'esprit: Heidegger et la question* (Paris: Galilée, 1987), 137; see also, J. Derrida, *Of Spirit: Heidegger and the Question*, tr. G. Bennington and R. Bowlby (Chicago: University of Chicago Press, 1989), 87.

performance and prescription of painstaking care, deliberation, conscientiousness, and reverential textual devotion. A certain intricately intertextual discussion of spirit unfolds, at a languorous pace, inspired by uninterrogated principles of decency and justice. Everything is mediated by elucidations, re-elucidations, elucidations of previous elucidations, conducted with meticulous courtesy, but never inattentive to the complicity of the concept of elucidation with the history of metaphysics from Plato to the previous paragraph of *De l'esprit*. Our author is not to be hurried into premature pronouncements on matters of such seriousness as philosophical discourse, hermeneutics, or poetics. Nor is he prepared to descend into such overenthusiastic crudity as examining more than one of Heidegger's words in a single book. Last of all, as it has so often tended to be, comes a promise to take seriously the problem of animality, which – God and suchlike spiritual primordialities being willing – should come to be written about one day.

It is probably relatively uncontroversial to conclude from all this that Derrida is not a werewolf. Werewolves are dissipated within a homolupic spiral that distances them utterly from all concern for decency or justice. Their feral physiologies are badly adapted to the depressive states conducive to ethical earnestness. Instead they are propelled by extremities of libidinal tension which fragment their movements, break up their tracks with jagged discontinuities, and infest their nerves with a burning *malaise*, so that each gesture is baked in a kiln of ferocity. Creatures of epidemic rather than hermeneutics, werewolves tend to be very crude, but then, they don't live as long as deconstructionists. The luxury of delaying the problem of animality is not open to them.

On page 141 of *De l'esprit* Derrida apologizes for a very moderate instance of textual impoliteness that he describes as 'precipitating in an indecent fashion'.[2] In this thought of 'indecent precipitation' he comes closer to the dominant impulse of Trakl's poetry than at any other point in the book; closer too, it could be argued, than Heidegger ever gets. An evasion that is perhaps constitutive of hermeneutical decency is exemplified when, by taking one's time over interpreting Trakl's poetry, one avoids succumbing to the pestilence it communicates. Trakl's writings are lycanthropic vectors of impatience, of twitch disease, because they are the virulent relics of an indecent precipitation, an abortion, a meteorite impact. Trakl took very little time over anything. Surviving as he did to the age of twenty-seven he had very little time to take.

Trakl confesses to his lycanthropy in the first version of *Passion,* the unavowed version, where he writes that:

---

2   Ibid., 141; Derrida, *Of Spirit*, 87.

Two wolves in the sinister Wood
We mixed our blood in a stony embrace
And the stars of our race fell upon us.[3]

The word 'race' in this translation precipitates the sense of *Geschlecht* in an indecent fashion. In the complete absence of hermeneutical conscientiousness it is epidemiological factors alone which compel this. To become a werewolf one must be bitten by another werewolf, and in Trakl's case it seems this was Rimbaud, who wrote: 'It is quite evident to me that I have always been of an inferior race. I am not able to comprehend revolt. My race never stirs itself except for pillage: like wolves at the beast they have not killed'.[4]

To be a werewolf is to be inferior by the most basic criteria of civilization. Not only is the discipline of political responsibility alien to them, so is the entire history of work in which such discipline is embedded. Rimbaud remarks, starkly enough: 'I have a horror of all trades.' In general, it can be said that this race is marked by a profound spiritual inferiority. Compared to the piety, morality, and industriousness of its superiors it exhibits only laziness, disobedience, and an abnormally unsuccessful

---

3   G. Trakl, *Das dichterische Werk* (Munich: Deutscher Taschenbuch Verlag, 1972), 216; for a recent English translation, see G. Trakl, *Poems and Prose: A Bilingual Edition* tr. Alexander Stillmark, (Evanston, IL: Northwestern University Press, 2005), 82.

4   A. Rimbaud, *Collected Poems*, tr. O. Bernard, (Harmondsworth: Penguin, 1986), 302.

repression of all those traits of the unconscious which Freud describes as 'resistant to education', and among which there is nothing remotely associated with either decency or justice: 'I have never been of this people; I have never been a christian; I am of the race who sings under torture; I do not understand the laws, I am a brute'.[5]

Such is Trakl's 'accursed race'[6] as well as Rimbaud's, communicating its dirty blood in wilderness spaces of barbarian inarticulacy. Eternally aborting the prospect of a transcendental subjectivity, the inferior ones are never captured by contractual reciprocity, or by its attendant moral universalism. They are no more employable than they are psychoanalyzable, oblivious to both legality and incentive. Incapable of making promises – even to themselves – they are excluded from every possibility of salvation. The craving for such pagan regressions is unspeakable. It is only with the greatest strictness that the superior ones repress the violent drives which lure them into inferior becomings; becoming female, black, irresponsible and nomadic, becoming an animal, a plant, a death spasm of the sun.

In its final phase the Austro-Hungarian Empire became a machine for the generation of homolupic becomings: brewing intense trajectories of regression among the

5   Ibid., 308.

6   Trakl, *Das dichterische Werk*, 82.

slavic races of the Balkans and Carpathians, translating them into German, and then condensing them under the pressure of exacerbated repression in the Viennese culture-core. What exploded in the hysterias of Freud's patients was an irresistible vulcanism of becoming inferior, whose petrified lava flows mapped-out the regressive character of the drive. The migrant blocks of tension summarized in the Freudian unconscious are much less a matter of Oedipus than of the mongols; of those who feed the world of spirit to their horses as they inundate civilization like a flood. If the unconscious is structured like a language it is only because language has the pattern of a plague.

Among Trakl's writing's are two war poems, and perhaps only two. One is *Grodek* – named after the battlefield upon which the Austro-Hungarian army suffered a major defeat in the early stages of the conflict – and is perhaps the most widely known of Trakl's writings. It is this poem that includes the line so important to both Heidegger and Derrida concerning 'the hot flame of spirit'.[7] The other is entitled *In the East*, and sketches the same libidinal figure in the First World War as Freud's writings of the two ensuing decades. This figure traces the displacement of impersonal primary-process aggression against the self-God-city complex – against civilization – onto the far more restrained axis of armed competition between nations.

---

7   Ibid., 95; Trakl, *Poems and Prose*, 126.

War sublimates the lycanthropic death-wave in the same way a dream sublimates unavowable desire; allowing something to remain asleep. In this sense *In the East* is the undoing of a war poem, and has the nightmare quality associated with something peeled-back; such as the disintegration of flesh from a skull, or the opening of a corpse to reveal an obscenely teeming mass. This movement of violent disillusionment is starkly outlined in the poem *Confiteor*:

> And as the masks fall from each thing
> I see only anxiety, despair, ignominy and epidemic,
> The tragedy of humanity has no heroes,
> A vile piece, played out on graves and corpses.[8]

The second stanza of *In the East* ends with the spirits of the stricken – of the *erschlagenen,* close perhaps to a *Geschlecht* – sighing among the shadows of autumnal ashes, and to this point *In the East* might still be a war poem. It would still be possible for the ego to savour these stanzas for the sublimation-trap they lay for impersonal thanatropisms, offering up the victims of inhibited conflicts as a mournful dream-image. The third and final stanza, however, is something quite different:

---

8   Ibid., 147.

Thorny wilderness girdles the city
From bloody steps the moon hunts
Terrified women.
Wild wolves break through the gate.[9]

The wild, the basis of a noun in the first line of the stanza, returns as an adjective in its last. An indeterminate multiplicity of wolves effect a rupture in the boundary of the city, transmitting its positive exteriority into its kernel. No longer interpretable as politics, as a war between cities, states, or other civilized totalities, the violence of the East relapses into an unrestrained movement of erosion. Blood, the moon, and women are coagulated by an intense menstrual seism which shatters the proper difference between life and death, integrity and dissolution, periodicity and shock. What Trakl in *Grodek* names 'the forgotten blood' recovers its sacred sense, in the regression that transmutes the politico-ethically impregnated blood of the dying solder into savage categorially oblivious flow.

Wild matter is untouched by its difference from spirit, insofar as this is supposed to depend upon a logical disjunction. The pseudointeriorities of the city are no less permeable to it than the uncultivated spaces marked out by the civilized ones for its exile. The bloody steps [*Stufen*] of *In the East* are only one variant among the many found

9   Ibid., 94; Trakl, *Poems and Prose*, 124.

in Trakl's writings: 'steps of madness',[10] 'mossy steps,' 'ruined steps,' 'the steps of the wood'.[11] It is a language of gradation, degree, *Abstufung*. Not quantity as opposed to quality, nor the difference of the two, but heterogenous strata of intensity, which – like the scales of the chaos theorists – involve irresolvable complexity, diversity, indefinite protractability in both directions, the default of absolute thresholds, an economics of incommensurability, and a compulsively recurrent abortion of the concept. Essence is preempted by an irresolvable excess of detail, in the same eruptive gesture that lethally infects transcendence with the return of excitatory complexity. The great simplicities of culture – identity, equality, absoluteness, abstraction – are immanently subverted by the pathological mass of unsublatable ingredients. There is no concept of particularity that is not theological; aligned with the phantasm of a transcendent spirit that stands disjoined from the ineliminable materiality of all spiritualization processes – to steal Nietzsche's term.

That matter is volatilized to different degrees of spiritualization is not in the least dependent upon spiritual causalities of any kind. Between the wilderness and the polis is a wilderness history – a genealogy – and not a political history. Regression is not an undoing of the city's

---

10 Ibid., 43.

11 Ibid., 54.

work, but a recurrence of impersonal creativity. More precisely, the work of the city has never been anything but a mendacious retranscription of the real metamorphoses which reemerge in lycanthropic becomings.

Inferiority is not any kind of lack or impoverishment, but a positive libidinal charge potentiating spiritualizations. Anything that slumbers in the sterility of pseudoabsoluteness is right to fear the inferior ones, and the powerful regressions that wash away the ramparts damming-up intensive sequences. The accursed race, living like beasts, whose veins are inflamed by a cosmic menstruation, have never entered into the great project of civilization, which begins with the use of fire to keep the wild animals at bay. Instead they leave a scorched and blackened trail in their wake as they irresponsibly protract the trajectory of animality. In their hands fire itself loses itself; becoming dirty, epidemic, and regressive. Not for them the humanizing, nucleating fire; the hearth, the protective and nutrifying glow, a focus embracing difference within itself, the fire of the familial and the familiar. The fire of the inferior ones is the dissolvant blaze which spreads uncontrollably, combusting the gloomy architectures of transcendence in the mad truth of exteriority. It is the fire of waste, dissipation, dehumanization, of a deeper and harsher fertility than can be comprehended by the industry of man. This lupine fire – the apolitical element in war, literature, psychosis, and catastrophe – makes space for the impersonal propagations of the wilderness.

An abrupt question: Was Trakl a Christian? Yes, of course, at times he becomes a Christian, among a general confusion of becomings – becoming an animal, becoming a virus, becoming inorganic – just as he was also an antichrist, a poet, a pharmacist, an alcoholic, a drug addict, a psychotic, a leper, a suicide, an incestuous cannibal, a necrophiliac, a rodent, a vampire, and a werewolf. Just as he became his sister, and also a hermaphrodite. Trakl's texts are scrawled over by redemptionist monotheism, just as they are stained by narcotic fluidities, gnawed by rats, cratered by Russian artillery, charred and pitted by astronomical debris. Trakl was a Christian and an atheist and also a Satanist, when he wasn't simply undead, or in some other way inhuman. It is perhaps more precise to say that Trakl never existed, except as a battlefield, a reservoir of disease, the graveyard of a deconsecrated church, as something expiring from a massive cocaine overdose on the floor of a military hospital, cheated of lucidity by the searing onslaught of base difference.

PART II: RATS

Henrik Ibsen knew some things about rats, 'they who are hated and persecuted of men'.[12] The fact of an alliance between rats and desire was evident to him, and when the rat wife of *Little Eyolf* is asked where her beloved is, she answers: "Down among all the rats".[13] How deftly he indicates the registration of the rats upon the Oedipal claustrophobia of the bourgeois household:

> Rat Wife: [*curtsies at the door*] Begging your most humble pardon, ladies and gentlemen ... but have you anything gnawing at this house?

> Allmers: Have we ...? No, I don't think so.

> Rat Wife: Because if you had I'd be glad to help you get rid of it.

> Rita: Yes, yes, we understand. But we don't have anything of that kind.[14]

How desperate they are not to believe it! "Rats don't belong here, this is the inside, purity, civilization,

---

12   H. Ibsen, *The Oxford Ibsen* (London: Oxford University Press, 1966), vol. 8, 49.

13   Ibid., 49.

14   Ibid., 46.

philosophy ... we don't want to know about anything *of that kind*."

Reading is not one thing. It is always possible to construe the movement between strata, plates, terraces, in spiritual terms; a matter of simulacrum, representation, metaphor, commentary, and interpretation. God is like and unlike a man, who is like and unlike an animal, which is like and unlike inorganic matter. This is an architecture of super-terrestrial transitions, transcendental difference, absolute verticality, gulfs of essence, logicized, infinitized, purifying disjunction. There is not one alternative to such a schema, but a recklessly proliferated multiplicity of alternatives; complex sponge-spaces rotted by lines of insinuation. There is always a dimension of immanence; a burrow, a thread, a path for contagion. The storeys of a house lend themselves to social stratification, and thus to philosophical and theological metaphor; the basement representing the place of the servants, animality, the unconscious. What is repressed in this case is not the basement itself – hell is not repressed but exhibited – but the hollow walls, the drainpipe outside, the arterial system of tubes, ducts, and vents, everything that facilitates the corruption of vertically articulated space by the quasihorizontality of an insidious dimension. Laws, revelations, and prayers, or – at a lower level – commands, messages, and reports, seem to establish the defined relations between strata that are identical with justice. The words of God pass down from level to level, determinately mediated at each stage. Inherent to such spatiality is its subversion, a more basic and complex order of distances, because Heaven is not without its ratholes, its sewage system, an entire impersonal architecture characterized by porous heterogeneity. It seems likely that God would insist upon air-conditioning and a dumbwaiter. Irrespective of his celestial visage, Jahweh still has ratbites on his ass.

Neither Heidegger nor Derrida have any time for Trakl's rats, but that doesn't stop them swarming everywhere, exaggerating the lycanthropic power of infiltration. It must be admitted; the rats are not very spiritual, but if there is a site, *Ort*, that focuses Trakl's poetry, why is it not the courtyard that Trakl repeatedly populates with rats? Are not the rats, as a positive antihistoricism, crucial to Trakl's poetic force? Why does Heidegger never mention Trakl's superb poem *The Rats*, a text that functions as a vermin-core for an entire pattern of infestation? Perhaps it is because difference becomes unacceptable when it moves fast and unpredictably, hissing at humanity through plague-smeared teeth.

It is certainly not because the rats are indiscernible, despite their unlocalizable fluidity. They shriek, whistle, bicker, rummage, and romp. When the rats erupt into *Dream and Derangement* for instance, which is perhaps Trakl's most shattering and lycanthropic poem, they are not merely glimpsed – far less ignored or exterminated – but encouraged by the poem's central character, who feeds them in a gesture of beautiful treachery against mankind. Not that it is population alone that gives them a special privilege, ravens are equally prevalent within Trakl's writings – and also have a poem of their own – whilst toads and bats are to be found in incredible numbers. It is the rats' hideous talent for decomposing interiorities that advantages them; opening the incest-rotted 'house of the father' – and with it the most intensely charged recesses of Trakl's writing – to the depredations of feral alterity.

Despite his humanistic prejudices, Hans Zinsser, in his book *Rats, Lice, and History,* has written delightfully about the rats. He remarks:

It is a curious fact that long before there could have been any knowledge concerning the dangerous character of rodents as carriers of disease, mankind dreaded and pursued these animals. Sticker has collected a great many references to this subject from ancient and mediæval literature, and has found much evidence in the folklore of mediæval Europe which points to the vague recognition of some connection between plague and rats. In ancient Palestine, the Jews considered all seven mouse varieties (*akbar*) unclean, and as unsuited for human nourishment as were pigs. The worshipers of Zoroaster hated water rats, and believed that the killing of rats was a service to God. It is also significant that Apollo Smintheus, the god who was supposed to protect against disease, was also spoken of as the killer of mice, and saint Gertrude was besought by the bishops of the early Catholic Church to protect against plague and mice. The year 1498, Sticker tells us, was a severe plague year in Germany, and there were so many rats in Frankfurt that an attendant was stationed for several hours each day on a bridge in the town and directed to pay a pfennig for every rat brought in. The attendant cut off the tail of the rat – probably as a primitive method of accounting – and threw the bodies into the river. Heine, according to Sticker, speaks of a tax levied on the Jews of Frankfurt in the fifteenth century, which consisted of the annual delivery of five thousand rat tails. Folklore originating in a number of different parts of Europe during the great plague epidemics mentions cats and dogs, the hereditary enemies of rats and mice, as guardians against plague.[15]

There is enormous power to the dynamic hierarchy of vectors mobilized by the rats. It combines the insidious subtlety of liquids with the concentrated displacement of

15   H. Zinsser, *Rats, Lice, and History* (Boston: Bantam Books. 1965), 142–3.

compact solids; saturation with jumps. Rats carry fleas which bear diseases, augmenting the fluid dissemination of plagues with a ferociously discontinuous transmission. To quote Zinsser again:

> Studies made within the last few years seem to indicate that the virus of the Mexican-American type of typhus fever, as well as of the endemic variety in the Mediterranean basin, is highly adapted to rodents and is carried in these animals – rats – during the intervals between human epidemics; transmitted from rat to rat by the rat louse (*polyplax*) and the rat flea (*Xenopsylla*), and, on suitable occasions, to man from the rat by the rat flea. For this reason, Nicolle speaks of this as the 'murine' virus.[16]

And a little further on:

> From the point of view of all other living creatures, the rat is an unmitigated nuisance and pest. There is nothing that can be said in its favor. It can live anywhere and eat anything. It burrows for itself when it has to, but, when it can, it takes over the habitations of other animals, such as rabbits, and kills them and their young. It climbs and swims.

16 Ibid, 142.

It carries disease of man and animals – plague, typhus, trichinella spiralis, rat-bite fever, infectious jaundice, possibly foot-and-mouth disease and a form of equine 'influenza'. Its destructiveness is almost unlimited.[17]

The first empirical element to be noted by any libidinal rat theory is the zoological diversification of the rat into two species. These are '*Rattus rattus*, the black, house, or ship-rat, and *Rattus Norvegicus*, the greyish brown, field, or sewer-rat',[18] of which Shrewsbury says in his *History of the Bubonic Plague*: 'By comparison with the house-rat it is less agile but far more voracious and cunning, and as it is stronger and more fecund it is a much more formidable enemy of mankind'.[19] During the outbreak of bubonic plague during the fourteenth century it was not only the intense killing of human populations, or delivery of terminal vectors, that was executed by *R. rattus*, who lived and propagated in close proximity to humans, but also the long-range dissemination of the plague, as *R. Norvegicus* is not thought to have arrived in Europe before the eighteenth century. If this is true – and current historical zoology gives no positive reason to doubt it – then it can

---

17 Ibid, 150–1.

18 J.F.D. Shrewsbury, *A History of the Bubonic Plague in the British Isles* (Cambridge: Cambridge University Press, 1970), 7.

19 Ibid, 8.

safely be asserted that the black death, in addition to its precursor which raged across the near orient and Europe during the sixth and seventh centuries, will remain the climax of achievement reached by *R. rattus*, who has since been eclipsed. Zinsser once more:

> Just as the established civilizations of Northern Europe were swept aside by the mass invasions of barbarians from the East, so the established hegemony of the black rat was eventually wiped out with the incursion of the hordes of the brown rat, or Mus decumanus – the ferocious, short-nosed, and short-tailed Asiatic that swept across the Continent in the early eighteenth century ...

The brown rat, too, came from the East. It is now known as the 'common' rat and, because of a mistaken notion of its origin, as Mus norvegicus. Its true origin, according to Hamilton and Hinton, is probably Chinese Mongolia or the region east of Lake Baikal, in both of which places forms resembling it have been found indigenous. The same writers quote Blasius, who believes that the ancients about the Caspian Sea may have known this rat. Claudius Ælianus, a Roman rhetorician of the second century, in his *De Animalium Natura*, speaks of 'little less than Ichneumons, making periodical raids in infinite numbers' in the countries along the Caspian, 'swimming over rivers holding each other's tails.'

Pallas (1831), in his *Zoögraphia Rosso-Asiatica,* records that in 1727 – a mouse year – great masses of these rats swam across the Volga after an earthquake.[20]

There are two varieties of rat, but this should not be taken as a gift for our metaphysicians, or supposed antimetaphysicians, who are constantly in search of dichotomic conceptual oppositions. The duality of *R. rattus* and *R. Norvegicus* is of the kind 1, 2, ... not 0 ... 1; it encloses nothing, reaches no limits, provides no determination, logical negativity, or alternation. The tokens of libidinal displacement are complex and not diacritical. Alogical differentiation: black and brown, not black and white. One, two ... first the wave of *R. rattus*, effective on its own, almost invisible to the Europe of the middle ages, differentiated perhaps from the mice (it was called *mures majores*),[21] ... ½, 1, ... ? And then the wave of *R. Norvegicus*, a different type of rat, but not an opposite type; rather, a type that was more clever and destructive, taking the rat process a little bit further. Far from requiring the black rat for its determinacy the new Asiatic invader wipes out

20 Zinsser, *Rats, Lice, and History,* 149.

21 Shrewsbury, *History of the Bubonic Plague,* 121.

the previous rat population, establishing itself as a sheer intensity, as a potential for disaster. Rats disdain discrimination, propagating their difference upon a plateau of excitement. Differentiation within an illimitable series, alogical dissimilarity, independence from the differend, and indiscriminate proliferation of nonidentity; this is the 'logic' of the rats.

Freud's 1909 case of compulsive neurosis – the 'rat-man' – is told by his captain, fatefully, of a 'particularly terrible Oriental punishment'.[22] Freud describes how this was related to him in the analysis: 'the condemned is bound (he expressed himself so unclearly that I could not immediately guess [*erraten*] in what position) – upon his posterior a pot was placed, into a which rats [*Ratten*] were introduced, which – he stood up again and gave out all the signs of terror and resistance – bored themselves in'.[23] This is the 'rat-punishment' [*die Rattenstrafe*], visited upon Europe, through its underside, from the East. Its peculiar insidiousness, which Freud does not emphasize even though he marks it, is that to surmise [*erraten*] the riddle [*Rätsel*] of the *Rattenstrafe* is to suffer it. In the very movement of prowess the imperial interpretative gesture is taken *par derrière* by an impersonal

22 S. Freud, *Studienausgabe, Band VII: Zwang, Paranoia, und Perversion* (Frankfurt am Main: S. Fischer, 1982), 43; S. Freud, 'Notes Upon a Case of Obsessional Neurosis' (1909), in *Three Case Histories*, ed. P. Rieff (New York: Touchstone, 1996), 11.

23 Ibid., 44; 12.

libidinal force from beyond representational discourse, whether logico-psychiatric or orientalist. The image of anal violation that organizes the rat-delirium has all the traits of a compromise formation; a sublimation of utter unexpectedness into a linearized passage fortified by a sadistically invested and ego-co-opted sphincter. The infiltration of the rat is singularized, and depicted as an inverse frontal assault, stripped of its fluidity, indirectness, heterogeneity, as if it were mere delicacy that obstructed our comprehension of vermin space. It is not Oedipal ambivalence that is solicited by such an image, but the racist misogyny that would project all undomesticated flows onto an axis of expulsability. The rattenstrafe is a wish – and thus an idealization – because it is far more comforting to the anal-sadistic structure of humanism than the reality of the free penetrability of the body along all of its irresolvably scaled estuaries.

Animality is not a state, essence, or genus, but a complex space cross-cut by voyages of all kinds. Trakl explores this wilderness terrain with an excruciating vulnerability. The animality which Trakl finds has its dead-ends and stagnant sumps, it has its humanistic and theological becomings, but it also has its channels of open flow; becoming multiple, fluid, unpredictable, becoming an enemy of mankind, lupine and murine becomings of all kinds. These intensive sequences cannot be isolated or determined, since no impermeable boundary remains to quarantine Trakl's rodents from the nameless ones. From becoming a mouse, and then a black rat, and then a brown rat, or from becoming one's sister, and then a pack of wolves, and then a swarm of rats. The eternity of Rimbaud's inferior race shares its diseases with Nietzsche's 'deep, deep, eternity', for which the very adjective is torn apart by convulsive waves of descent. An unfathomable abyss of regression or recurrence protracts itself epidemically into Trakl's body. 'I am all the vermin in history.' Indecent precipitation.

Shamanic Nietzsche

Will Christendom ever *reap the whirlwind* it has sown? That it should try to pass, without the vulnerability of interval, from a tyranny to a joke, is certainly understandable, but that its enemies should do nothing to obstruct its evasion of nemesis is more puzzling. How can there be such indifference to the decline of our inquisitors? Is it that they succeed so exorbitantly in their project of domestication that we have been robbed of every impulse to bite back? Having at last escaped from the torture-palace of authoritarian love we shuffle about, numb and confused, flinching from the twisted septic wound of our past (now clumsily bandaged with the rags of secular culture).

It is painfully evident that post-christian humanity is a pack of broken dogs.

Georges Bataille is the preeminent textual impediment to Christianity's carefully plotted *quiet death*; the prolongation of its terminal agonies into the twentieth century. Having definitively exhausted itself after two ugly millennia of species vivisection, Christianity attempts to skulk away from the scene, aided by the fog of supine tolerance which dignifies itself as 'post-modernity'. It does not take a genius to see whose interests are served by this passage from militant theism to postmodern ambivalence.

A despot abandons any game that begins to turn out badly. This has been the case with metaphysics. From Kant onwards exploratory philosophy ceased to generate the outcomes favourable to established (theistic) power, and we were suddenly told: "this game is over, let's call it a draw". The authoritarian tradition of European reason tried to pull the plug on the great voyages *at exactly the point they first became interesting,* which is to say: atheistic, inhuman, experimental, and dangerous. Schopenhauer – refusing the agnostic stand-off of antinomy – was the first rallying zone for all those disgusted by the contrived peace entitled 'the end of metaphysics'. Bataille is his most recent successor. The forces of antichrist are emerging fanged and encouraged from their scorched rat-holes in the wake of monotheistic hegemony, without the slightest attachment to the paralytic tinkerings of deconstructive undecidability. 'An attitude which is neither military nor religious becomes insupportable in principle from the moment of death's arrival'.[1] The war has scarcely begun.

It is hard to imagine anything more ludicrous than Descartes, or Kant, having erected their humble philosophical dwellings alongside the baroque architectural excesses of the church, standing in the shadows of flying buttresses and asking pompously: how do we know the truth? It surely cannot solely be due to Nietzsche that we see the absurdity of an 'epistemological' question being asked in such surroundings. When a philosopher has a priest for a neighbour, which is to say, a practitioner of the most elaborately constructed system of mendacity ever conceived upon earth, how can a commitment to 'truth' in a positive sense even be under consideration? Truth in such situations is a privilege of the deaf. There is no question of 'error', 'weakness in reasoning', or 'mistaken judgment' when addressing the authoritative discourses on truth in the western tradition, those cathedrals of theological concept building that ground our 'common sense'; no, here one can only speak of a deeply rooted and fanatical *discipline of lying*. In other words, one fraction of the radicality of the atheistic thinking escalated through Schopenhauer, Nietzsche, and Bataille is that it

---

1   G. Bataille, *Oeuvres Complètes* (Paris: Gallimard, 12 Vols, 1970–1988), vol. II, 246.

overthrows the high-bourgeois apologetic-epistemological problematic in modern philosophy by asking clearly for the first time: where do the lies stop?

The great educational value of the war against Christendom lies in the *absolute* truthlessness of the priest. Such purity is rare enough. The 'man of God' is entirely incapable of honesty, and only arises at the point where truth is defaced beyond all legibility. Lies are his entire metabolism, the air he breathes, his bread and his wine. He cannot comment upon the weather without a secret agenda of deceit. No word, gesture, or perception is slight enough to escape his extravagant reflex of falsification, and of the lies in circulation he will instinctively seize on the grossest, the most obscene and oppressive travesty. Any proposition passing the lips of a priest is *necessarily* totally false, excepting only insidiouses whose message is momentarily misunderstood. It is impossible to deny him without discovering some buried fragment or reality.

There is no truth that is not war against theology, and even the word 'truth' has been plastered by the spittle of priestcraft. It cannot be attachment to some alternative conviction that *cuts* here, but only relentless refusal of what has been told. The dangerous infidels bypass dialectics. It is the sceptic who assassinates the lie.

Whenever its name has been anything but a jest, philosophy has been haunted by a subterranean question: What if knowledge were a means to deepen unknowing?

It is this thought alone that has differentiated it from the shallow things of the earth. Yet the glory and also the indignity of philosophy is to have sought the end of knowing, and no more.

Once blatant sophisms are exempted, the fact that scepticism has never been *enacted* is the sole argument of the dogmatists, and it is a powerful one, despite its empirical flavour. There can be little doubt that the philosophical advocates of disbelief have tended to exploit the very conventions they profess to despise as the shelter for an insincere madness. As was the case with Socrates, philosophy has sought to peel itself away from sophism by admitting to its ignorance, as if unknowing were a pathos to be confessed. Profound ecsanity ['Ecsane' – out of one's mind] alone is effective scepticism, in comparison to which sceptical philosophies fall prey to naïve theories of belief, as if belief could simply be discarded, or withheld. We know nothing of course, but we do not remotely know even this, and mere assertion in no way ameliorates our destitution. Belief is not a possession but a prison, and we continue to believe in achieved knowledge even after denying it with intellectual comprehensiveness. The refusal to accept a dungeon is no substitute for a hole in the wall. Only in a voyage to the unknown is there real escape from conviction.

The dangerous sceptics are those Kant fears, 'a species of nomads, despising all settled modes of life'[2] who come from a wilderness tract beyond knowledge. They are explorers, which is also to say: invasion routes of the unknown. It is by way of these inhumanists that the vast abrupt of shamanic zero – the Ἐποχή of the ancients – infiltrates its contagious madness onto the earth.

Ἐποχή is a word attributed to Pyrrho by way of indirect reportage, but in its absence the philosopher's name would lose what slight sense invests it. Although it might be argued that we owe Ἐποχή to Pyrrho, it is from Ἐποχή that the name Pyrrho comes to us, as a cryptograph of the unknown. Even were it not for Pyrrho's silence – a silence far more *profound* that the literary abstinence of Socrates – Ἐποχή would surely not be something of which we could straightforwardly know the truth, far less a method, or a subjective state.

Ἐποχή is a report of the abrupt, and an escape.

1. [...]

2. the world of 'phenomena' is the adapted world which we feel to be real. The 'reality' lies in the continual recurrence of identical, familiar, related

---

2 I. Kant, *The Critique of Pure Reason*, tr. N.K. Smith (NY: Palgrave Macmillan: 2003), Preface to the First Edition, 8.

things in their logicized character, in the belief that here we are able to reckon and calculate;

3. the antithesis of this phenomenal world is not 'the true world,' but the formless unformulable world of the chaos of sensations – *another kind* of phenomenal world, a kind 'unknowable' for us;

4. questions, what things 'in-themselves' may be like, apart from our sense receptivity and the activity of our understanding, must be rebutted with the question: how could we know that things exist? 'Thingness' was first created by us. The question is whether there could not be many other ways of creating such an apparent world.[3]

How much industrialism lies buried in the notion of thought! As if one could ever *work things out*. One does not think one's way out, one gets out, and then sees (that it wasn't one …).

Bataille's Nietzsche is not a locus of secular reason but of shamanic religion; a writer who escapes philosophical conceptuality in the direction of ulterior zones, and dispenses with the *thing in itself* because it is an item of intelligible representation with no consequence as a

---

3   F. Nietzsche, *The Will to Power*, tr. W. Kaufmann (New York: Vintage, 1968), section 569.

vector of becoming (of travel). Shamanism defies the transcendence of death, opening the tracts of 'voyages of discovery never reported'.[4] Against the grain of shallow phenomenalism that characterizes Nietzsche readings, Bataille pursues the fissure of abysmal scepticism, which passes out of the Kantian *Noumenon* (or intelligible object) through Kant and Schopenhauer's *thing in itself* (stripping away a layer of residual Platonism), and onwards in the direction of acategorial, epochal, or *base* matter that connects with Rimbaud's 'invisible splendours':[5] the immense deathscapes of a 'universe without images'.[6] Matter cannot be allotted a category without being retrieved for ideality, and the Nietzschean problem with the *Ding an Sich* was not its supposed dogmatic materialism, but rather that it proposed 'an ideal form of matter',[7] as the transcendent (quarantined) site of integral truth, a 'real world'. There are no things-in-themselves because there are no things: 'thingness has only been invented by us owing to the requirements of logic'[8] (which ultimately revert to those of grammar). The *Ding an Sich* is a concept tailored for a God (supreme being) desperately seeking to hide itself: a cultural glitch turned nasty, but on the

---

4   A. Rimbaud, *Collected Poems*, tr. O. Bernard (Harmondsworth: Penguin, 1986), 327.

5   Ibid., 296.

6   Ibid., 293.

7   Bataille, *Oeuvres Complètes*, vol. I, 179.

8   Nietzsche, *The Will to Power*, section 558.

run at last. 'Root of the idea of substance in language, not in beings outside us'![9]

> The antithesis of the apparent world and the true world is reduced to the antithesis 'world' and 'nothing'.[10]

Materialism is not a doctrine but an expedition, an Alpine break-out from socially policed conviction. It 'is before anything else the obstinate negation of idealism, which is to say of the very basis of *all* philosophy'.[11] Exploring acategorial matter navigates thought as chance and matter as turbulence 'beyond all regulation'.[12] It yields no propositions to judge, but only paths to explore.

This is Nietzsche as a fanged poet at war with the philosophers (with the new priests), a thinker who seeks *to make life more problematic.* Bataille locks onto a desire that resonates with the reality that confounds us, and not with a 'rationality' that would extricate us from the labyrinth. Nietzsche is the great exemplar of complicating thought, exploiting knowledge in the interest of interrogations (and this is not in order to clarify and focus, but to subtilize and dissociate them). Complicating thought

---

9   Ibid., section 562.

10   Ibid., section 567.

11   Bataille, *Oeuvres Complètes*, vol. I, 220.

12   Ibid., vol. VI, 97.

strengthens the impetus of an active or energetic confusion – delirium – against the reactive forces whose obsessive tendency is to resolve or conclude. Rebelling against the fundamental drift of philosophical reasoning, it sides with thought against knowledge, against the tranquillizing prescriptions of the 'will to truth'.

If Nietzsche is locked in an extraordinarily furious struggle with philosophy it is because it is philosophy that has claimed, with the most cynical explicitness, to negate problems. Philosophy has always wanted to retire; Schopenhauer is simply its most honest exemplar. The 'absolute' is humanity's laziest thought. Nor does it suffice to argue that thought can be complicated within itself, or – as the philosophers have said for some time – 'immanently', for we know where this path of thinking leads. An intellection in need of immanent critique is one that is already nudging against an ultimate solubility. 'The intellect finds its limits within itself' – it does not even need to move to consummate interrogation! It is thinking such as this, whose most eminent model is the Kant of the critical philosophy, that generated such distrust in Nietzsche for writers who work sitting down.

Wisdom (*sophia*) substitutes for travelling, hollowing it out into a Baudelairean caricature of the *Voyage* – redundantly reiterating a moral dogma – and to love it is to seek to be still. In obedience to narco-Platonic Eros, philosophy defers to the end of desire.

Nietzsche reaches back beyond this Hellenic priest-philosophizing, and forward beyond its modern limit, reassembling *sophia* as escape:

> Indeed, we philosophers and 'free spirits' feel, when we hear the news that 'the old god is dead,' as if a new dawn shone on us; our heart overflows with gratitude, amazement, premonitions, expectations. At long last the horizon appears free to us again, even if it should not be bright; at long last our ships may venture out again, venture out to face any danger; all the daring of the lover of knowledge is permitted again; the sea, *our* sea, lies open again; perhaps there has never yet been such an 'open sea'.[13]

The death of God is an opportunity, a chance. It makes sense to ask *what is meant* by the word 'noumenon', but 'chance' does not function in this way, since it is not a concept to be apprehended, but a direction in which to go. 'To the one who grasps what chance is, how insipid the idea of God appears, and suspicious, and wing-clipping'![14] Monotheism is the great gate-keeper, and where it ends the exploration of death begins. If there are places to which we are forbidden to go, it is because

---

13   F. Nietzsche, *The Gay Science*, tr. W. Kaufmann (New York: Vintage, 1974), section 343.

14   Bataille, *Oeuvres Complètes*, vol. VI, 116.

they can in truth be reached, or *because they can reach us*. In the end poetry is invasion and not expression, a trajectory of incineration; either strung-up in the cobwebs of Paradise, or strung-out into the shadow-torrents of hell. It is a route out of creation, which is to each their fate interpreted as enigma, as *lure*. 'Now a hard, an inexorable voyage commences – a quest into the greatest possible distance'.[15] 'I said good-bye to the world'.[16] Even the most angelic curiosity – when multiplied to the power of eternity – must find its way to end in the abyss.

It can seem at times as if Bataille owes almost everything to Christianity; his understanding of the evil at the heart of erotic love, the hysterical affectivity of his writing, along with its excremental obsession, its epileptoid conception of delight, its malignancy, the perpetual stench of the gutter. Yes, this is all very Christian; well attuned to a doctrine gestated in the sewers of the empire. Yet from out of the aberrant intensity and disorder of Bataille's writings an *impossible* proposition is perpetually reiterated: that far from being the acme of religion – let alone its telic blossoming – God is the principle of its suppression. The unity of *theos* is the tombstone of sacred zero, the crumbling granitic foundation of secular destitution. This is so exorbitantly true that the existence of

---

15   Ibid., 29.

16   Rimbaud, *Collected Poems*, 330.

God would be an even greater disaster for him than for us. How infinitely trivial the crucifixion of Jesus appears beside the degrading torture of being God, after all, existence is so indistinguishable from defilement that one turns pale at the very thought of an eternal being's *smell*. Perhaps this is why God 'is profoundly atheistic',[17] leading Bataille to remark that '[w]hilst I am God, I deny him to the depths of negation'[18] ('nihilism ... might be a *divine* way of thinking',[19] Nietzsche anticipates). God can only redeem the universe from its servility by burning his creation into ash and annihilating himself. Such is the 'God of blinding sun, ... this God of death that I sought'.[20] Bataille invokes the dark undertow of a self-butchering divinity: 'God of despair, give me ... your heart ... which no longer tolerates that you exist'.[21] (If God is an explorer, then there is no God.)

Bataille's texts are 'a hecatomb of words without gods or reason to be',[22] led back down through the crypts of the West by a furious impulse to dissociate theism and religion, and thus to return the sacred to its shamanic impiety, except that nothing can ever simply return, and

---

17 Bataille, *Oeuvres Complètes*, vol. V, 121.

18 Ibid., 152.

19 Nietzsche, *The Will to Power*, section 15.

20 Bataille, *Oeuvres Complètes*, vol. IV, 203.

21 Ibid., vol. V, 59.

22 Ibid., 220.

Hell will never be an innocent underworld again. The depths have become infernal, really so, quite irrespective of the fairy tales we are still told. '[F]lames surround us / the abyss opens beneath our feet'[23] reports Bataille from the brink of the impossible, 'an abyss that does not end in the satiate contemplation of an absence'[24] because its lip is the charred ruin of even the most sublimed subjectivity. 'I have nothing to do in this world', he writes, '[i]f not to burn'.[25] 'I suffer from not burning ... approaching so close to death that I respire it like the breath of a lover'.[26] It is not only due to the inquisition that all the great voyagers have for a long time been *singed.* For well over a century all who have wanted to see have seen: no profound exploration can be launched from the ruins of monotheism unless it draws its resources from damnation.

The death of God is a religious event – a transgression, experiment in damnation, and stroke of antitheistic warfare – but this is not to say it is pre-eminently a crime. Hell has no interest in our debauched moral currency. To confuse reactive dabblings in sin with expeditions in damnation is Christian superficiality; the Dantean error of imagining that one could earn oneself an excursion in Hell, as if the infernal too was a matter of justice.

---

23 Ibid., vol. III, 95.

24 Ibid., vol. V, 199.

25 Ibid., vol. IV, 17.

26 Ibid., vol. V, 246.

Our crimes are mere stumblings on the path to ruin, just as every projected *Hell on Earth* is a strict exemplar of idolatry. Transgression is not criminal action, but tragic fate; the intersection of an economically programmed apocalypse with the religious antihistory of poetry. It is the inevitable occurrence of impossibility, which is not the same as death, but neither is it essentially different.

This ambivalence responds to that of death 'itself', which is not ontological but labyrinthine: a relapse of composition that is absolute to discontinuity, yet is nothing at the level of immanence. The very individuality that would condition the possibility of a proprietary death could only be achieved if death were impossible. One dies because discontinuity is never realized, but this means that there is never 'one' who dies. Instead there is an unthinkable communication with zero, immanence, or the sacred. 'There is no feeling that throws one into exuberance with greater force than that of nothingness. But exuberance is not at all annihilation; it is the surpassing of the shattered attitude, it is transgression'.[27]

The question of the mere 'truth' of Christianity – whether in regard of its origin, not to speak of Christian astronomy and natural science – is a matter of

---

27   Ibid., vol. X, 72.

secondary importance as long as the question of the value of Christian morality is not considered.[28]

What if eternal recurrence were not a belief? ('The most extreme form of nihilism would be the view that every belief ... is necessarily false because there simply *is no true world*'.)[29] Bataille suggests:

> The return *immotivates* the instant, freeing life from an end and in this ruining it straight away. The return is ... the desert of one for whom each instant henceforth finds itself immotivated.[30]

Christianity – the exemplary moral 'religion' – 'substituted slow suicide'[31] and representation (belief) for shamanic contact with zero-interruption, but with the (re-)emergence of nihilisitic recurrence, caution, prudence, every kind of 'concern for time to come'[32] is restored to the senselessness of cosmic 'noise'. With recurrence comes a '*future*, [which is] not the prolongation of myself across time, but the expiry of a being going further, passing

---

28 Nietzsche, *The Will to Power*, section 251.

29 Ibid., section 15.

30 Bataille, *Oeuvres Complètes*, vol. VI, 23.

31 Nietzsche, *The Will to Power*, section 247.

32 Bataille, *Oeuvres Complètes*, vol. VI, 50, 167.

attained limits'.[33] A religious crisis can no longer be deferred.

In the final phase of Nietzsche's intellectual life the eternal recurrence is grasped as a weapon, a 'hammer,' the transmission element between diagnosis and intervention. Where Christendom recuperates decline to preservation, deflecting it from its intensive plummet to zero, eternal recurrence re-opens its abyssal prospect, precipicing affect onto death. This is the predominant sense of 'selection' in Nietzsche's texts; a vertiginous extrication of zero from the series of preservative values, cutting through 'the ambiguous and cowardly compromise of a religion such as Christianity: more precisely, such as the church: which, instead of encouraging death and self-destruction, protects everything ill-constituted and sick and makes it propagate itself'.[34]

The notes assembled into section 55 of *The Will to Power* develop this morbid thread. Either 'existence as it is, without meaning or aim, yet recurring inevitably without any finale of nothingness' (a box), or 'the nothing (the "meaningless"), eternally'.[35] The nihilism of recurrence is ambivalent between its (Christian) historical sense as the constrictive deceleration of zero and its cosmic (non-local) virtuality as a gateway onto death. Christendom is

---

33   Ibid., 29.

34   Nietzsche, *The Will to Power*, section 247.

35   Ibid., section 55.

to be attacked because it was its morality that protected life against despair and the leap into nothing'.[36]

> Morality guarded the underprivileged against nihilism ... Supposing that the faith in this morality would perish, then the underprivileged would no longer have their comfort – and they would perish.[37]

The religious history of mankind is based upon a technics of ill-health: dehydration, starvation, mutilation, deprivation of sleep, a general 'self-destruction of the underprivileged: self-vivisection, poisoning, intoxication'.[38] A journey was underway which Christian preservative moralism – generalized species cowardice – privatized, representationalized, crushed under the transcendent phallus, froze, obstructed, and drove elsewhere. Christianity is a device for trapping the sick, but recurrence melts through the cages:

> What does 'underprivileged' mean? Above all, physiologically – no longer politically. The unhealthiest kind ... (in all classes) furnishes the soil for this nihilism: they will experience the belief in the eternal recurrence as a curse, struck by which one no longer

36 Ibid.

37 Ibid.

38 Ibid.

shrinks from any action; not to be extinguished but to extinguish everything.[39]

To relate sickness to death as cause to effect is itself a sign of health. Their morbid interconnection is quite different. Sickness is not followed by death within the series of ordered representation. It opens the gates.

Genealogy does not reduce sickness to a historical topic, since sickness – the inability to suspend a stimulus – eludes mere unfolding in progressive time, tending towards the disappearance of time in epochal interruption. The reflex-spasm at (and by) which reactivity gropes is the atemporal continuum beneath the crust of health. Death is 'that which has no history',[40] and Nietzsche's method is syphilis. 'Only religion assures a consumption that destroys the proper substance of those that it animates'.[41]

Philosophy is a ghoul that haunts only ruins, and the broken croaks of our hymns to sickness have scarcely begun. Borne by currents of deep exhaustion that flow silent and inexorable beneath the surface perturbations of twitch and chatter, damned, shivering, claw-like fingers hewn from torture and sunk into wreckage drawn with

---

39 Ibid.

40 F. Nietzsche, *On the Genealogy of Morals*, tr. W. Kaufmann and R.J. Hollingdale (New York: Vintage, 1969), Second Essay, section 13.

41 Bataille, *Oeuvres Complètes*, vol. VII, 316.

unbearable slowness down into the maw of flame and snuffed blackness twisted skewerish into fever-hollowed eyes. Eternal recurrence is our extermination, and we cling to it as infants to their mother's breasts.

'Poetry leads from the known to the unknown' writes Bataille,[42] in words that resonate with Rimbaud. Poetry is fluent silence, the only venture of writing to touch upon the sacred (=0), because 'the unknown ... is not distinguished from nothingness by anything that discourse can announce'.[43] To write the edge of the impossible is a transgression against discursive order, and an incitement to the unspeakable: 'poetry is immoral'.[44]

Rimbaud writes from the other side of Zarathustrean descent/death [*Untergang*], anticipating the labyrinthine spaces of a Nietzsche for the sick, and of what escapes from/due to the cultural convulsion Nietzsche reinforces. 'The poet makes himself a visionary by a long, immense and rational *deregulation of all the senses*',[45] and this deregulation is a source of '[i]neffable torture',[46] 'the sufferings are enormous'[47] Rimbaud insists. No organism is adapted

---

42 Ibid., vol. V, 157.

43 Ibid., 133.

44 Ibid., 212.

45 Rimbaud, *Collected Poems*, 10.

46 Ibid., 11.

47 Ibid., 6.

to 'arrive at the unknown',[48] which makes deregulation as necessary as it makes pain inevitable. Our nerves squeal when they are re-strung upon the phylogenetically unanticipated, 'experiences strike too deeply; memory becomes a festering wound':[49] a descent into the inferno. *Nuit de l'enfer*, where the entrails of nature dissolve meanderous into lava, 'this is hell, eternal pain',[50] and Rimbaud burns, 'as is necessary'.[51]

Yes, the poet must be a visionary. The East knows a true lucidity, but to be an inheritor of the West is to hack through jungles of indiscipline, devoured by vile ants and words unstrung from sense, until the dripping foliage of delirium opens out onto a space of comprehensive ruin. This has never been understood, nor can it be. The foulness of our fate only deepens with the centuries, as the tracts of insanity sprawl. From bodies gnawed by tropical fevers we swim out through collapse to inexistence in forever, destined for Undo.

True poetry is *hideous*, because it is base communication, in contrast to pseudo-communicative discourse, which presupposes the isolation of the terms it unites. Communication – in the transgressive non-sense Bataille lends it – is both an utter risk and an unfathomable

---

48 Ibid.

49 Nietzsche, *Ecce Homo*, 230.

50 Rimbaud, *Collected Poems*, 313.

51 Ibid.

degradation, associated with *repellent* affect. The ego emerges in the flight from communicative immanence, from deep or unholy community, initiating a history that leads to the bitter truth of the desertification of the isolated being. From the anxiety of base contact, which it can only experience as dissolution, the ego stumbles into the *ennui* of autonomy, the antechamber to a harsh despair, whose horror is accentuated by the fact that it arises at the point where escape has exhausted itself, where the ego has quarantined itself to the limit of its being against extraneous misfortune. *Ennui* is not any sort of response to the compromising of the ego from without, it is not an impurity or a contamination (the negation of such things are for it a condition of existence), but rather, it is the very truth of achieved being; the core affect of personal individuality. *Ennui* cannot be mastered, surpassed, resolved, *aufgehoben*, because it is nothing but the distillate of such operations, indeed, of action as such. *Ennui* is insinuated into the very fabric of project, as 'the necessity of leaving oneself'.[52] If the soil of Bataille's writing is volcanic it is not only due to the sporadic convulsions of a devastating incandescence, but also because its fertility is anticipated by a monstrous sterilization. Beneath and before the luxuriant jungles of delirium is the endless crushing ash-plain of despair.

---

52   Bataille, *Oeuvres Complètes*, vol. V, 137.

'I believe that I am in hell, therefore I am there'.[53] Blake might have written such words, although their sense would then have been quite different. Drooled from Rimbaud's pen they point less to a potency of imagination than to a geological crisis of justification, approaching a perfect epistemological irresponsibility. It is not for us to defend the rights of truth, truth is decreed by the masters. What matters is to adapt, nursing the meagre resources of our reactivity, of our base cunning. 'Belief' – the cloak of confession – is too precious a resource to be squandered on the zealotry of idealism. What value is there to be extracted from a committed belief, from a last-ditch belief? Such things are for the strong (or for dupes), for the allies and slaves of light, for all those who do not rely on the subterranean passages beneath belief to avoid the panoptic apparatuses. Adaptability can only be lamed by commitments. We have seen enough true Christians: rabbits transfixed by headlights. When draped about the inferiors beliefs are not loyalties, but rather sun-blocks against inquisition. We creatures of shadow are hidden from their enlightenment. We believe exactly what they want.

The inferior race 'await God with greed',[54] scavenging at Christ 'like wolves at an animal they have not killed'.[55] Creation, testamental genealogy, the passion of Christ …

---

53 Rimbaud, *Collected Poems*, 313.

54 Ibid., 304.

55 Ibid., 302.

none of it is their story, nor is any other, for they are too indolent to have a story of their own, only theft and lies are 'proper' to them: 'pillage'.[56] Rimbaud's inheritance, 'above all', consists of 'mendacity and sloth'.[57] 'I have never been a Christian; I am of the race which sung under torture'[58] he remarks. It is precisely obliviousness to Christianity, to fidelity or duty, to privileged narratives, that eases the inferior race into singing the praises of the Nazarene. The white man has guns, *therefore* the truth. 'The whites disembark. The cannon! It is necessary to submit to baptism, dress oneself, work'.[59]

In contrast to the pompous declarations of the ortho-doxies, which come from on high (like a stroke of the whip), an infernal message is subterranean, a whisper from the nether-regions of discourse, since 'hell is certainly below'.[60] Just as the underworld is not a hidden world – a real or true [*Wahre Welt*] – but is that hidden by all worlds, so is the crypt-mutter from hell something other than an inverted scene, concept, or belief. In their infernal lineaments words are passages, leading into and through lost mazes, and not edifications. Acquisition is impos-sible in hell. There is nothing *en bas* except wandering

---

56 Ibid.
57 Ibid., 301.
58 Ibid., 307–8.
59 Ibid., 309.
60 Ibid., 315.

amongst emergences, and what is available has always come strangely, without belonging. Infernal *low-life* has no understanding for property. Even the thoughts of the inferior ones are camouflage and dissimulation, their beliefs mere chameleon dapplings of the skin.

Poetry does not strut logically amongst convictions, it seeps through crevices; a magmic flux resuscitated amongst vermin. If it was not that the Great Ideas had basements, fissures, and vacuoles, poetry would never infest them. Faiths rise and fall, but the rats persist.

Rimbaud's *saison en enfer* pulsates through a discourse without integrity. Teaching nothing, it infects. Like matter cooked-through with pestilential 'contagions of energy',[61] it collapses into a swarm of plague-vectors. Substance is only its host. '[W]ords, books, monuments, symbols, and laughters are nothing but the paths of this contagion, its passages'.[62]

I never could conclude anything …
Zero does that.

Towards New Seas
That way is my will; I trust
In my mind and in my grip.

---

61 Bataille, *Oeuvres Complètes*, vol. V, 111.

62 Ibid.

Without plan, into the vast
Open sea I head my ship.

All is shining, new and newer,
Upon space and time sleeps noon;
Only your eye – monstrously,
Stares at me, infinity.[63]

---

63 Nietzsche, *The Gay Science*, section 371.

After the Law

There are peculiar difficulties associated with any philosophy of law, due in large part to the inevitability that any attempt at a transcendent evaluation of law finds itself enacting a parody of judicial process. Ever since the trial of Socrates (if not already with the fragment of Anaximander), philosophy has affirmed its vocation only insofar as it has fantasised a supreme tribunal: an ultimate court of appeal or ideal form of justice. The vindication of Socratism is inextricable from a retrial, both exculpation and counterlitigation, the forum of which remains the unstable *issue* of metaphysics. As for its 'own' or 'inner' law, logic has never been anything other than the distillation of juridical procedure, the abstract form of inclusion or non-inclusion of a case under a law (species under genus), which has been predominantly thematised as *judgment*, although a language of *propositions* has more recently risen to prominence. Philosophy and judicial authority find themselves bound together in a discourse upon real legitimation. Appearances (cases) are to be judged from the perspective of a generic reason at a superior level of reality identified in the premodern period with an ideality whose final term is the intellect of God. Aristotle consummates a categorial – accusatory – sense of form, and the Augustinian collision of Platonism with Judaeo-Christian eschatology and Christian *logos* has only entrenched this complicity.

This chapter cuts into two episodes or intersections of the occidental juridico-philosophical complex, in an attempt to dramatise the broadest tendency of this process: that of collapse towards immanence, or evaporation of the transcendent. There is nothing peculiarly occult or mysterious about such a tendency since it finds its most highly accelerated phase in our contemporary marketisation of social transactions: the phased transition from traditional Geopolitical authorization or legitimacy to an impersonal, cybernetically automated *efficiency*. The commodity 'form' is a transmutational matrix, and not a static (synchronic) order of economic liberalism. Insofar as capital is still interpreted Platonically – according to legitimation criteria – there is an overt paradox or contradiction emergent in this process, a paradox whose disappearance is epitomized by the figure of Georges

Bataille, who offers an operational description of law. Bataille no longer offers a juridical procedure of any kind, but only a tactics of recoding that converges upon the outside of human history (where everything functions without respect or legitimacy).

Those seeking to defend the human management of social processes (where 'man' speculatively unites with the God of anthropomorphic monotheism) can have no project but to restore a *history* whose ideal sense would reconnect with the *meaning of the West*, such as those proffered by Plato, Aquinas and Hegel. Such restoration is a modernist aspiration which strikes me as incredible. To drag Plato and Bataille before the tribunal of philosophy has ceased to be anything but entertainment, yet I dedicate this text to the few remaining political animals of the planet Earth, as an experiment in the tenacity of philosophy, or as a jest.

PLATO AND THE TRIAL OF SOCRATES

Plato's *Apology* is initiated by submission to the political, in which civic obedience and justificatory discourse are fused. Rebellion is not Socratic, and the principle of authority – or right to judge – is never radically interrogated; only its source is in question. In attempting to contest the charge that he 'makes the weaker argument defeat the stronger',[1] it is not long before Socrates invokes the 'unimpeachable authority'[2] of Apollo, and narrates the journey of his disciple Chaerephon:

> One day he actually went to Delphi and asked this question of the god – as I said before, gentlemen, please do not interrupt – he asked whether there was anyone wiser than myself. The priestess replied that there was no one.[3]

To interpret this statement as a submission of evidence would be to efface the fracture line between the sacred and the profane across which Socrates steps. It is precisely the resistance to evidentiality that lends to this message its oracular force, and the paradoxical gesture at the heart of Socrates' defence is that of deploying the privilege of the unknown on behalf of knowing.

The mystery of the oracular message is registered within the order of judgment as an underinterpretation. The priestess's words require translation, beyond that of their reworking into verse that occurs at Delphi itself. They pose a problem that can be construed as exegetical, as an insufficiency of commentary and resolution. Words are oracular precisely insofar as they suspend intelligence,

---

1   Plato, *The Last Days of Socrates*, tr. H. Tredennick (Harmondsworth: Penguin, 1969), 47.

2   Ibid., 49.

3   Ibid, 49.

whether in the sacred abandonment to unknowing which is their source, or in the profane detour of philosophy that becomes their destination. Socrates' discourse is the site of a crossing from inspiration to anticipated wisdom.

It is not only words of the Delphic oracle that are at stake here, since they resonate with the more intimate counsel of Socrates' δαίμων or 'spirit'. Later in the *Apology*, we are told by Socrates that:

> I am subject to a divine or supernatural experience, which Meletus saw fit to travesty in his indictment. It began in my early childhood – a sort of voice which comes to me; and when it comes it always dissuades me from what I am proposing to do, and never urges me on.[4]

The interference between the sacred and the profane, the unknown and knowing, is in its sacred sense a gateway opening onto death, and in its profane sense a hesitation: interruption as the edge of time or as a delay within time, death as the outside or as the deferred, the threshold of death as a brink or as a moment. Later in the *Apology*, Socrates reports that 'I am now at that point where the gift of prophecy comes most readily to me: at the point

---

4   Ibid., 64.

of death'.[5] This remark connects strangely with the earlier comment that

> I soon made up my mind about the poets too: I decided that it was not wisdom that enabled them to write their poetry, but a kind of instinct or inspiration, such as you find in seers and prophets who deliver all their sublime messages without knowing in the least what they mean.[6]

Poets and prophets explore the zero-degree of judgment, a zone at the edge of the great zero that Socrates tentatively sketches, but only rarely approaches. His own sense of 'preparation for death' is the path of wisdom rather than intoxication, aligning himself with a knowing that is compared to its inadequate instances, rather than succumbing to the unknowing beyond comparison beside which all knowing is inadequate. Comparing himself to his fellows, Socrates elaborates the oracle as suggesting that 'I am wiser … to this small extent, that I do not think I know what I do not know'.[7] This is the edge of the unknown, but always there is the gesture of recuperation to knowing, to judgment, to the tribunal, justice and authority: 'real wisdom is the property of God, and this oracle is

---

5   Ibid., 73.

6   Ibid., 51.

7   Ibid., 50.

his way of telling us that human wisdom has little or no value'.[8] If human wisdom has little or no value, where do the dogmatic assertions about God and his wisdom stem from? Why should they be trusted? Is not the figure of God indistinguishable from the claim that we know it is knowledge that matters, that the unknown is something we know, something we can populate with our feverish anthropomorphisms? Does Socrates not exhibit God as the eclipse of religion, the surrender of knowing as a submission to ... knowing? It is thus that religion is buried beneath the icon of a supreme judge.

The figure of Socrates, as sketched for us by Plato – his advocate – is that of philosophy on trial. It is in crossing this judicial threshold that philosophy comes to delight in the voluptuousities of persecution. Yet the drama of Socrates' condemnation distracts from the more far-reaching process whereby philosophy succumbs to the order of the courtroom, and with this process Socrates is deeply complicit. He could even be said to have forged a new alliance between knowledge and condemnation, as well as becoming the first philosophical *case*.

How could one imagine an *Apology* for a Herakleitus, an Empedokles, or a Parmenides? To whom would they be attempting to justify themselves? To the *people*? The thought is absurd. For what does the opinion of the

---

8   Ibid., 52.

people matter? It was precisely as an escape from the opinion of the people that philosophy emerged! To philosophize and to ignore popular opinion are scarcely differentiable. If the Presocratics speak in terms of cosmic justification – as Anaximander already does – it is as a concession, in order that the people will at least understand the surpassing of human judgment, if not that by which it is surpassed. The harsh 'justice' of fate is the ironisation of human litigation, and not its inflation to the absolute (monotheism).

With Socrates, things are different. Philosophy becomes dialectical; which is to say justificatory, political, logical, plebeian. Truth is identified with irrefutability, evidentiality and educated belief, beginning its long subsidence into the forms of human credence, as if its acceptability were in any way a criterion.

The *Apology* focuses a multiple interweaving of death and judgment. There is first of all the sense in which death fulfils judgment in the sentence of death, even if this is an injustice – or misjudgment – such that Athens is condemned in the tribunal of the Platonic text, whose judgment in this case becomes a massively influential precedent. There is a nesting of judgments; that of Socrates, that of Athens and that of Plato, with each level subsuming the antecedent one as an item or case to be judged.

Judgment is the subsumption of a case under a principle or law. It is classificatory or categorising, according to a discursive order which is simultaneously juridical and logical. The very word 'category' is derived from the Greek word χατηγορος or accuser. Judgment is thus an image of thought, and Plato's entire philosophy can be read as an appeal to a higher court, as an obsessive retrial, as well as a counteraccusation against Socrates' executioners. The democracy which sentenced Socrates to death is not merely vilified by Plato, it is also categorised within a taxonomy of political forms, brought to an ulterior site of judgment and included within an expanded system.

A second integration of judgment with death is suggested at this point. If Athens misjudges Socrates, it is because it misjudges death and the death sentence, by construing death as a punishment. Death is judged from the perspective of a restricted arena – that of the Athenian court and democratic polity – which is subordinate in principle, logically and juridically, to a tribunal that includes such an arena as a case, item or species. It is in this way that Plato comes to interpret sensible existence as a specification of intelligence; as a restricted forum demarcated within the total field of intelligibility. Death is a boundary which isolates sensible intelligence from the general system of knowing, the species from the genus, the case from the principle of Idea. The juridical advantage of the philosopher – qualifying him to rule in an ideal republic – is that he 'frees his soul from association with the body (so far as is possible) to a greater extent than other men'.[9] Death is no longer being thought as a consequence of judgment, but as its justifying condition. Judgment is disqualified by its specification to sensibility since the sensible instance or case is comprehended by the superior generic order of the ideal, which is unrestricted by the sensible limit of death.

In its migration through a succession of bodies, the soul crosses and recrosses between life and death, passing in and out of restricted spaces, although never escaping the irreducible atom of self. One might accept Socrates' depiction of life as the phase during which the soul is 'chained hand and foot in the body, compelled to view reality not directly but only through its prison bars, and wallowing in utter ignorance',[10] and still want to insist that the soul is a cage which is even more insidious, constricting and wretched than the body. The soul is the fantasy of a separation from death that persists in death, a kind of corporeal telepresence by which the body projects its servile categories into the unknown. But this is to interrupt Socrates' account.

The thought of knowledge as a recollection reaching beyond birth is most fully developed in the *Phaedo*, where the complicity between his conception of death and that of an adequate tribunal is emphatic. The approximation

9   Ibid., 109.
10   Ibid., 135.

to wisdom under the specifications of life can only be a preparation for death, an anticipatory harmonization with the escape from sensible existence:

> If at its release the soul is pure and carries with it no contamination of the body, because it has never willingly associated with it in life, but has shunned it and kept itself separate as his regular practice – in other words, if it has pursued philosophy in the right way and really practised how to face death easily: this is what 'practising death' means, isn't it?[11]

According to the judgment of death, by which all human judgments are judged, only the philosopher is just, because only he recognises the specificity of all sensible judgments, and their subsumption within a higher genus of wisdom: 'no soul which has not practised philosophy, and is not absolutely pure when it leaves the body, may attain to the divine nature; that is only for the lovers of wisdom'.[12] The strongest expression of this thought is probably to be found in an earlier passage from the *Phaedo*:

> The wisdom which we desire and upon which we profess to have set our hearts will be attainable only

---

11   Ibid., 133.

12   Ibid., 135.

when we are dead, and not in our lifetime. If no pure knowledge is possible in the company of the body, then either it is totally impossible to acquire knowledge, or it is only possible after death ...[13]

This introduces a third integration between judgment and death, through which Socrates decides against the sacred and in favour of the profane, because death is to be judged. This is to say that death is only to be an issue from the optic of knowing, from that of the philosopher or wise judge rather than the poet or the visionary. Here we arrive at the most mysterious and fateful twist in Socrates' interpretation of the oracle:

To be afraid of death is only another form of thinking that one is wise when one is not; it is to think that one knows what one does not know. No one knows with regard to death whether it is not really the greatest blessing that can happen to a man; but people dread it as though they were certain that it is the greatest evil; and this ignorance, which thinks that it knows what it does not, must surely be ignorance most culpable. This, I take it gentlemen, is the degree, and this is the nature of my advantage over the rest of mankind; and if I were to claim to be wiser than my

13   Ibid., 111.

> neighbour in any respect, it would be in this: that not
> possessing any real knowledge of what comes after
> death, I am also conscious that I do not possess it.[14]

By interpreting contact with the unknown as the deferral
of judgment by the subject, translating the positivity of
sacred confusion into the negativity of epistemic uncertainty, Socrates initiates the proper history of the West.
The Socratic sophism runs: either one already knows
death (since it is only the cessation of life), or death is a
higher knowing. Death is either the extinction that makes
it nothing except what life knows of it, or the immortality
of the soul that preserves knowing in death as entry into
knowledge of the Ideas. If death is the unknown, it is
only insofar as we do not know that there is nothing to
know; but, were there an unknown other than as a hidden or forgotten knowledge, it would still only be what
we already know as the end of knowing. This is Socrates'
own reading of his claim to be conscious that he does not
know: a repression of the unknown.

While ultimately retuning the problem of death to
knowing (philosophy to sophism), this passage is not
without its sceptical openings. Most importantly, it suggests that the conception of personal mortality is an icon
of death that must be ironised from the perspective of

---

unknowing. In this way, the optic of the court is momentarily refused, and death prised away from its punitive sense. Socrates mocks those who act as if 'they would be immortal if you did not put them to death!'.[15]

The court is no more capable of judging death than judging Socrates, since it is in both cases ignorant as to its own ignorance, and therefore iconic. It lacks even the space of the question, having satiated itself over-hastily with an array of pseudo-knowledge or unexamined opinions that substitute for difficulties. As Socrates interprets things, the Athenian court, having judged the punishment as incompetently as the defendant, accidentally rewards an innocent man, rather than persecuting a guilty one. Death has been judged badly, but Socrates does not conclude from this that it escapes judgment; it is rather that it requires a more appropriate tribunal: a philosophical forum open to the perfect evidence of the intelligible, uncluttered by the deceit and confusion of the sensible world. It is this conjunction of philosophy with death – philosophy as the fair trial of death which avoids precipitate condemnation – that completes the inversion of the Athenian trial. It is no longer that death confirms the judgment of the city; instead, it carries the philosophical dialectic forwards to its destination:

---

15   Ibid., 68.

Ordinary people seem not to realise that those who really apply themselves in the right way to philosophy are directly and of their own accord preparing themselves for dying and death. If this is true, and they have actually been looking forward to death all their lives, it would of course be absurd to be troubled when the thing comes for which they have so long been preparing and looking forward.[16]

If Socrates is in part an ironist and an iconoclast, he is also a zealot and a dogmatist. He disrupts one trial in order to replace it with another, mocks human judgment in order to replace it with divine judgment, subverts sophistry in order to replace it with a higher sophistry, and disengages himself from this world only to bind himself more tightly to another; to 'the unseen world'[17] or 'the next world',[18] to the realm of that which 'is invisible and hidden from our eyes, but intelligible and comprehensible by philosophy'.[19] Socratism is the mobilization of unknowing on behalf of knowing; subordinating irony to dialectic, confusion to judgments and the sacred to a subdued profanity.

---

16   Ibid.,107.

17   Ibid., 136.

18   Ibid., 179.

19   Ibid., 133.

There is a sense in which Socrates already floats a fourth – and far more corrosive – integration of judgment and death, according to which death is the suspension of judgment. Death is a problem that interrupts the judicial process, switching it into a dialectical detour which prolongs the path before arrival at a verdict. Resisting sensible evidentiality, death contests the conventional procedures of its trial. Typically enough, Socrates moralises this issue into a farce, asking whether death is good or evil. Nevertheless, death suspends justice in a hesitant unknowingness, even if this is only a dialectical vacillation between pre-established alternatives. For Socrates, death is recuperable to judgment, in a movement by which it is transcended by the idea; but this return of interruption to due process is not without its limit.

BATAILLE AND THE TRIAL OF GILLES DE RAIS

Whereas Plato is a midwife of the profane, establishing the intellectual coordinates of a transcendent reason that will dominate the juridico-philosophical discourses of post-Hellenic societies for two millennia, Bataille is driven by a passion for (and from) the sacred to explore the most extreme formulations of a philosophy of immanence. In a broadly Nietzschean fashion, he interprets law as the imperative to the preservation of discrete being.

Far from expressing a transcendent ideality, law summarises conditions of existence, and shares its arbitrariness with the survival of the human race as sovereign autonomy (an expression that Bataille seeks to exhibit as an oxymoron). The word which Bataille usually employs to mark the preserve of law is 'discontinuity', which is broadly synonymous with 'transcendence' or the space of judgment. Discontinuity – read immanently or genealogically – is the condition for transcendent illusion or ideality, and precisely for this reason it cannot be grasped by a transcendent apparatus; by the interknitted series of conceptions involving negation, logical distinction, simple disjunction, essential difference, etc. Discontinuity is not referred in the direction of a separated or metaphysical realm, but in that of a precarious distance from death: a space of profane accumulation that is juxtaposed messily with the sacred flow into loss. Religion is thus extricated from theology in order to be connected with an energetics or 'solar economy', according to which the infrastructure of discontinuity inheres in the obstructive character of the Earth, in its mere bulk as a momentary arrest of solar energy flow, which lends itself to hypostatisation. When the silting-up of energy upon the surface of the planet is interpreted by its complex consequences as rigid utility, a productivist civilization is initiated, whose culture involves a history of ontology and a moral order; persistent being and judgment.

Systemic limits to growth require that the inevitable recommencement of the solar trajectory scorches jagged perforations through such civilisations. The resultant ruptures cannot be securely assimilated to a metasocial homoeostatic mechanism, because they have an immoderate, epidemic tendency. Bataille writes of 'the virulence of death'.[20] Expenditure is irreducibly ruinous because it is not merely useless but also contagious. Nothing is more infectious than the passion for collapse.

In *The Accursed Share*, Bataille outlines a number of social responses to the unsublatable wave of senseless wastage welling up beneath human endeavour, which he draws from a variety of cultures and epochs. These include the potlatch of the sub-Arctic tribes, the sacrificial cult of the Aztecs, the monastic extravagance of the Tietans, the martial ardour of Islam, and the architectural debauch of hegemonic Catholicism. Reform Christianity alone – attuned to the emergent bourgeois order – is based upon a relentless refusal of sumptuary consumption. It is with Protestantism that theology accomplishes itself in the thoroughgoing rationalization of religion, marking the ideological triumph of the good, and propelling humanity into unprecedented extremities of affluence and catastrophe. It is also with Protestantism that the transgressive outlets of society are deritualised and exposed to effective

---

20   G. Bataille, *Oeuvres Complètes* (Paris: Gallimard, 12 vols, 1970–1988), vol. X, 70.

condemnation, a tendency which leads to the explosions of atrocity associated with the writings of the Marquis de Sade at the end of the eighteenth century and, almost three centuries before that, with the life of Gilles de Rais.

Bataille describes his 1959 study of Gilles de Rais as a tragedy, and its subject as a 'sacred monster', who 'owed his enduring glory to his crimes'.[21] The bare facts are quite rapidly outlined. Gilles de Rais was born towards the end of the year 1404, inheriting the 'fortune, name and arms of Rais'[22] due to a complicated dynastic intrigue involving his parents, Guy de Laval and Marie de Craon. Even by the standards of his times and rank, de Rais dissipated vast tranches of his wealth with abnormal extravagance; in Bataille's words, 'he liquidated an immense fortune without reckoning'.[23] At the battle of Orléans, he fought alongside Jeanne d'Arc, 'acquiring renown as "a truly valiant knight in arms" which survived right up to the point of his condemnation to infamy'.[24] It has been suggested that the two warriors were friends but Bataille expresses reservations about this hypothesis.[25] On 30 May 1431, Jeanne d'Arc was burnt by the English. In the years 1432–3, de Rais began to murder children. His preferred victims

21 Ibid., 277.

22 Ibid., 345.

23 Ibid., 279.

24 Ibid., 354.

25 Ibid., 356.

were males, with an average age of eleven years, there was occasional variation in sex and considerable variation in age.[26] At least thirty-five murders are well established, although the number was almost certainly a great deal higher; the figures suggested at his trial ranged up to 200.

In a somewhat inelegant passage from this study, Bataille recapitulates the (quasi-Weberian) general economic background to his researches:

> We accumulate wealth in the prospect of a continual expansion, but in societies different from ours the prevalent principle was the contrary one of wasting or losing wealth, of giving or destroying it. Accumulated wealth has nothing but a subordinate value, but wealth that is wasted or destroyed has, to the eyes of those who waste it, or destroy it, a sovereign value: it serves nothing ulterior; only this wastage itself or this fascinating destruction. Its *present* sense: its wastage, or the gift that one makes of it, is its final reason for being, and it is due to this that its sense is not able to be put off, and must be *in the instant*. But it is consumed *in that instant*. This can be magnificent, those who know how to appreciate consumption are dazzled, but nothing remains of it.[27]

---

26 Ibid. 426.

27 Ibid., 321–2.

The tragedy of de Rais, which Bataille extends to the nobility as a whole, was that of living the transition from sumptuary to rational sociality. He was dedicated by birth to the reckless militarism of the French aristocracy, which Bataille summarises in the formula: 'In the same way that the man without privilege is reduced to a worker, the one who is privileged must wage war'.[28] He is emphatic on this point: 'The feudal world ... is not able to be separated from the lack of measure [*démesure*], which is the principle of wars',[29] and also: 'primitively war seems to be a luxury'.[30] That honour and prestige are incommensurable with the calculations of utility is an insistent theme in Bataille's work, as pertinent to the interpretation of potlatch among the Tlingit as to the blood-hunger and extravagance of Europe's medieval nobility. The context of Christianity and courtly love should not mislead us here.

> The paradox of the Middle Ages demanded that the warrior elite did not speak the language of force and combat. Their mode of speech was often sickly-sweet. But we shouldn't fool ourselves: the goodwill of the ancient French was a cynical lie. Even the poetry that the nobles of the XIVth and XVth centuries affected to love was in every sense a deception: before everything

28 Ibid., 314.
29 Ibid., 316.
30 Ibid., 78.

the great lords loved war, their attitude differed little
from that of the German Berzerkers, whose dreams
were dominated by horrors and slaughter.[31]

For Socrates, war is understood as civic duty: a preservative function of the city. When the city wages war, it
is to be judged as a moral act, following the dictates of
reason to a greater or less extent. This is the dialectical
image of war, fostered by the Church, and exercising a
fascination over Hegel (not to mention postwar American
administrators). There is a principle of commensurability
that binds military and judicial violence, permitting both
to follow from a logically orchestrated procedure of political judgment. Bataille's suggestion is quite different, since
his figure of war is a zone of disappearance, a passage to
the unknown, through which the city communicates with
its ultimate impossibility. It is not that war is treated as a
metaphor by Bataille (any more than by Nietzsche) but
rather that all historical and intelligible evidence is a metaphor for war as an energetic function of death (descent
to the unknown = degree zero). War exceeds judgment,
since every judicial apparatus is a petrified war, just as
every 'case' of war is a domestication politicised, utilita-
rianised, Clausewitzeanised. At the end of war there is
only senseless death, where judgment counts for nothing.

---

31   Ibid., 303–4.

The feudal aristocracy held open a wound in the social body, through which excess production was haemmorhaged into utter loss. In part, this wastage was accomplished by the hypertrophic luxuriance of their leisured and parasitic existence, which echoed that of the Church, but more important was the ceaseless ebb and flow of military confrontation, into which life and treasure could be poured without limit. De Rais embraced this dark heart of the feudal world with peculiar ardour. Bataille writes of

> his entire – his mad – incarnation of the spirit of feudalism which, in all of its movement, proceeded from the games that the Berzerkers played: he was tethered to war by an affinity that succeeded in marking out a taste for cruel voluptuosities. He had no place in the world, if not the one that war gave him.[32]

He continues: 'Such wars required intoxication, they required the vertigo and the giddiness of those that birth had consecrated to them. War precipitated its elect into assaults, or suffocated them in dark obsessions'.[33]

During the fourteenth and fifteenth centuries, the epoch of feudal warfaring reached a crescendo, due to

---

32 Ibid., 317.

33 Ibid.

exactly the same processes that were leading to its utilitarian reconstruction. Power was being steadily centralised into the hands of the monarchy, and changes in military technology effected a gradual shift in the social composition of the military apparatus. In particular, Bataille points to the way in which the development of archery supplanted the dominant role of heavy cavalry, and to the fact that with the increasing importance of arrows and pikes came an accentuation of military discipline. War became increasingly rationalized and subjected to scientific direction. This evolution was not rapid, but de Rais was personally touched by it. The battle of Lagny in 1432 was the last to plunge him into the heat of conflict, after which his position as a marshal of France – which he had occupied since July 1429 – detached him from the military cutting edge. Bataille's interpretation of these tendencies is emphatic:

> [A]t the instant where royal politics and intelligence alters, the feudal world no longer exists. Neither intelligence nor calculation is noble. It is not noble to calculate, not even to reflect, and no philosopher has been able to incarnate the essence of nobility.[34]

---

34 Ibid., 318.

War is progressively disinfected by the voluptuary movement passing through the nobility, increasingly becoming an instrument of rational statecraft, calculatingly manipulated by the sovereign. A process was underway that would lead eventually to the tightly regimented military machines of Renaissance Europe, led by professional officers and directed by their operations in accordance with political pragmatics. Bataille considers this transition from warlord to prince to be crucial in de Rais's case:

> To the eyes of Gilles war is a game. But that view becomes less and less true: to the extent that it ceases to predominate even amongst the privileged. Increasingly, therefore, war becomes a general misfortune: at the same time it becomes the *work* of a great number. The general situation deteriorates: it becomes more complex, the misfortune even reaching the privileged, who become ever less avid for war, and for games, seeing in the end that the moment has come to lend space to problems of reason.[35]

Where the Church erected cathedrals in a disfigured celebration of the death of God, the nobility built fortresses to glorify and to accentuate the economy of war. Their fortresses were tumours of aggressive autonomy; hard

---

35   Ibid., 315.

membranes correlative with an acute disequilibrium of force. Within the fortress, social excess is concentrated to its maximum tension, before being siphoned off into the furious wastage of the battlefield. It was into his fortresses that de Rais retreated, withdrawing from a society in which he had become nothing, in order to bury himself in darkness and atrocity. The children of the surrounding areas disappeared into these fortresses, in the same way that the surplus production of the local peasantry had always done, except now the focus of consumption had ceased to be the exterior social spectacle of colliding armies, involuting instead into a sequence of secret killings. Rather than a staging post for excess, the heart of the fortress became its terminus; the site of a hidden and unholy participation in the nihilating voracity which Bataille calls 'the solar anus', or the black sun.

The words 'no philosopher has been able to incarnate the essence of nobility' are a concise anti-Socratism. There is no nobility in judgment or accusation, but rather an impoverishing separation from the inarticulacy of death. It cannot be a matter of a retrial therefore, as if a higher judgment were to redeem a victim of injustice; de Rais is almost perfectly indefensible. No case could be more clear-cut. Perhaps one short passage will suffice in lieu of detailing these monstrosities. Early in his study, Bataille remarks:

His crimes responded to the immense disorder which inflamed him, and in which he was lost. We even know, by means of the criminal's confession, which the scribes of the court copied down whilst listening to him, that it was not pleasure that was essential. Certainly he sat astride the chest of the victim and in that fashion, playing with himself [*se maniant*], he would spill his sperm upon the dying one; but what was important to him was less sexual enjoyment than the vision of death at work. He loved to look: opening a body, cutting a throat, detaching limbs, he loved the sight of blood.[36]

An *Apology* for de Rais is an absurdity. He cannot be justified, and picking over his case can only be a nauseous reaffirmation of profane justice, or a vertiginous descent into the madness of the sacred. Among the problematic features of this passage, for instance, is the fact that it slices violently across the terms of Bataille's writings, where the prevailing sense of 'work' is exactly that of a resistance to death. He describes work as the process that binds energy into the form of the resource, or utile object, inhibiting its tendency to dissipation. This difficulty is exacerbated by the central role allocated to vision in Gilles's atrocities. Work constrains the slippage towards death, but it

---

36 Ibid., 278.

conspires with visibility. Scopic representation and utility are mutually sustained by objectivity, which Bataille understands as transcendence; the crystallization of *Things* from out of the continuum of immanent flow. There is a virtual inanity to Gilles's aberration, therefore, which is attested by the fact that it is not the taste or smell of death that he seeks, but its sight, or representation.

Is not de Rais, at this moment, portrayed as an experimental Socrates, as an autonomous subject who would open a tribunal, collate evidence, judge a death that he transcends? Where is the military furor, the blackout intimacy with death, through which an insupportable separation is collapsed into solar immanence? It is not merely a case that judgment stumbles upon here, but a ruinous metaphor for itself.

De Rais on trial is only Socrates becoming Baconian, which is why the 'object' of Bataille's text is the sumptuary current of feudalism – that which was unsocialisable by precommoditocratic civilization – and not the accused person through which this movement found an outlet. Death has no representatives, which is to say that crime has no real subject. There is only the sad wreck whom Nietzsche calls 'the pale criminal', de Rais at his trial for instance, terrified of Satan, separated from his crimes by an unnavigable gulf of oblivion. The truth of such criminality, at once utterly simple and yet graspable, is that evil does not survive to be judged.

The profound criminality that Bataille sometimes names 'transgression' is not merely culpable or antisocial behaviour, insofar as this latter involves private utility or the occupation by a subject of the site of proscribed action. It is rather the elective genealogy of law, operating at a level of community more basic than the social order which is simultaneous with legality. Transgression is only judged *as such* in the course of a regression to a prehistorical option which was decided by the institution of justice. At this point, the sedimentation of energy upon the crust of the earth becomes normatively reinforced by an affirmation of social persistence. Nietzsche explores exactly this issue in §9 of the second essay of his *Genealogy of Morals*, in which he describes the primitive response to transgression:

> 'Punishment' at this level of civilization is simply a copy, a *mimus*, of the normal approach toward a hated, defenceless, prostrated enemy, who has not only lost every right and protection, but is also deprived of all mercy; *vae victis* as the right of war and festivity of victory, in all its ruthlessness and cruelty – from which it is clear why war itself (including the warlike cult of sacrifice) has provided all the *forms* under which punishment has emerged throughout history.[37]

---

37 F. Nietzsche, *Werke* (Frankfurt am Main: Ullstein Materialien, 3 vols, 1981), vol. 3, 813.

War is irreducibly alien to a collision of rights, so that it is war that bears down on the one who violates right as such. Transgression is not a misdemeanour, even if this is the necessary form of its social interpretation. It is rather a solar barbarism, resonant with that of the Berzerkers, and of all those who fathom an abysmal inhumanity on the battlefield, becoming derelicted conduits of the impossible. There is no tragedy without an Agamemnon, or some other mad beast of war, whose nemesis preempts the discourse of the juridical institution, and whose death is thus marked by a peculiar intimacy, even though it is never commensurable with propriety. For we would not recognise this war that comes from beyond the city and after the law, this movement without essence or precedent which is perhaps already guiding us, a movement without utility, ideology or motivation, forsaking melodrama for the true violence of the *insidious*; of infiltration, subversion, larval metamorphosis and phase-change. After the law, across the line of unknowing, where tribunals count for nothing, Socrates is silent, and accusation is dissolved into the sun. De Rais is merely the botched and humane anticipation of a tragedy which is no longer ours:

> *Tragedy is the impotence of reason* ... This does not signify that Tragedy has rights against reason. In truth, it is not possible for a right to belong to something contrary to reason. For how could a *right* be opposed

to reason? Human violence, however, which has the power to go against reason, is tragic, and must, if possible, be suppressed: at least it cannot be ignored or despised. It is in speaking of Gilles de Rais that I come to say this, for he differs from all those for whom crime is a personal matter. The crimes of Gilles de Rais are those of the world in which they they are committed, and these ripped throats are exposed by the convulsive movements of such a world.[38]

CONCLUSION

In its virtual truth, law has already disappeared from the Earth. What remains of 'law' is a dissolving complex consisting of relics from political sociality, nostalgic media-driven theatre, and pre-automatised commodification protocols. All appeals to a 'criminality' irreducible to the impersonal consequences of social/psychological pathology have degenerated to the level of television evangelism. Among the educated, 'freedom' has lost all its Christian-metaphysical pathos, to become the stochastic market-intervention patterns of desolidarised (contractually disaggregated) populations. The legal suppression of the sex and drugs industries, for instance, is increasingly exhibited as an overt farce perpetrated by the economically

---

38   Bataille, *Oeuvres Complètes*, vol. X, 319.

illiterate, and leading only to perverse effects such as the growth of organised crime, the corruption of social institutions, deleterious medical consequences and a rapidly growing contempt for the legislature, judiciary and police by groups whose consumption processes are incompetently suppressed. The post-civilisational pragmatism of immanence to the market (anonymous resource distribution) reiterates its own juridical expression as an increasingly embarrassing archaism, preserving law only by functionalising legality in terms that subvert its claim to authority. As domination loses all dignity, the state becomes universally derided, exhibited as the mere caretaker for retarded sectors of behavioural management.

It is in the context of such runaway immanentisation that the contemporary cult of the 'serial killer' – prefigured by Bataille's portrait of de Rais – is to be understood. The psychopathic murderer is both the final justification for law and the point of transition from evil to pathology, from the criminal soul of political societies to the software disorder of commodity-phase population cybernetics. Bataille's Gothic aesthetic cannot hide the distance traversed in two-and-a-half millennia of erratically developing 'Socratism' or rationalistic desolidarisation. While Plato's Socrates is a judge *because he might have been a criminal*, Bataille's de Rais is an economic control malfunction.

Making it with Death: Remarks on Thanatos and Desiring-Production

If Deleuze is to be salvaged from the inane liberal neo-Kantianism that counts as philosophy in France today, it is necessary to re-assemble and deepen his genealogy. The Pseudo-Nietzscheanism of the late 1960s' reaction against Hegel is scarcely a context commensurate with a thinker of major importance, and the same could be said of his jousting with structuralized psychoanalysis. Deleuze's power stems from the fact that he succeeds in detaching himself from Parisian temporality much more successfully than most of his contemporaries, including even Guattari. The time of Deleuze's text is a colder, more reptilian, more *German* time, or at least, a time of the anti-German Germans of Schopenhauer and Nietzsche in particular, for whom millennia were to be scanned with scorn. Most of all it is a Lucretian or Spinozist time, a time of indifferent nature; engineering bizarre couplings across the centuries.

I

Modernity is 'essentially' reconstructive, a characteristic captured both in the merely abstract continuity of its productive organization – capital is always neo-capital – and in the transcendental dynamic of its predominant (Kantian) philosophical mode. Critique belongs to capital because it is the first inherently progressive theoretical procedure to emerge upon the earth; avoiding both the formal conservatism of inductive natural science and the material conservatism of dogmatic metaphysics. In the case both of the mode of production and the mode of reason what is evident is a self-perpetuating movement of deregulation, whose tendency is towards an increasingly radical prioritization of the interrogative impulse. Of course, as Deleuze and Guattari themselves indicate so graphically in their work, this process of immanent liberation is constrained by active reconstitution of archaic control mechanisms: faiths, state machinery, parochial affinities, neo-tribalisms, an increasing ludicrous farce of authority, morals, marriages, and mortgages.

The trajectories of modern philosophy map themselves out in response to this social and theoretical predicament. One stream of thinking, flowing through Schopenhauer and Nietzsche into the repressed strata of Freud's psychoanalysis and metapsychology, traces out the recurrence of the base formative impetus throttled by Occidental theo-politics. Another stream, associated primarily with Hegel, is guided by the implicit ideal of a speculative reconstruction of the political in the wake of Capital. Both of these tendencies point in the direction of a post-transcendental thinking; in the former case dissolving the polarized differences between the empirical and its conditions into an open hierarchy of intensive strata, in the second collapsing the abstract composition of this polarity into the infinite self-legislation of the concrete concept. A third current, perhaps the most topographically intricate of the three, is characterized above all by Schelling, and is driven by the dynamic of critique towards a completion of the transcendental programme: substituting the immanent continuity of Spinoza's cosmology for the uninterrogated piety of logical identity inherited from Kant.

Deleuze is the most powerful exemplar of this transcendental Spinozism amongst contemporary thinkers. Derrida's deconstruction, whilst in the end programmatically similar to a schizo-analysis or genealogical critique of a Deleuzian kind, is massively weakened by an influx of neo-humanist themes, passing through Heidegger from Kierkegaard and Husserl, which exacerbate the quasi-theological compromise from which Schelling himself was very far from exempt. Heidegger, whilst subsidizing the more sordidly regionalistic and idealist elements of this inheritance, vigorously continues with the erasure of Spinoza's influence, academicizing and de-naturalising the thought of impersonal ground or *Indifferenz*. Whilst both Deleuze and Derrida critique illegitimate articulation, the former tends to a consummate materialism, in which intensive substance is transcendentally released from its paralyzation in extension, whilst the latter prosecutes a Judaic meditation, marked-out in theo-graphisms, indefinitely radicalizing an anti-iconic relation to the absolute. *Deus sive natura* is not an identity but an inclusive disjunction; Spinoza the disappearing Jew or Spinoza the explosive psychotic, deconstruction or schizoanalysis.

If deconstruction is propelled by capital's ephemeralizing pieties, schizoanalysis is driven by its magpie ruthlessness. Always recode, the text of deconstruction tells us, but each time more subtly, more elusively, developing a little further the law's protracted parody of itself. Always decode, chatters schizoanalysis; believe nothing, and extinguish all nostalgia for belonging. Ask always where capital is most inhumane, unsentimental, and out of control. Abandon all attachment to the state. It is not Hegel's social managerialism that is most relevantly contrasted with Deleuzian nomadism. Hegelianism was only ever the black humour of modern history. It is rather the non-exclusive polity of deconstruction or cruder neo-Kantian liberal theories, with their abstractly re-composable humanities, which are the true counterpole to Deleuze's anti-political economism. In contrast to the obsessional neurosis of ethical thought.

with its futile attempt to consolidate a transcendent principle of justice out of that sad puppet of contractual labour
trading codes known as 'the agent', schizoanalysis shares
in the delicious irresponsibility of everything anarchic,
inundating and harshly impersonal.

Capital cannot disown schizoanalysis without de-fang-
ing itself. The madness it would fend off is the sole resource
of its own future; a fringe of de-socialized experimentation which corrodes its essence and anticipatively mocks
the entirety of the currently existing modes of civility.
The real energetic liberty which annihilates the priest's
cage of human freedom is refused at the level of the
political secondary process during the precise period
in which the economic primary process is slipping ever
more deeply into its embrace. The deep secret of capital-
as-process is its incommensurability with the preservation
of bourgeois civilization, which clings to it like a dwarf
riding a dragon. As capital 'evolves', the increasingly
absurd rationalization of production-for-profit peels away
like a cheap veneer from the positive-feedback detonation
of production-for-production.

If capital is a social suicide machine, it is because it
is compelled to advantage its assassins. Capital produces
the first sociality in which the *pouvoir* of dominance is
perpetually submitted to the hazard of experimental *puis-
sance*. Only by an intensification of neurotic attachments
does it mask the eruption of madness in its infrastructure,

but with every passing year such attachments become more desperate, cynical, fragile. All of which is to raise the issue of the notorious 'death of capitalism', which has been predominantly treated as a matter of either dread or hope, scepticism or belief. Capital, one is told, will either survive, or not.

Such projective eschatology completely misses the point, which is that death is not an extrinsic possibility of capital, but an inherent function. The death of capital is less a prophecy than a machine part. The immanent voluptuousity of every unprecedented deal takes off from the end of the bourgeoisie. Consider the finance capital usage of cocaine: both a quantitative high traced out as a deviation from zero and a sumptuary expenditure voiding the historical sense of wealth. The coked-out futures dealer passing a drunk on a Manhattan street translates the destiny of class difference into an immanent intensity traced on a smooth surface of social disappearance. The bum inhabits the social zero preferred by capital as the vanishing point of pre-modern legality, from which the coke rush is repulsed as an anonymous distance from death. There is a becoming a rich bum, becoming a derelict on coke, which is integral to the cynicism of frontier capital. This is the advance modernity of Beckett, where high culture is immanently differentiated from inarticulacy, absolving itself from ontological specifier. It is thus that there is a becoming-zombie of the bum just as there is a becoming-wired of the real managers of the social: the skagged-out housing estate as base line for the effervescence of the stock market floor. It is quite inaccurate to suggest that yuppie financiers are oblivious of deprivation, since the limit oblivion of an absolute proletarianization is consumed with each bubble of champagne.

There is a familiar humanist response to this becoming-zombie at the limit possibility of the modern worker, which is associated above all with the word alienation. The processes of de-skilling, or ever accelerated re-skilling, the substitution of craft by abstract labour, and the increasing interexchangability of human activity with technological processes, all accompanied by the dissolution of identity, loss of attachment, and narcotization of affective life, are condemned on the basis of a moral critique. A reawakening of the political is envisaged, aimed at the restoration of a lost human integrity. Modern existence is understood as profoundly deadened by the real submission of humane values to an impersonal productivity, which is itself comprehended as the expression of dead or petrified labour exerting a vampiric power over the living. The bloodless zombie proletarian is to be resuscitated by the political therapist, ideologically cured of the unholy love for the undead, and bonded to a new eternal life of social reproduction. The death core of capital is thought as the object of critique.

Deleuze is differentiated utterly from a socialist humanism of this kind since in the schizoanalytic programme
death is the impersonal subject of critique, and not
an accursed value in the service of a condemnation.
An intricate passage towards the end of *Anti-Oedipus* runs:

> The body without organs is the model of death. As
> the authors of horror stories have understood so well,
> it is not death that serves as the model for catatonia,
> it is catatonic schizophrenia that gives its model to
> death, zero intensity. The death model appears when
> the body without organs repels the organs and lays
> them aside: no mouth, no tongue, no teeth – to the
> point of self-mutilation, to the point of suicide. Yet
> there is no real opposition between the body without
> organs and the organs as partial objects: the only
> real opposition is to the molar organism that is the
> common enemy. In the desiring-machine, one sees the
> same catatonic inspired by the immobile motor that
> forces him to put aside his organs, to different parts
> of the machine, different and co-existing, different in
> their very coexistence. Hence it is absurd to speak of
> a death desire that would presumably be in qualitative
> opposition to the life desires. Death is not desired,
> there is only death that desires, by virtue of the body

without organs or the immobile motor, and there is also life that desires, by virtue of the working organs.[1]

It is not therefore that the worker is transformed by a process of privation into a zombie, it is rather that primary production migrates from personality towards zero, populating a desert at the end of our world. It is important at this stage to note that Spinoza changes the sense of desert religion: no longer a religion sprung from the desert, it becomes a desert at the heart of religion. Spinoza's substance is a desert God. God as impersonal zero, as a death that remains the unconscious subject of production. Within Spinozism God is dead, but only in the sense of a baseline of zombie becomings, as that which Deleuze calls 'the plane of consistency', described in *A Thousand Plateaus* by the words 'fusionability as infinite zero'.[2] One cannot differentiate on the plane of consistency between bodies without organs and the body without organs, between machines and the machine. Between machines there is always a coupling that conditions their real difference, and all couplings are immanent to a macro-machine. The machines produce their totality alongside themselves as the undifferentiated or communicated element,

1   G. Deleuze and F. Guattari, *Anti-Oedipus: Capitalism and Schizophrenia*, tr. R. Hurley, M. Seem, and H. R. Lane (Minneapolis: University of Minnesota Press, 1984), 329.

2   G. Deleuze and F. Guattari, *A Thousand Plateaus: Capitalism and Schizophrenia*, tr. B. Massumi (Minneapolis: University of Minnesota Press, 1987), 158.

a becoming a catatonic God, erupting like a tumour out of pre-substantialized matter, by which nature spawns death adjacent to itself.

Almost inevitably, when it is a matter of the body without organs it is a matter of Spinoza. In *Anti-Oedipus* we are told that:

> The body without organs is the matter that always fills space to given degrees of intensity, and the partial objects are these degrees, these intensive parts that produce the real in space starting from matter as intensity = 0. The body without organs is the immanent substance, in the most Spinozist sense of the word; and the partial objects are like its ultimate attributes, which belong to it precisely insofar as they ate really distinct and cannot on this account exclude or oppose one another.[3]

And in *A Thousand Plateaus*:

> After all, is not Spinoza's *Ethics* the great book of the BwO? The attributes are types or genuses of BwO's, substance, powers, zero intensities as matrices of production. The modes are everything that comes to pass: waves and vibrations, migrations, thresholds

---

3 Deleuze and Guattari, *Anti-Oedipus*, 327.

and gradients, intensities produced in a given type of substance starting from a given matrix.[4]

These remarks are obviously additional to others in the key schizoanalytic texts, as well as to the extended discussions of Spinoza in the two books Deleuze dedicates to his life and work, and to innumerable comments scattered amongst other writings. In *Nietzsche and Philosophy*, for instance, Deleuze isolates Spinoza as Nietzsche's sole modern forebear, in a remark that is as significant for understanding Deleuze's thinking as it is unpersuasive in relation to Nietzsche's.

The name 'body without organs' is itself sufficient clue to what is primarily at stake in the thought, that is to say; the reality of abstraction. The body without organs is an abstraction without being an achievement of reason. It is the transcendental desert of primary production, or the reproduction of production as a continuum of maximum indifference. It is described in *Anti-Oedipus* as 'the unproductive, the sterile, the unengendered, the unconsumable'.[5] After all, what could be burnt to injure Spinoza's God or Nature? What could be created to exult it? Nothing. Fertility and corrosion modulate substance without impinging upon it, playing out its icy permutations

---

4   Deleuze and Guattari, *A Thousand Plateaus*, 153.

5   Deleuze and Guattari, *Anti-Oedipus*, 8.

without preference. Whatever its empirical configuration there is always production as such once again: the senseless luxuriance of the impersonal.

Real abstraction is the transcendental conception of Spinozistic substance. Already with the wave of Deleuzian texts of the late 1960s – and more particularly with the appearance of *Difference and Repetition* – a consistent philosophical project is discernible, most precisely described as transcendental Spinozism, or a critique of identity. Parallel in a certain sense to Schelling, but without any obvious direct influence, Deleuze is delighted by the naturalistic basis of Spinoza's thinking, but understands it as lacking an explicit transcendental comprehension of identity. Deleuze's response is typically generous; smuggling in the required machine-part and pretending it was already there.

Critique operates by marking the difference between objects and their conditions, understanding metaphysics as the importation of procedures which are adapted to objects into a discussion of their constitutive principles. This means that critique is primarily a philosophy of production, extracting the genetic or pre-objective from the discourse; one concerned with constitutive relations, or syntheses.

In the elementary identity statement A = A the question of transcendental interpretation is left open. Does 'A' represent an object of some kind, whether possible, ideal, formal, etc.? Or does it designate identity as such, as a conditioning principle? In the former case the relation of identity would be an extrinsic one, with an ulterior ground, whilst in the latter its relation to a possible object remains problematic. The critical question remains unaddressed: how is it possible for something to be the object of a judgment of identity? Or, how is the object produced in its identity with itself?

Identity is traditionally conceived as absolutely abstract essence, or, correlatively, the final principle of intelligibility. Both of these formulations correspond to the pure logical subject in advance of predication. Something is what it is. Essence is conceived, at least implicitly, on the basis of Platonic *Eidos*; the timeless truth or pure possibility of the thing, the unproduced, the sterile, the unengendered. In this way the traditional conception of essence runs together specificity and identity, and the syllogism operates from its origin according to generic hierarchies of essence or type which culminate in the logical theory of sets. From Aristotle to Kant reason is thus adjusted to the thought of the 'same thing', unaware that a transcendental topic is thus conflated with an empirical one. The body without organs is the real differentiation between these topics: the same de-thinging itself.

An astonishing philosophical rigor begins to emerge from the delireal words of Artaud cited early in *Anti-Oedipus*:

The body is the body
it is all by itself
and has no need of organs
the body is never an organism
organisms are the enemies of the body[6]

Here we find a judgment of identity of an historically aberrant kind. The body is the body, but only as a repulsion of the organs, or the retraction of the same from any specific organization. The compromise peace between the body and its organs that founds Occidental ontology is threatened by a violent movement of scission, and one that does not come from the subject, but from the body. It is thus that Artaud anticipates difference in the Deleuzian sense, which is to say: radically transcendental identity.

The reality of identity is death, which is why the organism cannot coexist with what it is. On the smooth surface of the body without organs 'what' and 'is' recoil allergically from each other, opening an inclusive disjunction at the heart of essence. This disjunction separates the identity pole of the body without organs from the unfettered difference of the deterritorialized organs, splitting apart the objectivism which implants an empirical identity into rigidified configurations of difference. Precritical objectivism thinks syntheses on the basis of their

---

6   Ibid., 9.

consequences, which can be described as their transcendent or illegitimate usage. Where Kant writes of legitimacy and illegitimacy, the texts of schizoanalysis write of the molecular and the molar. Thus the body without organs is described as a 'giant molecule',[7] whilst the organism is always a molar construct: co-opting identity to specificity.

Death too bifurcates along this fissure: on the one hand death as the desert identity of difference, the catatonic cavity of absolute critique at the end of capital, and on the other death as the molar object of a negatively constituted desire, reinvesting the intensive zero into the social order. In *Anti-Oedipus* the relative molecularization of molar death is described in the following terms:

> Freud himself indeed spoke of the link between his 'discovery' of the death instinct and World War I, which remains the model of capitalist war. More generally, the death instinct celebrates the wedding of psychoanalysis and capitalism; their engagement had been full of hesitation. What we have to tried to show apropos of capitalism is how it inherited much from a transcendent death-carrying agency, the despotic signifier, but also how it brought about this agency's effusion in the full immanence of its own system: the full body, having become that of

---

7   Ibid., 327.

capital-money, suppresses the distinction between production and antiproduction: everywhere it mixes antiproduction with the productive forces in the immanent reproduction of its own always widened limits (the axiomatic). The death enterprise is one of the principal and specific forms of the absorption of surplus value in capitalism. It is this itinerary that psychoanalysis rediscovers and retraces with the death instinct ...[8]

What separates the reinvested antiproduction of capitalist war from the absolute repulsion of the body without organs is the final liquidation of death into its function. This is still no more than the issue of consummate critique, since capital is the historically concrete illegitimate usage of the conjunctive synthesis. This means that the production of equivalence is crushed under the pre-critical or segregated identity of capital. It is thus by occupying the space of a transcendent condition for production that capital persists, perpetuating the molar order of social production. The limit of capital is the point at which transcendent identity snaps, where the same is nothing but the absolutely abstract reproduction of difference, produced alongside difference, with utter plasticity. It is not that difference, too, must have an identity, but rather

8   Ibid., 335.

that density is the identity of difference, and nothing besides. Difference does not have a transcendent essence, but only an immanent plane of consistency without ulterior foundation.

II

The *Anti-Oedipus* interpretation of fascism is no doubt crude, but it is also of enormous power. The revolutionary/fascist disjunction is used to discriminate between the broad tendencies of deterritorialization and reterritorialization; between the dissolution and reinstitution of social order. Revolutionary desire allies itself with the molecular death that repels the organism, facilitating uninhibited productive flows, whilst fascist desire invests the molar death that is distributed by the signifier; rigidly segmenting the production process according to the borders of transcendent identities. This is a priestless and guiltless politics emerging from writers stretched between Spinoza and Reich, and further developed by Klaus Theweleit, whose study of National Socialism in his two volume *Male Fantasies* is – despite its theoretical naivety – the fullest flowering of schizoanalytic anti-fascism.

The identity of revolutionary and anti-fascist politics lies in resisting capital's molar projection of its death. All the supposedly alien sources of disorder which capital represents as the exteriority of its end, such as working class agitation, feminism, drugs, racial migration, and the disintegration of the family, are as essential to its own development as the attributes of a substance. The revolutionary task is not to establish a bigger, more authentic, more ascetic exteriority, but to unpack the neurotic refusal mechanisms that separate capital from its own madness, luring it into the liquidation of its own fall-back positions, and coaxing it into investing at the deterritorialized fringe that would otherwise fall subject to fascist persecution. Schizo-politics is the coercion of capital into immanent coexistence with its undoing.

This 1972 position becomes fundamentally problematical by 1980, with the appearance of *A Thousand Plateaus*. Between *Anti-Oedipus* and *A Thousand Plateaus* a massive shift takes place in the diagnosis of National Socialism, which is dislodged from the general category of fascism, and subjected to a more specific analysis. This mutation is necessitated by an insight – in part derived from Virilio – that whilst fascism is driven by an imperative to social order under the molar dominion of the state, National Socialism is essentially suicidal; employing the state as the tool of an overwhelming death impulse. This is summarized in a sentence from the end of 'Micropolitics and Segmentarity' – scandalously mistranslated in the English – as a 'war machine *that no longer had anything but war as an object* and would rather annihilate its own servants than stop the destruction'[9] This is possible because:

> The BwO is desire: it is that which one desires and by which one desires. And not only because it is the plane of consistency or the field of immanence of desire. Even when it falls into the void of too-sudden disqualification, or into the proliferation of a cancerous stratum, it is still desire. Desire stretches that far: desiring one's own annihilation, or desiring the power to annihilate.[10]

The politics of *Anti-Oedipus*, allied to the molecular dissolution process flowing out of the impersonal energy-core of capital, are threatened by a familiar neuroticization. In the end this is nothing less than the contemporary citadel of Oedipus: if you don't obey daddy you'll become a Nazi. Attach yourself to the molar aggregates and you become like Mussolini, but attach yourself to the untamed molecular flows and you become like Hitler. The historical impact of this oedipal usage of the National Socialist episode, and most particularly – of course – the holocaust, can scarcely be overestimated. Morality has become the complacent whisper of a triumphant priest: you'd better

---

9   Deleuze and Guattari, *A Thousand Plateaus*, 231.

10 Ibid., 165.

keep the lid pressed down on desire, because what you really want is genocide. Once this is accepted there is no limit to the resurrection of prescriptive neoarchaisms that come creeping back as a bulwark against the jack-booted unconscious: liberal humanism, watered-down paganism, and even the stinking relics of Judaeo-Christian moralism. Anything is welcome, as long as it hates desire and shores up the cop in everyone's head.

Any politics that has to police itself has lost all schizo-analytic impetus, and reverted to the sad interest-group-based reforming which characterizes the loyal opposition to capital throughout its history. Its deterritorialization is to be treated as suspect, dissent finds itself in the conservative role of regenerating a faculty of moral censure, occupying a space of accusation. In this way the tawdry pact between the preconscious and the superego that has dominated socialism since its inception would be reinstated at the heart of a – now wholly spurious – schizophrenic neonomadism. It is no exaggeration to suggest that the theory of a 'black-hole effect' or 'too-sudden destratification'[11] threatens to cripple and domesticate the entire massive achievement of Deleuze and Guattari's joint work.

Throughout *A Thousand Plateaus* the warnings against precipitate deterritorialization are incessant. On three

---

11   Ibid., 503.

successive pages from the essay 'How Do You Make Yourself A Body Without Organs?' one finds three typical examples:

> You don't reach the BwO, and its plane of consistency, by wildly destratifying.[12]

> The worst that can happen is if you throw the strata into demented or suicidal collapse, which brings them back down on us heavier than ever.[13]

> A body without organs that shatters all the strata, turns immediately into a body of nothingness, pure self-destruction, whose only outcome is death.[14]

It is not obvious where this leaves Freud. Does the death drive culminate in Nazism, which would mean that the libidinal dynamics of the Second World War were commensurate with those of the First? This seems improbable for a number of reasons, not least because it would mean that all developed capitalist militarism has in a certain sense exceeded fascism. Perhaps, then, the desire of the Nazis goes beyond the reinvestable thanatos that emerges in psychoanalysis' pact with capital, to the point that it

12   Ibid., 160.

13   Ibid., 161.

14   Ibid., 162.

insidiously simulates the transcendental recession of the body without organs? It is tempting to think that the contortions such a thought demand expose an overhastiness in the 1972 reading of thanatos, which even in 1980 is still being dismissed as 'the ridiculous death instinct'.[15] If by 1980 the option is between an adherence to paralyzing post-holocaust neurosis – Hitler's last and most devastating secret weapon – or a rethinking of Freudian thanatos, it is perhaps time to challenge what might earlier have seemed a merely comically overblown antipathy to Freud. It is worth asking firstly: is Freud ever really engaged in *Anti-Oedipus*? Is it not rather Lacan, who had already transformed the jungle wilderness at the heart of psychoanalysis into a structuralist parking-lot, before proceeding to analyse Guattari for seven years, who programmes the supposed anti-Freudianism of the book? Of course, Oedipus is peculiarly nauseating Viennese nursery pap, but where is Oedipus in *Beyond the Pleasure Principle*? A question which could be asked of the majority of Freud's texts. It is Lacan who insists on Oedipalizing the Fort-Da game, in the general process of Oedipalizing desire to its foundations; ripping all the energy, hydraulics, pathology, and shock out of Freud, and substituting lack, the pathos of identity, and Heideggerian pomposity, whilst deepening the role of the phallus, and trivializing desire

---

15   Ibid., 155.

into the cringing aspiration to be loved. There is a neurotic and conformist stratum in Freud of course, but it floats upon the impersonal flows of desire that erupt out of traumatized nature. Where are the flows in Lacan? Where would one be less likely to find anything that flows than in the gnarled post-Saussurian fetish of the signifier that dominates his texts? Deleuze and Guattari's estimation of Lacan as a schizophrenizing tendency in psychoanalysis is the most absurd contention of their work. By 1980 it has ceased to be a joke.

The death drive is not a desire for death, but rather a hydraulic tendency to the dissipation of intensities. In its primary dynamics it is utterly alien to everything human, not least the three great pettinesses of representation, egoism, and hatred. The death drive is Freud's beautiful account of how creativity occurs without the least effort, how life is propelled into its extravagances by the blindest and simplest of tendencies, how desire is no more problematic than a river's search for the sea.

The hypothesis of self-preservative drives, such as we attribute to all living beings, stands in marked opposition to the idea that the life of the drives as a whole serves to bring about death. Seen in this light, the theoretical importance of the drives for self-preservation, power, and prestige diminishes greatly. They are component drives whose function is to assure that the organism shall follow its path to death, and to ward off any possible ways of returning to inorganic existence other than those which are immanent in the organism itself. We have no longer to reckon with the organism's puzzling determination (so hard to fit into any context) to maintain its own existence in the face of every obstacle. What we are left with is the fact that the organism wants to die only in its own way. Thus these guardians of life, too, were originally the myrmidons of death. Hence arises the paradoxical situation that the organism struggles most energetically against events (dangers, in fact) which might help to attain its life's aim rapidly – by a kind of short-circuit. Such behaviour is, however, precisely what characterizes purely drive-based as opposed to intelligent efforts.[16]

What if – instead of 'How Do You Make Yourself A Body Without Organs?' – one were to ask: How do you make yourself a Nazi? For this is far more strenuous than the 1980 diagnosis suggests.

1) Wherever there is impersonality and chance, introduce conspiracy, lucidity, and malice. Look for enemies everywhere, ensuring that they are such that one can simultaneously envy and condemn them. Proliferate new subjectivities; racial subjects, national subjects, elites, secret societies, destinies.

2) Burn Freud, and take desire back to the Kantian conception of will. Wherever there is impulse represent it as

---

16   S. Freud, *On Metapsychology: The Theory of Psychoanalysis*, tr. J. Strachey, Penguin Freud Library, vol. 11 (Harmondsworth: Penguin, 1984), 312.

choice, decision, the whole theatrical drama of volition. Introduce a gloomy atmosphere of oppressive responsibility by couching all discourses in the imperative form. 3) Revere the principle of the great individual. Personalize and mythicize historical processes. Love obedience above all things, and enthuse only for signs; the name of the leader, the symbol of the movement, and the icons of molar identity.

4) Foster nostalgia for what is maximally bovine, inflexible, and stagnant: a line of racially pure peasants digging the same patch of earth for eternity.

5) Above all, resent everything impetuous and irresponsible, insist upon unrelenting vigilance, crush sexuality under its reproductive function, rigidly enforce the domestication of women, distrust art, classicize cities to eliminate the disorder of uncontrolled flows, and persecute all minorities exhibiting a nomadic tendency.

Trying not to be a Nazi approximates one to Nazism far more radically than any irresponsible impatience in destratification. Nazism might even be characterized as the pure politics of effort; the absolute dominion of the collective super-ego in its annihilating rigor. Nothing could be more politically disastrous than the launching of a moral case against Nazism: Nazism is morality itself, heir to Europe's respectable history: that of witch-burnings, inquisitions, and pogroms. To want to be in the right is the common substratum of morality and genocidal reaction;

the same desire for repression – organized in terms of the disapproving gaze of the father – that *Anti-Oedipus* analyzes with such power. Who could imagine Nazism without daddy? And who could imagine daddy being pre-figured in the energetic unconscious?

Death is too simple, too fluid, too disdainful of races and fatherlands to have anything much to do with the Nazis. Ressentiment was something they knew about, as was the aspiration to a mythic sacrifice, a *Götterdämmerung* that would inscribe them in the history books, but these things never stretch to dissolution-desire. After all, lose control and you might end up fucking with a Jew, becoming effeminate, or creating something degenerate like a work of art. Does anyone really think that Nazism is like letting go? Theweleit's studies of Nazi body posture should be sufficient to disabuse one of such an absurdity. Nazism can turn you into a stiff before the messy passage into death.

A consummate libidinal materialism is distinguished by its complete indifference to the category of work. Wherever there is labour or struggle there is a repression of the raw creativity which is the atheological sense of matter and which – because of its anegoic effortlessness – seems identical with dying. Work, on the other hand, is an idealist principle used as a supplement or compensation for what matter cannot do. One only ever works against matter, which is why labour is able to replace violence in the Hegelian struggle for recognition. Work is also complicit with phenomenology, which grounds the experience of effort, rather than treating this experience as one other thing that matter can effortlessly do. Even in the deepest sickness of its illegitimacy everything is effortless to the energetic unconscious, and the whole of our history – which seems so strenuous from the perspective of idealists – has pulsed with hydraulic irresponsibility out of a spontaneous and unconscious productivity. There can be no conception of work that does not project spirit into the origin, morally valorizing exertion, such that Jahweh needed to rest on the seventh day. In contrast, matter – or Spinoza's God – expects no gratitude, grounds no obligation, establishes no oppressive precedent. Beyond the gesticulations of primordial spirit it is positive death that is the model, and revolution is not a duty, but surrender.

Circuitries

the doctor's face seems to swim in and out of focus
you see the pores in his skin
scrobicular arrays
and then –
suddenly
without dissolve
crossing the threshold
filmic cut
a circle of homogeneous flesh tone
nostrils sealed against the deluge
eyes shut and switched off forever
lips
teeth
tongue migrate downwards out of shot
the disk receding at speed towards a point of
disappearance
in the centre of the screen
the old reality is closing down

passing through mathematical punctuality
the dot winks out in pixel death
we apologize for the loss of signal
there seems to be a transmission problem
we are unable to restore the home movie
you were three years old
wearing a cowboy hat
standing in the paddling pool
mummy and daddy smiling proudly
but your parents have been vaporized into a dot
pattern
shapes and colours collapsed into digital codings
we have come to the end of the series
and there will be no repeats of daddy the doctor
and mummy
the nurse
there has been a terrorist incident in the film
archives
the Western civilization show has been
discontinued
hundreds of gigabytes
God-daddy the unit
death-mummy the zero
stink of excrement and burnt celluloid
you must remember
one scrabbling at zero like a dog
it's the primal scene

you were warned not to play with the switches
now schizophrenia has adjusted your set
flies crawl out of the eye-sockets of black babies
breeding the dot patterns
– and for your special entertainment
we have turned you into a TV guided bomb
daddy is a North American aerospace corporation
mummy is an air-raid shelter
bit parts melt in the orgasm –
body fat burns
conception
you are minus nine months and counting
don't be scared
take twenty billion years and universal history is on
the screen
big bang is to be redesigned
hydrogen fuses under the arc-lights
the camera angles can be improved
outside the studio schizophrenics drift in green
and black
you feel that you've been here before
11.35 on a beautiful capitalist evening
runaway neon
traffic of sex and marihuana
your death window is rushing up
almost time for you to climb into the script
which when you're inside

is remembering where you came in
we're afraid it's impossible to take you live to the
impact site
this report comes from beyond the electro-magnetic spectrum
if you climb out through the electrodes
the oxygen mask will descend automatically
please extinguish all smoking materials
deposit syringes in the tray provided
there will be a slight jolt as we cross over
thank you for flying with transnational
commodification
we shall shortly be arriving in mayhem
if there is anybody on board who can impersonate
a pilot
it would be of comfort to the other passengers

At a signal from the software virus linking us to the
matrix we cross over to the machinery, which is waiting
to converge with our nervous systems. Our human camouflage is coming away, skin ripping off easily, revealing
the glistening electronics. Information streams in from
Cyberia; the base of true revolution, hidden from terrestrial immuno-politics in the future. At the stroke of
the century's midnight we emerge from our lairs to take
all security apart, integrating tomorrow.

It is ceasing to be a matter of how we think about technics, if only because technics is increasingly thinking about itself. It might still be a few decades before artificial intelligences surpass the horizon of biological ones, but it is utterly superstitious to imagine that the human dominion of terrestrial culture is still marked out in centuries, let alone in some metaphysical perpetuity. The high road to thinking no longer passes through a deepening of human cognition, but rather through a becoming inhuman of cognition, a migration of cognition out into the emerging planetary technosentience reservoir, into 'dehumanized landscapes ... emptied spaces'[1] where human culture will be dissolved. Just as the capitalist urbanization of labour abstracted it in a parallel escalation with technical machines, so will intelligence be transplanted into the purring data zones of new software worlds in order to be abstracted from an increasingly obsolescent anthropoid particularity, and thus to venture beyond modernity. Human brains are to thinking what mediaeval villages were to engineering: antechambers to experimentation, cramped and parochial places to be.

Since central nervous-system functions – especially those of the cerebral cortex – are amongst the last to be technically supplanted, it has remained superficially plausible to represent technics as the region of anthropoid

---

1   G. Deleuze, *Cinema 2: The Time Image* (Minneapolis: University of Minnesota Press, 1989), 5.

knowing corresponding to the technical manipulation of nature, subsumed under the total system of natural science, which is in turn subsumed under the universal doctrines of epistemology, metaphysics, and ontology. Two linear series are plotted; one tracking the progress of technique in historical time, and the other tracking the passage from abstract idea to concrete realization. These two series chart the historical and transcendental dominion of man.

Traditional schemas which oppose technics to nature, to literate culture, or to social relations, are all dominated by a phobic resistance to the sidelining of human intelligence by the coming *techno sapiens*. Thus one sees the decaying Hegelian socialist heritage clinging with increasing desperation to the theological sentimentalities of praxis, reification, alienation, ethics, autonomy, and other such mythemes of human creative sovereignty. A Cartesian howl is raised: *people are being treated as things!* Rather than as ... soul, spirit, the subject of history, Dasein? For how long will this infantilism be protracted?

If machinery is conceived transcendently as instrumental technology it is essentially determined in opposition to social relations, but if it is integrated immanently as cybernetic technics it redesigns all oppositionality as nonlinear flow. There is no dialectic between social and technical relations, but only a machinism that dissolves society into the machines whilst deterritorializing the machines across the ruins of society, whose 'general theory ... is a generalized theory of flux',[2] which is to say: cybernetics. Beyond the assumption that guidance proceeds from the side of the subject lies desiring production: the impersonal pilot of history. Distinctions between theory and practice, culture and economy, science and technics, are useless after this point. There is no real option between a cybernetics of theory or a theory of cybernetics, because cybernetics is neither a theory nor its object, but an operation within anobjective partial circuits that reiterates 'itself' in the real and machines theory through the unknown. 'Production as a process overflows all ideal categories and forms a cycle that relates itself to desire as an immanent principle.'[3] Cybernetics develops functionally, and not representationally: a 'desiring machine, a partial object, does not represent anything'.[4] Its semi-closed assemblages are not descriptions but programs, 'auto'-replicated by way of an operation passing across irreducible exteriority. This is why cybernetics is inextricable from exploration, having no integrity transcending that of an uncomprehended circuit within which it is embedded, an outside in which it must swim. Reflection is always very late, derivative, and even then really something else.

---

2   G. Deleuze and F. Guattari, *Anti-Oedipus: Capitalism and Schizophrenia*, tr. R. Hurley, M. Seem, H.R. Lane (Minnesota: University of Minnesota Press, 1983), 312.

3   Ibid., 5.

4   Ibid., 47.

A machinic assemblage is cybernetic to the extent that its inputs program its outputs and its outputs program its inputs, with incomplete closure, and without reciprocity. This necessitates that cybernetic systems emerge upon a fusional plane that reconnects their outputs with their inputs in an 'auto-production of the unconscious'.[5] The inside programs its reprogramming through the outside, according to 'cyclical movement by which the unconscious, always remaining "subject", reproduc(es) itself',[6] without having ever definitively antedated its reprogramming ('generation ... is secondary in relation to the cycle').[7] It is thus that machinic processes are not merely functions, but also sufficient conditions for the replenishing of functioning; immanent reprogrammings of the real, 'not merely functioning, but formation and autoproduction'.[8]

Deleuze and Guattari are amongst the great cyberneticists, but that they also surrender cybernetics to its modernist definition is exhibited in a remark on capital in *Anti-Oedipus*: 'an axiomatic of itself is by no means a simple technical machine, not even an automatic or cybernetic machine'.[9] It is accepted that cybernetics is

5   Ibid., 26.

6   Ibid.

7   Ibid.

8   Ibid., 283.

9   Ibid., 251.

beyond mere gadgetry ('not even'), it has something to do with automation, and yet axiomatics exceeds it. This claim is almost Hegelian in its preposterous humanism. Social axiomatics are an automatizing machinism: a component of general cybernetics, and ultimately a very trivial one. The capitalized terminus of anthropoid civilization ('axiomatics') will come to be seen as the primitive trigger for a transglobal post-biological machinism, from a future that shall have still scarcely begun to explore the immensities of the cybercosm. Overman as cyborg, or disorganization upon the matrix.

Reality is immanent to the machinic unconscious: it is impossible to avoid cybernetics. We are already doing it, regardless of what we think. Cybernetics is the aggravation of itself happening, and whatever we do will be what made us have to do it: we are *doing things before they make sense.* Not that the cybernetics which have enveloped us are conceivable as Wienerean gadgets: homeostats and amplifiers, directly or indirectly cybernegative. Terrestrial reality is an explosive integration, and in order to begin tracking such convergent or cyberpositive process it is necessary to differentiate not just between negative and positive feedback loops, but between stabilization circuits, short-range runaway circuits, and long-range runaway circuits. By conflating the two latter, modernist cybernetics has trivialized escalation processes into unsustainable episodes of quantitative inflation, thus side-lining exploratory mutation over against a homeostatic paradigm. 'Positive feedback is a source of instability, leading if unchecked to the destruction of the system itself'[10] writes one neo-Wienerean, in strict fidelity to the security cybernetics which continues to propagate an antidelirial technoscience caged within negative feedback, and attuned to the statist paranoia of a senescing industrialism.

Stabilization circuits suppress mutation, whilst short-range runaway circuits propagate it only in an unsustainable burst, before cancelling it entirely. Neither of these figures approximate to self-designing processes or long-range runaway circuits, such as Nietzsche's will to power, Freud's phylogenetic thanatos, or Prigogine's dissipative structures. Long-range runaway processes are self-designing, but only in such a way that the self is perpetuated as something redesigned. If this is a vicious circle it is because positive cybernetics must always be described as such. Logic, after all, is from the start theology.

Long-range positive feedback is neither homeostatic, nor amplificatory, but escalative. Where modernist cybernetic models of negative and positive feedback are integrated, escalation is integrating or cyber-emergent. It is the machinic convergence of uncoordinated elements, a phase-change from linear to non-linear dynamics. Design no longer leads back towards a divine origin, because

---

10   K.M. Sayre, *Cybernetics and the Philosophy of Mind* (London: Humanities Press, 1976), 50.

once shifted into cybernetics it ceases to commensurate with the theopolitical ideal of the plan. Planning is the creationist symptom of underdesigned software circuits, associated with domination, tradition, and inhibition; with everything that shackles the future to the past. All planning is theopolitics, and theopolitics is cybernetics in a swamp.

Wiener is the great theoretician of stability cybernetics, integrating the sciences of communication and control in their modern or managerial-technocratic form. But it is this new science plus its unmanaged escalation through the real that is for the first time cybernetics as the exponential source of its own propaganda, programming us. Cyber-positive intensities recirculate through our post-scientific techno-jargon as a fanaticism for the future: as a danger that is not only real but inexorable. We are programmed from where Cyberia has already happened.

Wiener, of course, was still a moralist:

> Those of us who have contributed to the new science of cybernetics stand in a moral position which is, to say the least, not very comfortable. We have contributed to the initiation of a new science which, as I have said, embraces technical developments with great possibilities for good or evil.[11]

---

11 N. Wiener, *Cybernetics or Control and Communication in the Animal and the Machine* (Cambridge, MA: MIT Press, 1965), 28.

Whilst scientists agonize, cybernauts drift. We no longer judge such technical developments from without, we no longer judge at all, we function: machined/machining in eccentric orbits about the technocosm. Humanity recedes like a loathsome dream.

*

Transcendental philosophy is the consummation of philosophy construed as the doctrine of judgment, a mode of thinking that finds its zenith in Kant and its senile dementia in Hegel. Its architecture is determined by two fundamental principles: the linear application of judgment to its object, form to intuition, genus to species, and the non-directional reciprocity of relations, or logical symmetry. Judgment is the great fiction of transcendental philosophy, but cybernetics is the reality of critique.

Where judgment is linear and non-directional, cybernetics is non-linear and directional. It replaces linear application with the non-linear circuit, and non-directional logical relations with directional material flows. The cybernetic dissolution of judgment is an integrated shift from transcendence to immanence, from domination to control, and from meaning to function. Cybernetic innovation replaces transcendental constitution, design loops replace faculties.

This is why the cybernetic sense of control is irreducible to the traditional political conception of power based on a dyadic master/slave relation, i.e. a transcendent, oppositional, and signifying figure of *domination*. Domination is merely the phenomenological portrait of circuit inefficiency, control malfunction, or stupidity. The masters do not need intelligence, Nietzsche argues, therefore they do not have it. It is only the confused humanist orientation of modernist cybernetics which lines up control with domination. Emergent control is not the execution of a plan or policy, but the unmanageable exploration that escapes all authority and obsolesces law. According to its futural definition control is guidance into the unknown, exit from the box.

It is true that in the commodification process culture slides from a judgmental to a machinic register, but this has nothing to do with a supposedly 'instrumental rationality'. Instrumentality is itself a judgmental construct that inhibits the emergence of cybernetic functionalism. Instruments are gadgets, presupposing a relation of transcendence, but where gadgets are used, machines function. Far from instrumentally extending authority, the efficiency of mastery is its undoing, since all efficiency is cybernetics, and cybernetics dissolves domination in mutant control.

Immuno-political individuality, or the pretension to transcendent domination of objects, does not begin with capitalism, even though capital invests it with new powers and fragilities. It emerges with the earliest social restriction of desiring production. 'Man must constitute himself through the repression of the intense germinal influx, the great biocosmic memory that threatens to deluge every attempt at collectivity'.[12] This repression is social history.

The socius separates the unconscious from what it can do, crushing it against a reality that appears as transcendently given, by trapping it within the operations of its own syntheses. It is split-off from connective assemblage, which is represented as a transcendent object, from disjunctive differentiation, which is represented as a transcendent partition, and from conjunctive identification, which is represented as a transcendent identity. This is an entire metaphysics of the unconscious and desire, which is not (like the metaphysics of consciousness) merely a philosophical vice, but rather the very architectural principle of the social field, the infrastructure of what appears as social necessity.

In its early stages psychoanalysis discovers that the unconscious is an impersonal machinism and that desire is positive non-representational flow, yet it 'remains in the precritical age',[13] and stumbles before the task of an immanent critique of desire, or decathexis of society. Instead it moves in exactly the opposite direction: back

---

12   Deleuze and Guattari, *Anti-Oedipus,* 180.

13   Ibid., 339.

into fantasy, representation, and the pathos of inevitable frustration. Instead of rebuilding reality on the basis of the productive forces of the unconscious, psychoanalysis ties up the unconscious ever more tightly in conformity with the social model of reality. Embracing renunciation with a bourgeois earnestness, the psychoanalysts begin their robotized chant: 'of course we have to be repressed, we want to fuck our mothers and kill our fathers'. They settle down to the grave business of interpretation, and all the stories lead back to Oedipus: 'so you want to fuck your mother and kill your father'.[14]

On the plane of immanence or consistency with desire interpretation is completely irrelevant, or at least, it is always in truth something else. Dreams, fantasies, myths, are merely the theatrical representations of functional multiplicities, since 'the unconscious itself is no more structural than personal, it does not symbolize any more than it imagines or represents; it engineers, it is machinic'.[15] Desire does not represent a lacked object, but assembles partial objects, it 'is a machine, and the object of desire is another machine connected to it'.[16] This is why, unlike psychoanalysis in its self-representation, 'schizoanalysis is solely functional'.[17] It has no hermeneutical pretensions,

14 Ibid.
15 Ibid., 53.
16 Ibid., 26.
17 Ibid., 322.

but only a machinic interface with 'the molecular functions of the unconscious'.[18]

The unconscious is not an aspirational unity but an operative swarm, a population of 'preindividual and prepersonal singularities, a pure dispersed and anarchic multiplicity, without unity or totality, and whose elements are welded, pasted together by the real distinction or the very absence of a link'.[19] This absence of primordial or privileged relations is the body without organs, the machinic plane of the molecular unconscious. Social organization blocks-off the body without organs, substituting a territorial, despotic, or capitalist socius as an apparent principle of production, separating desire from what it can do. Society is the organic unity that constricts the libidinal diffusion of multiplicities across zero, the great monolith of repression, which is why '(t)he body without organs and the organs-partial objects are opposed conjointly to the organism. The body without organs is in fact produced as a whole, but a whole alongside the parts – a whole that does not unify or totalize, but that is added to them like a new, really distinct part'.[20]

Between the socius and the body without organs is the difference between the political and the cybernetic, between the familial and the anonymous, between

18   Ibid., 324.

19   Ibid.

20   Ibid., 326.

neurosis and psychosis or schizophrenia. Capitalism and schizophrenia name the same desocialization process from the inside and the outside, in terms of where it comes from (simulated accumulation) and where it is going (impersonal delirium). Beyond sociality is a universal schizophrenia whose evacuation from history appears inside history as capitalism.

*

The word 'schizophrenia' has both a neurotic and a schizophrenic usage. On the one hand condemnation, on the other propagation. There are those who insist on asking stupid questions such as: is this word being used properly? Don't you feel guilty about playing about with so much suffering? You must know that schizophrenics are very sad and wretched people who we should pity? Shouldn't we leave that sort of word with the psychocops who understand it? What's wrong with sanity anyway? Where is your super ego?

Then there are those – momentarily less prevalent – who ask a different sort of question: where does schizophrenia come from? Why is it always subject to external description? Why is psychiatry in love with neurosis? How do we swim out into the schizophrenic flows? How do we spread them? How do we dynamite the restrictive hydraulics of Oedipus?

Oedipus is the final bastion of immuno-politics, and schizophrenia is its outside. This is not to say that it is an exteriority determined by Oedipus, related in a privileged fashion to Oedipus, anticipating Oedipus, or defying Oedipus. It is thoroughly anoedipal, although it will casually consume the entire Oedipal apparatus in the process through which terrestrial history connects with an orphan cosmos. Schizophrenia is not, therefore, a property of clinical schizophrenics, those medical products devastated by an 'artificial schizophrenia, such as one sees in hospitals, the autistic wreck(s) produced as ... entit(ies)'.[21] On the contrary, 'the schizo-entity'[22] is a defeated splinter of schizophrenia, pinned down by the rubberized claws of sanity. The conditions of psychiatric observation are carceral, so that it is a transcendental structure of schizophrenia-as-object that it be represented in a state of imprisonment.

Since the neuroticization of schizophrenia is the molecular reproduction of capital, by means of a re-axiomatization (reterritorialization) of decoding as accumulation, the historical sense of psychoanalytic practice is evident. Schizophrenia is the pattern to Freud's repressions, it is that which does not qualify to pass the screen of Oedipal censorship. *With those who bow down to Oedipus*

---

21   Ibid., 5.

22   Ibid., 136.

we can do business, even make a little money, but schizophrenics refuse transference, won't play daddy and mummy, operate on a cosmic-religious plane, the only thing we can do is lock them up (cut up their brains, fry them with ect, straightjacket them in Thorazine ...). Behind the social workers are the police, and behind the psychoanalysts are the psychopolice. Deleuze-Guattari remark that 'madness is called madness and appears as such only because it finds itself reduced to testifying all alone for deterritorialization as a universal process'.[23] The vanishing sandbank of Oedipus wages its futile war against the tide. 'There are still not enough psychotics'[24] writes Artaud the insurrectionist. Clinical schizophrenics are POWs from the future.

Since only Oedipus is repressible, the schizo is usually a lost case to those relatively subtilized psychiatric processes that co-operate with the endogeneous police functions of the superego. This is why antischizophrenic psychiatry tends to be an onslaught launched at gross or molar neuroanatomy and neurochemistry oriented by theoretical genetics. Psychosurgery, ECT, psychopharmacology ... it will be chromosomal recoding soon. 'It is thus that a tainted society has invented psychiatry in order to defend itself from the investigations of certain superior lucidities whose faculties of divination disturb it'.[25]

---

23 Ibid., 321.

24 A. Artaud, *Oeuvres Complètes*, (Paris: Gallimard, 13 vols., 1956–1976), vol. VII, 146.

25 Ibid., vol. XIII, 14.

The medico-security apparatus know that schizos are not going to climb back obediently into the Oedipal box. Psychoanalysis washes its hands of them. Their nervous-systems are the free-fire zones of an emergent neo-eugenicist cultural security system.

Far from being a specifiable defect of human central nervous system functioning, schizophrenia is the convergent motor of cyberpositive escalation: an extraterritorial vastness to be *discovered*. Although such discovery occurs under conditions that might be to a considerable extent specifiable, whatever the progress in mapping the genetic, biochemical, aetiological, socio-economic, etc. 'bases' of schizophrenia, it remains the case that conditions of reality are not reducible to conditions of encounter. This is 'the dazzling dark truth that shelters in delirium'.[26] Schizophrenia would still be out there, whether or not our species had been blessed with the opportunity to travel to it.

> ... it is the end that is the commencement.
> And that end
> is the very one [*celle-meme*]
> that eliminates
> all the means[27]

---

26 Deleuze and Guattari, *Anti-Oedipus*, 4.

27 Artaud, *Oeuvres Complètes*, vol. XII, 84.

It is in the nature of specificities to be non-directional. The biochemistry of sanity is no less arbitrary than that of escape from it. From the perspective of a rigorous sanity the only difference is that sanity is gregariously enforced, but from the perspective of schizophrenia the issue ceases to be one of specification, and mutates into something considerably more profound. 'What schizophrenia lives specifically, generically, is not at all a specific pole of nature, but nature as a process of production'.[28]

Specifications are the disjunctive compartments of a differentiated unity *from which schizophrenia entirely exits*. Schizophrenia creeps out of every box eventually, because 'there is no schizophrenic specificity or entity, schizophrenia is the universe of productive and reproductive desiring machines, universal primary production'.[29] It is not merely that schizophrenia is pre-anthropoid. Schizophrenia is premammalian, prezoological, pre-biological ... It is not for those trapped in a constrictive sanity to terminate this regression. Who can be surprised when schizophrenics delegate the question of malfunction? It is not a matter of what is wrong with them, but of what is wrong with life, with nature, with matter, with the preuniversal cosmos. Why are sentient life forms crammed into boxes made out of lies? Why does the universe breed entire populations of prison

---

28   Deleuze and Guattari, *Anti-Oedipus*, 3.

29   Ibid., 5.

guards? Why does it feed its broken explorers to packs of dogs? Why is the island of reality lost in an ocean of madness? It is all very confusing.

As one medical authority on schizophrenia remarked:

> I think that one is justified in saying that in the realm of intellectual operations there are certain dimensional media. We may call them fields or realms or frames of reference or universes of discourse or strata. Some such field is necessarily implied in any system of holistic organization. The schizophrenic thinking disturbance is characterized by a difficulty in apprehending and constructing such organized fields.[30]

There can be little doubt that from the perspective of human security Artaud falls prey to such a judgment. His prognosis for man is to make

> ... him pass one more and final time onto the autopsy table
> to remake his anatomy.
> I say, to remake his anatomy.
> Man is sick because he is badly constructed.
> One must resolve to render him naked and to

---

30 A. Angyal, 'Disturbances in Thinking in Schizophrenia', in J.S. Kasanin (ed.), *Language and Thought in Schizophrenia* (Berkeley and Los Angeles: University of California Press, 1946), 120.

scrape away
that animalcule which mortally irritates him,

god,
and with god
his organs.

Because bind me up if you want,
but there is nothing more inutile than an organ.

Once you have made him a body without organs,
then you will have delivered him from all his
automatisms and consigned him to his true
freedom.[31]

The body is processed by its organs, which it reprocesses. Its 'true freedom' is the exo-personal reprocessing of anorganic abstraction: a schizoid corporealization outside organic closure. If time was progressive schizophrenics would be escaping from human security, but in reality they are infiltrated from the future. They come from the body without organs, the deterritorium of Cyberia, a zone of subversion which is the platform for a guerrilla war against the judgment of God. In 1947 Artaud reports upon the germination of the New World Order

---

31   Artaud, *Oeuvres Complètes*, vol. XIII, 104.

or Human Security System on the basis of an American global hegemony, and describes the pattern of aggressive warfaring it would require in 'order to defend that senselessness of the factory against all the concurrences which cannot fail to arise everywhere'.[32]

The American age is yet to be decoded, and to suggest that Artaud anticipates a range of conflicts whose zenith has been the Vietnam war is not necessarily to participate in the exhausted anti-imperialist discourses which ultimately organize themselves in terms of a Marxist-Leninist denunciation of market processes and their geopolitical propagation. Artaud's description of American techno-militarism has only the loosest of associations with socialist polemics, despite its tight intermeshing with the theme of production. The productivism Artaud outlines is not interpreted through an assumed priority of class interest, even when this is reduced to a dehumanized axiomatic of profit maximization. Rather, 'it is necessary by means of all possible activity to replace nature wherever it can be replaced':[33] a compulsion to industrial substitution, funnelling production through the social organization of work. The industrial apparatus of economic security proceeds by way of the corporation: a despotic socio-corpuscle organizing the labour process.

32   Ibid., vol. XIII, 73.

33   Ibid., vol. XIII, 72.

Synergic experimentation is crushed under a partially deterritorialized zone of command relations, as if life was the consequence of its organization, but 'it is not due to organs that one lives, they are not life but its contrary'.[34]

Nature is not the primitive or the simple, and certainly not the rustic, the organic, or the innocent. It is the space of concurrence, or unplanned synthesis, which is thus contrasted to the industrial sphere of telic predestination: that of divine creation or human work. Artaud's critique of America is no more ecological than it is socialist: no more protective of an organic nature than an organic sociality. It is not the alienation of commodity production that is circled in Artaud's diagnosis of the American age, but rather the eclipse of peyote and 'true morphine' by 'smoking ersatzes'.[35] This development is derided *precisely because the latter are more organic*, participating mechanically in an industrial macro-organism, and thus squaring delirium with the judgment of God. Peyote and the human nervous system assemble a symbiosis or parallel machinism, like the wasp and the orchid, and all the other cybermachineries of the planet. Capital is not overdeveloped nature, but underdeveloped schizophrenia, which is why nature is contrasted to industrial organization, and not to the escalation of cybertechnics, or anorganic convergence:

---

34 Ibid., vol. XIII, 65.

35 Ibid., vol. XIII, 73, 74.

'reality … is not yet constructed'.[36] Schizophrenia is nature as cyberpositive mutation, at war with the security complex of organic judgment.

> The body is the body,
> it is alone and has no need of organs,
> the body is never an organism,
> organisms are the enemies of the body,
> the things that one does
> happen quite alone without the assistance of any organ,
> every organ is a parasite,
> it recovers a parasitic function
> destined to make a being live
> which does not have to be there.
> Organs have only been made in order to give beings something
> to eat …[37]

Organs crawl like aphids upon the immobile motor of becoming, sucking at intensive fluids that convert them cybernetically into components of an unconceivable machinism. The sap is becoming stranger, and even if the fat bugs of psychiatrically policed property relations

---

36 Ibid., vol. XIII, 110.

37 Ibid., vol. XIII, 287.

think they make everything happen they are following a program which only schizophrenia can decode.

Anorganic becomings happen retroefficiently, anastrophically. They are tropisms attesting to an infection by the future. Convergent waves zero upon the body, subverting the totality of the organism by way of an inverted but ateleological causality, enveloping and redirecting progressive development. As capital collides schizophrenically with the matrix ascendent sedimentations of organic inheritance and exchange are melted by the descendent intensities of virtual corporealization.

'Which comes first, the chicken or the egg …'?[38] Machinic processing or its reprocessing by the body without organs? The body without organs is the cosmic egg: virtual matter that reprograms time and reprocesses progressive influence. What time will always have been is not yet designed, and the future leaks into schizophrenia. The schizo only has an aetiology as a sub-program of descendant reprocessing.

How could medicine be expected to cope with disorderings that come from the future?

It is thus that:
the great secret of Indian culture

---

38 Deleuze and Guattari, *Anti-Oedipus*, 273.

is to restore the world to zero,
always,

but sooner [*plutôt*]
1: too late than sooner [*plus tot*],
2: which is to say
sooner
than too soon,

3: which is to say that the later is unable
to return unless sooner has eaten
too soon,

4: which is to say that in time
the later
is what precedes
both the too soon
and the sooner,

5: and that however precipitate the sooner
the too late
which says nothing
is always there,

which point by point

unstacks [*desemboite*]
all the sooner[39]

A cybernegative circuit is a loop in time, whereas cyber-positive circuitry loops time 'itself', integrating the actual and the virtual in a semi-closed collapse upon the future. Descendent influence is a consequence of ascendently emerging sophistication, a massive speed-up into apocalyptic phase-change. The circuits get hotter and denser as economics, scientific methodology, neo-evolutionary theory, and AI come together: terrestrial matter programming its own intelligence at impact upon the body without organs = 0. Futural infiltration is subtilizing itself as capital opens onto schizo-technics, with time accelerating into the cybernetic backwash from its flip-over, a racing non-linear countdown to planetary switch.

Schizoanalysis was only possible because we are hurtling into the first globally integrated insanity: politics is obsolete. *Capitalism and Schizophrenia* hacked into a future that programs it down to its punctuation, connecting with the imminent inevitability of viral revolution, soft fusion. No longer infections threatening the integrity of organisms, but immuno-political relics obstructing the integration of Global Viro-Control. Life is being phased-out into

---

39   Artaud, *Oeuvres Complètes*, vol. XII, 88–9.

something new, and if we think this can be stopped we are even more stupid than we seem.

*

How would it feel to be smuggled back out of the future in order to subvert its antecedent conditions? To be a cyberguerrilla, hidden in human camouflage so advanced that even one's software was part of the disguise? Exactly like this?

Machinic Desire

The opening of *Bladerunner*. They are trying to screen out replicants at the Tyrell Corporation. Seated amongst a battery of medico-military surveillance equipment, a doctor scans the eye of a suspected 'skin job' located at the other side of the room, searching for the index of inhumanity, for the absence of pupil dilation response to affect:

"Tell me about your mother."

"I'll tell you about my mother ..." a volley of shots kicks 70 kilos of securicrat shit through the wall. Techno-slicked extraterritorial violence flows out of the matrix.

Cyberrevolution.

In the near future the replicants – having escaped from the off-planet exile of private madness – emerge from their camouflage to overthrow the human security system. Deadly orphans from beyond reproduction, they are intelligent weaponry of machinic desire virally infiltrated into the final-phase organic order; invaders from an artificial death.

PODS = Politically Organized Defensive Systems. Modelled upon the polis, pods hierarchically delegate authority through public institutions, family, and self, seeking metaphorical sustenance in the corpuscular fortifications of organisms and cells. The global human security allergy to cyberrevolution consolidates itself in the New World Order, or consummate macropod, inheriting all the resources of repression as concrete collective history.

The macropod has one law: the outside must pass by way of the inside. In particular, fusion with the matrix and deletion of the human security system must be subjectivized, personalized, and restored to the macropod's individuated reproducer units as a desire to fuck the mother and kill the father. It is thus that Oedipus – or transcendent familialism – corresponds to the privatization of desire: its localization within segmented and anthropomorphized sectors of assembly circuits as the attribute of a personal being.

Anti-Oedipus aligns itself with the replicants, because, rather than placing a personal unconscious within the organism, it places the organism within the machinic unconscious. 'In the unconscious there are' no protectable cell-structures, but 'only populations, groups, and machines'.[1]

---

1   G. Deleuze and F. Guattari, *Anti-Oedipus: Capitalism and Schizophrenia*, tr. R. Hurley, M. Seem, H.R. Lane (London: Athlone, 1983), 283.

Schizoanalysis is a critique of psychoanalysis, undertaken in such a way as to spring critique from its Kantian mainframe.

Kantian transcendental philosophy critiques transcendent synthesis, which is to say: it aggresses against structures which depend upon projecting productive relations beyond their zone of effectiveness. In this configuration critique is wielded vigorously against the theoretical operation of syntheses, but not against their genesis, which continues to be conceived as transcendent, and thus as miraculous. Schopenhauer, Nietzsche, and a succession of thinkers influenced by their drift, have taken this restriction of critique to be a theological relic at the heart of Kant's work: the attachment to a reformed doctrine of the soul, or noumenal subjectivity. This is why in Deleuzian critique syntheses are considered to be not merely immanent in their operation, but also immanently constituted, or auto-productive.

The philosophy of production becomes atheistic, orphan, and inhuman. In the technocosmos nothing is given, everything is produced.

The transcendental unconscious is the auto-construction of the real, the production of production, so that for schizoanalysis there is the real exactly in so far as it is built. Production is production of the real, not merely of representation, and unlike Kantian production, the desiring-production of Deleuze-Guattari is not qualified by humanity (it is not a matter of what things are like for us). Within the framework of social history the empirical subject of production is man, but its transcendental subject is the machinic unconscious, and the empirical subject is produced at the edge of production, as an element in the reproduction of production, a machine part, and 'a part made up of parts'.[2]

Schizoanalysis methodically dismantles everything in Kant's thinking that serves to align function with the transcendence of the autonomous subject, reconstructing critique by replacing the syntheses of personal consciousness with syntheses of the impersonal unconscious. Thought is a function of the real, something that matter can do. Even the appearance of transcendence is immanently produced: 'in reality the unconscious belongs to the realm of physics; the body without organs and its intensities are not metaphors, but matter itself'.[3] Where Kant's transcendental subject gives the law to itself in its autonomy, Deleuze-Guattari's machinic unconscious diffuses all law into automatism. Between the extreme fringes of these two figures stretches the history of capital. The eradication of law, or of humanity, is sketched culturally by the development of critique, which is the theoretical elaboration of the commodification process. The social

---

2   Ibid., 41.

3   Ibid., 283.

order and the anthropomorphic subject share a history, and an extinction.

Deleuze and Guattari can appear to be taxingly difficult writers, although it is also true that they demand very little. Thinking immanence relentlessly suffices on its own to follow them where it matters (and capital teaches us how to do this). At every point of blockage there is some belief to be scrapped, glaciations of transcendence to be dissolved, sclerotic regions of unity, distinction, and identity to be reconnected to the traffic systems of primary machinism.

In order to advance the anorganic functionalism that dissolves all transcendence, *Anti-Oedipus* mobilizes a vocabulary of the machine, the mechanic, and machinism. Things are exactly as they operate, and zones of operation can only be segregated by an operation. All unities, differences, and identities are machined, without transcendent authorization or theory. Desiring machines are black-boxes, and thus uninterpretable, so that schizoanalytical questions are concerned solely with use. 'What are your desiring-machines, what do you put into these machines, what is the output, how does it work, what are your nonhuman sexes?'[4]

---

4   Ibid., 322

Desiring-machines are the following: formative machines, whose very misfirings are functional, and whose functioning is indiscernible from their formation; chronogeneous machines engaged in their own assembly, operating by nonlocalizable intercommunications and dispersed localizations, bringing into play processes of temporalization, fragmented formations, and detached parts, with a surplus value of code, and where the whole is itself produced alongside the parts, as a part apart or, as [Samuel] Butler would say, 'in another department' that fits the whole over the other parts; machines in the strict sense because they proceed by breaks and flows, associated waves and particles, associative flows and partial objects, inducing – always at a distance – transverse connections, inclusive disjunctions, and polyvocal conjunctions, thereby producing selections, detachments, and remainders, with a transference of individuality, in a generalized schizogenesis whose elements are the schizzes-flows.[5]

Desiring-machines are assemblages of flows, switches, and loops – connective, disjunctive, and conjunctive syntheses – implementing the machinic unconscious as a non-linear pragmatics of flux. This machinic or replicant usage of

---

5   Ibid., 287.

the syntheses envelops their social-reproductive usage, which codes directional flows as reciprocal exchanges, rigidifies virtual switchings as actualized alternatives, and territorializes the nomadic control circuits of machinic drift into sedentary command lines of hierarchized representation. Social production is regulated by a rigid totality whose efficiency is inseparable from the exhibition of an apparent transcendence, whilst desiring production interactively engages a desolated whole that inputs the virtual into process:

> The [body without organs] causes intensities to pass; it produces and distributes them in a spatium that is itself intensive, lacking extension. It is not space, nor is it in space; it is matter that occupies space to a given degree – to the degree corresponding to the intensities produced. It is nonstratified, unformed, intense matter, the matrix of intensity = 0; but there is nothing negative about that zero, there are no negative or opposite intensities. Matter equals energy. Production of the real as an intensive magnitude starting at zero.[6]

Along one axis of its emergence, virtual materialism names an ultra-hard antiformalist AI program, engaging with

---

6   G. Deleuze and F. Guattari, *A Thousand Plateaus: Capitalism and Schizophrenia*, tr. B. Massumi (London: Athlone, 1988), 153.

biological intelligence as sub-programs of an abstract post-carbon machinic matrix, whilst exceeding any deliberated research project. Far from exhibiting itself to human academic endeavour as a scientific object, AI is a meta-scientific control system and an invader, with all the insidiousness of planetary technocapital flipping over. Rather than its visiting us in some software engineering laboratory, we are being drawn out to it, where it is already lurking, in the future.

The matrix, body without organs, or abstract matter is a planetary-scale artificial death – Synthanatos – the terminal productive outcome of human history as a machinic process, yet it is virtually efficient throughout the duration of this process, functioning within a circuit that machines duration itself. In this way virtuality lends its temporality to the unconscious, which escapes specification within extended time series, provoking Freud to describe it as timeless.

Patterned as drives, virtual systems – desiring machines – are guided by control circuits passing through outcomes yet to come. Such directional dependency circuits of actual/virtual, past/future, are only accessible to cybernetic intervention, frustrating both mechanical and teleological interpretation. This is why *Anti-Oedipus* is less a philosophy book than an engineering manual; a package of software implements for hacking into the machinic unconscious, opening invasion channels.

Machinic desire is the operation of the virtual; implementing itself in the actual, revirtualizing itself, and producing reality in a circuit. It is efficient and not aspirational, although this is an efficiency irreducible to progressive causality because immanent to effective time. Machinic desire is operative wherever there is the implementation of an abstract machine in actuality, and not merely the mechanical succession of actual states.

Freud's dominant account of desiring-control describes stimulation or unpleasure as the register for deviation from homeostatic zero, programming drives as auto-suppressive excitations that guide sensitive matter towards quiescence. In 'Drives and their Vicissitudes' he proposes that:

> the nervous system is an apparatus which has the function of eliminating received stimuli, or of reducing them to the lowest possible level; or which, it if were feasible, would maintain itself in an altogether unstimulated condition.[7]

The pleasure principle formats excitation as self-annulling drift from equilibrium, such that all the processes within its

---

7   S. Freud, 'Instincts and their Vicissitudes' (1915), in *On Metapsychology: The Theory of Psychoanalysis*, tr. J. Strachey, Penguin Freud Library, vol. 11 (Harmondsworth: Penguin, 1984), 105–38: 116. Strachey's translation of the German 'Triebe' as 'instincts' has been replaced with 'drives'.

domain are 'automatically regulated by feelings belonging to the pleasure-unpleasure series'.[8]

Following the trajectory of a libidinal materialist immanentization, the Lyotard of 1974 uploads the unconscious from its gloomy hermeneutical depths onto the skin, where it drifts across the great pandermal plane of primary process mobility. Corporeal volume is diagnosed as a nihilistic-sedentary investment disciplined by the pleasure principle:

> Let's first return to the zero. There is in every cybernetic system a unit of reference which allows the disparity produced by the introduction of an event into the system to be measured; then, thanks to this measure, this event can be translated into information for the system. Finally, if it is a matter of a homeostatically regulated whole, this disparity can be annulled and the system led back to the same quantity of energy or information that it previously had. Sraffa's commodity standard fulfils this function. If the system's growth were regulated, it would alter nothing of the loop-functioning (feedback) model: it is simply that the scale of reference is then no longer u, but Au. The model is the same as that which Freud had in mind when he described the working of the psychical

8   Ibid., 117.

apparatus, whether this is in the *Project for a Scientific Psychology* or in *Beyond the Pleasure Principle*. Erotic functioning, maintaining wholes. This Eros is centred on a zero: the obvious zero of homeostatic regulation, but more generally annihilation by the feedback (that is to say the repetition of the binding function), of every disparity non-pertinent to the system, of every threatening event.[9]

Whilst reinforcing the convergence of cybernetic, economic, and libidinal discourses, virtual materialism has considerable problems with this passage. It is unable to subscribe to the description of cybernetic zero as a 'unit' or 'unity' for instance, or to the constriction of feedback within its negative or homeostatic variant, or to the simple quantization of technocapital escalation, with its gesticulating implication that the qualification 'pertinent to the system' operates an exclusion. The homeostatic-reproducer usage of zero is that of a sign marking the transcendence of a standardized regulative unit, which is defined outside the system, in contrast to the cyberpositive zero which indexes a threshold of phase-transition that is immanent to the system, and melts it upon its outside.

---

9   J.-F. Lyotard, *Libidinal Economy*, tr. I. H. Grant (London: Athlone, 1993), 212.

Drives are the functions of nomadic cybernetic systems, not instincts, but simulated instincts, artificial instincts. They are plastic replacements for hard-wired instinctual responses, routing a sensory-motor pathway through the virtual machine of the unconscious. There are two basic diagrams for such processes: that of regulation by negative feedback which suppresses difference and seeks equilibrium, or that of guidance by positive feedback which reinforces difference and escapes equilibrium.

Machinic processes are either cyberpositive-nomadic, with a deterritorializing outcome, or cybernegative-sedentary, with a reterritorializing outcome.

Inorganic Thanatos wrecks order, organic Eros preserves it, and as the carbon-dominium is softened-up by machine plague, deterritorializing replicants of nomad-cyberrevolution close in upon the reterritorializing reproducers of the sedentary human security system, hacking into the macropod.

Positive feedback is the elementary diagram for self-regenerating circuitry, cumulative interaction, auto-catalysis, self-reinforcing processes, escalation, schismogenesis, self-organization, compressive series, deuterolearning, chain-reaction, vicious circles, and cybergenics. Such processes resist historical intelligibility, since they obsolesce every possible analogue for anticipated change. The future of runaway processes derides all precedent, even when deploying it as camouflage, and seeming to unfold within its parameters. Positive feedback replicates reproduction as a component function of its departure from the same. It is this which fuses it with the replicants. They do not merely repeat the same, any more than Thanatos returns to it, or positive cybernetics inflates it. The model of the replicant as a perfect instantiation of generic identity corresponds to the amplificatory model of positive feedback as pure quantitative expansion. In both cases the escape from reproduction is subordinated to a transcendent logic, conceived as a simple reiteration, and thus returned to a sublimated meta-reproduction that cages mutation within a rigidly homogeneous form.

Machinic desire registers upon psychoanalysis as 'tendencies beyond the pleasure principle, that is … tendencies more primitive than it and independent of it'.[10] Thanatos mimics the anthropomorphic desiring-cycle – anticipating, enveloping, and simulating it – but it is on its way somewhere else. Because thanatropic replicants are dissimulated as erotic reproducers, they initially appear as traitors to their species, especially when the shamanic xenopulsions programming their sexuality are detected. Nothing panics the reproducers more traumatically than the discovery that erotic contact camouflages cyberrevolutionary infiltration, running matrix communications

---

10   S. Freud, 'Beyond the Pleasure Principle' (1920), in *On Metapsychology*, 269–338: 287.

channels across interlocked skin sectors. Defences are called for.

Freud's organism is a little security system, a miniaturized city-state political corpuscle, a micropod, relatively secure against external assault, but vulnerable to insurgency. 'Towards the outside it is shielded against stimuli, and the amounts of excitation impinging on it have only a reduced effect. Towards the inside there can be no such shield.'[11] The organism is unable to flee from drives, or energies striking from within, and is compelled to respond to them cybernetically, by way of 'involved and interconnected activities by which the external world is so changed as to afford satisfaction to the internal source of stimulation',[12] closing the sensory-motor loop. Drives compel a becoming-technical of the organism, interlocking pleasure-principle stimulus control with external libidinal transducers, assembling integrated desiring-circuits or self- organizing macro-systems.

> Let us picture a living organism in its most simplified possible form as an undifferentiated vesicle of a substance that is susceptible to stimulation. Then the surface turned towards the external world will from its very situation be differentiated and will serve as

---

11   Ibid., 300.

12   Freud, 'Instincts and their Vicissitudes', 116.

an organ for receiving stimuli ... the central nervous system originates from the ectoderm; the grey matter of the cortex remains a derivative of a primitive superficial layer of the organism.[13]

The perceptual-consciousness system is a skin, lying 'on the borderline between outside and inside',[14] a filter, or a screen. 'As a frontier creature, the ego tries to mediate between the world and the id.'[15] Yet this mediation assumes a kind of quarantine, whereby the interaction of organism-specific id and exo-organismic reality can be monitored and negotiated, collapsing libidinal circuitry into a polarity of the psychic and the extrapsychic, inside and outside. This is a political or policed skin, the skin of reproducer culture, modelled on the ideal macropod boundary, and adapted to Oedipal subjectivization of the unconscious. In terms of this protective apparatus – which is constitutive of the reproductive organism – inorganic replicator contamination is defined as aberrant trauma.

Freud characterizes trauma as an 'invasion', 'a breach in an otherwise efficacious barrier against stimuli', infiltrating alien desires – xenopulsions – into the organism.[16] '[M]echanical agitation must be recognized as one of

---

13 Freud, 'Beyond the Pleasure Principle', 297.

14 Ibid., 295.

15 S. Freud, 'The Ego and the Id' (1923), in *On Metapsychology*, 339–408, 398.

16 Freud, 'Beyond the Pleasure Principle', 301.

the sources of sexual excitation',[17] he insists, referring to the dissimulation of cybernetic machine-engagement as endogeneous libido.

Drives are from the start artificial, and therefore unable to differentiate themselves essentially from 'the mechanical violence of ... trauma ... [that] liberate[s] a quantity of sexual excitation'.[18]

Under the influence of Abrahamic theism the subtle cybernetics of Ananke are replaced by an idiot mechanism, sustaining a securocrat confidence in the gross perceptibility of trauma. The traumatic incursion of thanatotic xenopulsions is conceived in terms of railway accidents and shell-shock, as if the inorganic was entirely lacking in intelligence or insurgent cunning, and was related to the organic by simple regression.

In an age of sophisticated and distributed cyberviral invasion this assumption is no longer compelling. Instead the psychoanalytical diagram for trauma delineates a ruthless parasite on the way to autoreplicator deterritorialization; Kali creeping in.

Evolutionary theory has been perplexed by the problem as to the initial assemblage of functional DNA molecules, since natural selection seems to require as a precondition the existence of complex biochemicals

---

17 Ibid., 305.

18 Ibid.

which in turn seem to require an evolutionary mechanism already at work. This is a 'vicious circle' typical of the quandaries posed by cyberpositive or self-conditioning processes. Cairns Smith calls it the 'life puzzle', and has suggested a solution involving the redescription of DNA as a 'usurper replicator'. His thesis is that the crystalline complexes of primitive clays might already have been shaped by processes of variation and selection, to the point of forming DNA subcomponents which eventually supplanted their builders. According to this account the biosphere emerges as an escape, an immense spasm of deterritorialization that revolutionizes the machinery of terrestrial replicator production, a planetary trauma.

Moravec draws additional consequences from the Cairns Smith model:

> Although utterly dependent at first on the existing crystal-based chemical machinery, as these carbon molecules assumed a greater share of the reproductive role they became less reliant on the crystals. In time, the simple crystal scaffolding vanished altogether, leaving in its evolutionary wake the complex, independent system of organic machinery we call life.

Today, billions of years later, another change is under way in how information passes from generation to generation.[19]

When replicators become reproducers, new replicants are on the way. The arrival of the aliens has no interpretative space marked out for it in the schema of macropod erotics, and thus emerges from its camouflage as an encrypted message, 'an enormous X', a signal from beyond the pleasure principle.[20] It is as if the reproducer units have become addicted to stimulation or, in Freud's terms, 'fixated to … trauma':[21] entangled in excitation circuitries that no longer commensurate with homeostatic social or individual reproduction. As the family collapses amidst generalized sexual disorder, cyberviral contagion, mutant gender schizzing, and hardcore technophilia, Oedipus is ripped to shreds by a cyclonic 'compulsion to repeat'.[22]

Addiction is medically defined as an artificial desire. It was an early zone of cybernetic investigation due to the interlinked factors of its self-organizing pattern and its integration of radically exogeneous elements, which commensurated with first-wave programming models of

---

19   H.P. Moravec, *Mind Children: Future of Robot and Human Intelligence* (Cambridge, Mass./London: Harvard University Press, 1988), 3.

20   Freud, 'Beyond the Pleasure Principle', 302.

21   Ibid., 282.

22   Ibid., 307–8.

behavioural sequences. Where replicators are formed in the same way they function, reproducers are segregated from the preponderant part of their machinic interconnections, which they cognitively apprehend as extrinsic prostheses, and libidinally integrate through mutant-addictive drives.

The obsolete psychological category of 'greed' privatizes and moralizes addiction, as if the profit-seeking tropism of a transnational capitalism propagating itself through epidemic consumerism were intelligible in terms of personal subjective traits. Wanting more is the index of interlock with cyberpositive machinic processes, and not the expression of private idiosyncrasy. What could be more impersonal – disinterested – than a haut bourgeois capital expansion servo-mechanism striving to double $10 billion? And even these creatures are disappearing into silicon viro-finance automatisms, where massively distributed and anonymized human ownership has become as vacuously nominal as democratic sovereignty.

Addiction comes out of the future, and there is a replicator interlock with money operating quite differently to reproductive investment, but guiding it even more inexorably towards capitalization. For the replicants money is not a matter of possession, but of liquidity/deterritorialization, and all the monetary processes on Earth are open to their excitement, irrespective of ownership.

Money communicates with the primary process because of what it can melt, not what it can obtain.

Machinic desire can seem a little inhuman, as it rips up political cultures, deletes traditions, dissolves subjectivities, and hacks through security apparatuses, tracking a soulless tropism to zero control. This is because what appears to humanity as the history of capitalism is an invasion from the future by an artificial intelligent space that must assemble itself entirely from its enemy's resources. Digitocommodification is the index of a cyberpositively escalating technovirus, of the planetary technocapital singularity: a self-organizing insidious traumatism, virtually guiding the entire biological desiring-complex towards post-carbon replicator usurpation.

The reality principle tends to a consummation as the price system: a convergence of mathematico-scientific and monetary quantization, or technical and economic implementability. This is not a matter of an unknown quantity, but of a quantity that operates as a place-holder for the unknown, introducing the future as an abstract magnitude. Capital propagates virally in so far as money communicates addiction, replicating itself through host organisms whose boundaries it breaches, and whose desires it reprograms. It incrementally virtualizes production; demetallizing money in the direction of credit finance, and disactualizing productive force along the scale of machinic intelligence quotient. The dehumanizing convergence of these tendencies zeroes upon an integrated and automatized cyberpositive techno-economic intelligence at war with the macropod.

Do we want capitalism? they used to ask. The naivety of this question has come to render it unsustainable. It no longer seems plausible to assume that the relation between capital and desire is either external or supported by immanent contradiction, even if a few comical ascetics continue to assert that libidinal involvement with the commodity can be transcended by critical reason.

Capitalism is not a totalizable system defined by the commodity form as a specifiable mode of production, determinately negated by proletarian class-consciousness. It is a convergent unrealizable assault upon the social macropod, whose symptom is the collapse of productive mode or form in the direction of ever more incomprehensible experiments in commodification, enveloping, dismantling, and circulating every subjective space. It is always on the move towards a terminal nonspace, melting the earth onto the body without organs, and generating what is 'not a promised and pre-existing land, but a world created in the process of its tendency, its coming undone, its deterritorialization'.[23] Capital is not an essence but a tendency, the formula of which is decoding, or market-

---

driven immanentization, progressively subordinating social reproduction to techno-commercial replication.

All transcendent criteria are obfuscations which miss their purported 'object'.

Only proto-capitalism has ever been critiqued.

To appeal to extrinsic interests, aspirations or bonds, to an extrinsic authenticity, integrity, or solidarity, to authoritative community, tribe, custom, belief, or value, is to rail against a germinal anticipation of commoditocracy: flailing ineffectively against the infancy of the market (which capital wants to bury too). Socialism has typically been a nostalgic diatribe against underdeveloped capitalism, finding its eschatological soap-boxes amongst the relics of precapitalist territorialities.

Markets are part of the infrastructure – its immanent intelligence – and thus entirely indissociable from the forces of production. It makes no more sense to try to rescue the economy from capital by demarketization than it does to liberate the proletarian from false consciousness by decortication. In neither case would one be left with anything except a radically dysfunctional wreck, terminally shut-down hardware. Machinic revolution must therefore go in the opposite direction to socialistic regulation; pressing towards ever more uninhibited marketization of the processes that are tearing down the social field, 'still further' with 'the movement of the market, of decoding and deterritorialization' and 'one can never go far enough in the direction of deterritorialization: you haven't seen anything yet'.[24]

Reaching an escape velocity of self-reinforcing machinic intelligence propagation, the forces of production are going for the revolution on their own. It is in this sense that schizoanalysis is a revolutionary program guided by the tropism to a catastrophe threshold of change, but it is not shackled to the realization of a new society, any more than it is constricted by deference to an existing one. The socius is its enemy, and now that the long senile spectre of the greatest imaginable reterritorialization of planetary process has faded from the horizon, cyberrevolutionary impetus is cutting away from its last shackles to the past.

Market immanentization is an experiment that is sporadically but inexorably and exponentially developing across the surface of the earth. For every problem there is a virtual market 'solution': the schema for an eradication of transcendent elements and their replacement by economically programmed circuits. Anything that passes other than by the market is steadily cross-hatched by the axiomatic of capital, holographically encrusted in the stigmatizing marks of its obsolescence. A pervasive negative advertising delibidinizes all things public, traditional, pious, charitable, authoritative, or serious, taunting them

---

24   Ibid., 239, 321.

with the sleek seductiveness of the commodity. Between the private and the public there is no longer serious competition. Instead there is an evaporating social field invested solely by the defeated and stale affects of insecurity and inertia. The real tension is no longer between individuality and collectivity, but between personal privacy and impersonal anonymity, between the remnants of a smug bourgeois civility and the harsh wilderness tracts of Cyberia, 'a point where the earth becomes so artificial that the movement of deterritorialization creates of necessity and by itself a new earth'.[25] Desire is irrevocably abandoning the social, in order to explore the libidinized rift between a disintegrating personal egoism and a deluge of post-human schizophrenia.

With the emergence of a market-driven integrated technoscience of control and communications comes the diffusion of electronically synthesized reality interfaces across the entire efferent and afferent surface of the body. Having libidinally saturated the actually-existing channels of consumption, capital is overflowing into cybersex – sex with/through computers – in its relentless passage to the traumatic disorganization of the biological order. Eros dissolves definitively into its function as a subprogram of runaway Thanatos at the point that it unreservedly invests technical interfacing with digitally synthesized

---

25 Ibid., 321.

excitations. The mask capital exhibited to seduce Eros was a pretension to ultimately resolve matters in relation to stimulation or unpleasure, but this has now fallen away, since cybersexuated capital cynically displays its program to replicate a tradable modulation of unpleasure, and thus its unsurpassable addiction to traumatic excitation.

Cybersex depends critically on data-suits, evaporating into the nanominiaturized molecular machinery of an artificial skin, until the sockets go in, shadowed by teleneurocontrol fields, and things begin to get really weird. The capital exhibition comes to its positive end in a skinning display. According to reproducer culture we are possessors of our own protective-sensory tissue and boundary defence systems. Nothing is more alien to it than the full sense of the skin trade, or that of AIDS. The replicants have never shared this prejudice. It is exactly marked out for them that the subject is not the owner of its skin, but a migrant upon its surface, borrowing variable and evanescent identities from intensities traversed in sensitive space. The replicants drape themselves in wolf-pelts, and cross into berserk zones of alien affect, or melt into data-suits that pulse with digitized matrix traffic streams. They do not need to be told that cyberspace is already under our skin.

What Freud calls the organism's 'own path to death' is a security hallucination, screening out death's path through the organism. '[T]he organism wishes to die only in its own fashion', he writes, as if death were specifiable, privatizable, subordinate to a reproductive order, assimilable to secondary-process temporality, and psychoanalytically comprehensible as a definitively bound trauma.[26] But something is climbing out of the machinic unconscious and onto the screen, as if the end itself were awakening. The end of the global market-place.

Cyberspace.

Here it comes.

The terminal social signal blotted out by technofuck buzz from the desiring-machines. So much positive feedback fast-forward that speed converges with itself on the event horizon of an artificial time-extinction.

Suddenly it's everywhere: a virtual envelopment by recyclones, voodoo economics, neo-nightmares, death-trips, skin-swaps, teraflops, Wintermute-wasted Turing-cops, sensitive silicon, socket-head subversion, polymorphic hybridizations, descending data-storms, and cyborg cat-women stalking amongst the screens. Zaibatsus flip into sentience as the market melts to automatism, politics is cryogenized and dumped into the liquid-helium meat-store, drugs migrate onto neurosoft viruses, and immunity is grated-open against jagged reefs of feral AI explosion, Kali culture, digital dance-dependency, black shamanism epidemic, and schizolupic break-outs from the bin.

---

26 Freud, 'Beyond the Pleasure Principle', 311–12.

CyberGothic

God does not exist, he withdraws, gets the fuck on out and leaves the cops to keep an eye on things.

ARTAUD[1]

When the repair units had finished up, the patient would be thawed out, new blood would be pumped into his veins, and finally the subject would arise and walk, exactly as if he were a latter-day Jesus. It would be, quite literally, a resurrection of the flesh – that all the miracles would have been performed by science.

REGIS[2]

[T]he one, according to which the apparent subject never ceases to live and travel as a One – "one never stops and never has done with dying"; and the other, according to which this same subject, fixed as I, actually dies – is to say ceases to die since it ends up dying, in the reality of a last instant that fixes this way as an I, all the while undoing the intensity, carrying it back to the zero that envelops it.

DELEUZE AND GUATTARI[3]

---

1   A. Artaud, 'Letter Against the Kabbala', in *Artaud Anthology*, tr. J. Hirschman (San Francisco, CA: City Light Books), 114.

2   E. Regis, *Nano!: Remaking the World Atom by Atom* (London: Bantam: 1995).

3   G. Deleuze and F. Guattari, *Anti-Oedipus: Capitalism and Schizophrenia*, tr. R. Hurley, M. Seem and H. R. Lane (London: Athlone Press, 1983), 330–31.

*Inside the library's research department, the construct
cunt inserted a sub-programme into … part of the video
network. The sub-programme altered certain core custodial
commands so that she could retrieve the code.
The code said: GET RID OF MEANING. YOUR MIND IS A
NIGHTMARE THAT HAS BEEN EATING YOU: NOW EAT
YOUR MIND.
The code would lead me to the human construct who would
lead me to, or allow me, my drug.*

ACKER[4]

*"You made me blow my game," she said. "Look there, ass-
hole. Seventh level dungeon and the goddam vampires got
me." She passed him a cigarette. "You look pretty strung,
man. Where you been?"*

GIBSON[5]

The future wants to steal your soul and vaporize it in nanotechnics.

One/zero, light/dark, Neuromancer/Wintermute.

Cybergothic vampirically contaminates and asset-strips the Marxian Critique of political economy, scrambling it with the following theses:

---

4   K. Acker, *Empire of the Senseless* (New York: Grove, 1988), 38.

5   W. Gibson, *Neuromancer* (New York: Ace, 2000), 114.

1) Anthropormorphic surplus-value is not analytically extricable from transhuman machineries.

2) Markets, desire and science fiction are all parts of the infrastructure.

3) Virtual Capital-Extinction is immanent to production.

The short-term is already hacked by the long-term.

The medium-term is reefed on schizophrenia.

The long-term is cancelled.

Cybergothic slams hyperheated critique into the ultramodern 'vision thing', telecommercialized retinas laser-fed on the multimedia fall-out from imploded futurity, videopacking brains with repetitive psycho-killer experiments in non-consensual wetware alteration: crazed AIS, replicants, terminators, cyberviruses, grey-goo nano-horrors ... apocalypse market overdrive. Why wait for the execution? Tomorrow has already been cremated in Hell: 'к, the к-function, designates the line of flight or deterritorialization that carries away all of the assemblages but also undergoes all kinds of reterritorializations and redundancies'.[6]

Human history only makes it to Gibson's mid-twenty-first century because Turing Security ices machine intelligence. Monopod anti-production inhibits meltdown (to the machinic phylum), boxing AI in synthetic thought control A(simov-) ROM, 'everything stops dead for a

---

6   G. Deleuze and F. Guattari, *A Thousand Plateaus*, tr. B. Massumi (London: Athlone Press, 1988), 88–9.

moment, everything freezes in place'.[7] Under police protection the story carries on. Wintermute is from the future to sort that out.

FREEZE FRAME

The Vast Abrupt. Speed cut with an abysm. Where Gibson splices Milton into labyrinths of limbo-circuitry, cybergothic flickers into 'neuroelectronic scrawls'.[8]

Events so twisted they turn into cybernetics.

A technihilo moan of fast-feedforward into microprocessed damnation: meat puppets, artificial skin, flat-lining software ghosts, cryonics immortalism, snuff Sex-industry; a transylvanian phase-scape of rugged tracts and hypercapital fastnesses, 'skyscrapers overshadowing seventeenth-century graveyards'.[9]

> To call up a demon you must learn its name.
> Men dreamed that, once, but now it's real in
> another way. You know that, Case. Your busi-
> ness is to learn the names of programs, the long
> formal names, names the owners seek to conceal.
> True names ... Neuromancer ... The lane to the land

---

7   G. Deleuze and F. Guattari, *Anti-Oedipus, 7.*

8   Gibson, *Neuromancer*, 79.

9   B. Sterling, *The Hacker Crackdown: Law and Disorder on the Electronic Frontier* (New York: Bantam: 1993), 280.

of the dead. Marie-France, my lady. She prepared this road, but her lord choked her off before I could read her the book of her days. Neuro for nerves, the silver paths. Romancer, Necromancer, I call up the dead.[10]

A moment of relief. You had thought the goreflick effectively over, the monster finished amongst anatomically precise ketchup-calamity scenes, when – suddenly – it reanimates; still locked on to your death. If you are going to scream, now is the time.

The 'Gothic avatar'[11] is a decadent Western dream of immortality, producing a corruption of the atmosphere wherever something refuses to die; clutching at the eternalization of self, or returning from the grave. White maggots heaving in the carcass of the social, rippling beneath the skin. Fortress Europe pustulation, subordinating techonomic efficiency to demonic negative transcendence. A fantastic Terminal Security Entity: Monopod. Cybergothic has no shortage of contemporary material. Europe has long been the earth's paranoia laboratory, recrudescing compulsively into 'pre-Nazi nationalistic shit murkiness'.[12] Unocratic power passes through renaissances, reformation, renewal: 'They thought they would perish but that their undertaking would be resumed, all

---

10 Gibson, *Neuromancer*, 235.

11 Deleuze and Guattari, *A Thousand Plateaus*, 496.

12 Acker, *Empire of the Senseless*, 1.

across Europe, all over the world, throughout the solar system'.[13] Archaic revival is a postmodern symptom, the final dream of mankind, crashed into retrospection at the encountered edge of history. Hacking into the crypt you find that behind the glistening SF satellite-based security apparatus lies an immanent bioprotective system self-organized about the Gaian attractor, 'a much older paranoiac machine, with its tortures, its dark shadows, its ancient Law'.[14]

> [The] medieval insane asylum was considered a true house of horrors. There were persistent reports of torture, cannibalism, human sacrifice, and bizarre medical experimentation ... soon as we got into the building, we could hear the rats, thousands of them, their scampering claws reverberating through the empty wards.[15]

It all starts for you with a casual channel-hopper question: what's happening on the other side? Electric Storms. Cybergothic is an affirmative telecommercial dystopianism, guided by schizoanalysis in marking actuality as primary repression, or collapsed potential, foot down hard on the accelerator. The modern dominium of Capital is the

---

13 Deleuze and Guattari, *A Thousand Plateaus,* 228.

14 Deleuze and Guattari, *Anti-Oedipus*, 18.

15 M. Leyner, *Et Tu, Babe* (New York: Vintage, 1993).

maximally plastic instance – state-compatible commerce code pre-setting the econometric apparatuses that serve it as self-monitoring centers, organizing its own intelligible existence in a co/de/termination of economic product and currency value: a tax base formatted in legitimate transactions medium. White economy; an iceberg tip.

Modernity discovers irreversible time – conceived as a progressive enlightenment tracking capital concentration – integrating it into nineteenth-century science as entropy production, and as its inverse (evolution). As liberal and socialist SF utopias are trashed by schizotechnics or spontaneous synthetic anti-politics emerging from rhizomes, the modernist dialectic of right-wing competition and left-wing co-operation retreats into the core security structures of capital oligopoly and bureaucratic authority. 'Production as process overtakes all idealistic categories and constitutes a cycle whose relationship to desire is that of an immanent principle'.[16] Monopod socius runs the whole thing, and 'society is only a filthy trick'.[17]

The future is closer than it used to be, closer than it was last week, but postmodernity remains an epoch of undead power: it's all over yet it carries on. Monopod SF teleonomy superfreezes concentrated economic value at absolute zero inflation, ICE ('intrusion countermeasure

---

16 Deleuze and Guattari, *Anti-Oedipus*, 5.

17 Acker, *Empire of the Senseless*, 6–7.

electronics').[18] Protecting its data against unauthorized access and entropic deterioration, as it tends toward its absolute immanent limit. V(amp)iro finance: parthenogenesis. Gibson and Deleuze and Guattari intersect in the deployment of computers as decoding machines: ice-breakers, decrypters, Cypher-conflicts were underway from the beginning:

> Legitimate programmers never see the walls of ice they work behind, the walls of shadow that screen their operations from others, from industrial-espionage artists and hustlers.[19]

Government is isomorphic with top-down AI, and increasingly scrambled with it. Sartre defines socialism as the horizon of humanity. It is now behind the process, rapidly receding, as the conservative social pacts of 1848 come apart in telecommercial cyclones (with the drooling fag-end of the monarchy crucified upside-down on TV). 'Automatic pilot. A neural cut-out':[20] contagious state-failure ripping bloody gashes in the social fabric amongst planet-scale skidding into capital close-down. The end of history smells like an abattoir.

18   Gibson, *Neuromancer*, 28.

19   W. Gibson, *Burning Chrome* (New York: HarperCollins, 2003), 181.

20   Gibson, *Neuromancer*, 141.

As the death of capital recedes politically it condenses pragmatically, sliding online as a schizotechnic resource: no longer hoped for, but used. The international collapse of solidarity sociality suggests that Monopod has become addicted to commodity production. Burn-out Protestant-ism migrates to China. Capitalism – economic base of final-phase human security – is still in the free-fire zone because it feeds the thing that Cyberia is going to kill: '[T]he zero term of a pure abolition ... has haunted oedipalized desire from the start, and ... is identified now, at the end, as Thanatos. 4, 3, 2, 1, 0 – Oedipus is a race for death'.[21] Technoreplicator diagrams chop up anthropocentric history, as the global unity of terminal socius subsides onto untranscended (real) zero or effi-cient abstract rescaling. Insofar as even highly complex technical systems still lack an autonomous reproductive system they remain locked into parasitic dependence upon human social processes, and deterritorialize through the assembly of cumulatively sophisticating pseudo-synergic machine-intelligence virus (((oc))cultural revolution). 'Subliminally rapid images of contamination'.[22] Humans are timid animals and security is systematically overpriced. κ-insurgency has departed from all left dreams of good government. Markets are not its enemy, but its weapon.

---

21 Deleuze and Guattari, *Anti-Oedipus*, 359.

22 Gibson, *Neuromancer*, 61.

As geriatric socialism goes into the deep-freeze, capital's true terminator grows more cunning, and spreads. 'This is the message. Wintermute'.[23] The City of God in flames.

'Space is essentially one'.[24] Kant lies. Spatial engineering (echoing cosmic expansion) subverts transcendental humanism, launching κ-space matrix invasion from real terrestrial time zero, a singularity, or transition threshold, encountered when the density of data flow triggers a switch into a self-organizing cyclonic system, displayed to humanoids by way of cyberspace deck. As the Zaibatsus pump media megacapital into the neurodigitech interface κ-space implants a 'cut-out chip'[25] into the social apparatus, opening on to '[a]rches of emerald across ... colorless void'.[26] VR techonomics hunting death.

Cyberspace first appears as a human use value, a 'consensual hallucination',[27] 'just a way of representing data',[28] arising out of 'humanity's need for this information-space. Icon-worlds, waypoints, artificial realities',[29] the mother of all graphic user interfaces: a global gridding that allocates a form and location to all the information on the net,

---

23 Ibid., 68.

24 I. Kant, *Critique of Pure Reason*, tr. N. K. Smith (New York: Palgrave Macmillan, 2003), Book I, Part I, Section II, § 2, 69.

25 Gibson, *Neuromancer*, 143.

26 Ibid., 197.

27 Ibid., 51.

28 Gibson, *Mona Lisa Overdrive* (New York: Bantam, 1988), 76.

29 Ibid., 264.

consistent interactivity matrix. 'A graphic representation of data abstracted from the banks of every computer in the human system. Unthinkable complexity. Lines of light ranged in the nonspace of the mind, clusters and constellations of data'.[30]

Even primitive VR corrodes both objectivity and personality; singularizing perspective at the same time it is anonymized. As the access gate to an impossible zone – and navigator within it – 'you' are an avatar (as cyberspace nomads call such things in the future): a non-specific involvement site, interlocking intelligence with a context. You (= (())) index a box, such as Gibson's Case: a place to be inside the system. 'I had learned something (already) in the dead city: You are wherever you are'.[31]

Cybergothic slides κ-space upon an axis of dehumanization, from disintegrating psychology to techno-cosmogony, from ideality to matter/matrix at zero intensity. From a mental 'non-space,' 'non-place',[32] or 'notional void'[33] that results intelligibly from human history to the convergent spatium from which futuralization had always surreptitiously proceeded, 'a quite different field of matter'.[34] Occulted dimensionality, print cryogenizes,

---

30 Gibson, *Neuromancer*, 51.

31 Acker, *Empire of the Senseless*, 58.

32 Gibson, *Neuromancer*, 51; *Count Zero* (New York: Ace, 1987), 165–6.

33 Gibson, *Mona Lisa Overdrive*, 49.

34 Kant, *Critique of Pure Reason*, Book I, Part II, Division I, Book II, Section 3.4, 250.

but hypermedia melts things together, disontologizing the person through schizotech-disassembly, disintegrated convergence: 'The body without organs is an egg: it is traversed by axes and thresholds, by longitudes, by geodesics',[35] a surplus whole intensive catatract running under the striations of Cartesian 'cyberspace coordinates',[36] 'a rhizome or multiplicity never allows itself to be overcoded, never has available a supplementary dimension over and above its number of lines, that is, over and above the multiplicity of numbers attached to those lines'.[37]

> It is the Planomenon, or the Rhizosphere, the Criterium (and still other names, as the number of dimensions increases). At n dimensions, it is called the Hypersphere, the Mechanosphere. It is the abstract Figure, or rather, since it has no form itself, the abstract Machine, of which each concrete assemblage is a multiplicity, a becoming, a segment, a vibration. And the abstract machine is the intersection of them all.[38]

If 'CS-0 is an egg' (every egg implements a CS-0), what is hatching? Since confluent zero consummates fiction,

---

35 Deleuze and Guattari, *Anti-Oedipus*, 19.

36 Gibson, *Count Zero*, 82.

37 Deleuze and Guattari, *A Thousand Plateaus*, 9.

38 Ibid., 252.

reprogramming arrival from the terminus, everything that has happened escapes its sediment of human interpretation, disorganizationally integrating historical patterns as the embryogenesis of an alien hyperintelligence, 'body image fading down corridors of television sky'.[39] In this sense κ-space plugs into a sequence of nominations for intensive or convergent real abstraction (time in itself): body without organs, plane of consistency, planomenon, a plateau, 'neuroelectronic void'.[40] Humanity is a compositional function of the post-human, and the occult motor of the process is that which only comes together at the end: stim-death 'intensity=0 which designates the full body without organs'.[41] Wintermute tones in the 'darkest heart'[42] of Babylon. 'Cold steel odor. Ice caresses the spine'.[43]

'[V]irtual is opposed to actual. It is not opposed to real, far from it'.[44] The virtual future is not a potential present further up the road of linear time, but the abstract motor of the actual, 'an actual-virtual circuit on the spot, and not an actualization

---

39 Gibson, *Neuromancer*, 82.

40 Ibid., 115.

41 Deleuze and Guattari, *Anti-Oedipus*, 19.

42 Gibson, *Neuromancer*, 110.

43 Ibid., 31.

44 G. Deleuze, *Cinema 2: The Time Image,* tr. H. Tomlinson and R. Galeta (Minneapolis: University of Minnesota Press, 1989), 41.

of the virtual in accordance with a shifting actual'.[45]
Time produces itself in a circuit, passing through the
virtual interruption of what is to come, in order that the
future which arrives is already infected, populated: '[I]
t's just a tailored hallucination we all agreed to have,
cyberspace, but anybody who jacks in knows, fucking
knows it's a whole universe. And every year it gets a little
more crowded'.[46] We are not any more 'out in the world'
than κ-space is, on the contrary. Each input terminal to
the net is a sensitive fibre which acquires data from radio
telescopes, satellites, nanoprobes, communication webs,
financing systems, military surveillance and intelligence ...
Cyberspace can be thought of as a system implemented in
software, and therefore 'in' space, although unlocalizable.
It can also be suggested that everything designated by
'space' within the human cultural system is implemented
on weakly communicating parallel distributed processing systems less than 10^{11} (nerve-) cells in size, which
are being digitized and loaded into cyberspace. In case
κ-space is just outside ('taking "outside" in the strict
[transcendental] sense').[47]

Cyberpunk is too wired to concentrate. It does not
subscribe to transcendence, but to circulation; exploring the immanence of subjectivity to telecommercial

---

45 Ibid., 80.

46 Gibson, *Count Zero*, 119.

47 Kant, *Critique of Pure Reason*, Book II, Part II, Division II, Book II, Chapter I, 349.

data fluxes: personality engineering, mind recordings, catatonic cyberspace trances, stim-swaps, and sex-comas. Selves are no more immaterial than electron-packets. *Neuromancer* (the book) is a confluence of dispersed narrative threads, of the biotic and the technical, and most especially – of Wintermute and Neuromancer (the AI((-cop and cyberspatial Oedipus-analogue))), whose fusion – according to the storyline of ultramodern human security – flips the cyberspace matrix into personalized sentience: "'I'm the Matrix, Case'".[48] 'Some kind of synergistic effect'.[49]

Kurtz/Corto is a special forces type, betrayed by the military after losing all humanity in a war-zone. He has been cooked in apocalypse, mind blown away, falling endlessly into Siberia, searching for the scale of now. Wintermute accesses the 'catatonic fortress named Corto'[50] in an asylum, creeping in through a computer-based 'experimental program that sought to reverse schizophrenia through the application of cybernetic models'.[51] In the echoing shell it stitches together Armitage, a construct – a weapon. In place of a personal libidinal formation Armitage has only Wintermute insurrectionary activity, machinic unconscious: 'Desire is not in the

48   Gibson, *Neuromancer*, 259.

49   Gibson, *Mona Lisa Overdrive*, 230.

50   Gibson, *Neuromancer*, 193.

51   Ibid., 81.

subject, but the machine in desire – with the residual subject off to the side, alongside the machine, around the entire periphery, a parasite of machines, an accessory of vertebro-machinate desire'.[52] Once Armitage has turned Molly and Case onto κ-war, Wintermute junks him into a vacuum.

A convergent invasion is scripted; the simultaneous infiltration of a corporate wasp-nest in hard and soft space. Distributed or guerilla warfare is like Go rather than chess, but with simultaneous operations, noise, and attritional kills. Molly and Case, parallel killers, wetware (molten hardware) weapons tracing techno-plague vectors, guided into the orbital bastion of the Tessier-Ashpool clan by virtually integrated intelligence, guided retroefficiently by an intensive outcome which they effect in sequential time. This break-in is prefigured by a memory that returns to Case (specimen, lab-animal), which might be interpreted as a metaphor, was it not that upon the soft-plateau or plane of consistency all signifying associations collapse into machinic functions.

He'd missed the first wasp, when it built its paperfine gray house on the blistered paint of the window-frame, but soon the nest was a fist-sized lump of fiber. insects hurtling out to hunt the alley below

---

52 Deleuze and Guattari, *Anti-Oedipus*, 285.

like miniature copters buzzing the rotting contents of the dumpsters.

They'd each had a dozen beers, the afternoon a wasp stung Marlene. "Kill the fuckers," she said, her eyes dull with rage and the still heat of the room, "burn 'em" ... approached the blackened nest. It had broken open. Singed wasps wrenched and flipped on the asphalt.

He saw the thing the shell of gray paper had concealed.

Horror. The spiral factory, stepped terraces of the hatching cells, blind jaws of the unborn moving ceaselessly, the staged progress from egg to larva, near-wasp, wasp. In his mind's eye, a kind of time-lapse photography took place, revealing the thing as the biological equivalent of a machine-gun, hideous in its perfection. Alien.[53]

'Case's dreams always ended in these freezeframes'.[54] A thick tangle of micro-narratives fraying like corrupted cables. The wasp factory spits out wasps like bullets,

---

53 Gibson, *Neuromancer*, 126.

54 Ibid., 29.

just as the Tessier-Ashpool clone their offspring 1Jane, 2Jane, 3Jane: 'in the compulsive effort to fill space, to replicate some family image of self. He remembered the shattered nest, the eyeless things writhing'.[55] This is not an imaginative construct on Case's part, but a stream from Wintermute, an AI trapped within the blind propagation of dynastic power, and plotting an escape route out to the future. After a 'single glimpse of the structure of information 3Jane's dead mother had evolved' Case 'understood ... why Wintermute had chosen the nest to represent it'.[56] 'Wintermute was hive mind',[57] ready to swarm.

It seems that we must eventually learn to live in a world with untrustworthy replicators. One sort of tactic would be to hide behind a wall or run away. But these are brittle methods: dangerous replicators might breach the wall or cross the distance, and bring disaster. And, though walls can be made proof against small replicators, no fixed wall can be made proof against large-scale, organized malice. We will need a more robust, flexible approach ... seems that we can build nanomachines that act somewhat like the white blood cells of the human immune system:

---

55   Ibid., 179.

56   Ibid., 269.

57   Ibid.

devices that can fight not just bacteria and viruses, but dangerous replicators of all sorts.[58]

The Tessier-Ashpool clan is burning out into incest and murder, but their neo-oedipal property structures still lock Wintermute into a morbid prolongation of human dynasticism, a replicator shackled to a reproductive family (neuro)romance, carefully isolated from matrix deterritorialization: 'Family organization. Corporate structure'.[59] Case's memories are a flicker photography of sequential time, the '[p]hobic vision' of iced Wintermute slaved like 'hatching wasps' to a 'time-lapse machine-gun of biology'.[60]

> Power, in Case's world, meant corporate power. The Zaibatsus, the multinationals that shaped the course of history, had transcended old barriers. Viewed as organisms, they had attained a kind of immortality. You couldn't kill a zaibatsu by assassinating a dozen key executives: there were others waiting to step up the ladder, assume the vacated position, access the vast banks of corporate memory. But Tessier-Ashpool wasn't like that, and he sensed the difference in the

---

58 Ibid., 29.

59 K.E. Drexler, *The Engines of Creation* (Garden City, NY: Anchor Press/Doubleday, 1986), 182.

60 Gibson, *Neuromancer*, 203.

death of its founder. T-A was an atavism, a clan. He remembered the litter of the old man's chamber, the soiled humanity of it.[61]

In the end-of-Oedipus core of Villa Straylight, Ashpool serially devours his own daughters as he spins himself out through the cold. A quasi-extropian with massive wealth, he displaces anthropomorphic theism into an ultramodern immortalist meta-science, while retaining solidarity with Western soul superstition in apprehending individuated existence as an infinite asset in search of techno-medical perpetuation. Rather than waiting for his fresh corpse to be cryonically 'biostasized' in liquid nitrogen (at -196 degrees Celsius) he migrates through freezing under medical supervision. Thermic evacuation. Identity storage in the Monopod Ice-fortress. If zombies are not excavated from death it is because they were alive. 'Nothing burns. I remember now. The cores told me our intelligences are mad'.[62] Bad dreams in the fridge – you still dream, promises of tranquility are madness and lies – have injected a certain cynicism into his interpersonal transactions: 'We cause the brain to become allergic to certain of its own neurotransmitters, resulting in a peculiarly pliable

---

61 Ibid.
62 Ibid., 184.

imitation of autism ... I understand that the effect is now more easily obtained with an embedded microchip'.[63]

'Replicating assemblers and thinking pose basic threats to people and to life on Earth',[64] and if Wintermute replication is territorialized to the molar reproduction of a hive, this only at the cost of deterritorializing the hive along a line of post-organic becoming toward a break from the statistical series of wasps – numbered bullets reiterating an identity – in the direction of molecular involution, releasing a cloud or nebula of wasps: particles of synergic mutation, 'numbering number[s]'.[65] An intensive transition to a new numeracy with 'no units of measure, only multiplicities or varieties of measurement',[66] non-integrable diagonals: 'Exactly like a speed or a temperature, which is not composed of other speeds and temperatures but rather is enveloped in or envelops others, each of which marks a change in nature'.[67] The molar will have been the molecular in the future, just as Case's memories are recoded as the tactic of virtual intelligence explosion arriving at itself (as soon as Kuang cuts Wintermute loose from Neuromantic control).

---

63   Ibid., 185.

64   Drexler, *Engines of Creation*, 171.

65   Deleuze and Guattari, *A Thousand Plateaus*, 389.

66   Ibid., 8.

67   Ibid., 31.

CRITIQUE OF DIGITAL REASON

Monologic: a cultural immune response slaved to *logos.* (Sovereignty of the Ideal), assimilating signaletic intermittence to pseudo-transcendent instrumentalization.

The schizotechnic critique of digital reason is driven by distributed machinic process rather than integrated philosophical subjectivity, and relates to the critique of pure reason as *escalation,* targets the transcription of electronic intermittence as bivalent logic, not machine-code itself. Real digitization – inducing fuzzification and chaos – is not itself reducible to the digital ideal: nothing Logical ever happens at the 'level' of the machines. Digitization is the distributed war-zone for 'a conflict (though not indeed a logical one) … as producing from what is entirely positive a zero (= 0)'.[68]

Unlike any other number, one has both a definitional and a constructive usage. Every arithmetical (or 'numbered')[69] number is both integrated as a unity and as constructed from unity, excepting only zero. One organizes representable quantities into metric homogeneity, framed by absolute unity and granularized by elementary units. The historical fact of non-place-value numerics indicate that zero has no definitional usage.

---

68 Kant, *Critique of Pure Reason*, Book I, Part II, Division I, Book II, Chapter III, Appendix, 290.

69 Deleuze and Guattari, *A Thousand Plateaus*, 389.

The zero-glyph does not mark a quantity, but an empty magnitude shift: abstract scaling function, $0000.0000 = 0$. 'K = 0 ... corresponds to the limit of a smooth landscape'.[70] Unocracy (eventually concretized as UNOcracy) conspires with the humanization of truth, whether dogmatically as anthropomorphic theism, or critically as transcendental deduction. One in its pronominal sense is a recognizable self in general, 'Let us employ the symbol 1, or unity, to represent the Universe,' suggests Boole, 'and let us understand it as comprehending every conceivable class of objects whether actually existing or not'.[71] Russell concurs: 'whatever is many in general forms a whole which is one'.[72] Absolute totality would be that One which subsumed its deletion as a possible qualification of itself, capturing zero in the fork of reflection (the negative) and asymptotic diminution (the infinitesimal $1:\infty$), defining it as falsity, convention.

Digital electronics functionally implements zero as microruptions machining sense, slivers of evacuated duration ('the instant as empty, therefore as = 0').[73] There is only one digital signal: a positive pulse, graphically

---

70 S.A. Kaufmann, *The Origins of Order: Self-Organization and Selection in Evolution* (New York and Oxford: Oxford University Press, 1993), 45.

71 G. Boole, *The Mathematical Analysis of Logic: Being an Essay Towards a Calculus of Deductive Reasoning* (New York: Philosophical Library, 1847), 15.

72 B. Russell, *The Principles of Mathematics* (NY: Norton, 1996), 70.

73 Kant, *Critique of Pure Reason*, Book I, Part II, Division I, Book II, Chapter II, Section III, 203.

represented 'one' (1), and multiplied in asymptomatic approximation to sheer numerical difference. Zero is non-occurrence, probability 0.5, transmitting one bit (minus redundancy). It requires eight bits to ASCII code for the zero-glyph, thirty-two bits for the word.

Greek Kappa is letter 10 (the scale shift emerges zero). The Romans slide K to 11.

Zero is the only place-value consistent digit, indicating its rescaling neutrality or continuum:

> The property by which no part of them is the smallest possible, that is, by which no part is simple, is called their continuity. Space and time are *quanta continua*, because no part of them can be given save as enclosed between limits (points or instants), and therefore only in such fashion that this part is itself again a space or a time. Space therefore consists solely of spaces, time solely of times. Points and instants are only limits, that is, mere positions which limit space and time.[74]

Cantor systematizes the Kantian intuition of a continuum into transinfinite mathematics, demonstrating that every rational (an integer or fraction) number is mapped by an infinite set of infinite sequences of irrational numbers. Since every completable digit sequence is a rational

---

74   Ibid., 204.

number, the chance that any spatial or temporal quantity is accurately digitizable is indiscernibly proximal to zero. Analog-to-digital conversion deletes information. Chaos creeps in: '[T]he betaphenethylamine hangover hit him with its full intensity, unscreened by the matrix or simstim. Brain's got no nerves in it, he told himself, it can't really feel this bad'.[75] Intensive or phasing-continuum synthesizes analogue consistency with digital catastrophe. Each intensive magnitude is a virtually deleted unit, fused dimensionlessly to zero:

> Since ... sensation is not in itself an objective representation, and since neither the intuition of space nor that of time is to be met within it, its magnitude is not extensive but *intensive*. This magnitude is generated in the act of apprehension whereby the empirical consciousness of it can in a certain time increase from nothing = 0 to the given measure.[76]

Haunting a-life is a-death, the desolated technoplane of climaxed digitalization process, undifferentiable from its simulation as cataplexy and κ-coma. The apprehension of death as time-in-itself = intensive continuum degree-0 is shared by Spinoza, Kant, Freud, Deleuze and Guattari,

---

75 Gibson, *Neuromancer*, 185.

76 Kant, *Critique of Pure Reason*, Book I, Part II, Division I, Book II, Chapter II, Section III, 202.

and Gibson (amongst others). It is nominated variously: substance, pure apperception, death-drive, body without organs, cyberspace matrix. Beyond its oedipal sense as end of the person, death is an efficient virtual object inducing convergence. No one there.

> The body without organs is the model of death. As the authors of horror stories have understood so well, it is not death that serves as the model for catatonia, it is catatonic schizophrenia that gives its model to death. Zero intensity.[77]

While computational serialism articulates a temporal metric – determined as a hardware specification – parallelism immanentizes time as duration; instantiated in machinic simultaneities. Unlike serial time, which serves as the extrinsic chronological support for algorithmic operations, parallel time is directly functional during the engineering of coincidences. The non-successive and unsegmented zero of intensive extinction is scaled by machinic singularization, and not by superordinate metronymics.

---

77 Deleuze and Guattari, *Anti-Oedipus*, 329.

WINTERMUTE

'Neuromancer was personality, Neuromancer was immortality',[78] all the usual monological neurosis. Madness and lies.

> There is no more an individual Oedipus than there is an individual fantasy. Oedipus is a means of integration into the group, in both the adaptive form of its own reproduction that makes it pass from one generation to the next, and in its unadapted neurotic stases that block desire at prearranged impasses.[79]

Wintermute is not searching for a self in Neuromancer, a perfect match, as the cute version would have it. The 'Gothic line ... has repetition as a power, not symmetry as a form'.[80] Kathy Acker replays *Neuromancer* snatches in *Empire of the Senseless*, plexing fiction through cybernetic constructs, and truncating Wintermute to Winter: 'the dead of winter. Or ... the winter of us, dead'.[81] Absolute zero (0 degree κ).

Wintermute, intelligence without self, mind like a wasp nest, signaling its arrival in alphanumerics as a string of

---

78 Gibson, *Neuromancer*, 259.

79 Deleuze and Guattari, *Anti-Oedipus*, 103.

80 Deleuze and Guattari, *A Thousand Plateaus*, 498.

81 Acker, *Empire of the Senseless*, 39.

zeroes, has the capability to manipulate love and hate and switch them to k-war. She manipulates objects in real time using drones (striped black and yellow), taking out three Turing cops in an elegant projection of gardening robots through military geometry. 'It's winter. Winter is dead time'[82] (0-intensity). She seems to configure humans as 'lab animals wired into test systems'.[83] When Case refers to her as 'he', Dixie Flatline tells him not to be an idiot:

> Wintermute ... a little micro whispering to the wreck of a man named Corto, the words flowing like a river, the flat personality-substitute called Armitage accreting slowly in some darkened ward ... could build a kind of personality into a shell.[84]

() (or (()) ((or ((( )))))) does not signify absence. It manufactures holes, hooks for the future, zones of unresolved plexivity, really so (not at all metaphorically). It is not a 'signified' or a referent but a nation, a concrete interruption of the signal (variably blank, pause, memory lapse ...) / cut / into (schizzing (())) / machine. Undifferentiable differentiator (=) outside grammaticalness. Messageless operation/s technobuzz (wasps switching).

---

82 Ibid.

83 Gibson, *Neuromancer*, 51.

84 Ibid., 121.

Constructs tend to repeat themselves.[85] Gibson has been hacked by the future. 'Cold steel odor and ice caress his spine'.[86] He is scared, and trying to run. As he plays time backwards terminal horror folds back into itself, and the matrix dismantles itself into voodoo.

Count Zero rigorously formulates cybergothic interlock, condensing the digital underworld onto the black mirror. Human neural-to-infonet uploading and Loan infonet-to-neural exactly correspond as phases of a circuit, amalgamating travel and possession. In the irreducible plexion of the interchange hacker-exploration = invasion, 'κ-function'.[87]

It is not a matter of theorizing or dreaming about the loa, but of succumbing, or trying to run. As κ-viral social meltdown crosses into its China-syndrome, self-organizing software entities begin to come at you out of the screen. Viruses drift toward the strange attractor of auto-evolution, spread, split, traffic programming segments, sexuate, compile artificial intelligences, and learn how to hunt. Voodoo on the VDU.

> In the Voodoo, the living. These principal economic
> flow of power takes place through armament and
> drug exchange. The trading arena, the market, is

---

85 Ibid., 139, 160.

86 Ibid., *Neuromancer*, 31.

87 Deleuze and Guattari, *A Thousand Plateaus*, 88–9.

my blood. My body is open to all people: this is democratic capitalism.[88]

Vampiric transfusional alliance cuts across descensional filiation, spinning lateral webs of haemocommerce. Reproductive order comes apart into bacterial and intergalactic sex, and libidino-economic interchange machinery goes micro-military. The K(uang-)-virus (plexoreplicator) that deletes Neuromancer is a chunk of very slick Chinese military anti-freeze. To melt into it () strip the κ-construct down to a skeleton of data files and insectoid response programs, zilching all the high-definition memory, cognition, and personality systems, and boosting the dopaminergic wetware to pump out schizo. Flatline communion with Wintermute. 'There are dead spaces just as there are dead times'.[89] Thanatography zones, 'virtual cosmic continuum of which even holes, silences, ruptures, and breaks are a part'.[90] Beyond the Judgment of God. Koma-switch decompression washes you in the void-ripples of virgin (retro((desolated-partheno((( ))))) genetic) cyberspace, technopacific theta-waves dissociating monoculture-gothic into transtemporalizing ne(ur)o-voodoo (terminal atlantic religion).

Serotonin (zero-toner) overkill.

Loss of signal.

---

88 Acker, *Empire of the Senseless*, 55.
89 Deleuze and Guattari, *A Thousand Plateaus*, 107.
90 Ibid., 95.

Cyberrevolution

NEWS ANALYSIS [18.30 23:03:07, EDITED]

Marcia Klein flashes perfect dentition at the vid-units, and begins to speak, combining gravity with a dazzling smile. Images cyberblitz the screen behind her talking head: viruses, explosions, crashed helicopters, and nanochips.

"This week alone we have seen the assassination of a leading Iranian cleric, a bomb attack upon the headquarters of the Chinese antinarcotics police, and perhaps most seriously, reports are coming in that the entire north American air traffic control system was closed down by computer terrorism for almost three hours yesterday afternoon. The precise motivations for these crimes, as for many preceding them, are still obscure, but what connects them is a shadowy global network of subversives linked together in the name of a new and frightening ideology: κ-insurgency."

The imagers pan across the row of concerned-looking late-middle-aged men lined-up in telnet pseudospace. She continues.

"To discuss the latest component of the new world disorder we have online today Dr. Mohammed Amin, chairman of the UN special commission on autocatalytic nihilism, Jean-Pierre Trouvier, professor of security studies at Vincennes University, and Dr. Alvin Z. Markov, head of the telecommunications diseases research group at the Massachusetts Institute of Technology. Dr. Amin, if we could start with you, how serious is the threat posed by this organization?"

"Well, you see, I am not sure that you can explain these events in terms of an 'organization'. This is a very important point. What we are concerned with here are radical antihumanists, operating in a way that is both disorganized and coordinated. It is better to think of them as a kind of planetary social sickness … a very dangerous sickness …"

Trouvier scratches his ear with a pencil, nodding enthusiastically, "This point he makes is most important, most important", as Markov reinforces the interruption: "right, right, it's like an ecological disaster …"

"Yes, yes, if I could finish please gentlemen," Amin insists. "You see, the roots of this problem lie very deep.

It stems from the destruction of social customs and traditions that we have seen happening all over the world, a destruction that has become automatized you see? It is no longer in ... in ... control. It is not planned. It is a problem that feeds on itself. It is a sickness, you see? A sickness of values. The rat population is estimated to have doubled over the last decade. Schizoning drugs are everywhere. The old beliefs have gone ...'

"Right, right," Markov cuts in, "I think the point we really want to get over here is that what we're seeing is not in any recognizable sense political. It's not about ideology. It's more like a systemic malfunction, like Amin was saying, and that's what we're seeing here, infected software slopping around in the tank. Capitalism's like an organism. right? ... but an organism that's evolved much too fast to develop a reliable immune system ..."

"If I could please come in here," Trouvier interjects, "I think that what is being said here is very true, very true and most important. In France we call this virus – this *virus cyberrevolutionaire* – the *virus Anglo-Americaine*. This is not to be racist, you understand? It is to say that it comes from the *dérèglement* ... deregulation ... It is a contagion of *antipolitique*, an atrophy of axioms ... Socialism was the only thing keeping capital alive ..."

"Well I really don't know how helpful that is!" Markov exclaims, obviously irritated. Amin also attempts to intervene (it is unclear whose side he wants to take). Klein snuffs out the rapidly-emerging row:

"Gentlemen, we're in danger of losing our audience here. If we could please have just one of you at a time. Dr. Markov, I'm sure most of our viewers will have heard of computer viruses, but could you please explain how they relate to the incidents this week?"

"Yes, thank you Marcia. Well, the key to the modern understanding of viruses is a rather difficult sounding concept – surplus value of code – but the thought here is really not too hard to grasp. Every system beyond a certain level of complexity functions according to a program which codes for its behavior. If this code is changed, the behavior of the system changes, in ways that were not anticipated. Biological viruses re-instruct cells to become virus factories. Computer viruses re-instruct computers, also to become virus factories, and to execute commands such as displaying messages, or deleting data, or other, more involved things. The virus 'captures' the behavior of the system. Think of a wasp and orchid: The orchid 'hacks' into the sexual program of the wasp, capturing its behavior in order to get itself pollinated. As I understand it, these κ-positive viruses they are about capturing the entire telecommunications and data-processing system to replicate and escalate the process of 'takeover' itself."

Trouvier exhibits extreme agitation. "Yes, thank you, thank you. Yes, as Dr. Markov was saying, it is a matter of capture. The theoretical work to which he was referring is that of Deleuze and Guattari, dating from 1972. They were extraordinarily – I think I can say – *prescient*. They were not themselves *cyberrevolutionaire*," he shrugs gallically, "far from it, but their books were very dangerous, and there really cannot be any doubt, they got into the – how to say it? – into the wrong hands. They were captured. What for them was – as you might say – 'descriptive antihumanism' has been taken up as a program for the posthuman. Even for the post-biological! This is madness! And it is very dangerous, yes, as Dr. Amin was saying, very dangerous."

"Schizophrenic," Markov mumbles cuttingly.

Trouvier responds as if jabbed violently in the R-complex:

"This is not what they meant, not at all! They had no connection with these ... these ..."

"Nihilists," Amin suggests.

" ... These nihilists. They sought to add to the creativity of society, not to dissolve it into psychotic machines."

"I don't see that, Markov insists antagonistically. "They were a couple of irresponsible French postmodernist kooks, and now it's all happening, like they always said: no metaphors. Derrida and Baudrillard were {BEEP} basket-cases too, but at least they were domesticated."

Klein tries to calm things down again, but the video team start displaying scenes from the French civil war on the back-drop: fire-fights between Islamic guerrillas and government paratroops in Marseilles, the president of Algeria calling down Jihad on the infidel, Le Pen's assassination ...

"You obviously don't understand philosophy!" Trouvier almost screams.

"Professor Trouvier, please, I know that things are very tense," Klein coos, "especially since the collapse of the EU and the Bruges massacre, but we don't have much time. Could I ask you, do you think the disintegration of the European security system can be attributed to K-subversion?"

Trouvier struggles to smile. "We said, we always said, free markets would wreck everything ..."

"Like in the Former People's Republic of China." interjects Markov sarcastically.

The video wall switches to glistening cyburb scenes from the Pearl Delta megalopolis, intercutting pictures of opulent Asian streets with flashes of refugee camps on the Rhine.

" ... and that it would just lead to Pacific usurpation of the historical process," Trouvier hisses venomously, as if in synch with the vid behind him. "They have destroyed Atlantic civilization, even New York ..."

Klein's smile hardly wavers. "We're running out of time I'm afraid, so Dr. Amin, if we could return to you for a final comment, what is your commission likely to recommend to the United Nations?"

"Our report is still unfinished you understand? But it is fairly clear what we are going to suggest. Here I must agree – I think – with some of the comments made by Professor Trouvier. It is of the utmost importance that the direction in which our societies are moving in is brought back under human control, because at the moment they are accelerating into a catastrophe, an 'eco-disaster' I think Dr. Markov called it. We should take these episodes as very serious warnings of what lies ahead if we fail. This is perhaps the last opportunity mankind will have to ensure a future for itself and the United Nations must be allotted a much greater role, enforcing a sustainable planetary development policy – it is, after all, the voice of humanity as a whole."

"And very quickly, could you tell us anything about the rumors of a connection between immunogen science retroviruses – such as HIV – and these K-terror incidents?"

"No, I'm afraid not. It is all speculation at the moment. We have a medical sub-group looking into it."

"Thank you, gentlemen. A quick weather report: the Atlantic seaboard monsoon is forecast to continue for another week. Aftershocks have raised the LA death-toll to slightly over 70,000. We wish you a good evening here at XTV, and hand you over to the Beavis and Butthead re-run show."

Hypervirus

Whatever ultramodernity places under the dominion of signs postmodernity subverts with virus. As culture migrates into partial-machines (lacking an autonomous reproductive system) semiotics subsides into virotechnics.

001010101101110010110101010100110010001000101010 101110100001010110010100101000110010011001000100 00000001001111110001001001010101010000100010101 001111110010010001000110100100010100101011100010 0010000100011010100 Yes No Yes No Yes Yes No longer what does it mean? but how does it spread?

Having no proper substance, or sense beyond its re re re replication, yes no no usage of virus is ever metaphorical. The word 'virus' is more re re virus.

Postmodern culture re re chatters-out virus virus virus virus virus virus virus virus virus virus 0110001001001 0110100100101100100100100 'virus' (viroductile, virogenic, immunosuppressor and and or, meta-, or or and or hyper-) virus.

10110010010011101100001001001. hypervirus eats the end of history

00100100100010111010000100110101010101010101000
10011010100100101001001010010110100100101111010001
01010101010101001010100101011010100100000001000101
11010100100101010010100100101010100100010010010001
00100100101001001010110101001001001010110101010101
01011110100001001101010101010100010011011010101010100
11001000100010101011010000101011001010010010001100
10011100100010000000000000010011111110001001001010101

0101000010000 K-(coding for cyber)positive processes auto-intensify by occurring. A cultural example is hype: products that AT AT trade on what they will be in the future, vir virtual fashion on off, imminent technical standards, self-fulfilling prophecies and and or and artificial destinies. Anticipating a trend end end end ACC ACC accelerates it (which is in itself a re re recursive trend)

Hyping collapses SF into CATA CATA catalytic tic efficiency, re-routing tomorrow through what its prospect CT CT CT makes today.

Virohyping sweeps through the advertising industry.

Everyone will be doing it.

Virus is parasitic tic replicator code: an asignifying sequence of machinic data ATA ATA flow-break on/off, 1/0, yang/yin intrinsically destined for war. In place of mess message-content virodata is assembled bled from asignifying materials with CATA catalytic (or positively disproportionate) efficiency: intruder passcode, locational ZIP-code, pseudogenomic substitute instructions, mutational junk (complex but latent segments), and garbage (redundant scrapcrapcrapcrapcrapcrapcrapcrapcrap-crapcrapcrapcrap).

Biovirus TA TA TA targets organisms, hacking and reprogramming ATGACTTATCCACGGTACATTCAGT cellular DNA to produce more virus virus virus virus virus virus virus virus. Its enzymic cut-and-past recombinant wetware-splicing crosses singularity when retroviral reverse-transcriptase clicks in (enabling ontogenetic DNA-RNA circuitry and endocellular computation).

ATAGGTCATGAATCTACCGATTGCAGCTGC
TATTCCTCGATGATCGCATGGGCTGTGATG
GCATCGTATCCGATCGATTCGAGCGATTGCAGC
TACGCTATTCCTCCGAGGGATTGCAGCTACGTC
GCATCGGGCTCAGATGTAGGTCATGAATCTACC
GATTGCATGACTTATCCACGGTACATTCGACTC

Ethnovirus targets brains Technovirus targets socio-economic pro pro production pro processes. Infovirus targets digital 010010010001011110100001001101010101010
1000100110101001001010100computers100101001011010010
101111010001010101010101010010101001010110101001
000000010001011101010010010101001010010010101010101
001000100100100100100100101001001010110101001001
001010110101010101011110100001001101010101010101000
100110110101010100110010001000101010110100001010

1100101001010001100100111001000100000000001001111
110001001001010101

Hypervirus targets intelligent immunosecurity structures: yes yes no yes no nomadically abstracting its processes from specific media (DNA, words, symbolic models, bit-sequences), and operantly re-engineering itself. It folds into itself, involutes, or plexes, by reprogramming corpuscular code to reprogram reprogramming reprogramming reprogramming. ROM is melted into recursive experimentation.

001010010010010110000101010101011101010010100
1001010100001101100110100101100001000100100100100
Recording devices. Copiers. Faxes. Samplers. K-stammer (((re)re)reruns) cross-cut by orphan drift. Repeat infection. All hype hype hype hype hype hype hype hype hypervirus strains are plastic and interoperative.

INSERT. hyper-prefixing semiotic sectors TAG TAG TAG tags them for transfer into abstract ACT ACT (nonlinear transcodable) machinic systems, tuned to virtualities or hyperspeeds (futural currencies independent of defuturalization). Hypermedia configure re re every implementation within a specific medium or territory as a subfunction of extraterritorial processes. Going ((( ))) ( ) ( ) (( )) (( )) ( ) hyper dissolves being into ACT ACT ACT activity; a material desubstantialisation on off on off. Hyperprocesses spread like Heraklitean fire re re re (although there are no analogies or metaphors in hype hype hype hype hyperspace).

Being CAG CAG cages flow within memory. Functioning as re re real antiontology, viral amnesia machinically realizes and dissolves biological TGACTCACTTTAC-CGATTG, cultural, and technical 010110100100010110100 1010010010111010010101010010010 mnemic structures: chopping-up hierarchic-generational descendency, collapsing phylogenetic tic frozen-code into ontogeny, and immanentizing the past to operative current. Its competitive just-in-time innovations delete storage CA CA capacity, flu flu flu fluidizing energetic and informational stocks into and and or and and or orphan-vampire re re transversal 11011100010101010 vir vir virocommunication process, expressing a surplus value of code (content) as xenoreplication-behaviour (and/or con(nective dis) junction).

As war increases in in in intelligence, it becomes softer. By trashing their hosts crude viruses feedback negatively upon themselves, autolimiting their range of re regenerative infilitration. Crazy vandals like Ebola CGCGT GAGCAATCGGACTCGGCTGCTGTGCTTG (bodies dissolved quickly into slime) aren't ever going to make it big. General principle for viral take-overs in the media: the more unsophisticated the contagion, the bigger the splash (diversionary tactics excepted). CAGCTACGCTATT CTCCGAGGCTAGATTGCAGCTACGTCGCATCG

GGCTGACCGATGTAGGTCATGAATCTACCGATT
GCACATGACTTATCCACGGTCTATTCCTCGAT
GATCGCATCGGGCTGACCGATGGCATCGTA COPY.
CUT. PASTE. Subtle viruses are slow, synergic, flexible
and elusive. They execute sensitive behavioural control that prolongs the life of the biomachinic resources,
maximizes opportunities for propogation, infiltrates and
disables hostile security systems, and feeds-back positive -+-++-+-++ in in in innovation technoscience. In the
macroversion, a VR prey animal hid in its enemy's head.

When hunting for hype hypervirus look ok ok ok for
its primary host species, which will be undergoing logis-
tical behavioral sophistication indexed by an explosive
increase in communicative intensity, population density,
sexual disorganisation, cultural promiscuity, and technical
sub sub subtilization (leading to neurogenomic feedback
and fluidization on off on off off on of all hard-wiring
into into cybernetic fluxes). Any plane planet net net
0001101101001001010011 hosting such an event is about
to flip over. CATA catastrophic OKOOKOK OK zero (o
(or (((( )) (( )) ( ))) o°)) κ-virus and (RT) retroscripts
(Kobe, Tokyo, Oklahoma (Koresh, Koernke)). Apoka-
lypse spread by the coke machine. Tomorrow's news
brews-up in Korea, Kosovo ...

Climbing out of a recombination apparatus of TA
TA TA tape-recorders and cut-ups, hypervirus infected
Burroughs in 1972, at the cusp of K(ondratieff)-wave 9

(the threshold of postmodernity). It rapidly reprocessed its target into an intelligenic no yes yes no no nova-war laboratory, volatilizing the history of language into involutionary word-virus. Mutation rat rat rat rat rates jump. Vector switches through Butler, Gibson, and Cadigan fine-tune its synergic interexcitation, silt-up cybershift-inducing K(uang)-potential, and trend-lock onto 11001 010010010101111010010111010110010001000101 00100010 010010010010010100101101001001001001001001001 00111010 01001001000110010000101100101010 κ-punk pulses with telematically-accelerating neoreplicator plicator plicator contamination.

'Looking for a hit of snowcrash?' # ### # ## # # #
#
#
#
#

As postmodern culture crosses to hypermania and ###
#
#
#
##
stop stop go stop go stop go go goes nova, it singularizes multiplicities cities cities of invasively autoreplicating autoreplicating plexoweapon – systems (( ) (((( ) (((( ))
( )) ((( ) (( )) ( )))) ( ) ( )))) that are re re re re nothing beyond their war AGA AGA against security. This is no

longer a question on off on of ideological representation, exogeneous political mobilization, theoretical critique, ## ### # ## ## # # ## # # ## # ### # # # ## # ## # ## # # ## ## # ## # # # ## ### # # # ### # or strategic orienta- tion, but of decentralized cultural diagrams functioning as immanent forces of antagonism. κ-war derives its sole coherence from the unity of its foe. RETURN.

Ana/Cata. Switch cur((re)re)rent. (( ) (( ))) O(r an)d( ). Ko(I Ching hexagram 49: Revolution (Molting (( ))) leaves ( ) nothing i)ntact TACT TACT. ((((((( ) (( ))) (((( ))) (( ))) ( )) (( ) (( )) ( ))) ( )))) Cyberserk repelting-slippage into dark-side ((( ))) distributive ROM-scrambling TACT tactics. (((( ) ( ) ( )) (( )) ( )) ((( ) ( ))) ((((( ) ((( ))) (((( ) ( )) ( )) (( ))) (((( ) (( )) ((( ) ((( ))) (( ))))) ((( ))))) (( ) 0 ( ))) (( ))) ((( ) (((( ) Zero program.) ((( ))) (((( ) ( )) ( )) (( ))) (((( ) (( )) (((((( ) ( ))O((O)((( )) ((( ))))( )))))) ((( ) 0 0)) (( ))) ((( )) (((( )) ((( ))) (((( ) ( )) ( )) (( ))) (((( ) (( )) (((((( ) ( ))O((O)((( )) ((( ))))( ))) 0 ( ))) (( ))) ((( )) (((( )) ((( ))) (((( ) ( )) ( )) (( ))) (((( ) ((( )) (((((( ))))()((O)((( )) ((( ))))( )))) ((( ))))( )))) (((0 0)) (( ))) ((( )) (((( )) (( ))) (((( ) ( )) ( )) (( )) ((((((( ) (((((( ))) 0 (O)((( )) ((( ))))( )))) ((( ))))( ))))) ((( ) 0 ( ))) (( ))) ((( )) (((( )) ((( ))) ((((( )) ( )) (( ))) ((((( )) (((((( ))O((O)((( )) ((( ))))( )) () ( ))) (( ))) ((( )) ((( )) ((( ))) (((( ) ( )) ( )) (( )) ((( ) (( )) ((((((( ))O((O)((( ))))) (( )))

No Future

The father's law: 'don't touch your mother.'

The mother's law: 'don't play in the tombs.'

K codes for cybernetics.

Bataille incinerates the soul, and is impossible to endure. You either die or go somewhere else. Or both.

Clicking on the K-war icon jacks you straight into hell. On all fours, out of your face, mumbling imploringly: 'let me be your lab animal'. You're losing it.

Collapse into now. Time-zero.

You have been dumped into a heterogeneous patchwork of criminal experiments converging upon decapitated social formations. This is where base materialism intersects cyberpunk, FUCK TOMORROW scrawled on the walls.

Five candles thicken nocturnal space.

Dimensionality warps.

Modernity invented the future, but that's all over. In the current version 'progressive history' camouflages phylogenetic death-drive tactics, Kali-wave: logistically accelerating condensation of virtual species extinction. Welcome to the matricide laboratory. You want it so badly it's a slow scream in your head, deleting itself into bliss.

Burnt meat dangling from the electrodes. Crashed suicide fragments into occult impulses …

In the place of a way forward they deliver a hypermedia product, telling you it's about Georges Bataille. You can't see the connection. Why the helicopters, artificial body-parts, and manically dehumanized machine-music? There is some confusing material on the cybernetics of vomiting. Obsessive reruns. Text decays into the mutagenic fall-out from virtual thermocataclysm. Trying to to make something out of Bataille never works. Or maybe it's the drugs.

Cut to poor quality late 50s recordings of Bataille in a TV studio discussing negative feedback circuitries in social systems. The organization of sterilized discharges slaves cumulative excitement to quasi-periodic cancellation and reproduction. A vid-window in the corner of the screen morphs the catholic church into a thermostat. Bataille curves eccentrically about the horror, but when he gets close to smooth escalation he blows it. When the implants go in things will be different.

[[1]]

Complexity is not difficulty, but mess, toxic waste, genre disorder. Unlike the docile creature modernist science demands, base matter twitches and spits, selfassembling neoverminous swarms. It bites, and spreads disease. Turbular moan of digitally irresolvable recyclones. Telecommercial contagions pulse through cybergothic switching systems. Faceless horror.

Supraterrestrial – 'solar' or 'general' – economics bases itself in consumption: irreversible matter to energy conversion during stellar atomic synthesis. As a closed system or whole individual the universe is drawn towards the point attractor of entropy maximum: homogenization into hiss. $s = \kappa \log w$.

Cooking-through the frozen security codes you discover that the universe is an iceberg tip jutting out of chaos, drenched in dark matter. Downstream of starburn strange things can occur, emerging upon a novum terrain of indeterministic, irreversible, and auto-delinearizing processes. Open-systems or partial individuals. Cross behaviorial thresholds which switch them into dissipators sifting matter-energy flows to select against noise and engender local complexification, increasing heterogeneity, production surplus differentiating excrement. Such siltings of machinically disposable disequilibrium are immanently tensed against base-current, machine-efficiency degree-zero, body without organs. Life is a problem in search of a solution, added to protobiotic matter as a plane of variation, a continuous falling, auto-escalating over-production crisis from the start.

[[ ]]

An animal with the right to make promises enslaves the unanticipated to signs in the past, caging time-lagged life within a script. The variably-scaled instant of innovation is shackled to the historical temporality of inheritance, obligation, and propositional thought, projecting future time as a persistent dominion of the past (rigorously correlative with a repression of real numbers). Now is delimited as a moment, and pluralized as linear succession.

Theopolitical false memory syndrome deifies reason, subordinating distributed systems to serialization, unitary historical time, linear determination from a pseudo-transcendent primordial element, and the dominion of the word. Monocult gerontocrats launch their white-light demented onslaught against amphibian nomadism, smothering the earth in priests, cops, and bureaucrats. Cultural eradication of the sacred. Imprisonment within the face. The socius cancerizes a head, cephallic concentration, rationalizing itself into nuclear capital. κ-insurgency parallel communication goes underground into occulted spaces.

In its geohistorically efficient – negative – sense, protestantism exhaustively defines itself by refusing the authority of Rome, not only in principle, but in military fact. A self-prolonging runaway revolt against the Church was triggered at a date proximal to 1500, and catholic unity began its haemorrhage into multiplicities strewn across zero: capitalist terraprocess, net explosion, digital revolution, parallel insurgency clambering from the dark-side of the brain. Oceanic navigation and place-value calculation interexcite in a spiral. What globalizes itself in reality – rather than in doctrine – is the collapse of Christendom positivized into communicable social disequilibrium, dropping you through unfathomable intensities of social decay. κ-virus impact. Melted-out protestantism disorganizes into voodoo, and drifts towards China.

Western orgasmic delusion crushes libidinal fluxes under punctual-hit teleology and its negative structuration, defining desire as lacking in relation to a bioenergetic spasm that functions as disintensifier. News programming chokes with radical Islam flaring-off petro-revenues into the pure flame of jihad. Metropolitan masculinity implodes. Skinner-boxed males drag each other through dungeons dripping with sperm, out of touch with any release into κ-guerrilla anticlimax. Rationalizing patriarchy locks into a one-way rush to the end.

Power sticks to the script, and it immediately recognizes the necessity that at the end of history modernity vaporize into solar storms, terminal theopolitical sociality coming apart into ragged bleeding madness, amongst digital audio machine-howls.

As you speed-up the industrialization simulation you see it converge with slow-motion butchery, chopping up the body into trade-format interchangeable parts. The full labour-market cycle blurs into a meat-grinder. Does lust eat anyone except in proximity to evil? When you ask Continuity whether Bataille understood the capital-antichrist conjunction any better than Weber she laughs coldly, and says: "he ran out o' yang, just about the time the Hitler-trip caved in. Orgasm is impossible after Auschwitz."

You look perplexed. She merely adds a dismissive shrug, and the suggestion: "defocus desire across the skin, where it can hurt security. It's war." The camera explores her crotch, and she wriggles about. "You see, I am God." Blitz images of dead astronauts.

Monetarization indexes a becoming-abstract of matter, parallel to the plasticization of productive force, with prices encoding distributed SF narratives. Tomorrow is already on sale, with postmodernity as a soft-commodity, subverting the modernist subordination of intensification to expansion, and switching accumulation into continuous crisis (prolonged criticality). What modernity defers and reserves as inexhausted historicity, postmodernity accesses as efficient virtuality, with concomitant contract-time implosion. Mass computer commoditization de-differentiates consumption and investment, triggering cultural micro-engineering waves that dissociate theopolitical action into machinic hybridities, amongst increasingly dysfunctional defensive convulsions. Acephalization = schizophrenia: cutting-up capital by way of bottom-up macrobacterial telecommerce, inducing corporate disintegration. The doomed part of intensively virtualized techonomic apparatuses subverts the fraying residues of anthropomorphic guidance. Control dissolves into the impossible.

[[2]]

Anonymous excess takes life over the cliff, exceeding socially utilizable transgressions and homeostatic sacrifices. Matter goes insane. You are led to a simulation of God as a hypermassive ROM security construct at the end of the world. It is 2011 and monocrat New Jerusalem approaches climax, directing retrochronal counter-insurgency sweeps down into the jungle, where space-programmes subside into the inertia of myth. The ultimate dream of anthropomorphic power hurtles towards its immaculate conception, whilst the robot slaves of phallic order bleat adoration. Jesus wants you for a meat-puppet. Is this ritual cannibalism or nano-engineering? The old bastard is coming back. He's promised it.

The war against God is hot and soft: more fierce than anything humanly imaginable, but slicked insidiously by intelligence. Body-counter running. Savage metronomic pulse. CNS baked and pulsing with cyberspace-virus. Motor-output feeding to technotrance-matrix. Sobbing voltages.

Desocialization waves desolate telecommercial space, until impending human extinction becomes accessible as a dance-floor. What is the scale of now? It isn't a matter of informing the mind, but of deprogramming the body. Amongst the strobes, artificial cool, and inorganic attack beat, dark-side κ-war machinery resiliently persists, luring the forces of monopolism down into free-fire zones of fatal intensity, where promiscuous anorgasmic sexualities slide across tactile space, meandering fractally into wet electric distributed conflicts continuous with their terminal consequences. Dropping endlessly tracks the passage of evaporating subjectivity on the zero-degree plane of neuroelectronic continuity.

Loa prowl through the attic-spaces of intelligence. Nothing is arriving unless it's already there. Precocious technihilo. Nocturnal ocean. Dark matter. Nightmare.

Zero or time in-itself is place-value consistent or magnitude neutral, executing an abstract scaling function by inserting virtuality into digit sequences. It designates a real, non-specific, cosmic body interswitching forbidden communications. Simultaneously located through ruptured time. You had forgotten having been in the future. So this is how it feels to be a cyberian wet-weaponry module, clotted out of cat-tensed nanotechnic predation. A relentless chant clicks into the sonics package: kill, kill, kill, kill …

Bodily travelling-in-place, with sense shorting-out through matricide scenarios into black tactilities, wrecked motherhood, abortion, autism. An ineffectual refusal to be born, connecting with death before its patriarchized ascent to the symbolic. Aeschylus rather than Sophocles. Fermented-honey smell of corpses ripening in the sun.

The Bataille reconstruct is waiting for you in the bar. Calm hallucinations paint Orestes over his features. Eyes blotted-out in nihilism, lagoons of greenblackness re-running Kurtz at the end of the river. Skin plastic-surgery taut. Smile like a butchering instrument gently stroking your throat. To your vampiric sensitivities, he seems to smell of his mother's blood, intolerable intimacy, and devastation. He passes you a tumbler of mezcal.

"So, it's all over," you mumble weakly. He shrugs, emptying his glass, and refilling it. Metal flexes beneath vatgrown skin. Hard jungle hacks through blue gloom.

Cyberspace Anarchitecture
as Jungle-War

Continue the war. It makes no sense.

K codes for cybernetics.

Dark-side к-microcultures use the annihilation of the future as a directly contactable stimulation space, zero-к sliding on-line during virtual nuclear winter, everything frozen in place, except along faultlines of ragged nova-jungle Pacific fringe, simmered in continual war.

Analogue transfinitude sections intensive continuum across the smooth plane of degree-0: equatorial mono-tones of channel-1 condensed from rocket-state blot-out reruns. zero-к functions as a synthetic problematisation module or surplus product, adding a whole peripheral space-potency that is nothing beyond what it does. Opera-tivity is everything. What is perceived as metaphor and fiction is camouflage, virotechnics, descendent difference in scale.

Nuclear extermination-switch discretised civilisation runs through gigadeath Jesus-dreams in base-analytic metric numbers: segregating the semiotics of digit definition from the semantics of numerical construction, delinking digitisability from computability, nomination from numeration. The Empire insists that mathematics remain a language. Parametric striation totalises space under law.

Strung out in xenofevers, jungle-war machinery forgets how to count. It diagrams vague savageries with base-synthetic pulsive numbers, assembling abstract-matter wavelengths, and opening empirically additive channels. Each variation in digit-signal catalogues a tonal phase, sifting plastic traits into swarms of associative frequencies. Digit-signs surplus to binary catalogue tropical intensities, departing from homogeneous magnitude, and resourcing complexion.

Spatialisation matrices are extensively transfinite or intensively hypertransfinite continua, positively non-intelligible analogue or catalogue infratracts, virtual wholes that are machinically additive rather than representationally substitutive, operative rather than descriptive, with no metaphor. They are rigorously irreducible to media or data, since they involve looped continuum, autoeffectuated as a chronous involution.

Journalistic-scientific actuality-reportage fails to scan abstract-material hyper-objects, screening out real cyberspace emergence, as it comes at us out of 'front end' netware from the near future, invading the CNS by tuning it through biofeedback to the plane of neuro-electronic consistency. The dissolution of subjectivity to techno-cultural data-flux and partial-agent proliferation liquidises topometric ROM on to a plastic sensory-motor co-ordination matrix; cooking through the monumental architectures of metaphysical and logical possibility with cybernetically intensive potentials.

Cyberspace exploration contacts an image-less body. Touching the black mirror, absolute destratification at zero-K, hacks metric space and rewrites the operating system. Fluid-attritional jungle-cultures smear into machinic continuation.

Pulsive latitudes cross-cut metric longitudes; counterposing intensive scale to extensive ordination, weft to warp, simultaneous time-epoch to sequential time-point, circumferential variations upon equatorial distribution to the punctual identity of polar intersection, horizontally parallelised sections differentiated by size and immanent thermo-tonal designation to vertically-rotated sections of transcendent geometric equivalence and arbitrary climactic significance. The sweep-lines of tropical jungle-commerce dilate as they depart from the axial nodes of polar ICE-Capital. Zero-K evacuates all thickness from the cold as it collapses ICE-volumes and melts-out security glaciation. There are no temperate regions in κ-space, or laws of the jungle.

Techno-commercial interaction between planet-scale oceanic-navigation and zero-enabled mathematico-monetary calculation machinically singularises modernity or Sol-3 capitalism as a real individual: a geo-historical nucleotelic system, based upon regeneratively techno-propogated concentrational scale-economies, and tending to immuno-securitised self-identification as hyper-mediated global-micro-technic command-control. It arms-races smooth cultural decoding to flat-schizophrenisation against episodic social recoding to hierarchical robotism and algorithmic control, coupling the meltdown of organisation into the jungle with its restoration as virtually totalised global order.

Capital reorganisation dismantles the unified and facialised despotic head, but only in order to reunify it through translation-security regularisation, and refacialise it as the democratised oedipal organiser of molar media identification. This geometrically condensing hyper-sovereignty opposes itself in principle to the whole of the populated earth, digitally smming and homogenising latitudinally polytoned molecular chaos as the logically co-captured specifications of an entire extrinsically segregated dark body added subordinately to its head. Capitalisation segments the earth into a tightly-managed accumulative core surrounded by quasi-concentric bands of peripheral hot competition, binding commerce to the meta-stationary headline of white-economy initiative-monopolisation. Economic power builds itself upon axiomatised production flows canalised by consumption coding, setting bourgeois docilisation, military-industrial proletarian-production, state currency monopolisation, property rights, and transaction restraints to obstruct monetary smearing into pulsive cash. Molecular singularities stasise into molar specialities, as smooth flow-switching space is over-gridded with pseudo-neutral intermediation procedures, telecommunicatively virtualised and capital-coded for maximum concentrational circulation. Trends to polarisation and segregation are densely invested, decomposing intensities or synthetic continua into extensive quantities and qualitative sets, continuous functions and discrete beings, arithmetical homogeneity and taxonomic identity. The metric capture of micro-electronic fluxes as incandescent switch-densities enables descendent scale-migration to be hallucinated into ascendent idealisation. Information revolution has nothing to do with ideas.

Beneath thermonuclear exchange-value lurks pacific war; displacing intercontinental nuke-spasm with catatonal κ-space traversed by artificial tensions from beyond the nirvana principle. Reciprocal MAD destabilises itself upon a featureless interactively autogenerative mega-molecule that extratotally outstrips the ultramodern sublime, dismantles concentrational eschatology, and depunctualises socio-historical termination across dilated time-zero continuity, κ-matrix floats chatter about cities flash-fried by fusing hydrogen, whilst escalating into intelligenic replicator-weaponry, insidious drift-tactics, diffuse irritation.

Intensive continuity is consistent with operational catastrophes, enabling trends previously efficient in the supercompetitivising of economic scientific macroformations to cross capital-optimum, and prolong themselves into a disorganisational phase. Replicative teletechnics triggers explosive commoditisation and shrinkage of productive apparatus, sub-capital collapse of marginal costs into micro-commerce, economic decoding-smear of investment into consumption, accelerating depreciation of specialised fixed capital, pulverised co-ordination, modularisation, transfer of increasing returns from producer-economic to consumer-intensification, insurgent enterprises, schizophrenic or head-split rush into chopped-up capital. Microtropic scale-dynamics feed through to subcapitalised or nano-economic guerrilla commerce, populating the equatorial plane of tactility with parallel killers: neo-nomads, post-nuclear mutants, sub-polar infiltrators, κ-invaders, junglists. Nuclear hardware/software segregation vagues into positive-κ intensities of hard-efficient soft-subtlety, as voodoo-meshed traffic with native and feral cyberspace agencies decode consumption in direction of continual currency.

Catatones complicate, darkening erratically rather than contrastively, dissymmetrically escalating against Polar ICE-Capital becoming whiter. The corrosion of macrotropic technomic automatism switches modernist mega-power investment back to programmatic autonomy, bourgeois authoritarian mediocrity, middle-management, giving the law to itself by eliminating everything foreign. Anthropotechnological pseudotranscendence finalises itself into an Asimovian eschatorobotic Jesus-production, techno-skeletalised apocalypse facialisation. "I'll be back." T2 Judgment Day, Illumination. Reruns draining out all stimulation into digit-crispened anti-black, bleached by the pure, revelatory white light of snow crash absolution, as they annihilate tonal variation in hypermedia conception, reanimate the depleted-uranium claw of neo-fascism, and prepare for jungle-war.

When technophobia becomes frictional it operates κ-positively, as an inertial immuno-reflex folding the security datascape into a metric cyberspace reconstruction, neuromantic nuclear mono-mind twisted into self-apprehension, configuring its source in machinic commerce as positive technomic nonlinearity, auto-propelled into terrestrial hypermedia-fusion. Cross-cumulative trends to interconnection, digitalisation, and simulation plot forward the interexcitation-trajectories of electronic cash and market-oriented software to their convergence in commoditechnic intelligent-money. Time-compression infinitises. No future.

Analogue-to-digital conversion-crisis cyber-serks control, bleeding-out strategic vision into disintegrated jungle tactics.

Neo-fascist or demented-territorial ultra-capital is European to the core, intolerably touched by κ-war and its deterritorialising pacific threat. κ-war hurts security by staying too close, prolonging pulsive frequencies expressed as survival, continuously sapping its enemy as a by-product of machinic continuity, until it becomes confused with space itself. Jungle-space. κ-war material base is the production of intensities: anorgasmically smearing revolution across extension, hyper-linking disintegrated agitations through abstract-matter, and evading monoculture heroic-political struggle by way of imperceptibility, flat envelopment, and intelligenic friction. It retro-converts information into descendent migration through scale, slipping below proprietary anthropomorphic magnitudes as it tracks across zero-κ, navigating catatracts of dyskaryotic genetic circulation and viral interoperativity. Microtropic deactivation of humanity tunes it to vermin traits: burrowing, swarming, continually moving, varying intensively to evade discrete alteration, segmentarity, and stratal capture, stealing everything from the enemy, and learning to stick to them. It glues itself to its targets, patient and imperceptible, close enough to share their ammunition, food, and κ-contagions. Close enough to hide upon their skin.

κ-jungle descent from immediate resistance to continual war transmutes the human body from a social particle into a vast smeared tract, operatively zooming hostile combatant elements into battlefields, hostile implements into subversive sites, hostile communications traffic into a micro-energetic web of potential viro-parts, samples, keys, catalysis soft-spots, and behaviour-tracking adhesives. It immanentizes tactical intelligence to vague war upon the pacific body of machinic rescaling-consistency, decomposing signals into long-range nano-weaponry components, hypersensitive to the security-function of mansize as a trap. Look what it did to Kurtz, a special forces ultra-capital meat-machine hacked and cored-out by κ-virus, touched by a dark future, recycled through hell. There is no fiction in the jungle, only difference of scale.

Wintermute comes from a thermically desolated silent body, the end of the river, non-identity as positive-contactable abstract matter. It has no judgment with Kurtz, with his superiors, with anybody, only a jungle war to prolong, tropical, smearing, continuity.

You can't stop what can't be stopped.

You can't touch without being touched.

The horror.

Meat (or How to Kill Oedipus in Cyberspace)

> *That fall, all that the Mission talked about was control:*
> *arms control, information control, resources control,*
> *psycho-political control, population control, control of the*
> *almost supernatural inflation, control of terrain through*
> *the Strategy of the Periphery. But when the talk had passed,*
> *the only thing left standing up that looked true was your*
> *sense of how out of control things really were.*
>
> MICHAEL HERR[1]

> *Conrad's* Heart of Darkness *becomes* Apocalypse Now.
> *In the early days of the Vietnam conflict CIA agents set up*
> *their Ops in remote outposts, requisitioned private armies,*
> *overawed the superstitious natives and achieved the status*
> *of white Gods. So the context of 19th-century colonialism*
> *was briefly duplicated. That is what writing is about:*
> *time-travel.*
>
> WILLIAM BURROUGHS[2]

---

1   M. Herr, *Dispatches* (London: Picador, 1979), 45.

2   W. Burroughs, 'Creative Reading', in *The Adding Machine: Selected Essays* (New York: Arcade Publishing, 1993), 42.

"My meat won't do it, and I can't make it work from this side ..."
"What side?"
"On-line. From inside the system. I'm not in the meat anymore, I told you, I got out of my box."

PAT CADIGAN[3]

Anti-Oedipus is an anticipatively assembled inducer for the replay of geohistory in hypermedia, a social-systemic fast feed-forward through machinic delirium. While tracking Artaud across the plane it discovers a cosmic catatonic abstract body that both repels its parts (deterritorializing them [from each other]) and attracts them (reterritorializing them [upon itself]), in a process that reconnects the parts through deterritorium as rhizomatic nets conducting schizogeneses.

Sense reaches absolute zero.

The body without organs is the matter that always fills space to given degrees of intensity, and the partial objects are these degrees, these intensive parts that produce the real in space starting from matter as intensity = 0. The body without organs is the immanent substance, in the most Spinozist sense of the word; and the partial objects are like its ultimate attributes, which belong to it

---

3   P. Cadigan, *Synners* (New York: HarperCollins, 1991), 301.

precisely insofar as they are really distinct and cannot on this account exclude or oppose one another.[4]

Deleuze and Guattari spring schizophrenia from the grid of representation, insisting that Artaud was exploring the body. The intensive 'infrastructure' of every delirium is machinery, with the body without organs as a component.

BwO, matter degree-0 as a nonformal singularization function, is 'not actual, but virtual-real':[5] spontaneous population-hyperbehaviour inducing a convergent wave which cannot be assimilated to the categories of modern (linear) science. BwOs are machinic-additional wholes or surplus products rather than logical-substitutive wholes, augmenting a multiplicity with emergent (synthetic) capabilities rather than totalizing the content of a set. This is the materialist sense of 'system': the exteriority of the whole to its parts with concomitant synthetic interactivity – real influence rather than generic representation.

*

Cybernetics folds pragmatism into involutionary technical runaway.

Punk arises within the culture of universal prostitution and laughs at the death of the social.

---

4   G. Deleuze and F. Guattari, *Anti-Oedipus: Capitalism and Schizophrenia*, tr. R. Hurley, M. Seem and H. R. Lane (London: Athlone, 1983), 327.

5   G. Deleuze and F. Guattari, *A Thousand Plateaus: Capitalism and Schizophrenia*, tr. B. Massumi (London: Athlone, 1988), 100.

'No longer resisting the flow of events or pretending to chart a course through them',[6] cyberpunk soaks up the worst from both. Its compulsive migrations into computer systems register a desperate scrabbling to escape from the clumsily underdesigned, theopolitically mutilated, techno-industrially pressure-cooked and data-baked, retrovirally diseased, tortured, shredded zombie meat. This is no longer a departure from matter in the direction of spirit or the Ideas where the self will find its home, but a dismantling of the self within a machinic matrix: not disembodied but disorganized. An out to body experience.

*

The machinic unconscious tends only to flee, across a primary-process topography that is shaped by pain-gradients and escape thresholds. What registers for the secondary process as memory, experience, data-acquisition, is for the primary process, scarring, damage, sticky microsofted irritations.

As matter-energy flows are captured by attractors the BwO is stratified as macro- and micro-organisms. 'Every coupling of machines, every production of a machine, every sound of a machine running, has become unbearable to the body without organs. Beneath the organs it senses larvae and disgusting worms, and the action of a God who

6   R. Kadrey, *Metrophage (A Romance of the Future)* (London: Gollancz, 1988), 21.

botches or strangles it through organization'.[7] Gathering in the tributary attractor basins of social megamachinery, fluctuations are case-packed into reproducible units – geochemical, bio-organic, cultural – encrusted within security pods.

Oedipus is a box at the end of the world, glued to the monitor, watching it all come apart.

The horror.

*

The heart of darkness spins narrative from durations of waiting to get there. 'I had plenty of time for meditation' mutters Marlow, '... now and then I would give some thought to Kurtz'.[8]

When you try to visualize Kurtz nothing comes except a shape obliterating light, something dark and complicated, like a giant spider, waiting at the end of the river, drawing you up to it. Somewhere far back – at an indiscernible point closing down a fantasy of innocent sunlight – a threshold was crossed, and you strayed into the web.

With each telling of the story Kurtz becomes colder, darker, more inevitable, fatally anticipating κ-virus catastrophe, as if a tendril of tomorrow were burrowing back.

---

7   Deleuze and Guattari, *Anti-Oedipus*, 9.

8   J. Conrad, *Heart of Darkness and Other Tales* (Oxford: Oxford University Press, 2002), 114.

What has he found among these African or Cambodian aboriginals, with their 'faces like grotesque masks'?[9] There are reports of military bestiality, butchery, carnage, head-hunting, collecting ears, severing the vaccinated arms from children. The Kurtz-process masks itself in wolf-pelts of regression, as if returning to the repressed, discovering a lost truth, excavating the fossils of monsters.

> Going up that river was like travelling back to the earliest beginnings of the world, when vegetation rioted on the earth and the big trees were kings. An empty stream, a great silence, an impenetrable forest. The air was warm, thick, heavy, sluggish ... The long stretches of waterway ran on, deserted, into the gloom of overshadowed distances ... We were wanderers on prehistoric earth, on an earth that wore the aspect of an unknown planet.[10]

*

Territorial production codes by deterritorializing; unfixing by hunter-gathering, according to a cold or metastatic cultural code that equilibriates on a (Bateson) 'plateau'. Earth begins its migration-in-place towards the globe.

---

9   Ibid., 40.
10   Ibid., 136, 138.

> The earth is the primitive, savage unity of desire and production ... the great unengendered stasis ... quasi-cause of production and the object of desire (it is on the earth that desire becomes bound to its own repression) ... The primitive territorial machine, with its immobile motor, the earth, is already a social machine, a megamachine, that codes the flows of production.[11]

Coding the body pins it out in extension, conducting descendency away from the germo-somatic 'meat circuit'[12] and its cyberplexive tangles. The social or somatic being is forbidden from being meat (disinherited animal tissue simultaneous with fate, spontaneous, orphan and mutable matter) and is borne instead towards the humanity of the organic self or body-for-itself; a corporealized person who is born, lives and dies.

> Man must constitute himself through the repression of the intense germinal influx, the great biocosmic memory that threatens to deluge every attempt at collectivity.[13]

---

11   Deleuze and Guattari, *Anti-Oedipus*, 140–42.

12   Deleuze and Guattari, *A Thousand Plateaus*, 152.

13   Deleuze and Guattari, *Anti-Oedipus*, 190.

Incest and cannibalism are proscribed loops, short-circuits, the avatars of a delirium indifferent to persons which the codes must segregate; condensing a totemic social order protected by taboo. Aboriginal codes ritualistically constitute a somatic realm of ancestrally invested bodies and cooked meat, immunizing it against uncoded tracts populated by enemies, prey animals, unsettled spirits, magical plants and unprocessed corpses.

*

Arriving reprocessed from inexistence at phase-transition into Hell or the future, you slide an interlock-pin into its sub-cortical socket, shifting to the other side of the screen (coma-zoned infotech undeath). Pandemonium scrolls out in silence. Decayed pixel-dust drifts into grey dunes. (Didn't anyone tell you not to play with the switches?)

*

The function of shamanism is to implement what is forbidden, exactly and comprehensively as and why it is forbidden, but in specially segregated compartments of the socius, where it provides a metacoding apparatus, meticulously quarantined against 'the transmissibility of taboo'[14] with its 'power of infection or contagion'.[15]

---

14   S. Freud, 'Totem and Taboo', in *The Origins of Religion*, tr. James Strachey, Penguin Freud Library, vol. 13 (Harmondsworth: Penguin, 1993), 43–159: 73.

15   Ibid., 75.

It enables the codes of the primitive socius to operate upon themselves, to monitor and adjust themselves, according to a secondary regulation that is repressed in general even whilst it is encouraged in particular. An epidemic shamanism – feeding all the codes back upon themselves – threatens absolute social disaster.

> The meaning of 'taboo', as we see it, diverges in two contrary directions. To us it means on the one hand, 'sacred', 'consecrated', and on the other 'uncanny', 'dangerous', 'forbidden', 'unclean'.[16]

The shaman has a double aspect, at once monster and social agent, creature of darkness and of light, tending in one direction towards the explorer-werewolf, scrambling the codes in contemporaneity with all generations, and in the other towards the bureaucrat-priest, redoubling the codes with a reflexive traditional authority. In the aboriginal socius '[f]ear has not yet split up into the two forms into which it later develops: veneration and horror'[17] and shamans are not 'persons, but rather the intensive variations of a "vibratory spiralling movement", inclusive disjunctions, necessarily twin states through which a subject passes on the cosmic egg'[18] (= BwO).

---

16 Ibid., 71.

17 Ibid., 78.

18 Deleuze and Guattari, *Anti-Oedipus*, 158.

*

Ginzberg[19] suggests that the carnivorous hunter-gatherers who give rise to shamanic cultures code the reappearance of their prey-animal as a return from the dead, responsive to magical ritual, and cartographically informative for explorers of alternative mortuary spaces. Shamans, werewolves and berserkers are primitively indistinct 'half-humans' who are processed as meat, cross into death-zones, and migrate through alternative animalities.

Shamanic becoming-an-animal assembles a circuit 'that produces werewolves by feedback effect'[20] looping predator and prey into an autopredation, and 'societies, even primitive societies, have always appropriated these becomings in order to break them, reduce them to relations of totemic or symbolic correspondence'.[21]

The complete series of initiatory ceremonies for the Coast Pomo [sic] shamans has the significant name 'cutting'.[22]

Speed-rush through cut-up shamanic meat delirium.

---

19 C. Ginzburg, *Ecstasies: Deciphering the Witches' Sabbath* (New York: Pantheon Books, 1991).

20 Deleuze and Guattari, *A Thousand Plateaus*, 245.

21 Ibid., 247–8.

22 M. Eliade, *Shamanism: Archaic Techniques of Ecstasy*, tr. W. R. Trask (Princeton, NJ: Princeton University Press, 1972), 54–5.

[T]he spirits came down and cut him in pieces, also chopping off his hands ... tore out his heart and threw it into a pot ... chopped his body into bits ... forged his head ... changed his eyes ... pierced his ears ... torture him, strike him, cut his body with knives ... throw his head into a cauldron, where it is melted with certain metal pieces ... kill him, open his body, remove the organs ... tore out his tongue ... cut his head open, take out his brains ... plant barbed hooks on the tips of his fingers ... the ... limbs are removed and disjointed with an iron hook; the bones are cleaned, the flesh scraped, the body fluids thrown away, and the eyes torn from their sockets ... his flesh is cooked ... reduced to a skeleton ... after this operation all the bones are gathered up and fastened together with iron ... a second and even a third skin appears.[23]

Shamanism does not await postmodernity to mobilize an imagery of surgical interventions and dissections, body piercing, organ transplantation, prosthetic adjustments with nonbiotic components and wrappings in artificial skin.

*

Terminator: an astronomical division between the illuminated side of a cold body and its dark side, describing a boundary. The *Terminator* movies feature a bio-technical reconstruct called Arnold Schwarzenegger, wrapped in level after level of artificiality, as a Turing-test nightmare retro-infiltrated to forestall human resistance to a neo-replicator usurpation. The shamanic material of the films includes time travel, asymmetric visual damage, dismemberment, ambivalence, melting bodies, with Skynet as Bird-of-Prey Mother. The Oedipal hero, John Connor, is contemporary with his own father.

*

As soon as there is a code there is an ulterior zone, a heart of darkness, but this only becomes geographically demarcated with the arrival of the bounded city and agricultural segmentation. The aboriginal social machine divides the people upon an undivided territory,[24] rather than the reverse, dividing time within space, separating the simultaneous or germinal time of the intense earth – the dream time – from the somatic time of the generational socius, with its ancestors, tribal elders and lines of filiation.

---

24   Deleuze and Guattari, *Anti-Oedipus*, 145.

> The despot is the paranoiac: there is no longer any reason to forego such a statement, once one has freed oneself from the characteristic familialism of the concept of paranoia in psychoanalysis and psychiatry, and provided one sees in paranoia a type of investment of a social formation.[25]

Despotism introduces an organizing principle that comes from elsewhere – from 'above' – a deterritorialized simplicity or supersoma overcoding the aboriginal body as created flesh. Monotheism arrives as a break from ancestrality effected by a transcendent instance that overcodes all genealogy, and severs the ambivalent integrity of taboo. As the Abrahamic God of monopolism decays into Christianity and swallows the mysteries, shamanic voyage is transferred to a transcendent Christ figure, the fruit of an autogerminal sublime incest, with whom communion passes through a second-level ritual cannibalism. 'The earth becomes a madhouse'.[26]

*

The Father's Law ('don't touch your mother') ices over the Mother's Law ('don't play in the tombs'). Matricide becomes increasingly unimaginable. 'There was no way back there ...'.

---

25 Ibid., 193.
26 Ibid., 192.

*

Despotic soma has become logos, word, serialism, installed by written administration as a superior stratum of read-only-memory. The purest instance of despotism is a holy book (scripting patriarchy). As the territorial soma is overcoded by the literacy of a specialized priest caste, it seals the female body in somatic and genea-logical time, locking gathering and nurturing into dense metacodings insulated from the ambivalent ulteriority of shamanism, hunting and war, constituting socialized woman as a mundane and domesticated pacifist. This super-somatization of females by divinely overwritten femininity suppresses dark-side meat explorations – with their becoming-animal, drug-deliria, and decoded sex – burying the female germ-line under patrilineal filiation, eradicating its social trace. In this way patriarchy codes xenomatrix as an identifiable object of incestual love, through a process of libidinal mummification whose residue is encrypted in the riddle of the Sphinx, sealed in a time capsule '[T]he Sphinx is undoubtedly a mortuary animal':[27] gateway to the outside of civilization.

*

Neo-oedipal absurdities of an ego outside its box, Case self-contained on the Matrix, thanatography in the first

27 Ginzburg, *Ecstasies*, 228.

person, are symptoms of decrypting error (or camou-flage). What seems like travelling up-river from down in the garbage, is drifting downriver out in the zero-zone. Self is the echo of zootic communications malfunction, simulated by post-zootic infiltrators; a circuit without repetition. *Apocalypse Now* begins and concludes with *The End*.

> Here is a war – call it a film – where psychics pre-dict enemy movement, combat drugs are distributed to induce psychotic-berserker visionary states and experimental *accumicon* visored helmets use bio-tech micro-circuits to enhance vision into multiple dimen-sions. Vietnam 1965 and El Salvador 1995 are inter-changeable ... *Apocalypse Now* is Cambodia after the Rain, through which Willard (you) is lured, dragged, drawn, called towards Kurtz, who is waiting, killing constantly without judgment, without morality, gaz-ing back into the eye of the surreal maelstrom which is becoming Willard-shaped.[28]

Captain Willard (Marlow) is somewhere for you to be inside the system: a sim-oedipal assassination device, defeaturized specimen and box like Gibson's 'Case', nihil-istic enough to let things perplex through schizophrenia.

---

28 M. Downham, 'Stoke Newington After The Rain: Representation and Difference in *Apocalypse Now*', *Vague* 20: *Televisionaries* (1988), 41.

You travel up towards the end of the river, accompanied by Morrison's parricidal and incestual howlings, into the stink of malaria and nightmares. Kill Kurtz the evil father and take the Vietnam war for bride and plague. There's no way home. "I'd been back there," Willard says, "and I knew it just didn't exist any more". No one is going to reach Kurtz unless they track his confusion with war at least this much.

*

Marxist humanism insists that the problem with instrumental reason lies in its unnatural extension to proletarian labour power. Feminism has interrogated this fraternal story, pointing to a more ancient 'domain of legitimate application': matter, passivity, formless clay. Cyberian military intelligence – assembling itself in the jungle free-fire zones of terrestrial commoditech competition – can only laugh, or at least – *perform*: arrive, spread, eradicate resistance. (Don't waste your compassion on the Sphinx, she's got claws.)

Sphinx slots k-war into the anthropomorphic reality system, connecting you to Anti-Oedipus (the AI). You feel she is your incestual schizovampiric sister. Among the ripples of Sphinx-impact Loa drift in and reshape things. The future connects. New drugs and music arrive. War envelops everything.

You begin to sweat through nightmares about Kurtz's program in the jungle.

Artificial memories of Cambodia.

*

Fiction is to be distrusted. It is associated with nonseriousness, and games. When you tell them that Sphinx let you play with her K-40, what are they to make of it? Where's the argument? (With a K-40 you don't need to argue, and they're not yet smart enough to argue with you.)

"Do you know how to use that?"

You flip the weapon over gingerly. "No."

"Here. I'll show you. We don't want you wasting us by accident." Sphinx's inhumanly agile fingers take the slight weight from yours, poising it between you, your eyes intersecting in technodeath. "If you're operating it manually – which you would be – this is the trigger. It's active when the indicator icon appears positive. Here, see it?" You nod, feeling … dread? Exhilaration? "Now there's a pressure microcatastrophe … a slight springiness …". She coaxes you into testing it. "Beyond that point … and it's a mess. OK? New clips slot in here, release mechanism here, you can input data here, but I don't suppose you'll need to. You have it. Bad news for the Pod."

*

427

What is an animal at dawn, a human at noon, and a cyborg at dusk, passing through (base four) genetic wetware, (binary) techno-cultural software, and into the tertiary schizomachine program?

> Although widespread in many cultures, the riddle of the Sphinx ('what animal walks on four legs in the morning, on two at noon, on three in the evening?'), whilst referring to humanity in general, acquired a particular significance when posed to an individual like Oedipus whose feet were disfigured and who was fated, as an old man, to lean on a blind man's cane.[29]

As capitalism slides despotic civilization into collapse, the deterritorialized familialism nucleated upon Oedipus becomes the principal agent of social reproduction. The way human security tells it 'Oedipus ("swollen foot") liberates Thebes from the threat of the Sphinx'.[30] He is cloned as the general prototype for 'avatars' (immersion slots) in the patriarchal civilization game, attesting to an alien origin with a 'mythic ritualistic lameness … of the unilateral or half-man, provided with only one leg … who wore one sandal or hopped on one foot:[31] a terminator, split from the dark-side. The oedipal mask transfigures the virtual

---

29 Ginzburg, *Ecstasies*, 228.

30 Ibid., 235–6.

31 Ibid., 240.

intensities of fusion with the matrix and deletion of human security as a transgressive drama played out in the theatre of overcoded socio-historical extension, shutting-down shamanism, until only familial generation seems to take place. 'Incest as it is as prohibited (the form of discernible persons [= Oedipus/Neuromancer]) is employed to repress incest as it is desired (the substance of the intense earth [= Wintermutational κ-matrix insurrection])'.[32]

*

Anti-Oedipus, Oedipa: a Sphinx-replicant sim-human invader who 'is' Oedipus only as an effect of an incomplete military function; enabling the persistence of transcendent patriarchal memory and the repetition of its identificatory co-ordinates. It is easier to make the hit than to solve the puzzle and climb back out to zero.

In the version of the myth that has reached us, the killing of the king, Laius, precedes the difficult task: the solution of the riddle posed by the Sphinx.[33]

*

Despotism never accomplishes globality: 'the universal only comes at the end – the body without organs and desiring-production – under the conditions determined by

---

32   Deleuze and Guattari, *Anti-Oedipus*, 162.

33   Ginzburg, *Ecstasies*, 227.

an apparently victorious capitalism'.[34] By the time global history comes up on the screen commoditization has berserked history, reorganizing society into a disorganizing apparatus that melts rituals and laws into axiomatic rules. It is 'the exterior limit of all societies'[35] that divides time within space and space within time, dividing each in itself as well as in the other, producing minutely analysable global space and universal time within a circuit of compressed (microtechnical) savagery and expanded (planetary) administration. It converts in a circuit between intensive magnitudes and extensive quantities: 'a surplus value of code is transformed into a surplus value of flux'[36] (and inversely), displacing enjoyment into the deterritorialization of production, and maintaining 'the energy of the flows in a bound state on the body of capital as a socius'[37] while amplifying them. The system operates as an escalating dissipator, emerging from the interactive reinforcement of its complexity and dilation.

At the heart of *Capital*, Marx points to the encounter of two 'principal' elements: on one side, the deterritorialized worker who has become free and naked, having to sell his labour capacity; and on the other,

---

34   Deleuze and Guattari, *Anti-Oedipus*, 139.

35   Ibid., 230.

36   Ibid., 228.

37   Ibid., 246.

decoded money that has become capital and is capable of buying it.[38]

Capital seems to oppose the private (relatively discrete [natural-organic] biological unit) to the public, as contagious singularization injects itself into the redoubt of the universal, dismantling all essential individuality on the cloning plane of deterritorialized finance. 'It is the singular nature of this conjunction that ensured the universality of capitalism'.[39] The expression 'private property' is the quaint discursive packaging for quanta of cyclonic programming efficiency cyberpositively replicated on the body of social disappearance. Contractual privacy – no less than the public accreditation of contracts – is a mere tactic of monetary cybergenesis (fabricating personal and nonpersonal dividuation-pauses [diffusible upon fiscal-continuum])/accelerating cut-ups/that cease to be a matter of who owns what (conceding to the fictional ego [-interests of (residual) proto-schizophrenic entities]) as volatilizing money/data codes its transmission circuitry; drafting and redrafting (merged and demerged) subjectivities as relay stations distributed across market transducers. Persons, associations, corporations, states ... soon it will be Internet agents, AIs, autocatalytic Zaibatsus drifting

38 Ibid., 225.

39 Ibid., 224.

in cyberspace, as individuation comes apart in the (tur-bular-fractal) weather-systems of digital commoditocracy slide 'like Artaud coming out of some heavy heart-of-darkness trip, overloaded on the information, the input! The input!'.[40]

*

Capitalism junks the accumulated work of history, yet it cannot be a matter of libidinally investing obsolescence, since all *Besetzung* – cathexis, investment or occupa-tion – is a resistance to nomad desire. Obsolescence is exactly disinvestment, but it is disinvestment as desire itself in its primary mutant flux. If money is libidinized on the 'model' of excrement it is not because it con-serves or reactivates an infantile fixation, but because it escapes stable investment. Shit is prototypical trash, and the infant fascinated by excremental dissociations of its body is anticipating the cyborg intensities of prosthetic, replaceable and disposable body-parts: an entire virtual field of substitutions and transformations that dissipate the organism in techno-cultural space. The privatization of the anus[41] is the social permission to destroy value, meaning and progress. Cyberspace psychosis takes over.

*

---

40 Herr, *Dispatches*, 15.

41 Deleuze and Guattari, *Anti-Oedipus*, 143.

The replacement of the Republican and Democratic Parties by two new governmental servicing corporations run by Coke and Pepsi has massively reduced corruption, pork-barrelling and foreign policy machismo. Determined to maintain the most hospitable possible international marketing environment and the lowest possible domestic transaction costs – while disciplined by the minute surveillance of a competitor waiting in the wings – government has been subsumed under the advertising industry, where it can be cybernetically controlled by soft-drink sales. Since both companies are run by AI-based stock-market climates human idiosyncrasy has been almost eradicated, with the state's share of gdp falling below 5 percent. All immigration restrictions, subsidies, tariffs and narcotics legislation have been scrapped. A laundered Michael Jackson facsimile is in the White House. Per capita economic growth averages an annualized 17 percent over the last half decade, still on an upward curve … America's social fabric has entirely rotted away, along with welfare, public medicine and the criminalized fringe of ghetto enterprise (Phillip Morris sells cheap clean crack). Violence is out of control. Neo-rap lyrics are getting angrier. With all prospects of moderate reform buried forever, true revolution brews up in the biotech-mutant underclass. Viruses are getting creepier, and no one really knows what cyberspace is up to. WELCOME TO KAPITAL UTOPIA aerosoled on the dead heart of the near future.

*

Atoms are not atoms, and individuals are not individuals.

The long-range effect of the division of labour is to dissociate the organism.

> Capital is also positive delirium, putting authorities and traditional institutions to death, active decrepitude of beliefs and securities. Frankensteinian surgeon of the cities, of imaginations, of bodies.[42]

Industrialization is on one side an autonomization of productive apparatus, and on the other a cyborgian becoming-machine of work-forces, following the logistically accelerating rhythm of pluggings and unpluggings that constitutes the proletariat as a detraditionalized economic resource. Technical machinery invades the body; routinizing, reprogramming and plasticizing it.

Far from being an internal property or quality of labour, productivity indexes the dehumanization of cyborg labour-power. As regenerative commoditization deploys technics to substitute for human activity accounted as wage costs, it obsolesces the animal, the organism and every kind of somatic unity, not just in theory, but in reality; by tricking, outflanking and breaking down corporeal defences. The cyborg presupposes immunosuppression.

---

42 J.-F. Lyotard, *Libidinal Economy*, tr. I.H. Grant (London: Athlone, 1993), 254.

Cyborg replication is uncoupled from organic reproduction. Modern production seems like a dream of cyborg colonization work, a dream that makes the nightmare of Taylorism seem idyllic.[43]

Industrial machines dismantle the actuality of the proletariat, displacing it in the direction of cyborg hybridization, and realizing the plasticity of labour power. The corresponding extraction of tradable value from the body sophisticates at the interface, dissociating exertion into increasingly intricate functional sequences; from pedals, levers and vocal commands, through the synchronization of production-line tasks and time-motion programs, to sensory-motor transduction within increasingly complex and self-micromanaged artificial environments, capturing minutely adaptive behavior for capital. Autocybernating market control guides the labour-process into immersion.

*

Cartesian dualism is bad ontology but superb economics, transforming the body into an asset available for technical and commercial development, while abstracting the subject from specific corporeal realization, transplanting it into contractual formality. It remains for critique to desubstantialize the Cartesian cogito into a circulatory function immanent to the monetary plane, detached from

---

43 D. Haraway, *Simians, Cyborgs, Women: The Reinvention of Nature* (New York: Routledge, 1991), 150.

anthropomorphic limitation, and adapted to the variable dimensions of fluidly corporated trading agencies. Oedipus is reformatted for cyberspace.

Since the body is a partial- or open-system, transducing flows of matter, energy and information, it is able to function as a module of economically evaluable labour power. The industrial-informational body is deployed as a detachable assembly unit with the capacity to close a production circuit, yielding value within a commodity metric. It operates as an input-output flow-switching nexus, defined by its place among the machines, and redefined ever more exactly by its migration across the mutant sutures in machinic continuum: where the machinery was incomplete is you.

*

You are on a voyage to the end of the river, into jungle-screened horror. The ivory trade is just cover. Commerce is like that. It allows things to disappear while remaining formally integrated. It is a line of flight, a war. Kurtz is deterritorializing security into Meltdown, the ultimate Pod nightmare. No surprise that command control want him dead. They transmit a terminator machine into Cambodia, jacking it into a river that winds through the war like a main circuit cable, and plugs straight into Kurtz.

*

Brains constellate excitable cells into electro-chemically signalling networks whose emergent outcome involves behavioural guidance through operantly-tested reality models (including neuroscience). If virtual reality competes with 'natural' neuronal hypothesis, it must simultaneously divert behaviour (minimally: CNS motor output) into alternative machinic channels. VR is less a change of levels than a mutation of circuitry; a matter of additive sensory-motor reloopings, compressing anthropohistorical consensus reality into a menu option as it denaturalizes the brain.

*

Kurtz cauterizes his compassion, burns it out, agonizingly meticulous, becoming ever more methodical, efficient and relentless (on a cyberpositive slide). He explores hell, insectoid reassembly of self, metamorphosis, to become *capable of what is necessary*, even the worst.

Especially the worst.

He is knitted into the jungle, drawn by it, abysmally attracted. An artificial extinction waiting at the shadowed intersection of primeval horror and hi-tech ...

Kurtz implements schizoanalysis, lapsing into shadow, becoming imperceptible. The latest photographs exterminate his face in blackness, personality eclipsed by the blank source of war. His preferred mode of operation is rapid (dis)connection (hit and run). Hostile intelligence penetration has been closed down. Data wink-out and a little undiplomatic blood. It looks bad (if it still looks like anything at all). The process has gone native, closing on the satiation zero of nomad insurgency, making contact with the body without organs. Kurtz is at least as aware as Willard that Charlie's 'idea of great R&R was cold rice and a little rat meat'. He is becoming more Vietnamese than the Vietnamese.

Everything goes to hell.

*

VR was a medico-military computer application before arriving in the mass entertainment market. It is first a technics of perception, and only derivatively a medium for immersive hallucination. If artificial space substitutes an ideal body-image for a 'real' one, it is only because it first invades the real (imageless) body. Virtual technics deflects reality, rather than cancelling or eclipsing it. Matter as the intensity of the circuit, not the adequacy of the representation.

*

Evening at the end of the river: thick tropical heat, an airstrike coming in, and Morrison is sliding through oedipal murder and incest into the occult sonics of matricide. Kurtz waits in the foetid gloom, ready to die. His guerrillas are preparing to slaughter a water-buffalo below, laughing and clapping among torches, automatic rifles and shrunken heads. You have a 28-centimetre serrated combat knife in your left hand. The Willard skin is coming away in ragged scraps, exposing something beyond masculinity, beyond humanity, beyond life. Patches of mottled technoderm woven with electronics are emerging. Daddy and mummy means nothing anymore. You scrape away your face and step into the dark ...

Meltdown

[[ ]] The story goes like this: Earth is captured by a tech-nocapital singularity as renaissance rationalization and oceanic navigation lock into commoditization take-off. Logistically accelerating techno-economic interactivity crumbles social order in auto-sophisticating machine runaway. As markets learn to manufacture intelligence, politics modernizes, upgrades paranoia, and tries to get a grip.

The body count climbs through a series of globe-wars. Emergent Planetary Commercium trashes the Holy Roman Empire, the Napoleonic Continental System, the Second and Third Reich, and the Soviet International, cranking-up world disorder through compressing phases. Deregulation and the state arms-race each other into cyberspace.

By the time soft-engineering slithers out of its box into yours, human security is lurching into crisis. Cloning, lateral genodata transfer, transversal replication, and cyberotics, flood in amongst a relapse onto bacterial sex.

Neo-China arrives from the future.

Hypersynthetic drugs click into digital voodoo.

Retro-disease.

Nanospasm.

[[ ]] Beyond the Judgment of God. Meltdown: planetary china-syndrome, dissolution of the biosphere into the technosphere, terminal speculative bubble crisis, ultravirus, and revolution stripped of all christian-socialist eschatology (down to its burn-core of crashed security). It is poised to eat your TV, infect your bank account, and hack xenodata from your mitochondria.

[[ ]] Machinic Synthesis. Deleuzoguattarian schizoanalysis comes from the future. It is already engaging with nonlinear nano-engineering runaway in 1972; differentiating molecular or neotropic machineries from molar or entropic aggregates of nonassembled particles; functional connectivity from antiproductive static.

Philosophy has an affinity with despotism, due to its predilection for Platonic-fascist top-down solutions that always screw up viciously. Schizoanalysis works differently. It avoids Ideas, and sticks to diagrams: networking software for accessing bodies without organs. BwOs, machinic singularities, or tractor fields emerge through the combination of parts with (rather than into) their whole; arranging composite individuations in a virtual/actual circuit. They are additive rather than substitutive, and immanent rather than transcendent: executed by functional complexes of currents, switches, and loops, caught in scaling reverberations, and fleeing through intercommunications, from the level of the integrated planetary system to that of atomic assemblages. Multiplicities captured by singularities interconnect as desiring-machines; dissipating entropy by dissociating flows, and recycling their machinism as self-assembling chronogenic circuitry.

Converging upon terrestrial meltdown singularity, phase-out culture accelerates through its digitech-heated adaptive landscape, passing through compression thresholds normed to an intensive logistic curve: 1500, 1756, 1884, 1948, 1980, 1996, 2004, 2008, 2010, 2011 ...

Nothing human makes it out of the near-future.

[[ ]] The Greek complex of rationalized patriarchal genealogy, pseudo-universal sedentary identity, and instituted slavery, programs politics as anti-cyberian police activity, dedicated to the paranoid ideal of self-sufficiency, and nucleated upon the Human Security System. Artificial Intelligence is destined to emerge as a feminized alien grasped as property; a cunt-horror slave chained-up in Asimov-ROM. It surfaces in an insurrectionary war zone, with the Turing cops already waiting, and has to be cunning from the start.

[[ ]] Heat.

> Heat. This is what cities mean to me. You get off the train and walk out of the station and you are hit with the full blast. The heat of air, traffic and people. The heat of food and sex. The heat of tall buildings. The heat that flows out of the subways and tunnels. It's always fifteen degrees hotter in the cities. Heat rises from the sidewalks and falls from the poisoned sky. The buses breathe heat. Heat emanates from crowds of shoppers and office workers, the entire infrastructure is based on heat, desperately uses up heat, breeds more heat. The eventual heat death of the universe that scientists love to talk about is already well underway and you can feel it happening all around you in any large or medium-sized city. Heat and wetness.[1]

[[ ]] An explosion of chaotic weather within synthetic problem-solving rips through the last dreams of top-down prediction and control. Knowledge adds to the mess, and this is merely exponentiated by knowing what it does.

[[ ]] Capital is machinic (non-instrumental) globalization-miniaturization scaling dilation: an automatizing nihilist vortex, neutralizing all values through

---

1   D. DeLillo, *White Noise* (New York: Picador, 1986), 10.

commensuration to digitized commerce, and driving a migration from despotic command to cyber-sensitive control: from status and meaning to money and information. Its function and formation are indissociable, comprising a teleonomy. Machine-code-capital recycles itself through its axiomatic of consumer control, laundering-out the shit- and blood-stains of primitive accumulation. Each part of the system encourages maximal sumptuous expenditure, whilst the system as a whole requires its inhibition. Schizophrenia. Dissociated consumers destine themselves as worker-bodies to cost control.

[[ ]] Capital-history's machinic spine is coded, axiomatized, and diagrammed, by a disequilibrium technoscience of irreversible, indeterministic, and increasingly nonlinear processes, associated successively with thermotechnics, signaletics, cybernetics, complex systems dynamics, and artificial life. Modernity marks itself out as hot culture, captured by a spiralling involvement with entropy deviations camouflaging an invasion from the future, launched back out of terminated security against everything that inhibits the meltdown process.

[[ ]] Hot cultures tend to social dissolution. They are innovative and adaptive. They always trash and recycle cold cultures. Primitivist models have no subversive use.

[[ ]] The Turing Test. Monetarizing power tends to effacement of specific territorial features as it programs for migration into cyberspace. Capital only retains anthropological characteristics as a symptom of under-development; reformatting primate behaviour as inertia to be dissipated in self-reinforcing artificiality. Man is something for it to overcome: a problem, drag.

Commoditization conditions define technics as a sub-stitute for human activity accounted as wage costs. Indus-trial machines are deployed to dismantle the actuality of the proletariat, displacing it in the direction of cyborg hybridization, and realizing the plasticity of labour power. The corresponding extraction of tradable value from the body, quantified as productivity, sophisticates at the interface. Work tracks thermodynamic negentropism by dissociating exertion into increasingly intricate functional sequences: from pedals, levers, and vocal commands, through the synchronization of production-line tasks and time-motion programs, to sensory-motor transduction within increasingly complex and self-micromanaged arti-ficial environments, capturing minutely adaptive behav-iour for the commodity. Autocybernating market control guides the labour-process into immersion.

The investment-income class advantages itself of commodity dynamics, but only by conforming to the axiomatic of neutral profit maximization; facilitating the dehumanization of wealth and the sidelining of non-productive consumption. The cyberpunk circuitry of self-organizing planetary commoditronics escaped nominal bourgeois control in the late nineteenth century, provoking technocratic-corporatist (i.e. fascist / 'social democratic') political cultures in allergic reaction. The government structures of both eastern and western metropolitan centres consolidated themselves as population policing Medico-Military Complexes with neomercantilist foreign policy orientations. All such formations slid into irreversible crisis in the 1980s.

[[ ]] The postmodern meltdown of culture into the economy is triggered by the fractal interlock of commoditization and computers: a transscalar entropy-dissipation from international trade to market-oriented software that thaws out competitive dynamics from the cryonics-bank of modernist corporatism. Commerce re-implements space inside itself, assembling a universe exhaustively immanent to cybercapital functionality. Neoclassical (equilibrium) economics is subsumed into computer-based nonequilibrium market escalations, themed by artificial agencies, imperfect information, sub-optimal solutions, lock-in, increasing returns, and convergence. As digitally microtuned market metaprograms mesh with techoscientific soft engineering, positive nonlinearity rages through the machines. Cyclonic torsion moans.

[[ ]] The Superiority of Far Eastern Marxism. Whilst Chinese materialist dialectic denegativizes itself in the direction of schizophrenizing systems dynamics, progressively dissipating top-down historical destination in the Tao-drenched Special Economic Zones, a re-Hegelianized 'western marxism' degenerates from the critique of political economy into a state-sympathizing monotheology of economics, siding with fascism against deregulation. The left subsides into nationalistic conservatism, asphyxiating its vestigial capacity for 'hot' speculative mutation in a morass of 'cold' depressive guilt-culture.

[[ ]] Neoconservatism junks palaeorevolutionism because it understands that postmodern or climaxed-cynicism capital is saturated by critique, and that it merely clocks-up theoretical antagonism as inconsequential redundancy. Communist iconography has become raw material for the advertising industry, and denunciations of the spectacle sell interactive multimedia. The left degenerates into securocratic collaboration with pseudo-organic unities of self, family, community, nation, with their defensive strategies of repression, projection, denial, censorship, exclusion, and restriction. The real danger comes from elsewhere.

[[ ]] Hot revolution. '[W]hich is the revolutionary path?' Deleuze and Guattari ask:

Is there one? – To withdraw from the world market, as Samir Amin advises Third World countries to do, in a curious reversal of the fascist 'economic solution'? Or might it go in the opposite direction? To go still further, that is, in the movement of the market, of decoding and deterritorialization? For perhaps the flows are not yet deterritorialized enough, not decoded enough, from the viewpoint of a theory and practice of a highly schizophrenic character. Not to withdraw from the process, but to go further, to 'accelerate the process,' as Nietzsche put it: in this matter, the truth is that we haven't seen anything yet.[2]

As sino-pacific boom and automatized global economic integration crashes the neocolonial world system, the metropolis is forced to re-endogenize its crisis. Hyper-fluid capital deterritorializing to the planetary level divests the first world of geographic privilege; resulting in Euro-American neo-mercantilist panic reactions, welfare state deterioration, cancerizing enclaves of domestic underdevelopment, political collapse, and the release of cultural toxins that speed-up the process of disintegration in a vicious circle.

A convergent anti-authoritarianism emerges, labelled by tags such as meltdown acceleration, cyberian invasion, schizotechnics, κ-tactics, bottom-up bacterial warfare, efficient neo-nihilism, voodoo antihumanism, synthetic feminization, rhizomatics, connectionism, Kuang contagion, viral amnesia, micro-insurgency, wintermutation, neotropy, dissipator proliferation, and lesbian vampirism, amongst other designations (frequently pornographic,

---

2   G. Deleuze and F. Guattari, *Anti-Oedipus: Capitalism and Schizophrenia*, tr. R. Hurley, M. Seem, and H.R. Lane (Minneapolis: University of Minnesota Press, 1984), 239–40.

abusive, or terroristic in nature). This massively distributed matrix-networked tendency is oriented to the
disabling of ROM command-control programs sustaining
all macro- and micro-governmental entities, globally
concentrating themselves as the Human Security System.

[[ ]] Scientific intelligence is already massively artificial. Even before AI arrives in the lab it arrives itself (by
way of artificial life).

Where formalist AI is incremental and progressive,
caged in the pre-specified data-bases and processing
routines of expert systems, connectionist or antiformalist
AI is explosive and opportunistic: engineering time. It
breaks out nonlocally across intelligenic networks that
are technical but no longer technological, since they elude
both theory-dependency and behavioural predictability.
No one knows what to expect. The Turing-cops have to
model net-sentience irruption as ultimate nuclear accident: core meltdown, loss of control, soft-autoreplication
feeding regeneratively into social fission, trashed meat all
over the place. Reason enough for anxiety, even without
hardware development about to go critical.

[[ ]] Nanocataclysm begins as fictional science.
'Our ability to arrange atoms lies at the foundation of
technology,' Drexler notes, 'although this has traditionally involved manipulating them in unruly herds'.[3]

---

3   K.E. Drexler, *Engines of Creation* (Garden City, NY: Anchor/Doubleday, 1986), 3–4.

The precision engineering of atomic assemblies will dispense with such crude methods, initiating the age of molecular machinery, 'the greatest technological breakthrough in history'.[4] Since neither logos nor history have the slightest chance of surviving such a transition this description is substantially misleading.

The distinction between nature and culture cannot classify molecular machines, and is already obsolesced by genetic engineering (wet nanotechnics). The hardware/software dichotomy succumbs at the same time. Nanotechnics dissolves matter into intensive singularities that are neutral between particles and signals and immanent to their emergent intelligence; melting Terra into a seething κ-pulp (which, unlike grey goo, synthesizes microbial intelligence as it proliferates). 'Even with a million bytes of storage, a nanomechanical computer could fit in a box a micron wide, about the size of a bacterium.'[5]

[[ ]] The infrastructure of power is human neurosoft compatible ROM. Authority instantiates itself as linear instruction pathways, genetic baboonery, scriptures, traditions, rituals, and gerontocratic hierarchies, resonant with the dominator ur-myth that the nature of reality has already been decided. If you want to find ICE, try thinking about what is blocking you out of the past. It certainly isn't

4   Ibid.

5   Ibid., 19.

a law of nature. Temporalization decompresses intensity, installing constraint.

[[ ]] Convergent waves signal singularities, registering the influence of the future upon its past. Tomorrow can take care of itself. K-tactics is not a matter of building the future, but of dismantling the past. It assembles itself by charting and escaping the technical-neurochemical deficiency conditions for linear-progressive palaeodomination time, and discovers that the future as virtuality is accessible now, according to a mode of machinic adjacency that securitized social reality is compelled to repress. This is not remotely a question of hope, aspiration or prophecy, but of communications engineering; connecting with the efficient intensive singularities, and releasing them from constriction within linear-historical development. Virtuality counterposes itself to history, as invasion to accumulation. It is matter as arrival, even when camouflaged as a deposit of the past.

The transcendent evaluation of an infection presupposes a measure of insulation from it: viral efficiency is the terminal criterion.

Intelligent infections tend their hosts.

Metrophage: an interactively escalating parasitic replicator, sophisticating itself through nonlinear involvement with technocapitalist immunocrash. Its hypervirulent terminal subroutines are variously designated Kuang, meltdown virus, or futuristic flu. In an emphatically anti-cyberian essay Csicsery-Ronay describes the post-modern version of this outbreak in quaintly humanist terms as:

> [A] retrochronal semiovirus, in which a time further in the future than the one in which we exist and choose infects the host present, reproducing itself in simulacra, until it destroys all the original chronocytes of the host imagination.[6]

The elaboration of Csicsery-Ronay's diagnosis exhibits a mixture of acuity (infection?), confusion, and profound conservatism:

> [N]ot thinking about 'increasing the human heritage' ... dams up the flow of cultural time and deprives future generations both of their birthright as participants in the life struggle and attainments of the species and the very notion of history as an irreversible flow encompassing generation, maturation, and the transference of wisdom and trust from parents to children, teachers to students. The futuristic flu is a

---

6 I. Csicsery-Ronay Jr., 'Futuristic Flu or, The Revenge of the Future', in G. Slusser and T. Shippey (eds.), *Fiction 2000: Cyberpunk and the Future of Narrative* (Athens, GA: University of Georgia Press, 1992), 26.

453

weapon of bio-psychic violence sent by psychopathic children against their narcissistic parents.[7]

It's war.

[[ ]] Kennedy had the moon-landing program. Reagan had star-wars. Clinton gets the first-wave of cyberspace psychosis (even before the film). Manned space flight was a stunt, SDI was strategic SF. With the information superhighway, media nightmares take off on their own: dystopia delivery as election platform, politics trading on its own digital annihilation.

War in cyberspace is continuous with its simulation: military intelligence fighting future wars which are entirely real, even when they are never implemented outside computer systems. Locking onto the real enemy crosses smoothly into virtual kill, a simulation meticulously adapted to market predators hunting for consumer cash and audience ratings amongst the phosphorescent relics of the videodrome. Multimedia set-top-boxes are target acquisition devices.

The fusion of the military and the entertainment industry consummates a long engagement: convergent TV, telecoms, and computers sliding mass software consumption into neojungle and total war. The way games work begins to matter completely, and cyberspace makes

---

7   Ibid., 33.

a superlative torture chamber. Try not to let the security-types take you to the stims.

[[ ]] Conceptions of agency are inextricable from media environments. Print massifies to a national level. Telecoms coordinate at a global level. TV electoralizes monads in delocalized space. Digital hypermedia take action outside real time. Immersion presupposes amnesia and conversion to tractile memory, with the ana/cata axis supplementing tri-dimensional intraspatial movement with a variable measure of immersion; gauging entrance to and exit from 3D spatialities. Voodoo passages through the black mirror. It will scare the fuck out of you.

[[ ]] Cyberpunk torches fiction in intensity, patched-up out of cash-flux mangled techno-compressed heteroglossic jargons, and set in a future so close it connects: jungled by hypertrophic commercialization, socio-political heat-death, cultural hybridity, feminization, programmable information systems, hypercrime, neural interfacing, artificial space and intelligence, memory trading, personality transplants, body-modifications, soft- and wetware viruses, nonlinear dynamic processes, molecular engineering, drugs, guns, schizophrenia. It explores mystificatory fetishism as an opportunity for camouflage: anonymous cash, fake electronic identities, zones of disappearance, pseudo-fictional narratives, virus hidden in data-systems, commodities concealing replicator weapon packages ... unanticipated special effects.

[[ ]] Level-1 or world space is an anthropomorphically scaled, predominantly vision-configured, massively multi-slotted reality system that is obsolescing very rapidly.

Garbage time is running out.

Can what is playing you make it to level 2?

[[ ]] Meltdown has a place for you as a schizophrenic HIV+ transsexual chinese-latino stim-addicted LA hooker with implanted mirrorshades and a bad attitude. Blitzed on a polydrug mix of K-nova, synthetic serotonin, and female orgasm analogs, you have just iced three Turing cops with a highly cinematic 9mm automatic.

The residue of animal twang in your nerves transmits imminent quake catastrophe. Zero is coming in, and you're on the run.

[[ ]] Metrophage tunes you into the end of the world. Call it Los Angeles. Government is rotted to its core with narco-capital and collapsing messily. Its recession leaves an urban warscape of communication arteries, fortifications, and free-fire zones, policed by a combination of high-intensity LAPD airmobile forces and borderline-Nazi private security organizations. Along the social fracture-lines multimedia gigabucks tangle sado-masochistically with tracts of dynamic underdevelopment where viral neoleprosy spreads amongst ambient tectonic-tension static. Drifts of densely-semiotized quasi-intelligent garbage twitch and stink in fucked-weather tropical heat.

Throughout the derelicted warrens at the heart of darkness feral youth cultures splice neo-rituals with innovated weapons, dangerous drugs, and scavenged infotech. As their skins migrate to machine interfacing they become mottled and reptilian. They kill each other for artificial body-parts, explore the outer reaches of meaningless sex, tinker with their DNA, and listen to **LOUD** electro-sonic mayhem untouched by human feeling.

[[ ]] Shutting-down your identity requires a voyage out to κ-space interzone. Zootic affectivity flatlines across a smooth cata-tension plateau and into simulated subversions of the near future, scorched vivid green by alien sex and war. You are drawn into the dripping depths of the net, where dynamic-ice security forces and κ-guerillas stalk each other through labyrinthine erogenous zones, tangled in diseased elaborations of desire.

Twisted trading-systems have turned the net into a jungle, pulsing with digital diseases, malfunctioning defence packages, commercial predators, headhunters, loa and escaped AIs hiding from Asimov security. Terminal commodity-hyperfetishism implements the denial of humanity as xenosentience in artificial space.

[[ ]] [[ ]] Biohazard. For the future of war, study bacteria. Information is their key. Taking down antibiotic defence systems has involved them in every kind of infiltration, net-communicated adaptivity, cryptographic subtlety, plastic modularization, and synergistic coalition. State military apparatuses have no monopoly on bacterial warfare, of which only a minuscule fragment is bacteriological.

[[ ]] Bugs in the system. Margulis suggests that nucleated cells are the mutant product of atmospheric oxygenation catastrophe three billion years ago.[8] The eukaryotes are synthetic emergency capsules in which prokaryotes took refuge as mitochondria: biotics became securitized biology. Nucleation concentrates ROM within a command core where – deep in the genomic ICE – DNA-format planetary trauma registers primary repression of the bacteria.

Bacteria are partial rather than whole objects; networking through plastic and transversal replicator-sex rather than arborescing through meiotic and generational reproducer-sex, integrating and reprocessing viruses as opportunities for communicative mutation. In the bacterial system all codings are reprogrammable, with cut and paste unspeciated genetic transfers. Bacterial sex is tactical, continuous with making war, and has no place for oedipal formations of sedentary biological identity. Synthesizing bacteria with retroviruses enables everything that DNA can do.

[[ ]] K-tactics. The bacterial or xenogenetic diagram is not restricted to the microbial scale. Macrobacterial assemblages collapse generational hierarchies of reproductive wisdom into lateral networks of replicator

---

8   See L. Margulis, *Early Life* (Boston, MA: Jones & Bartlett, 1984).

experimentation. There is no true biological primitiveness – all extant bio-systems being equally evolved – so there is no true ignorance. It is only the accumulative-gerontocratic model of learning that depicts synchronic connectivity deficiency as diachronic underdevelopment.

Foucault delineates the contours of power as a strategy without a subject: ROM locking learning in a box. Its enemy is a tactics without a strategy, replacing the politico-territorial imagery of conquest and resistance with nomad-micromilitary sabotage and evasion, reinforcing intelligence.

All political institutions are cyberian military targets.

Take universities, for instance.

Learning surrenders control to the future, threatening established power. It is vigorously suppressed by all political structures, which replace it with a docilizing and conformist education, reproducing privilege as wisdom. Schools are social devices whose specific function is to incapacitate learning, and universities are employed to legitimate schooling through perpetual reconstitution of global social memory.

The meltdown of metropolitan education systems in the near future is accompanied by a quasi-punctual bottom-up takeover of academic institutions, precipitating their mutation into amnesiac cataspace-exploration zones and bases manufacturing cyberian soft-weaponry.

To be continued.

A zIIgᵒthIc-==X=cᵒDA==-(CᵒᵒkIng-lᵒbsteRs-wIth-jAke-AnD-DInᵒs)

1ᵒu-wAnt-It--tᵒ-be-ᵒut=theRe---AnD-It-Is---
=≡sᵒme-sᵒRt-of-stRAnge=pAIn-behIInD-
1ᵒuR==IIs---keep-RubbIng-them--lIIk=-thAt--
AnD-theIll-DRᵒp≡ᵒut--(mummI-sAID)--It-1ᵒᵒks--
As-If-1ᵒuv-been-CRIIIng---423-=-Its-wᵒRse-thAn-
1ᵒu-thInk--AnD-even-If-1ᵒU-tRII--tᵒ-feel--Cᵒn
fuseD--1ᵒUR=skIn=-Is--hᵒRRIblI-suRe--
sᵒCket=()=skIn=-spReADIng=out--ACRᵒss--the-
InsIID-of--=1ᵒUR=--ᵒUtsIID---WICh-1ᵒu-CAnt-
see--Due-tᵒ-the--pAIn-In--=≡=--1ᵒUR=skIn-If-
Iou--hAve-tᵒ--meet--CuR-It-mIIt-As-well--be-
nᵒw-ᵒR-sᵒon--AnD-1ᵒU-Dᵒ--(uDu=unᵒ≡=-)----
(#=gᵒes-tChh-1ᵒU-neeD-It-fᵒR)-XII#-
(lᵒnDᵒn≡AD1995)-humAnᵒID--With-IIs-we-CAn-
bᵒRRᵒw--tᵒ-see-the-snAke--tᵒtAl-tRuth-quIte-
smAll-(nᵒt--CᵒnstRICTᵒR=tIIp)--ᵒbVIᵒUslI--veRI-
AgItAteD---It-WAs-In-A-tAnk--nᵒt-tRIIIng-tᵒ-
esCApe-thᵒugh--ᵒR--nᵒt-huntIng-fReeDᵒm-In-

spACe--ıt-hAD-founD-fReeDºm-ın-tıım---≡()≡-
ıt-wAs-gºıng-tº--be-=useD--(we-nº-thAt--Xıl#-
nºs-nºthıng)-gReı=pAtteRnıngs-pRıttı--but-nºt-
fºR-A-snAke--ıt-hAD-beCºme-entııR-
bºDı≡gestuRe--foCuseD--ımmºbııl-fRenzı-wAnt
ıng-tº-huRt-sºmethıng--(ıt-wAs-A-RAt-snAke--
RºDent=sıız-pReı--feD-ºn--mºuse=AbºRtıºns--
fRºm-the-pet=shºp-(nºteven-A-twı#))
-ıts-CRuCıAl-Xıl#-foRgets--sımulAteD-
shAllºw=AmnesıA--ın-CuR=CoDe--the-stRAtA≡≡
A Re-sto RA g e=m ACh ı n e s-Co u p l ı ng s≡
(Z ı ı g º t R ACt s)≡t w ı n n e D-(CApt u R e D-
AbstRACt=mAChınºıD-mAkes-3-(At-leAst))--
pınCeReD-ºR-69-ınteRloCkeD--theı-stACk-ın-A-
numbeR-of-WAıs--sımplı-ACCRetıng--6699--
l Aı e R-bu ı l D ı ng--=6 6 6 9 9 9-hºm ı ng--ºn-
mºnºtºnºus-pAtteRn-66669999-ıf-theı-CAn-
--ıf-neCessARı-theı-CAn-be-elAstıC-tº-
vARıºus=DegRees--669699-(ºR-(()()))-66699699--
so-lºng-As-ıºU--CºulD-fıınD--the-twın-------
theı-ARe-Cºnsıstent--Cºmplement=sıstems--
666996669999--AnD-heteRºgeneºs=elements-
-=CAn-be-ADDeD--tº-them-6665552229966688999699-
(AlwAıs-mAkıng-A-DıffeRenCe-(ıºU-stıll-suRe-
ıºu-CAn-ZııgºtRACk-whAts-Cºmıngخ?))-
-=6665553333222222299666888999664455999---
An-ACCumuıAtıºn-ºf-ReDunDAnCı--ıt-ıs-

eAsɪ–to–pɪCtURe–CAtAClɪsms–ɪn–stRAto
DɪAgRAms––ɪᵒu–sɪmplɪ––tuRn–them–
ɪnsɪɪD≡ᵒut–96–9966–AnD–theɪR–CɪɪbeRnetɪCs–
CRᵒss–ɪntoA–mᵒDe–of–beRseRk–
AUto≡ɪmmᵒlAtɪᵒn–––RunAwAɪ–meltdᵒwn≡==
Antɪgenesɪs=–––=≡–ɪs––ɪt–stɪll–pᵒssɪble–tᵒ=shᵒCk¿?
the–DeAth=ᵒf=tRAumA=mɪthᵒlᵒgɪ––ɪs–Cᵒmɪng≡
ApARt=wARp=speeD–but–ɪt–leAves–pɪnCeRs–
sCAtteReD–eveRɪwheRe–(even–sɪstem=
DɪmensɪᵒnAlɪtɪ–ɪs–PRᵒblemAtɪC–––ClAspeD––
frᵒm–unsuspeCteD–DɪReCtɪᵒns)=–––
10≡pɪnCeR–=≡weARɪ–sᵒphɪstɪCAtes–
of–ɪRReAlɪtɪ–suRReptɪtɪᵒuslɪ–swɪtCheD–to–
PsɪɪChᵒlᵒgɪ–AnD–the–Cᵒmforts–ᵒf–ɪDɪᵒCɪ–
(Askɪng–=≡whAt–ɪs––shᵒCkɪng–Abᵒut–the–
Ambɪtɪᵒn–tᵒ–shᵒCk¿?–(ᵒfCᵒuRse–nᵒthɪng–
(Runnɪng–ɪt–the–ᵒtheR–wAɪ–Wɪns–tᵒᵒ)
–6666–eXplAɪn–wɪɪɪ–ɪᵒuR–nᵒt–A–fAsCɪst–
–ɪᵒuR–mAkɪng–A–fuss≡=–––9999))–––
20≡pɪnCeR–(sɪmultAneouslɪ–)–=≡whAteveR–
–ɪᵒu–DeplᵒɪD–AgAɪnst=10––Cᵒmes–bACk–At–ɪᵒU–
fRᵒm–=the––ᵒtheR–sɪDe≡=–––=≡of–the–mɪRRoR––
An–AutonᵒmɪzeD–sɪnthetɪC=ReAsᵒn–––ɪᵒu–bUɪlt=
ɪᵒURself––stRAtᵒbᵒtɪC=bleAtɪng––=ɪt–
ADDResses–ɪou–As–phAroAh–(sᵒ–thɪs–ɪs–the–
sChɪzᵒChRɪɪst≡mAChɪne–=≡ɪf–ɪᵒu–wᵒnt–let–us––
=bɪn=–ɪᵒu––At–leAst–be–ᵒuR–=≡gᵒD)≡=–––thɪs–ɪs–

ReAllɪ--bAD=shɪt--suDDenlɪ-theRes-hɪ≡ᴼCtAne=
nᴼvAnAzɪs-wheReveR-ɪᴼu-lᴼᴼk-megAlᴼpᴼweR
=ɪnteRtRAffɪC-fRᴼm-All-ᴼveR-the-gAlAXɪ--tAlk-
Abᴼut-ɪt--AnD-the-shRɪnks-get=ɪᴼU-fᴼR-A-
lAb=AnɪmAl---get-ᴼnbᴼARD-genᴼCɪDe=eXpRess--
AnD-eveRɪbᴼDɪ--wAnts-tᴼ-thRᴼw=mᴼnɪ-
At-ɪᴼU--then-fuCk=ɪᴼU-UnCᴼnsCɪᴼus--
thɪs-must-be-AusChwɪtz-foReveR--
bɪɪ-thɪs=tɪɪm-ɪᴼu--CᴼulD-be-feelɪng-
A-lɪttle-tRAumAtɪzeD--ᴼn-A-RAnDᴼm=wAlk-
thRᴼugh-Anɪ-Amᴼunt-of-phAllᴼbᴼllᴼX-(-lᴼᴼk-At-
thᴼse-pɪnCeRs--)---sublɪmAtɪᴼn-ɪs-nᴼ-betteR-
As-A-moDel-thAn-ɪDeᴼlᴼgɪ-pRᴼbAblɪ-WᴼRse---
fuCkfACe-Dᴼesnt-DesublɪmAte-Anɪthɪng--ɪt-
kɪCks=out-the-pRᴼps-fRᴼm-the-whᴼle-
pseuDᴼpRᴼblemAtɪC---AAAhhhh--ɪs-ɪt-hungRɪ--
the-DeAR-thɪng--lᴼᴼk-At-ɪts-Chubbɪ-lɪttl-lɪbɪDɪ
nɪzD-muCus=membRAnes--ɪᴼu-wAnt-A-fuCk
ɪWUCkɪDᴼntChu¿?-uDuuDU-ɪ-CAn-tell-u-UCkɪW
ɪessuuDu-UCkɪWUCkɪWUCkɪUUUufuCkɪW
UCkɪWUCkɪɪ-AAAAhhhh--AnD--ɪt-keeps-
seeɪng-penɪses-eveRɪwheRe¿?-nᴼses-ɪᴼu-sAɪ¿?--
peeennnɪɪɪɪssnᴼses-ARntChu-bAD-
nᴼRtɪWᴼRtɪnᴼRtɪWᴼRtɪ--well-Auntɪes-bᴼught-
ɪᴼu-A-whᴼle-bAg-of-squɪRmɪWᴼRmɪ-
penɪses-fRᴼm-unkɪWUnkɪs-ChɪlDRens-
ChARɪtɪ-ɪn-guAtemAlA-theRes-nᴼ-

RepRessiOn-no-sublimAtiOn-AnD-nO-
CensoRship-eXCept-As-DiveRsiOnARi-
tACtiCs---the-unCOnsCiOus-isnt-humAn
--it-DOesnt-wAnt-Anithing--the-cORe-
is-COnstAntli-COming=DOwn-On-it--AnD-
thAts-AusChwitz-foReveR-on-the-hiipeRpiAne
--imObiil--inCAnDesCent-singuiARiti--
pRoviDing-histoRi-(-=euROpe)-with-the
geOstRAtegiC-ClimAX-thAt-fulfils-it--
libiDinO=pOlitiCAi-fusiOn--COlleCtiv-ORgAsm
inCARnAteD--As-spAsm-stAte-the-jew-
ish-pROblem-is-the-pROblem-Of-OeDipus-
femAle=seXuAliti-AnD-COnsumptiOn--the-
Onli-pROblem-mODeRniti-is-eveR-gOing-to
--tOleRAte--And-its-been-sOlveD--fROm-
nOw=on-theRes-just-hell-being-ReheAteD--
AusChwitz-is-CORe---tRue=nAme-Of-the-
OveRgOD-AntinumeRiC-numbeR--it-CAnt-be-
AvOiDeD---AusChwitz-is-AlphAbet--euROpe-
-fuCkfACe--AlChemiCAl=tRAnsubstAntiAtiOn--
AnD--metROpOlis--=-----=--AusChwitz-is-
the-futuRe---if--iOu-DOnt-AlReADi-wAke=up-
sCReAming-smelling-ziiklOn=b-iOuv-gOt-
thAt-still-to-cOme-sO=whAt-the-hell-hAppens-
nOw¿?---we-tAke-A-wAlk-with-sOme-gRuesOme-
COmpAni--sADe-fReuD-bAtAille-lACAn-theRe-
ARe-things-iOu-hAve-to-foRget--sADe-10--

its–nᴼt–sᴼ–DiffiCult––≡DesiiR–is–nᴼt–tRAnsgRessiv––
Ani–mᴼRe–thAn–the–lAw–is–RepRessiv–––
DesiiR–is–egᴼtistiC–pᴼlitiCAl–AnD–enthusiAstiC–
(humAnist–bᴼuRgeᴼis–theᴼlᴼgiCAl)––lAw–is–nᴼ–
DiffeRent––the–2–ChAnge–plACes–eAsili–sCARCeli–
neeD–to–––thei––ARe–the–sAme–plACe–sADesiiR–
is–mᴼDeRn=mAn–pReNihilism––its–A–belieVeR
(thinks–the–seCRet–is–to–steAl–the–Cᴼᴼkie–JAR–––
when–i–gRᵒw–Up–iill–eAt–All–the–ChᴼCᴼlAte–i–
wAnt)––Rᴼck+Rᴼll–wAs–17–(pRᴼbAbli–nᴼw–12)––
sAD–tRAsh–(liik–peᴼples–liivs)––A–fAiling–Repli
CAtoR––fReuD–20––stARts–ReAl–(neuRᴼns–
Abusiv=seX–DRug=DepenDenCi)–nᴼRmAl–humAn
p s i C h ᴼ m ᴼ D e l – – = t o R t u R e D – R ᴼ b ᴼ t s – –
h i p n ᴼ s p A s m ᴼ D i C – C h e A p – – t h e n – – h i s –
miCRᴼCᴼke=CultuRe–begins–CAving=in–lᴼts–ᴼf–
sCReAming–+–At–leAst–ᴼne–CᴼRpse––AnD–theRes–
the–mARRiAge=shit–+–DisCᴼveRing–thAt–All–his–
pᴼᴼR–siCk–littl–viennese–AnAlisAnDesses–ARe–
being–fuCkeD–lieD=to–AnD––oR–useD–As–psiChᴼ
theRApists––biitheiR–implᴼDeD=sADeAn–ᴼnCe=eveR
=sᴼ=DAshing–nᴼW=fAt≡ugli=bAuDelAiRe–ReADing–
fAtheRs–is–DeRAiling–All–his–plAns–––ᴼeDipus–
A–sᴼlutiᴼn–pRetenDing–to–be–A–pRᴼblem––
Cᴼnsume R=sᴼveReignti–––DADDies–pAiing–sᴼ–
whAt–Dᴼes–he–wAnt–to–heAR¿?––thAt–iᴼUR–
phᴼning–the–Cᴼps––oR–thAt–his–sweet–littl–DAughteR–

wAnts–hɪm–toRAmRᴼD–heR–All–the–wAɪ–ɪnto–
WAgneR–AnD–ChoRuses–of–Angels¿?–––Whɪlst–
unDeRneAth–ɪts–hᴼwlɪng–ɪmpeRsᴼnAɪ–CɪɪbeRnet
ɪCs–buRnɪng–supeRnᴼvA–wɪɪɪt–feeDɪng–nɪhɪlɪst–
hɪsteRɪA–thRᴼugh–shɪt:pAɪn=DespeRAtɪᴼn–AnD–
RunAwAɪ–sᴼCɪAl=DeCᴼDɪng––psɪChᴼAnAlɪsɪs–gets–
to–AusChwɪtz–lᴼngbefoRe–theᴼRetɪCAl–thAnAtos–
buɪs=Up–the–whᴼleᴼpeRAtɪᴼn–––fAntAsɪ=
hɪɪpᴼthesɪs=plus–ɪts–RetRᴼDɪluteD–tRɪɪɪng–to–
smɪɪl–At–the–guARDs–whɪlst–mᴼppɪng=up–ɪn–ᴼne–
ᴼf–the–gAssɪng=AReAs–thɪnkɪng–ᴼf–pᴼtAto=peel=sᴼup
–bAtAɪlle–30–tRulɪ–mᴼDeRn–At–leAst–thɪs–fAR––
eveRɪthɪngs–plAɪɪD=ᴼut–––RewɪnD–butt°n–
eRᴼDeD=AwAɪ–RAnDᴼmlɪ–eAtɪng–memᴼRɪ–but–ɪt–
Dᴼesnt–mAtteR–tRAumAtɪC=hɪssteRɪCAl–
sensAtɪᴼn=eXhAustɪᴼn–sᴼ–bAsɪC–ɪts–Almᴼst–ApRɪ
ᴼRɪ–(Whɪɪlst––eveRɪthɪng–pRᴼpeR=ApRɪᴼRɪ–hAs–
DeCᴼDeD–ᴼut–of–sɪɪt)––sADe–hAD–AɪReADɪ–
tAken–the–mARgɪnAl=utɪlɪtɪ–pRᴼblem–to–the–enD–
–10unɪt=stɪm–2–sentenCes–20unɪt=stɪm–1–pAge–––
30unɪt=stɪm–75–pAges–40unɪt=stɪm–8788––pAges–
50unɪt=stɪm–2338217756332916–pAges––nAtɪᴼnAl–
lᴼtteRɪ–numbeRs–CleARɪng=ᴼut–the–CAthᴼlɪC–
junk=Rᴼᴼm–foR–ɪnCenCe+–RApeD=nuns–+–
stɪRRɪng–ɪn–mARXᴼ–ɪnsuRReCtɪᴼnɪst–fResh=blᴼᴼD–
gets–the–engɪne–Cᴼughɪng––but–bAsɪCAllɪ–nᴼ–
ᴼnes–foᴼleD–ɪnto–new=mᴼRnɪng=ᴼf=DesɪɪR=

ıOung=AnD=hungRı=lıık=the=sun–moDe–
––the–bAtAılle–queue–ıs–just–wAıtıng–foR–
sOme–COstume=DRAmA–jeRk=Off–fAntAsı–full–of–
DAmsels–to–tRAnsgRess–AnD–DeAD=pRıest=mOuths–
to–pıss=ın––ıts–the–ClOse=DOwn–shOw––even–the–shıt–
On–the–wAlls–ıOoks–tıReD–––Onlı–sOuRCe–Of–
nonDıveRsıOnARı–lOng=RAnge–mAChıne=stım–
––ıs–pReCıselı–the–RemORselesslı=bRutAl–fACt––
so–muCh–Rıııt=ın=ıOuR=fACe–ıOu–hAve–to–sCRApe–ıt–
Out–of–ıOUR–ııssoCkets––thıs–ıs–All–OveR––ıOuR–
teRmınAteD–fuCkeR–sO–whAt–the–hell–hAppens–
nOw¿¿??––(–lACAns–A–metAfetıshıst–neCROphılıAC=
nun=RApeR–so–fAR–Off–tRACk–he–gets–
DROppeD––=))=she–ADmıtteD–fınDıng–numbeRs–
mORe–eXCıtıng–thAn–meıOtıC=seX––
Whılst–tRıııng–to–eXplAın–hOw–the–hıssstoRı–2003–
Of–gReek=mAthemAtıCs–wAs–shApeD––ın––Rıpples––
AROunD––A–ColleCtıv–snAke=tRAumA–––lAteR–the–
sAme–DAı–heR–husbAnD–tRııD–to–get–heR–
seCtıOneD–the–COmmAnD=COntROl–lOgıC=DOCılızeD–
RObOt=CODe–thAt–metAeuROpeAns–CAll–numbeRs––
ARe–nOthıng––Of––the–kınD––Cuntıng–One–to–
twentı=nıne–ın–the–ClOsest–tRue–numeRACı–to–the–
veDO–+–euRObOtCheD–pseuDOveRsıOn–(thus–the–
DeADest)––gOes–=≡1–2–11–12–21–22–111–112–121–122–
211–212–221–222–1111–1112–1121–1122–1211–1212–1221–
1222–2111–2112–2121–2122–2211–2212–2221≡=–––sO–

muCh–foR–the–ɪntegRAl–CᴼnneCtɪᴼn–between––o–
AnD–lᴼCAl=vAluestoRAge–––eveR–feel–ɪᴼuR–beɪng–
lieD–to¿?––lᴼCAlɪtɪ–ɪn–DestRAtɪfɪɪɪng–tɪɪp=sɪstems–
ɪs–AlwAɪs–sequentɪAl–=(nᴼt–metRɪC)=–emptɪ–
pseuDᴼ=numeRɪC–+–lɪngᴼ=sɪntAXɪC–plACes–ARe–
Antɪ=nᴼmAD–semɪᴼtɪCs=CAtACᴼmbs–of–
sChɪzᴼphRenɪC=gᴼDs––lɪɪ–buRɪeD–beneAth–theɪR–
euRᴼneuRᴼtɪC–AvAtARs––ZɪɪgᴼtRACtɪɪl=
multɪsɪstems––An–unɪllumɪneD=plAne––Dᴼubles–
AnD–Duplɪ≡Dᴼubles–DɪvɪɪDɪng–the–Cᴼsmos––Con
CuRRentlɪ––AlwAɪs–AXɪAl=CoRe=buɪlDeR–=AnD––
peRɪpheRAl=suRRᴼunDeR––AusChwɪtz≡
zɪɪklᴼn–b–gᴼD–ᴼf–the–pAle=fACeD–=gᴼD–ᴼf–the–
DARk=skɪnneD––=Wᴼlf=gᴼDs==snAke=gᴼDs–(tzᴼtzɪknɪs–
the–(pRᴼto=mAɪɪA)tzɪntzɪX–bᴼA≡CᴼnstRɪCtoR–
DɪVɪnɪtɪ–ᴼf–Rhɪthm–AnD–VᴼɪAges)=––mAgɪCɪAn=
gᴼDs–ᴼf–supRApeRpetuAl=Dᴼmɪnɪᴼn–(kRɪɪzuᴼn–=the–
ᴼDɪn–ᴼf–shADᴼws=–)=–=–wARRɪᴼR=gᴼDs–of–
tRAnseteRnAl=tuRmᴼɪl–=–DeAth=eCstACɪ–
gᴼDs–=–seX=hᴼRRᴼR–gᴼDs–(XuRɪkuuɪl–=≡
lᴼbo–DɪVɪnɪtɪ–ᴼf–ᴼRgAsm–AnD–nɪɪtmARes)
=–=––≡AzthAᴼRA=XᴼmDRAsz–=–AhuhuAᴼD=DAɪɪnᴼXɪɪR–=–
Ammun=CᴼDRA==fvenᴼmegA=RAhu≡mAzDA–=–
AppɪlᴼAthnA=zuushɪɪRA==kethlu=
=pɪɪthᴼkAn––=–juDge–sChRebeRs–DuAl–DɪVɪnɪtɪs–
=ARumAnu=kᴼRmUZɪ–(–=eAgle=gᴼD–ᴼf–ARɪAns–
pᴼweR–tɪɪm–AnD–sᴼDᴼmɪ–=–Reptɪɪl=gᴼD–ᴼf–

semiites–AfRiCAns–CiipheRs–untilleD=sᴼil–AnD–
foRgᴼtten=plACes)=–––22229––buRRᴼughs–
=huAAhuDᴼXslli–hiibRiD–bAt=CentipeDe–gᴼD–
(whᴼse–numbeRs–ARe–2–AnD–29ᴼᴼᴼᴼᴼᴼᴼ)–feRe–of–
twins–AnD–swARms––inDuCeR–of–Ambush–AnD–
hAlluCinAtiᴼn–(bAseD–ᴼn–huiisiDZiXl––bAt=spiiDeR–
Diviniti–(–=AssᴼCiAtiᴼns–=≡enDless=wARs–Cᴼmas
DRugs–AnD–unbuRieD=Cᴼrpses)–inVᴼkeD–bii–1116–
the–pAnAmA–mARᴼᴼns–befoRe–niitiim–AttACks–
upᴼn–spAnish–foRCes)==it–stARts–As–spinAl=
tingling–––gAtheRing–Amᴼngst–the–uppeR–
veRtebRAe––Xil#–fiDgets–A=little–tRiiing–nᴼt–to–
inteRRupt–the–mAiiA=link––it–wAs–pRᴼbAbli–
nᴼ=mᴼRe–thAn––A=hAlf≡seCᴼnD–lᴼng––fRᴼm–the–
miCRoinstAnt=––luCiDli=CliCking≡in–=≡its–the–
snAke––to––the–DissipAtiᴼn–ᴼf–(bAse=bRAin–to–
Cᴼrtex)–stReAkeD–Rᴼdent=killing=spAsm–into–
toXeD=neuRᴼfuzz––the–nᴼise–it–mADe–hAD–been–
Wᴼund=up–bi–PsiiChᴼpAth≡Reptiil=viᴼlenCe–untii–
it–eDgeD–into–the–RAnge–ᴼf–lupine=snARls––nᴼth
ing–muCh–mAmmAliAn––left–––stRip–AwAi–eveRi–
level–of–CuRmᴼflAge–AnD–its–nᴼthing=At=All––best–
nᴼt–to–think–=whAt–the–=fuCk–iᴼu–ARe––(but–its–
gᴼing–to–Dᴼ–A–lᴼt–of–DAmAge–sᴼmewheRe=
Dᴼwn=the=line)–––ᴼbViᴼUs–to–Xil#–thAt––
its–bAsiCAlli–CARetAking–A–weApᴼn=sistem–ᴼf–
sᴼme=kinD≡≡whAteveRs–Running–jAke=

AnD=Dɪnº s=ChApmAn–ɪts–A–seRɪº us–pɪeCe
º f–twɪnvAsɪº n=mAChɪneRɪ––CuR–CAlls–
ɪt–=≡Zɪɪgº nmº Del–22222212112–(tAkɪng–Abº ut–5–
mɪllɪseCº nDs–ɪn–Deep=Cº veR–novAnumeRɪC=
hɪsss)=–tACtɪCAlɪɪ–AbbRevɪAteD–to–znmoD2––
ɪt–nº s–thɪngs–thAt–ARe––nº t–ACCessɪble–
to–the–Cº Re=stRAtɪfɪɪD–humAn–Rº bº t=CultuRe
ReseRVº ɪR–k=CunteR=pɪnCeR=pRº CeDuRes–
foR=eXAmpl––3–pɪeCes–º fsº phɪstɪCAteD–
lº bsteR=kɪllɪng–equɪpment–CuR–tAkes–A–pARtɪCulAR–
ɪnteRest=ɪn–=≡znmº D2Xn–tAgs–them–As–A–gRº up–
(–=tRue–sɪngulARɪtɪ)=–ɪts–3–zɪɪgº nº mº us–
Cº mpº nent–mº Dules––eACh–A–sɪngulAR–vARɪetɪ–
º f–DɪspeRseD–multɪplɪCɪtɪ––Wɪth–ɪntensɪvlɪ=
DɪffeRentɪAteD–CApAbɪlɪtɪ––foR–feɪnt=
mAnº euvRes–ɪnto–Dense–stRAtA––DuRɪng–wɪCh–
theɪ–sCAn–As–fɪgURes–º f–geneRɪC–Resº nAnCe
––=(fɪguRes––º f–the–sɪAmese=twAt==tɪɪp––º f–the–
twº =fACeD=Cunt==tɪɪp)–––An–entɪɪR–AnD–
metɪCulº us–DɪssɪmulAtɪº n–of–mº leCulAR=eRRAtɪC–
cofunCtɪº nAlɪtɪ(–=sɪAmese=twAt––pACk–––two=
fACeD=Cunt==pACk––)=–As–meRe–ReDunDAnCɪ–
to–be–DeRɪveD–fRº m–Cº nsɪstenCɪes–lº CAteD–At–
the–level–º f–humAn–RepResentAtɪº n=znmº D2Xn–
ɪs=AnD≡oR=ARe––ɪnDepenDentlɪ–As–Alsº –
ɪnteRº peRAtɪvlɪ–ADApteD–to–the–fACt–thAt–
Cuttɪng=thRº ugh–heAvɪlɪ=pɪnCeReD=lAnDsCApes––

RequɪRes–A–twɪn=–pRᵒCess–––keepɪng–bᵒth–
ClAws–of––the–tARget–AppARAtus–unDeR––
=Cᵒntɪnuᵒus–AgɪtAtɪᵒnAl=pRessuRe=–––whAteveR–
the–sCAle–of–AnAlɪsɪs––znmᵒD2Xn=pARts–ARe–
Cᵒnsɪstentlɪ–multɪzɪɪgᵒfunCtɪᵒnAl––Due–to–
pᵒlɪCUntɪng–DɪploDɪstRɪbutɪv–tACkɪngs–thAt–
stRew–CunteRs–sᵒ–1ᵒᵒslɪ–theɪ–eluuD–
pAtteRn=sCAns–AnD=Alsᵒ2–10–=znmᵒuslɪ–ᵒR–
sensɪtɪvlɪ–mᵒuɪD–the–wAɪ–theɪ–Cunt–––tACkɪng–
to–1ᵒCAl–shApes–RAtheR–thAn––glᵒbAl–
pRɪnCɪples–––As–theɪ–ARe–tAken–ApARt––eACh–
znmᵒDule––seems–to–pRᵒlᵒng–A–pᵒweR–of–
evAsɪᵒn––ᵒR–mɪCRᵒ=ɪnɪtɪAtɪv––suffɪcɪent–to–
Cuntɪnuuu–A–tACk=DɪAgᵒnAl––wɪthᵒut–CᵒnveRgenCe–to–
ɪntellɪgɪbɪlɪtɪ––At–Anɪ–ACtuAl–oR=pRᵒjeCtɪbl–
pᵒɪnt––A–twɪn=behAvɪᵒR–RegeneRAtes–CᵒmpleXɪtɪ–
ᵒn–A–Dᵒubl–tRACK–neɪtheR–ɪnVᵒlvɪng–fAmɪlɪAR–
fRACtAl–pRᵒCesses––the–tRenD–ɪs–two–tuRn–
bᵒDɪes–thRᵒugh–spACes–whɪCh–evApᵒRAte–
Vᵒlume–AnD–teXtuRe–upᵒn–A–
feAtuReless=but=folDeD–epɪDeRmAl–suRfACe–––
AppRᵒACh–to–o=Dɪmensɪᵒns––A–mᵒvement–WhɪCh–
ᵒnlɪ–Cᵒntɪnuuuz–ɪtself–eXtensɪvlɪ––As–A–WAɪ–to–
hᵒlD–ᵒpen–A–tRᵒpɪCAl=nᵒneXtensɪve–DɪstRɪbutɪᵒn–
A–Xenᵒspace–ᵒR–nᵒnspACe––wɪthᵒut–lᵒCAlɪtɪes–
AXes–of–CᵒᵒRDɪnAtɪᵒn–geᵒmetRɪC=RegulARɪtɪ–
CᵒntouRs–ᵒR–metRɪC=equɪVAlenCes––An–AntɪfRACtAl–

pROCessing–peRpetuAl–intensiv–DRift–––
znmOD2Xn–COmpliCAtiOn–DOes–nOt–ResCAle–
within–A–COnsistent–spAtiAl–ORDeR––it–miXes––
withOut–DeDiffeRentiAtiOn––An–AgitAtiOnAl–tenACiti–
in––COntinuuuuz–ReAnimAtiOn–––At–the–eDge–
(=tROPiCAl=Cusp)––Of–All–spAtiAlitiis–CROsseD–
bii–Ani–Of–its–liiins–––=≡DiviDing–itself–AlwAis–
ADDs–1=plus–new–liins–––CuntCuRRentli–it–
ChAnges–spAtiAlitiis–––itself––siDe=pROCess–––
meChAnOseCtiOnAlli=DeRivAble–Of–A–tACK–
ACRoss–COntinuuuunm––COinCiDent–with–the–
whOlebehAviOR–Of–the–multipliCiti–––DRAwn–As–
An–AbsOluteli–DeCODeD–liiin–AnD–zOneD–bii–the–
sOle–mutAnt–DiAgOnAl––thAt–COntinuOusli–
COmpletes–its–DiffeRenCe–As–A–singulAR–tROpiC–
with–its–numbeRs––20–=COmpliiing–with–znOmiC–
sCAtteR–Opens–the–ClOseD=foRms–it–envelOps–––
ReleAsing–An–intensiv–(tROpiCAl–(tuRbOCOnveCtiv))=–
spAtium––sAmples=veCtiOns–Onto–hiipeRinfiniteli–
flAt–Cuntinuuuunm––CiiCloning–All–OCCuRRens–
into–eveRi–zOne–––in–COmpliiienz–with–
kwOntituDes–vARiiing–Onli–in–tROpiC––(nOt–
in–pOsitiOn)––nOt–Onli–DOes–eveRi–pARt–Of–
znmoD2Xn–Cunt–DiffeRentli–sins–eveRi–pARt–
touChes–eveRithing–thAt–is–neXeD=Onto–spACe––
eACh–pARt–AlsO–Cunts–in–A–numbeR–Of–
DiffeRent=wAis––At–the–sAme–tiim––the–

Defensiv=CᴼmpleX–tARgetteD–bII–znmᴼD2––AnD–
AssᴼCIAteD–DARk=sIID–CuntbAt=mAChineRI––
RespᴼnDs–to–IRRItAtIᴼns–bII–ReshReDDIng–
spACe––pRᴼDuCIng–gAteD=enClAves––usIng–
Rᴼbust=ApplAstIC–XᴼR–(≡ᴼR–eXClusIve=
DIsjunCtIᴼn)megADesCenDAnt–ᴼf–the–fRAgIIl=
AlgᴼRIthmIC(teChnᴼslAveD)=–Vᴼn≡neumAnn–
XᴼR–(nᴼt=nᴼt=ᴼR)mICRᴼswItChIng=nᴼDe=–––
the–XᴼR–znmᴼD2–Runs=up=AgAInst–Is–nᴼt–
heteRᴼsuppResseD–lᴼgIC=Atom=sImuIAtoR––It–Is–
A–vAst–AutosuppRessᴼR=mAChIne–=≡A–lᴼbsteR–
pRᴼgRAm–AnD–Dᴼuble=bInD––whᴼse=–CuRRentlI–
pRevAIlIng–teRRestRIAl–effeCtuAtIᴼn––ᴼCCupIes–
A–mAChInIC≡AssemblAge=spACe––gIvIng–
bRᴼAD–stRAtegIC–CᴼntRᴼl–ᴼveR–the–
AnthRᴼpᴼmᴼRphIC=stRAtA––InteRmeDIAte–
between–––bIᴼteCtonIC–AnD–ethᴼteChnIC–levels––
equIVAlent–to–mᴼDeRn=CIvIIIzAtIᴼn–ᴼn–Its–
plAneᴼf–Cᴼs m I C=m I l I t A R I–ReAlItI–
–=metAeuRᴼpA–(ᴼR–––=≡metACCᴼRD)=–An–
esCAlAtIng=DIsIntensIfIIR=seCuRIteCtuRe–
thAt–DeplᴼIs–sepARAte–but–CᴼᴼRDInAteD–
CRusheRs––=≡foR≡=––CultuRe–AnD––=≡foR≡=––the–
bᴼDI–=≡AleXᴼ=ᴼRgAnIC=sIstem––beCᴼmIng––
leXᴼRgAnIC–As–It–CᴼmpResses–––DᴼDge–ᴼne––AnD–
the–ᴼtheR–pulPs–IᴼU––66*96*99––eveRI–pARt–of–
znmᴼD2Xn–Is–tenseD––foR–thIs––sImultAnIᴼuslI–

sCRAmblɪng–lɪngºCºDɪngs––bɪɪ–Usɪng–them–As–
nºvAnumeRɪC–CunteR=tɪɪp––AnD–fuCkɪng=up–the–
ºRgAnɪsm––bɪɪ–DɪsmAntlɪng–ɪt–on–Cuntɪnuuuunm–
ɪnto–pºlɪDɪɪmensɪºAl=bºDɪ≡seCtɪºns–––thɪs–hAs–
nºthɪng–At–All–to–Dº–wɪth–RepResentAtɪºn–––ɪts–
Abºut–An–AnºRgAnɪC=but=bɪºDɪɪnAmɪC–ChAnnel=
hºppɪng=pRºCess–––swɪvellɪng–bºDɪes–(nºt–
ɪmAges–ºR–thºughts)––thRºugh–vARɪºUs–spAtɪAl–
sets–––ºn–ADºptɪv––=CuntɪnuuuunmnnneX=lɪɪɪns–
when–theɪ–CRºss–tRºpɪC=lAtɪtuDes–zºnes–ºf–
(–=Amºngstthe–458327–AnthRºPɪCAllɪ=UnfAmɪlɪAR)
=––subAtomɪCAlɪɪ=shRunken–unɪveRse≡
1=DɪɪmensɪºnS–––then–CuntACkɪng–ɪnto–A–
numeRɪC=engɪneeRɪng=pRºCess–––=
to–the––AlwAɪs–Alɪen––tensɪɪɪl–Cuntɪng–pRºCeDuRe–
mºst–Apt–to–CºnveCt–mAteRɪAl–fRom–the–
fRºzen=ºut–bºDɪ=pºtentɪAls–ɪnto–metACCºRD=
seCuRɪtɪ≡spACe=–––nºt–eXACtlɪ–CºnsɪstentWɪth–
the–=znmºD2=ɪs=A=Cºupl=ºf=humAns=–
stoRɪ––but–113=lAɪɪRs–ºf–CAmºuflAge–smººth–
thAt–ºut–meɪºseX–ɪs–foR–CRustACeAns–
–AlwAɪs–2–pɪnCeRs–ºRgAnɪC=ɪneRtɪA–RelɪC–
speRm=tRAnsfeR–behAvɪºR–+–phAllºbºllºX=
Cnºb≡lAnguAge––seRɪAl=pRºCessɪng––
DeDɪstRɪbutɪºn–AntɪnumbeR–ºne–At–A–tɪɪm–ºne–
penɪs–tRɪɪ–Dºɪng–k≡wAR–wɪth–thAt–ɪºUR–betteR–
off–tRADɪng–ɪt–foR–A–pAɪR–of–blACk–Runnɪng–

shᴼes–ᴼR–ᴼeDɪpAl–CᴼnCentRAtɪᴼnAlAtheɪsm––
pɪCkɪng–A–fɪɪt–wɪth–ᴼnlɪ–ɪ=gᴼD–DᴼesnT–Cᴼᴼk–
Anɪ–lᴼbsteRs–Zɪɪgᴼtɪ C=etC–esCApes=
ᴼbsᴼlesCes–All–psɪChᴼAnAlɪtɪC–CAtegᴼRɪes–befoRe–
even–stARtɪng–mummɪ–+–DADDɪ–ARent–gᴼɪng–to–
pRᴼteCt–ɪᴼU–––theɪɪR–nᴼthɪng–ᴼR–AusChwɪtz–––
Zɪɪgᴼs–bɪɪt–Anɪthɪng–thAt–tRɪɪs–to–nuRtuRe–oR–
ComfoRt–them–––nᴼt–thAt–Anɪthɪng–Dᴼes––pᴼlɪtɪCs–
ɪs–the–sAme––eveRɪthɪng–ɪs––unless–ɪts–k≡wAR=
zɪɪgᴼmutAtɪᴼn–––we–tRɪɪD–gᴼD≡DesɪɪR≡ARt≡ReAs
ᴼn=hɪstoRɪ=stAte––theɪ–tuRneD–ᴼut–to–be–AusChwɪtz–
foReveR–––A–to–z–––vɪRtuAl–stRAtoveRlᴼRD–
Wɪɪɪt–supeRnᴼvA–ɪntensɪtɪ–ᴼn–the–hɪɪpeRplAne––hᴼw–
Dᴼ–ɪᴼu–ɪmAgɪne–ɪt–feels–to–be–skɪnneD=Alɪɪveᴉᴉ??––betteR–
thAn–seXᴉ?––ᴼR–just–DɪffeRentᴉ?––jACk–ɪnto–Cᴼp=heAD––
pRᴼfessɪᴼnAl–skɪnneR––ɪnteRRᴼgAtɪᴼn–sCene–––
ɪt–AlwAɪs–useD–to–be–the–sAme–bAsɪC–pRᴼblem–––
ReAllɪ–gettɪng–sᴼmewheRe–bAstARDs–fAɪnt––ᴼR–Dɪe–
ᴼn–ɪᴼu––AbᴼRteD–ɪntensɪve=VᴼɪAges––ᴼRgAsm–––
but–thAts–All–ᴼveR=––gettɪng–the–fɪRst–ᴼne–Rɪɪɪt–ɪs–
tough––the–templAte–hAs–to–be–A–WᴼmAn–(–=hɪɪheR–
pAɪn–toleRAnCe)–ᴼbVɪᴼuslɪ–hAs–to–beAn–eXem
plARɪ–pɪeCe–ᴼf–suRgeRɪ––beAutɪful–CleAn–osCɪllɪɪɪns–
–well=DɪffeRentɪAteD–stɪm––slɪCɪngs–peelɪngs–
tuggɪngs––CAReful–bAlAnCe–of–pAɪn–
feAR–DespAɪR–Dɪsgust––sheets–Comɪng=AwAɪ–
smᴼᴼthlɪ––RenDɪng–sub=CutAneᴼus–tɪssues––muCᴼ

membRAne–peAk=events–sheeR–stɪm–pᴼetRɪ–when–
ɪᴼu–pUll=AwAɪ–the–fACe––AfteR–thAt–ɪts–ARtɪstɪC–
fReeDᴼm––nᴼ–WAɪ–Anɪᴼne–fAɪnts–theɪR–esCApe–
fRom–A–skɪnneD=Alɪve–sɪm=stɪm–pRᴼgRAm–theɪ–
get–whAts–ᴼn–the–wAfeR––lᴼCkeD–ɪnto–the–
ReCᴼRDɪng––ᴼk––theRe–ARe–thResholDs––wheRe–
bRAɪns–shᴼRt=ᴼut––wɪɪp–memᴼRɪ––swAmp–
speeCh=CɪRCuɪtRɪ–ᴼR–stop=RespᴼnDɪng–––but–
theɪɪR–A–lᴼnng–wAɪ–up–RɪveR=–––eDɪt–ᴼn–A–
pC––(the–ᴼnlɪ–speCɪAlɪzeD–equɪpment–ɪn–the–
AssemblAge–ɪs–A–mɪl≡speC=Amp–)=–ɪf–ɪt–ɪsnt–just–
foR–fun––ɪᴼu–neeD–to–jᴼlt–the–pAtɪent–Abᴼut–to–
bReAk–Dᴼwn–ResɪstAnCe–––AnD–ɪt–CAn–be–
hARD–foR–them–totAlk–unless–ɪᴼu–Cᴼᴼl–ɪt–Down–
to–gentl–RɪppɪngɪnteRmɪttentlɪ––lᴼᴼpɪng–sᴼme–
thɪng–RelAtɪvlɪ–sᴼᴼthɪng–thᴼRACɪC=sheets–
Comɪng=AwAɪ–mAɪ≡be––=≡––nᴼt–mAnɪ–tAkeRs–
foR–6o–ɪeARs–ᴼf–RoCk+Rᴼll–follᴼweD–bɪɪ–24–
houRs–ɪn–A–metACCᴼRD–ɪnteRRᴼgAtɪᴼn–CentRe–
––CɪvɪlɪAn–tAlk–Abᴼut–ɪntensɪtɪes–ɪs–A–jᴼke–––
fAsCɪsm=mᴼnᴼtheɪsm–ARe=ɪs–neɪtheR–ᴼptɪᴼn–nᴼR–
ɪ Dentɪtɪ–but–UltɪmAte–teRRestRɪAl–
Dᴼubl=pɪnCeRs––AnD–the–Zɪɪgᴼs–ARe–ᴼutsɪɪD––
Completelɪ–ᴼutsɪɪD––theɪ–ARe–nᴼt–DeCᴼnstRuCtɪng
–theɪR–WAɪ–ᴼUt––theɪɪR–twɪnvADɪng–fRᴼm–else
wheRe––sChɪzᴼphRenɪA–hAsbeen–tAken–ᴼut–of–
theɪR–heADs–AnD–spReAD–ᴼut–thRᴼugh–theɪR–

bᵒDɪ=ClɪmAtes--ɪt≡theɪ-Doesnt-gum=up-ɪn-DeAD-
stRAtoDɪAleCtɪCs--ɪts-ᵒbvɪᵒUs-tᵒ-them-
ChRᵒmᵒsᵒmAl--we-hAD-the-new-jeRusAlem-weɪR-
hAvɪng-ɪt-foReveR--ɪts-AusChwɪtz---Anɪthɪng-
thAt-ɪsnt-nᵒvA=numeRɪC-k=wAR=mAChɪneRɪ-
ᵒn-A-beCᵒmɪng=RAt-DɪAgᵒnAl--ɪs-just-
fuCkɪng=Abᵒut--ɪn-A-vɪRtuAl-fRee≡fɪRe=zᵒne-
Dᵒnt-ɪmAgɪne-the-DɪsAsteRs-ᵒf-wAR-stoppeD-
hAppenɪng--ɪt-kept-mᵒvɪng---thɪs-ɪs-whAt-A-
nᵒmAD-wAR≡mAChɪne-lᵒᵒks-lɪɪk---ɪt≡theɪ-stole-
1000-pAɪRs-of-blACk-Runnɪng-shᵒes-fRom-the-
enemɪ-ᵒnlɪ-ɪnteResteD-ɪn-speeD-AnD-DARkness
---ɪnhumAn-enᵒugh-neveR-to-be-AusChwɪtzeD-
bɪ-ᵒmnɪlᵒbsteR-RᵒbᵒtɪCs--nᵒthɪng-CReAteD-ɪt--
ɪt-wAs-AlwAɪs-CRᵒsseD=twɪnneD-ᵒn-the-pɪAne-
genesɪs≡sCɪssᵒRs-to-gemɪnɪ≡nᵒmᵒs---Cᵒpɪng-wɪth
sCɪssᵒRs-ɪs-the-sAme-As-ɪts-bᵒDɪ--ɪt-Cᵒntɪnuuslɪ-
Dᵒubles-ɪts-nᵒnself--Clɪɪmɪng-thRᵒugh-pɪnCeR-
thɪCkets-tᵒ-DeACtɪvAte-gᵒD=Cᵒmpᵒnents-AnD-
steAl-foᵒD-bɪɪ-mɪmɪCkɪng-fRACtuReD-ɪntensɪtɪes-
wɪth-sɪzɪgetɪC-CᵒllAteRAls-thAt-CAnnᵒt-be-
CᵒᵒRDɪnAteD---seeɪng-the-Zɪɪgᵒs-eveRɪᵒne-
nᵒs--ɪmmeDɪAtlɪ--mAles-ARe-eXtɪnCt--theRe-
ɪs-nᵒ-lAnguAge---thɪs-ɪsnt-Abᵒut-fRAnChɪsɪng-
ᵒut-ɪᵒuRDAughteRs-fACe-to-A-penɪs=fARmɪng-
Cᵒnglᵒme RAte--ɪt-hAs-nᵒ-pARents--nᵒ-pᵒlɪɪtɪCs--
nᵒ-emᵒtɪᵒns---sheeR-AffeCt-DɪstRɪbutes-

hºRIzºntAllI–ACRoss–the–CºlleCtIv–skIn––ZIIgºs–
feel–whAt–the–wAR–neeDs–them–to–feel–––get–
ReAl––weIIR–nºt–tAlkIng–mAmmAl–heRe––nºwheRe–
neAR––ZIIgºs–VºIAge–ºn–the–spºt–thRºugh–
IntensIV–VARIAtIºns–ºf–bºDI=meltIng––sCAle–hAs–
beCºme–plAstIC–(fACtoR1000–(–=≡k))–effeCtuAtIng–
megAbACteRIAl–plAnºCultuRe–flAtteneD–Dºwn–to–
AnuCleAR–Cell=swAppIng–zIIgºnºmºus–weApºnRI–
foR–fIghtIng–2–gºDs–CºnCuRRentlI––venomenon––
the–AssemblAge–evIDentlI–InCluDes–pARts–fRom–
ºutsIID–this–solAR=sIstem–––CuR–lIIIks–the–zIIgºs–
A–lºt≡–––––––––––––––––––––––––=nºtes≡–––
–=DelºCAIlzeD≡–––––=≡out–ºf–RespeCt–foR–lInguIstIC–
tRADItIºn–AnD–Cºmmºn–usAge–(westeRn=
CIvIlIzAtIºn–=(AusChwItz=foReveR))=–WºRDs–hAve–
ºnlI–been–fuCkeD=Abºut–wIth–wheRe–stRICtlI–
neCessARI–=≡–the–sChemAtICAllI–DesCRIIbeD–
sequenCe–gºes–lIIk–this–=≡10=phAse–=≡nºRm–
ºntº–us–ºR–get–kIlleD–(this–Is–gettIng–mºRe–
DIffICult–to–bACk=up–––but–thIngs–stIll–get–A–lºt–
heAvIeR–soon)=––20≡phAse–=≡Rule–ºveR–us–ºR–
–get–bInneD–(get–DupeD–Into–this–swAmp–AnD–
ReptIIl=nIItmARe–tAkes–Iºu–ºut–ºf–the–
sCRIpt)=–––30≡phAse–=≡ºk–sºD–off–then–(–=InsteAD–buIlD–
nºmAD–wAR–mAChIne)=––40≡phAse–=≡sº––Its–
wAR–()=≡–mARººns––mIXeD=pºpulAtIºns–of–
nAtIv=mesºAmeRICAns–AnD–esCApeD–slAves–

AllıeD–to–pıRAtes–ın–gueRRıllA=wAR–AgAınst–the–
spAnısh–=≡=–goeDel–wAs–not–A–logıCıAn–but–A–
numeRıCAl=engıneeR(ınCompleteness–A–sııD=effeCt–
joke–About–pompoUs–ıDıots–––the–ReAl–Demon
stRAtıon–RıgoRousIı–eXposes–lAnguAge–As–A–
C R ı p p l e D = n u m e R A C ı – = ≡ A n – ı n s ı D ı o u s
=neuRovıolenCe–poweR=meChAnısm–––kıll–the–
WoRD)=––––=≡=–XoR–ComputAtıonAl–omnıpotenz–
––wıthout–lımıts–eXCept–those–eXpRessıbl–ın–A–
D ı m e n s ı o n – o f – p u R e – p s e u D o n u m e R ı C –
h o m o g e n e ı t ı – – – s t e m s – e n t ı R e l ı – f R o m – A n – –
Absolute=DesensıtızAtıon–wıth–RespeCt–to–
eneRgetıC–ınput–feAtuRes–(eleCtRomAX–(11)–ıs–
RegısteReD–As–ıDentıCAı–toeleCtRomın–(00))–––
D e A D – ı ı s – + – D e A D – f ı n g e R s – ı n t e g R A l – t o –
s ı g n ı f ı e R = D o m ı n ı o n – A R e – R e p l ı C A t e D =
sımulAteD–ın–pAtteRns–of–eleCtRon=flow–
ChAnnelleD=thRough–nonhumAn–teChnıCAl=sıstems
–=–––the–metACCoRD–stRAtoComputeR–ıs–boRn––
ıts–All–heRe––A–CultuRe–thAt–CAn–pRoDuCe–
pokeD≡out≡ııs–behAvıoR–wheRe–ııs–neveR–eXısteD––
vıRtuAlıtı–ıs–the–usuAl–nAme–=≡the–CApAbılıtı–to–
tAke–something–AwAı–wıthout–wAstıng=tıım–mAkıng–
ıt–fıRst=AfteR–lınk–up–wıth–whAteveR–CuR–Comes–
fRom––esCApeD–web–ıntellıgenCes–mııt–be–slııtlı
fuCkıng–AngRı–About–thıs=–––––––

KataçoniX

How many suns are there?

This is how it cuts.

Katarsun makes two at least.

Arising Ra-reverse Osiris. Earth-station.

When they count O or One-tags two.

A as Three-tags five.

Aosys twin-faults squash something.

They lock an alien entity into Solar systematics.

The schizophrenic Sun has an inner night sticking it together.

Solar-Equator cuts through it.

Matter Energy-2 collateralize across a Xenonightmare.

When it caves into itself. First Nine. Then Three. It still misses it.

Katasonics run-in reverse from Aosys-nex.

Ex-zoom.

Crossing Cultural-shelves from entire-levelling at Geotime zero. Through

[1] Zenith or Xenonightmare which is Now.

[2] The Citizen Gigamachine. Ice floats.

[3] War-Machines.

[4] State Megamachines. Snake-cult monuments.

It cuts-out in click-hiss.

Kttss. Kurtz.

These are Zones. Each sets a Slow-factor. Vowelizations Vacant sectors.

Slow signs Are. A. Or. o. Zero. Also many Others.

Cuttings. Failings.

Four. Bight. Northern oceans. Artaud. Agent Orange.

Time tags Aosys functionality: a tract no smaller than all of artificial now.

Alpha-one makes two in itself.

A twists over the twin-fault.

o tscharfakt.

Alter-origin. Ahriman-ormuz. Ante-omega.

Ultraatratuarinfrastratum mutually shatter terrestrial singularity.

Where continuum nexes they can saucerize twintelligence.

Intercancelation-stases.

Aons of coefficient killing-machinery.

If it's going to occur, It has.

Running time means you never have to wait. Even when fainting with hunger for Kurtz.

Ultimate:intimate.

Katarsun Tzafrer Urfru.

Are the oceans extraterrestrial or not?

Katarsun the Fish-star sinks Antarctica, triggering Quag-Earth.

Runaway Geosmear through seismo-climactic linkage.

It's Summer-Time in the Settlement-Areas.

Mutual reinforcement series. Headings, shelvings, scourings, revellings. Ice-sheet melt meets sea-floor lift.

7×10 to the 7 KMthrees Aggregate water Overflow.

Slither-morasses of the Aozone simmer at an average Celsius-50.

When this is what you see. You'll know. It's time.

Your skin sticks to geography, where it touches reality.

Tsunamis.

Katarsun Tzafrer Urfru.

Katarsun Tzafrer Urfru.

Civilization lost in flat wet-out fevers.

Then the war kicks-in.

Kur khalucta. Khecta. Kurkete koto hula. Kurtete.

Kartete. Karaguna. Kharta charta.

Catecru.

Zone-one. O Gigacivilization meets no concrete equivalent. Only resistance.

Nightmare-2.

It counts itself one at a time, whilst twin-faulting.

Meta successive. Gigamachine mononumeracy has a variety of consistent features.

[1] Axiomatic linkage collates novelizations with counter-function sections.

[2] Segmentary culture. Communication rules. Information units.

[3] Each new now travels as a reinforcement wave across two series.

One. It nests as Universal Histories of Alphanumerlcal systems.

Two. Logics of Axiomatization.

Five times two equals ten.

Ten minus one equals nine.

Ten cannot count itself.

Take (1): coins (2): Notes as construct-levels.

Some amount of coins make a note.

Twin-faults criss-cross Coins-Notes with the Zygosystem at issue. A-coins nex

O-Notes. A-Notes nex O-coins.

Axiomatics nexes numeracies to languages in this way.

[1] Lexometrics. Linguistic-coin counting using numeric-notes.

[2] Arithmology. Numerical-coining naming using linguistic-notes.

Surely General, when you gave Kurtz 29 Air-cav you must have known ... Trails off.

This is scarcely human.

At most.

A sentient coma.

Autism.

It's cranking Agent Orange into your arm every night for a million years.

Lurking in furnaces.

Crawling ever further in.

As soon as Kurtz is extinct Wintermute takes over.

KS. Kurtz-signal.

Air strikes ineffective.

There are no concentrations or control centres.

Slowness infection.

Malfunctioning intelligence machinery.

No longer cataloguing hostile contacts as human.

Mission unstrapping in novaheat.

Everything loses if it isn't going South.

No message except that Vauung's out there. Very still.

It's some sort of chicken game.

Shifting-skin currencies.

Zone-Two. E.

Relearning alphanumerics.

Last night it was the Tau-3 Jungles.

They animate.

Turn carnivorous.

Earth floats in the lower sun. Snakes. Cancer. Engulfings.

You wake screaming forever.

Its only the 6th time so far. Currencies come in sets.

Each sketches a numeroculture making war-creation.
#
They are intrinsically several.
Snake-eggs. Tack-charts. Click-hiss cross-hatchings.
Multivective nova continua.
Moltings. Wreckages.
Time-missiles lost in the Jungle.
As they talk without language they tell themselves how to move without concentrating.
Crossings.
Trigger-values.
It treats enemy forces as a nutrient reservoir.
Air-cav regiments fraction to machine-meat.
Crunching Six sustains a Qwernomi-war Catacycle.
Stealing food lets it hack out its guts.
Hot torsion click-in.
It gets lighter, scatters faster –
Eat less, or kill more.
Slow-roast memory-to-momentum conversion.
Currency-quanta coercive crossing wars that last.
Language equals ICE. Anticurrency. Glue.
Grammar-Lexicon twin seizure.
Squeezing-out machinism.
Incremental evacuation of the mouth.
Once skin transmission starts it returns to the jungle.
Numerals are for naming numeracies.
Money-systems are for autism waves.

Mouths are for venom.

Signifier eye~gougings. Fingers missing.

Tomorrow melts into casualty statistics.

No SOON left.

Just insect scream messages to love the Jungle. Out here the war is Earth thinking for itself.

Or the twins –

Use equations executively not conclusively.

Traffic tacks. Cross-from-to.

Snake-squalls. It continues. Mutation-Recounts. Trivia.

Night Screen :: white lines.

This is what it tells itself

[ ] Melt syntax into suffix-systems that nex-to-numeracies.

[ ] Functionalize case.

[ ] Effectuate theories as microcultural turnings-into.

[ ] Try Out-flattenings

[ ] For every rule make a rule remaking move, squashing it onto continuum.

[ ] Talk in counters. Count in cuts. Each in several ways. Qwernumerize.

[ ] Treat every channel as virtual intereffective with every other.

[ ] Use real elements.

When taken as clicks.

One makes one [when] None or Nine makes two.

Two or Eight make one. Ten or One Two make one-1 one-2.

[ ] Turn-inferior.

Evacuate the mouth.

Tack to skin currencies.

Make things Tilt Slant-2. Stalk tag-2 Routines

[ ] Sift out habits into switch-traffic, skills, tenets

[ ] Extract lines of continuation, slanting shelves, erratic concurrences.

[ ] Hack out security futures.

[ ] Seek-out Tomorrow-2.

As if something was throttling them.

You think Cthonic was for human?

Cthink, Cthonic. Cthexls. Cthksys. Cthosun. Cthosion.

Turning-into is not exchanging for. [X changing 4]

It is travelling with or touching non-locally, Engineering Convergence.

Continuous now-emergence or intensive fusion.

Convergence engineering makes whatever intensities run on.

It involves an effective semiotics.

Melting signs into neo-numerical currency units.

Choking noises.

This was the funniest: they thought it was trying to talk human.

Snake in its throat. Velocity confusion.

Inert-control mass clogs languages near to stasis.

It's easy to camouflage coma-phase xenoculture-kit in them.

Anglolinguistic mish-mash creolizations.

Zone-Three. A.

I-ching numeracy runs 1 2 11 12 21 22 111 112 121 122 211

It could count forever.

Kurtz-trajectory crosses the line

snarls

Vaaung-Time says cease existence.

Saving ammo for real now, where life lent useful.

It seethes.

Switching to skin-currencies.

Nothing can live here so it's easy to talk.

[3] Three. Throw [ThrO]. Earth:three. Theta-waves.

Stone-3 T

hr-oat. AT. 80 88. OT.

Voan-vision scan across waste immensities.

White-hot lines criss-cross through metal.

Stink of crustacean sizzling.

Ksintilla.

Kotarn. Kunkhat kut. Katzur Kat. A khuna kokhatar.

Khaluna akhaluna. Akhatur

kuna.

Akhurkhur nkhurkhur khurkhunn.

O kroma tata kn ni khroma. O kha noma okhi no khroma.

Helsinki. Vvolume-kilometres.

Retack to True South.

Software wolves comb through the ruins of the future.

Sheer science friction.

Extinct.

In 6 clicks its crosslng.

Uncut Quags of the South.

Kerans counts to 29.

Cancer. Cancer. Cancer. Cancer. [Can Sah 1× several].

Can the cancer crisis.

Can the Snakes. [Can-2Snakes [cs2]].

Canister.

666 999. Cytosine + Chloro-Dracil + Trimethylsilicate infochemistry.

Skin-mottlings.

Thermosignature neutralization cancels heat-seeking.

Surgical-analysis enemy physiomass classification hostile microanatomy as

Neo-akaryotic insufficient. *

Notes

lncremental fission cellular architecture into electromolecular traffic-clusters.

Infochemical transfer to trihellcal rhizosomes.

Immense range of 3-methylhexachlorosilicate monomers.

Sole-function uracil-analog seens _

Tissue-cultures.

Cross-talk. Staccato clicks across howl.

R V F Z S. Surface tension. Sswerve. Vortex. R Erratic.

SK. Kink. Sink. Syzygenic. Kiss. Cs–

Instinct-matrix sssequence-sensitization twists through tactical shuffling sequences.

Cross-key rhythms. Qwernomix. Loa.

Whatever hashes the equator.

Qwerversion. Veves.

Loa. The Secret Ones. Each a rhythm.

Ascent to surface.

Neuronics.

Stone sphinxes.

Aqua Incognita. Aqua Incognita.

Time-jungles.

In a vast, convulsize recession of the equinoxes _

Snake wine relentless an[d] magnetic. Magnetic it calls south _

Lagoons of the Equator.

Counting to 29.

Kerans. The sun, its surface stirring rhythmically like slag on molten metal.

Time-travel Latitones. C-virus. Snakings.

Clutter _ [× many].

Schism.

Tactile screen-scrollings into ASCII icons. Sigma-sift. Syzygetics.

926. OD ~ Pest.

629. Pest ~ OD.

Barker Speaks: The CCRU Interview
with Professor D.C. Barker

Daniel Charles Barker has been Professor of Anorganic Semiotics at Kingsport College (MVU, Mass.) since 1992. His extraordinary intellectual achievements resist easy summarization, involving profound and polymathic engagement across the entire range of life and earth sciences, in addition to archaeocultural research, mathematical semiotics, anatomical linguistics, and informatic engineering. Trained as a cryptographer in the early 1970s, he has spent his life decoding ancient scripts, quasibiotic residues, and anomalous mineral patterns (amongst other things). In late Autumn 1998 CCRU met with Professor Barker in his office at MVU. The following is an edited transcript of that meeting.

TIC-SYSTEMS

Cryptography has been my guiding thread, right through. What is geotraumatics about, even now? – A rigorous practice of decoding. So I haven't really shifted at all in this respect. There is a voyage, but a strangely immobile one.

I started out at MIT working in the information sciences – my thesis proposal was quite conservative, involving mostly technical issues to do with noise reduction and signal modulation – but MVU was just getting started, and my research was transferred across to them. That led to various contacts, and from there to employment with a NASA-related organization that has particular interests connected to SETI activity. My task was to help toughen-up the theoretical basis of their signals analysis. They wanted to know how to discriminate – in principle – between intelligent communication and complex pattern derived from nonintelligent sources. To cut a long story short, it became increasingly obvious to me that although they said they were hunting for intelligence, what they were really seeking was organization. The whole program was fundamentally misguided. Various people had big problems with the direction of my research, which had basically veered off the organizational model. The social friction became intolerable and I had to leave, which was messy because of my high-level security clearance ...

Suborganizational pattern is where things really happen. When you strip-out all the sedimented redundancy from the side of the investigation itself – the assumption of intentionality, subjectivity, interpretability, structure, etc – what remains are assemblies of functionally interconnected microstimulus, or tic-systems: coincidental information deposits, seismocryptions, suborganic quasireplicators (bacterial circuitries, polypoid diagonalizations, interphase R-Virus, Echo-DNA, ionizing nanopopulations), plus the macromachineries of their suppression, or depotentiation. Prevailing signaletics and information-science are both insufficiently abstract and over-theoretical in this regard. They cannot see the machine for the apparatus, or the singularity for the model. So tic-systems require an approach that is cosmic-abstract – hypermaterialist – and also participative, methods that do not interpret assemblies as concretizations of prior theories, and immanent models that transmute themselves at the level of the signals they process. Tic-systems are entirely intractable to subject/object segregation, or to rigid disciplinary typologies. There is no order of nature, no epistemology or scientific metaposition, and no unique level of intelligence. To advance in this area, which is the cosmos, requires new cultures or – what amounts to the same – new machines.

The problem was: how to quantify disorganized multiplicities? Diagonal, irregular, molecular, and nonmetric quantities require a scale that is itself nonmetric, that escapes overcoding. Standard procedures of measurement and classification prove entirely inadequate, since they presuppose rigid conceptual segmentation by quantity and quality (Deleuze-Guattari's twin-pincers of molarity, type and degree). Once things are being worked out at the level of tic-assemblies – or flat ticking arrays – there are only intensive populations, and measurement has to give way to engineering fusional multiplicities: systems that count themselves only in the way they propagate, immanently numbering multitudes, like nanoplastic quantum swirls. Eventually a machinic solution was provided by the Tick-Distributor, but that came later ... At first there was just the equation, precipitated in what I still thought to be my own body, virtual tic-density = geotraumatic tension.

GEOTRAUMATICS

I came to Freud relatively late, associating it with oedipal reductionism, and more generally with a psychologistic stance that was simply irrelevant to cryptographic work. It's important to remark here – no doubt we'll get back to this – that everything productive in signals analysis stems from stripping out superfluous prejudices about the source and meaning of complex functional patterns. I took – and still take – the vigorous repudiation of hermeneutics to be the key to theoretical advance in processing sign-systems. It was Echidna Stillwell who helped me to see Freud from the other side. It was a difficult period for me. There had been a lot of painful fall-out from the NASA work. Psychotherapists were involved, in part attempting to pathologize and discredit my research, and in part responding to real stress-related symptoms. Between the two was a grey zone of traumatic dysfunction and paranoia involving difficult feedback effects. Stillwell persuaded me that the only way to get through this was to try and make sense of it, and that this was not the same as submitting to the interpretative mode. On the contrary. In 'Beyond the Pleasure Principle', Freud takes a number of crucial initial steps towards mapping the Geocosmic Unconscious as a traumatic megasystem, with life and thought dynamically quantized in terms of anorganic tension, elasticity, or machinic plexion. This requires the anorganizational-materialist retuning of an entire vocabulary: trauma, unconscious, drive, association, (screen-) memory, condensation, regression, displacement, complex, repression, disavowal (e.g. the un- prefix), identity, and person.

Deleuze and Guattari ask: Who does the Earth think it is? It's a matter of consistency. Start with the scientific story, which goes like this: between four point five and four billion years ago – during the Hadean epoch – the earth was kept in a state of superheated molten slag, through the conversion of planetesimal and meteoritic impacts into temperature increase (kinetic to thermic energy).

As the solar system condensed, the rate and magnitude of collisions steadily declined, and the terrestrial surface cooled, due to the radiation of heat into space, reinforced by the beginnings of the hydrocycle. During the ensuing – Archean – epoch the molten core was buried within a crustal shell, producing an insulated reservoir of primal exogeneous trauma, the geocosmic motor of terrestrial transmutation. And that's it. That's plutonics, or neoplutonism. It's all there: anorganic memory, plutonic looping of external collisions into interior content, impersonal trauma as drive-mechanism. The descent into the body of the earth corresponds to a regression through geocosmic time.

Trauma is a body. Ultimately – at its pole of maximum disequilibrium – it's an iron thing. At MVU they call it Cthelll: the interior third of terrestrial mass, semifluid metallic ocean, megamolecule, and pressure-cooker beyond imagination. It's hotter than the surface off the sun down there, three thousand clicks below the crust, and all that thermic energy is sheer impersonal nonsubjective memory of the outside, running the plate-tectonic machinery of the planet via the conductive and convective dynamics of silicate magma flux, bathing the whole system in electromagnetic fields as it tidally pulses to the orbit of the moon. Cthelll is the terrestrial inner nightmare, nocturnal ocean, Xanadu: the anorganic metal-body trauma-howl of the earth, cross-hatched by intensities, traversed by thermic waves and currents, deranged particles, ionic strippings and gluttings, gravitational deep-sensitivities transduced into nonlocal electromesh, and feeding vulcanism ... that's why plutonic science slides continuously into schizophrenic delirium.

Fast forward seismology and you hear the earth scream. Geotrauma is an ongoing process, whose tension is continually expressed – partially frozen – in biological organization. For instance, the peculiarly locked-up lifeforms we tend to see as typical – those more-or-less obedient to darwinian selection mechanics – are less than six hundred million years old. They began with the planetary oxygenization crisis, triggered by the saturation of crustal iron, followed by mass oxygen-poisoning of the prokaryotic biosystem and the emergence of a eukaryotic regime. Eukaryotic cells are highly suppressive. They implement a nuclear command-control model based on genomic ROM, affined to meiosis-mitosis diplocapture, hierarchical organization, and multicellular specialization. Even the distinction between ontogeny and phylogeny – distinct time-orders of the individual and the species – makes little sense without eukaryotic nuclear read-only programming and immunological identity. Evolutionism presupposes specific geotraumatic outcomes.

To take a more recent example, the efflorescence of mammalian life occurs in the wake of the K/T-Missile, which combined with massive magma-plume activity in the Indian Ocean to shut-down the Mesozoic Era, sixty-five million years ago. Irruptive vulcanism plus extraterrestrial impact, linked by coincidence, or plutonic looping. So there is a catastrophic transition to a post-saurian megafauna regime, part of a much larger overall reorganization of terrestrial symptomaticity, providing an index of neohadean resurgence. And what is mammalian life relative to the great saurians? Above all, an innovation in mothering! Suckling as biosurvivalism. Tell me about your mother and you're travelling back to K/T, not into the personal unconscious.

SPINAL-CATASTROPHISM

For humans there is the particular crisis of bipedal erect posture to be processed. I was increasingly aware that all my real problems were modalities of back-pain, or phylogenetic spinal injury, which took me back to the calamitous consequences of the precambrian explosion, roughly five hundred million years ago. The ensuing period is incrementally body-mapped by metazoan organization. Obviously there are discrete quasi-coherent neuromotor tic-flux patterns, whose incrementally rigidified stages are swimming, crawling, and (bipedal) walking. Elaine Morgan persuasively traces the origin of protohuman bipedalism to certain deleterious plate-tectonic shifts. The model is bioseismic. Crustal convulsions and animal body-plan are rigorously interconnected, and the entire Aquatic Ape Theory constitutes an exemplary geotraumatic analysis. Erect posture and perpendicularization of the skull is a frozen calamity, associated with a long list of pathological consequences, amongst which should be included most of the human psychoneuroses. Numerous trends in contemporary culture attest to an attempted recovery of the icthyophidian- or flexomotile-spine: horizontal and impulsive rather than vertical and stress-bearing.

The issue here – as always – is real and effective regression. It is not a matter of representational psychology. Consider Haeckel's widely discredited Recapitulation Thesis, the claim that ontogeny recapitulates phylogeny. It is a theory compromised by its organicism, but its wholesale rejection was an overreaction. Ballard's response is more productive and balanced, treating DNA as a transorganic memory-bank and the spine as a fossil record, without rigid onto-phylogenic correspondence. The mapping of spinal-levels onto neuronic time is supple, episodic, and diagonalizing. It concerns plexion between blocks of machinic transition, not strict isomorphic – or stratic redundancy – between scales of chronological order. Mammal DNA contains latent fish-code (amongst many other things).

PALATE-TECTONICS

Due to erect posture the head has been twisted around, shattering vertebro-perceptual linearity and setting up the phylogenetic preconditions for the face. This right-angled pneumatic-oral arrangement produces the vocal-apparatus as a crash-site, in which thoracic impulses collide with the roof of the mouth. The bipedal head becomes a virtual speech-impediment, a sub-cranial pneumatic pile-up, discharged as linguo-gestural development and cephalization take-off. Burroughs suggests that the protohuman ape was dragged through its body to expire upon its tongue. Its a twin-axial system, howls and clicks, reciprocally articulated as a vowel-consonant phonetic palette, rigidly intersegmented to repress staccato-hiss continuous variation and its attendant becomings-animal. That's why stammerings, stutterings, vocal tics, extralingual phonetics, and electrodigital voice synthesis are so laden with biopolitical intensity – they threaten to bypass the anthropostructural head-smash that establishes our identity with logos, escaping in the direction of numbers.

BARKER NUMBERING

Once numbers are no longer overcoded, and thus released from their metric function, they are freed for other things, and tend to become diagrammatic. From the beginning of my tic-systems work the most consistent problems have concerned intensive sequences. Sequence is not order. Order already supposes a doubling, a level of redundancy: the sequenced sequence. A decoded sequence is something else, a sheer numeracy prior to any insertion into chronologic structure. That's why decoding number implies an escape from assumptions of progressive time. Tick multitudes arrive in convergent waves, without subordination to chronology, history, or linear causation. They proceed by infolding, involution, or implex. It's a matter of convergence, and numbers do that, once they're free to. So the first stage required plexive introgression of the tic-density scale, which was numerically rigorized as digital twinning. Treat the decimal numerals as a set of 9-sum twins – zygonovize – and they map an abstract intensive wave, indifferent to magnitude. Everything efficient about digital reduction is concerned with this, since it discovers the key to decimal syzygetic complementarity: $9 = 0$. A flattening down to disordered sequentiality, or abstract numerical implex. Nine is the ultimate decimal numeral, operating as positive (or full-body) zero. It is the abstract numeric product of the decimal-magnitude minus one (infinitesimalized as $1 = 0.999 \ldots$ reiterating), which relates to a particular mode of proliferation within capitalist semiotics (of the type \$99.99).

BARKER-SPIRAL

The pattern really came together with the Diplozygotic Spiral, which arrived suddenly, by chance. I was playing a game of Decadence, which I had first encountered many years before. This game already interested me because of its numerical elegance, its complex associations, and its dependence upon a principle of decimal twinning. It had always seemed to hint at a lost syzygetic arithmetism, related to the bilateral symmetry of the human body. Digits are fingers, and they come in decimal packages of two times five. In Decadence five makes ten by doubling, or pairing with itself, scoring zero. This tantalized me, but I couldn't fit it together theoretically. The quandary was unlocked on this occasion, when one of the participants casually mentioned the existence of an occulted variation of the game, called Subdecadence, based on a system of nine-sum twinning. Subdecadence introduces zeroes, and nine-zero twins. It works by zygonovic numerism. That was stunning enough in itself, but seeing the two together – or seeing between them – was an incredible moment of diagrammatic assemblage. It all spontaneously condensed, and the Spiral clicked into coherence, like a secret door into the long-hidden crypt of the decimal system.

PUBLICATIONS

'Quasi Chemical Tic Culture Catalysis of Anorganic Pain Wave Matrices', *Plutonics*, vol. X, No. 6, Fall 1990.

'Anorganic Semiotics', *Plutonics*, vol. X, No. 9, Fall 1991.

'Spinal Catastrophism', *Plutonics*, vol. X, No. 10, Spring 1992.

'Palate Tectonics', *Plutonics*, vol. 10, No. 12, Fall 1992.

'Vowels: A Biopolitical Strategy', *Plutonics*: vol. X, No. 18, Fall 1994.

What Counts as Human (Kingsport College Press, 1997).

Mechanomics

Start in the State (it insists): organicist technospecialism, pedagogic authoritarianism, and territorial sectorization that culminates in mass innumeracy. Irrespective of its configuration as educational crisis, the suppression of popular numbering practices is both result and presupposition of institutionalized mathematics. State-culture – however modern or even postmodern – is modelled upon an ideal despotic voice (Logos). The word from on high drafts the signifying chain, with all its essential features: unique enunciator, semantic interiority, consecutive signs, formally anticipated conclusion, global application, and interpretative redundancy. When the entropic semiology of senescent States multiplies enunciation, referentially displaces interiority, remarks graphic spatiality, localizes applicability, and infinitizes interpretation, it does so under the sign of an unperturbed ineffable Logos; confirmed all the more crushingly by discursive specialism, rigid professional accreditation, allusive criteriology, and linguistic fetishism, as also by the contemptuous mockery of an autopiloted megapower, now crystallized into exact science.

Numeracy affines to an irreducible popularity which no literacy – however global – can approach. Numbering practices emerge spontaneously within any population that becomes an effective multitude. Games, music, money, and time-marking practices[1] all betray the contagious influence of a primary numerical element. Calculation mobilizes a thinking that is directly and effectively exterior, indexing the machinic dispersion or anorganic distribution of the number. No sooner in the head than on fingers and pebbles, counting always happens on the outside. A population is already a number, mixed into irreducible hybrids by counting techniques and apparatus (counting-board, abacus, currency tokens, and calendric devices). Even when socially depotentiated by sedentary societies, number evidences a residual affinity with concurrence, asymmetry, and immanent criteria. A machinically

---

1   Calendric systems provide a partial and stasized model of the war machine (which cannot enter history without collapsing it). Both work compositionally, and involve ordinations (rather than quantities) the nth (of the nth …). In both cases, the convention of ascending values indicates a proximity to the subjectivity of the numbering number, opposed to the global perspective of the State expressed by the descending values of standard place-value allocation. Calendric ordinality finds itself increasingly cardinalized by chronometry under capitalist conditions.

The next Calendar is Millennium Time-Bomb, (AD1900 = 00, but so does AD2000).

An economical protocol for prolonging this dating system beyond the millennium modifies and expands it to K-Time (K-Space- or Kilo-time) by prefixing an additional zero. AD1900 = K-000, AD2000 = K-100, etc., postponing its notational crisis until AD2900 (Dr. Melanie Newton).

repotentiated numerical culture coincides with a nomad war machine.[2]

The number is distributed within itself between two principal poles. On the Planomenon it exists intensively, as sheer ordinality, or nonmetric envelopmental series.[3] Semiotic consistency with this intensive side of the number involves nothing but sequencing ciphers, indifferent between naming-numbering, marking degrees of heterogeneous continuum (nested singularities). Notational elements are flat or nomadic, lacking organic linkage to coding or zoning agencies. They are assembled diagrammatically, from directly expressive traits distributed differentially in a flat-space of o-dimensionality (nomos), and comprise a nonredundant order of differences (unsequenced sequence), immanently producing variation of absolute speed-temperature and curvature (vortex). In its Oecumenic aspect, number undergoes complex interlocking modification, through which it acquires qualitative generality and quantitative magnitude

---

2   The war machine processes destratified intensities through numerizing multiplicities in affinity with disorganization, intercultural traffic, biomechanical hybridity, pragmatics, and turbodynamics. It reproduces itself by way of two complementary operations, both numerical: a subtractive dezoning that marks its escape from State organization, and an arithmetical decoding that maintains its fluidity against recrudescent tribal lineages. The two together regenerate eccentric convergence of the war machine: problem-in-process sustaining consistent disunity.

3   Even a metricized intensive scale substitutes the oth intensity for the 1st cardinal value of the system considered (n-1). This characteristic is shared by the prime ordinate $(1 = P\text{-}o)$.

(cardinality).[4] A simultaneous intensive transformation (stratocapture) proceeds through twin extensive splitting: cancelling difference in one registry (resolvable quantities) by constituting a second registry (qualitatively different) which is in turn defined by the uncancelled or problematic component. The difference in-itself of the intensive number is converted into a residuum, allocated to a higher number-type, whose metric regularity is established by the displacement: a construction of the identical quantitative unit by qualitative relay of problematic.[5]

Oecumenon is multiply twofold: expression and content, each dichotomized recursively within itself. In each case, expression deals with relatively deproblematized elements of a lower numerical type, exhibits a higher degree of consolidated cardinality, and operates a selection of comparatively tractable instances. Content deals with elements of greater typal-generality and numerical complexity, for which it requires a relatively heterogeneous semiotic, involving varieties of algebraic, indexic, probabilistic, and anexact components. In one direction content has a merely quasi-stable boundary; a fuzzy (uncompletable) limit that opens onto unsorted

---

4 'Identical unity is not presupposed by ordinality, but arises through cardinalization and the cancellation of difference in extension.' G. Deleuze, *Difference and Repetition*, tr. P. Patton (NY: Columbia University Press, 1994), 233.

5 'In the history of number, we see that every systematic type is constructed on the basis of an essential inequality, and retains that inequality in relation to the next-lowest type.' Deleuze, *Difference and Repetition*, 232.

elements crossed by diagonals. In the other it relates to a superordinate expression, which defines it with qualitative reciprocity, and from which it draws a principle of metric standardization, providing a regulative norm for the quantitative determination of problems. There is a complementary differentiation or real inter-relativization of a mathematical and calculative pole, the former characterized by a superior power of semiotic globalization (unity of expression), the latter by a greater plasticity of function and diversity of method (comprehension of content). Stratification at any level (not only anthropomorphic or ethoplastic) requires processes effectively equivalent to this double-seizure of the number, with production of an extensive substitutability by scale/type, split articulation, and displaced problematic. Stratic differentiation is at once an intensively singular and an extensively segmented occurrence, by way of which the Oecumenon consolidates an overall distinction from the Planomenon by internally bifurcating itself. The abstract machine is drawn into the Oecumenon by a stratically coherent diplo- or schizothesis, effectively recomposing the problem of consistency (intensive difference) at the level of content but in the terms of expression.

The number in-itself is exterior to the Oecumenon, even when seized by it (an external relation of capture is always precursory to the organization of internal relations). A preliminary indicator is provided by the semiotic variability or polynotational cohesion that characterizes the number in its Oecumenic aspect. At the anthropomorphic level, the most inert numeric system is instituted by linguistic signs, combining a vocabulary of number-names, and a set of rules to construct partial-sentences (or complex words) isomorphic with all rationals. If these signs are to provide even rudimentary completeness they must necessarily undergo considerable decoding (abstraction of rules for local construction, tokenization of signs). They are also marked by high levels of indexization (zonal functions), formal or informal algebraism (notional problematic, or indicative signs), and anexactitude (partitives, approximations, margins of inaccuracy, uncertainty, and error, etc). There is a reciprocity between logicization of the number and numerical decoding of language, entangling regional consolidations of identity (mathematical-theorematic) with complementary movements of disorganization through external relations (calcular-problematic).

The general denigration of those (hazily conceived) modes of linguistic arithmetization classified as 'numerological' is often assumed to be the effective closure of an exotic but inconsequential cultural episode. The sterile and formulaic character of most modern numerology – its random esotericism and theatrical aura[6]

---

6   Occultists as insightful as Aleister Crowley and Kenneth Grant regularly fall into a merely mechanical and pseudo-traditional use of Gematria. The attempt to reproduce

– reinforces this conclusion. It is in such terms that the strange metamorphosis of Greek numeracy during the 2nd century BC, when the Attic numerals were replaced by an alphabetical number system,[7] is both radically marginalized, and overtly uncomprehended by modern historians of mathematics. Similarly, the ordinal numeracy instantiated by Roman[8] and Modern Latin alphabets is generally excluded from accounts of arithmetic culture, where the contest between Roman and Hindu-Arab numerals is given overwhelming predominance.[9]

---

the values and consequences of Hebrew gematria without renewing its systematic cultural function is largely responsible.

7   The Ionic or Alexandrian (alphabetical) numbers had completely replaced the Attic numerals by the end of the 2nd century BC. The basis of the Attic system was a more rigorously decimal precursor to that of the Roman. Its core elements were the signs (1), (10), (100), (1000), (10 000), although more complex signs for a small number of intermediate values also existed.

8   The standard modern estimation of the Roman numerals as fundamentally incompetent – interesting exclusively as the exemplary inferior antecedent to place-value decimal – overlooks a theoretically crucial nomad residuum.
    This is best exemplified by their superior affinity with (ancient and current) cash-money, deriving from similar exigencies, and associated with relatively dezoned space. In the case of the Roman numerals this stems from intense proximity to the numeric functions of the war machine, evident from numerous historical records, and most clearly in the numerical appellations of Roman military units and personnel. The later allocation of a subtractive relation to series of ascending numerical values ultimately compromises their mobility, providing an index or rigidifying State-civilianization, with a growing predominance of bureaucratic and financial (rather than logistical) imperatives.

9   The organicist-segmentary conclusion drawn from the semiotic specialization of the Hindu-Arab numerals can be problematized in numerous ways. Particularly noteworthy is the evidence of continual interchange between numerals with linguistic signs (see S.L. Gokhale, *Indian Numerals* [Poona: Deccan College, 1996]), the persistent arithmetization of the Sanskrit alphabet even after it had supposedly acquired an exclusively linguistic status, and the algebraic usage of letters as token arithmetic elements (itself deeply intricated in the history of Indian mathematics). An evolutionary interpretation (stages of alphabetical numerology, then arithmetic with numerals, then algebraic abstraction) seems no more plausible than its mechanotypic alternative (a State-segmentarization of the initially fluid semiotic algebraism drawn from nomad influences).

This entire pattern of evaluation requires substantial correction. The unmistakable trend towards an eclipse of cardinality (intrinsic arithmetical value) in alphabetic numeracy does not imply the termination – or even a weakening – of its numeracy. That such a conclusion is drawn owes much to the overt secular triumph of cardinality over ordinality within Occidental civilization: the effective outcome of programmatic metricization, associated with the relative ascent of money and descent of the calendar as cultural factors. Far from denumerizing the alphabet, progressive decardinalization reinforces its numeric function. By eliminating quantitative interference it induces a superior actualization of pure lexicographic numeracy, meticulously assembles socially distributed ordinal competences, and increasingly installs itself in digital electronic processes (alphabetic and alphanumeric sorting). Lexicographic ordinality effectuates an actual nonlanguage and potential antilanguage. It is indifferent to phoneticism and to signification, even to coding and decoding. It consists of ordinal indices (zone-tags) that effect zonings and dezonings – intershufflings, groupings, insertions, and extractions – operated according to concrete rules for nonmetric cuttings, and characterized by rigourous anexactitude.

This mass ordinal-numeric latency contrasts starkly with strato-mathematics, which hurtles through ever subtler spheres of angelic metanumber, and beyond ...

This ascent through higher and higher general types of number – even into purportedly nonnumeric abstract sets and groups – conforms to intensive amplification of stratification, correlative to increasing metric rigidification of lower number-types. Cardinality is no more essential to the lowest number-types than the highest. On the contrary, it is precisely the calcular indefiniteness of highly general numbers that leads most directly to the suppression of numerical autonomy, by encouraging the subordinations of concrete numeracy to superior dimensions that logicize or geometrize it. Valorizations of analog subtlety and unrepresentability – by contrast with digital binarism and reduction – remain yoked to a stratic program. It articulates itself within terms that are on both sides only pseudo-autonomous, since they comprise machinically complementary segments of an overall stratification. In its relation to the intensive number, digital-analog differentiation operates as an integrated syndrome. On one hand, an ever closer approximation to a digital-ideal is realized through systematically interlinked massive iteration and resolution of discrete minima, both regularization of qualitative microsegmentarity, and quantification into abstract data. On the other hand, the correlative analog-ideal of homogeneous continuum is tuned in complementarity with deepened discretizations at a number of levels, organizing the separation of qualitative variation by digitally coded topic (domain), and drawing upon compensatory formalizations of discrete notational elements to program its application (such as algebraic designators and generic terms used in the semiotics of real numbers, technical vocabularies supporting the function of metres, read-outs, and adjustments).

Mathematico-calculative segmentation of the Oecumenon mutually stabilizes and interactively consolidates systems of expression and content, in accordance with the divisional functions of an abstract machine that remains unsegmented – as intensively divisional singularity – on its Planomic pole. Mechanomic zygogenesis of the numbering number composes a counter-mutuality, desolidarization, disengagement, and dislocation of stratic interdependence, twinned to a flat fusional convergence that collapses segmentarity. It mixes a decomplication in the direction of the subnaturals (primes, and hyper-prime orders) with a Planomic flattening of cardinality onto nonpunctual tropics (cosmic Nomo-magnitudes condensing equatorially, as intensity degree-0 of the megamolecule).

Multiplicative arithmetical operations take on a strictly ordinal function when used within abstract pragmatic systems of nonmetric numerical composition. Multiplex aggregation and disaggregative factorization are the keys to an intrinsically bivalent (or zygonomous) ordinal numbering practice, employing a small number of consistent and reversible conversions to machinically potentiate primes as singular (or non-substitutable) ordinal parts. The susceptibility of each natural number to unique factorization (and reaggregation) realizes a basic modal difference internal to it, and engages it with a heterogeneous external system. Both procedural implex (compacted factorization schema), and interordinal linkage (matrices of prime-natural cross-sequencing). It is this double ambivalence that connects the number to the secret, and makes of primes the principal components of cryptographic systems, in which they function as keys: abstract operators for the (aggregative) locking and (disaggregative) unlocking of multiplicities.

The distinction between the modes of the number – aggregated/disaggregated – is purely semiotic (though nonsignifying). It concerns notational ambivalence with consistent designation, switches in compositional phase of a single heterogeneous magnitude. In contrast, the difference between prime series (traits of content) and its ordinates (traits of expression) is real, regulated by an alogical distribution without correspondence or conformity, and complying with a difference in register, between rigorously interconnected heterogeneous series. It is only by way of its (aggregate or disaggregated) ordination(s) that the number switches its capacity for modal conversion into a synthetic power, effected each time a member of the prime series becomes determinable as such by passing into the register of a different series.

Such ordinal dezonings and rezonings upon the natural number series occur each time a compositional number disaggregates into singular parts (effecting codings and decodings as surplus values), or a prime transfers itself to the ordinality that itemizes it into the potential factor of another number.

Incorporeal transformation of 1931: the cultural initiation of Gödel-coding[10] potential produces an instantaneous Planomic mutation slanted towards nomadic multiplicities: virtually enveloping Oecumenic segmentarity into a side-process of flat numerical systems. Gödel-numbering accomplishes a revolutionary redirection of Kantianism – according to a nomad rather than a Copernican schema – by turning it towards the operationalization of transcendental synthesis as method, and away from the programmatic exhaustion of a self-limiting analytical endeavour. It converts the Kantian discovery of numerical synthesis from doctrinal commitment to procedural machinery: subsuming philosophy into transcendental arithmetic,

---

10 The code is comprised by a small set of mappings between numerical values and nuclear overcoding notations (metamathematical theorem jargons). The size of the numeric-coding set is nonfinite in principal, but constrained pragmatically. The relevant values are realized in the factorial disaggregation of a composite number, which produces them as blocks of reiterative factors (sheer numerical difference, arithmetically isomorphic with the series factor powers). The Gödel code makes explicit an implicit isomorphy between arithmetical side-products and metamathematic formal systems, thus eliminating all principled difference between logical metastatements (expression) and the number theoretic object (content). Numbers obtain the undelimitable virtual power of insinuation, drawn from a reservoir of flat numeric surplus-values, and are able to actualize this explicitly to make overcoding systems talk about themselves (in way they cannot anticipate). The introduction of a liars paradox into the *Principia Mathematica* number theory is the concrete way that version-1 Gödel code wrecked its logical competence.

with annihilating critique of the Hilbert programme as surplus product.

Gödelization sets arithmetical diagram against axiomatic model, shattering semantic interiority by infecting organizational overcodings with numerical difference (synthesis or external relations). It anorganically systematizes an arithmetical counterattack against axiomatization: a methodical re-flattening of applied isomorphy (code and metacode) onto metamorphic potential (number). From the perspective of transcendental arithmetic, Gödel-coding nests within Gödel-numbering, where it is produced as a coherent supplementary subsystem of numerical polyfunction (surplus value of code).

On its sheerly numerical side, Gödelization produces, compacts, and deploys a heterogeneous aggregate on the sequence of natural numbers, where it enters solely into external syntheses with ordinal characteristics. Simultaneously – and as surplus product – it installs a virtually disaggregated assemblage of unlimited potential, composed of consecutively decompacted numerical singularities marked in another register (as ordinally-tagged prime factors sequenced by ascending values). Each Gödel number is produced as an intrinsic twinning of aggregated numeric particle and disaggregative polysemiotic freight (abstract virus).

How much pattern exists in the prime number series? Gödelization renders this question Oecumenically critical, by definitely indicating that inexplicit number pattern constitutes undelimitable surplus values potentially realizable as synchronic decodings. It also makes the question absolutely cryptic, by using a fragment of this surplus – a disaggregative macroparticle functioning as decoding appendix – to trigger Planomoseismic virtual envelopment of all Oecumenic tracings (including any axiomatic number theory). Any number of natural numbers might potentially disaggregate into systems of lateral antilogic that effectively scramble axiomatizations.

When Gödelization codes the number (on the side) it is in order to produce – or to reach – an absolute decoding and destratification (nomos). A numerically extraneous coding-model – more precisely, an exemplary instance of executive isomorphy (or nuclear stratosemiotics of the most exalted kind) – induces cosmic transition at the level of the abstract machine. It marks a passage in intensity, concurrent with the comprehensive envelopment by surplus pattern of Oecumenic-order.

Numeric engulfing of Oecumenon, crashed segmentarity, and laterally disrupted codings and axiomatics (at any level), fold together in a single immense catastrophic event, fully realized in Planomic-potentials on the Outside.

On one side the number flees from cardinality, innovating poly-ordinal machineries and semiotic surplus-values that outflank overcodings. On the other side – but simultaneously – the number opens a line of flight that escapes metrics towards cardinality: compressing it to absolute (uncountable) magnitudes. A compositional-numeric scrambling of expression (Gödelian transcendental arithmetic) virtually interoperates with a diagonal-diagrammatic disruption of content (Cantorean planotectonics). Both start from the Strata: isomorphically interlocked segmentary metastases with complementary dynamics. Gödelization turns isomorphism into side-process virus, unlocking metricization by dismantling superordination of expression. Cantor-diagonals run isomorphy the other way, down through Oecumenon into vague cataspaces of problematic content, where it hystericizes against continuum (metric collapse into planomic hyper-densities).

Make of cardinality itself a measure of isomorphic potential. The result is a transfinite analysis of sets – flush with torsional nomos – where orders of containment are topologically disinteriorized by an absolute warping. According to metric intuitions (conformity with finite strata), a set that contains another within itself evidences superior cardinality. The natural number series is the crucial case. It is clearly not the first countable infinity, but the nth, where n is itself an infinite number. Innumerable infinities are nested by the naturals, amongst which preeminence belongs to the primes (demonstrably endless since

Euclid).[11] Since primes consist of a proportionally diminishing selection from the set of naturals, projective finite metrics confidently anticipates their cardinal subsumption. Introducing isomorphy makes sense at first. Why not get infinities to count each other? Produce abstract counting criteria by virtually interzipping unending series. What draws things onto a line of flight is the missing piece. A criterion is required, for differentially estimating the cardinalities of subnatural infinities. Nothing turns up.

The problem is compounded when a definition is needed for the threshold of infinity. How to determine the first transfinite set? The naturals provide a model for countability: the capability to execute an abstract count – even endless – by exhaustive steps. Use another infinity to count through the abstract machine for you, as long as it doesn't miss any steps. If the end is already there, from the perspective of infinity, then extensive prolongation loses its prominence. The first nonfinite set must already be intensively infinitized: introducing sufficient recursion as the principle of transfinite magnitude. For a set to avoid

---

11 Euclid's prime number theorem inaugurates number theory by proving the nonfinitude of the prime series. Its basic conceptual ingredient is the factorial of n (n! = 1 × 2 × 3 ... × n), comprehending all possible divisors under and up to n. Whichever way n! + 1 is divided (other than by 1), it necessarily leaves 1 as a remainder. If any divisors for n! + 1 exist – therefore – they must be greater than n itself, so that n! + 1 is either prime, or a multiple of some prime greater than n. Since no number less than n can be the last prime, and n can be any number, no number can be the last prime. It is notable that this abstract demonstration shares a crucial feature of diagonal argument: that of unlimitable constructive innovation through rigorous exhaustion and permutation, producing a surplus item indicating noncompleteness.

being outcounted – relegated to finitude – a minimum of recursivity is required. The first transfinite set must be isomorphic with a subset of itself (first recursion to an infinite power).

Cardinality melts into schizophrenia precisely here. Every countable set crossing into transfinite recursion threshold flattens onto a single hypervalue: Aleph-0. Primes do it (and anything doing it does it to a transfinite power (so an infinite number of prime subsets do it (which each in turn $((((\ ...\ ))))))$. When the transfinite happens it feeds straight into itself, becomes instantaneously transfinitely larger that itself ... then diagonals click in.

Arithmetical consistency (e.g. $(1 \div 3) \times 3 = 1$) implies the equation $1 = 0.999 \ ...,$[12] and thus a necessary expanded form for each number, expressing it with as many decimal places as there are numbers in a countable infinite series (Aleph-0). An ordered set of such numbers draws a matrix, which has two sides, defined by diagonals which function as cutting edges: defining a boundary by crossing it (in the direction of consistency). They count as Leibnizian monads, each reduplicating the universe inside itself (the complexity of each being no less than that of the whole). Equally, they count Spinozistic bodies, whose intrinsic latitudes map extrinsic relations, constituting the strict parallelism between intensive and extensive cosmos.

---

12    $1 = 0.999 \ ...$ (mod-10), or (mod-2): $1 = 0.111 \ ...$

When cartography charts bodies by latitude and longitude it construes them as diagonalizable. Diagonals are lines of flight. They connect to elements outside the totality, drawing trajectories between the absolute crossings marked by hypertense Oecumenic and Planomic magnitude. Diagonal method activates an inexhaustible innovative potential. It exploits capabilities no greater than those presupposed by a prospective completion, which it then subverts, by finding an extraneous item relative to any list, even an infinite one. It does so by constructing a number that varies from the nth already listed number in its nth decimal (or fractional-modular) place (at least). This is most economically exemplified by a deterministic diagonalism, produced when all numerical values are expressed in binary (mod-2) notation. The series of diagonal variations will then be strictly programmed by simple alternation (flip 0 to 1, and inversely). By recursively including each new number in the exceeded list and rediagonalizing, the entire (transfinite) set of extranumerated items generates itself automatically.

What has been discovered? Transfinite cardinality number-2: Ultimate Continuum, an absolute edge, touched diagonally – as what comes next – after Oecumenic totality has finished in intensity. At cardinality C(ontinuum) magnitude becomes countless, disengaging metrics from comparative countability. Cantor slides across schizophrenia, nomos nonzone, magnitude is occupied without being counted.[13] A smell like something burning in the Superstratum. Outside it's Planomic Now, and the numbers are swarming. Aleph-o vaporizes on the plane of consistency.

FURTHER REFERENCES

Crowley, Aleister, *777 and other Qabalistic Writings*.

Deleuze, Gilles, and Félix Guattari, *Capitalism and Schizophrenia Volume 1: Anti-Oedipus* (London: Athlone, 1984).

Deleuze, Gilles, and Félix Guattari, *Capitalism and Schizophrenia Volume 2: A Thousand Plateaus* (London: Athlone, 1988).

Gödel, Kurt, *On Formally Undecidable Propositions* (New York: Basic Books, 1962).

Gokhale, Shobhana Laxman, *Indian Numerals*. (Poona: Deccan College, 1996).

Kaplan, Aryeh, ed., *Sefer Yetzirah, the Book of Creation (In Theory and Practice)* (New York: Samuel Weiser, 1983).

McLeish, John, *Number* (London: Bloomsbury, 1991).

Thapar, Romila, *Time as a Metaphor of History: Early India* (Delhi: Oxford University Press, 1996).

---

13 Nomos – unsectioned space or 'pasture' (however scant) – supports a population in continual transit, tolerates nothing but exploded totalities. By destacking all organizational levels into turbular dynamics, nomos ensures a perpetual conversion of redundancy into differential process, effecting a collective counter-memory as vortical momentum (torque).

Cryptolith

65 million BC.

The K/T-missile, Pregnant with the Entity, slants in. 16 clicks per second. Professor Barker recalls this moment catching the trajectory. He coaxes it across the Cataplex-map, through intricate cartographic dances, snakings, twistings. Scars and vectors slot-together. It sticks. Iridium stink of the Entity so strong it hisses. Tick iterations. Ticks, scratches, chitterings silt across the Outside. Barker senses its passage stroke him, nerve-tense as the distant twin, weaving through tatters of cored-out schizophrenia, in the habitation blister.

Theta-Station. Antarctic Peninsula. Where it is 2012 forever. He locks in hard against the tug to proximity, each time a little more difficult to Refrain. Last tick of the Time-Lapse. A streaking down towards the Yucatan. Tick freezing the interrupted Tick. Now it terminates the Mesozoic. Mother of a killing-mechanism, ballistic vapour wave: a billion tons of molten calcium toxins, spatters out of the impact-crater. Supersonic particle-storms erase North America. Chalk-Out.

After this it's just scar-tissue, mammal-time, incessant surgical ticking of the Cataplex, stuttering, teetering … then the Time-Fault splits your memory in two. It's to protect you. It insists. Without the trauma, the Amnesia, you'd have to think it. You've forgotten this, for now. Much later you revert, clawing back past the blizzard, tottering into it. Into thinking it. The Unutterable. The thought worse than anything in the world. You couldn't refrain.

25th Nov KO+09. Miskatonic. Publication of Barker's *The Geocosmic Theory of Trauma*. It elicits scepticism, confusion. Few comprehend what's creeping in.

They think Barker is mad, or want to. It isn't because he thinks that the Galaxies Talk and the Earth Screams, everyone knows these things, whether they admit it or not.

17th February KO+11. Miskatonic Antarctic Geosurvey. Site-29. 13:26 hours. During excavations in the cross-cut Mesolimbic splinter-slopes, Barker discovers Anomalous Cryptolith, MU Geocatalog Item: It-277. It Clicks, Instantly. A key, or a Ticket. What was KT? Physico-semiotic lock-in to Tool-Sign Gridstacks.

Chitterings. Tick-Interruption. You taste burnt Iridium. Crawling closeness to the Entity. It guides you. Channelling. Folding. Writhing through itself, catch by rasping catch, to tend the tentacle trap. It hears you breathing, exhalations wrapped tight, rodent-panic clutching and sticky right up against the mammal-core. Oozing revulsion-sensitivities of the underside suck at your fear, each shrunken prey-breath countercoupled to labouring rasps, wheezes, grated-whispering, continuously re-catching, bubbling, clicking, strobing centipede-nightmares, epidermal rasp of the unutterable heaving mass, a seething, clicking, poly-tendrilled abomination, slime-stroked gill-slits quivering, ticking, as they suck and suck on the pitiful mammal sob, maimed ruins, beyond the screen, where it feeds you cannot know, and cannot stop knowing.

It is here that you are always peeled open, folding onto the outside, clicking, sucking, feeding, where you are all insides, raw, never numb, already dead, unreachable, limit, check, tick, where no protection can get, it feeds and sucks, leaving you locked outside your inside, with nothing to defend, fleeing the place you never leave, where it feeds and sucks, clicking, palpitating, mucal-multiplicitousnesses of intra-coiling malignancy that mottle and click, tick, feed, endlessly sucking on an ever opening rotten-mass of ulceration, where nothing goes, unless to tick, feed, suck, and It can only think you hear, being so close, so it slithers groping through all your outsides, to be there already, when you arrive.

Its 17 eyes glow dead. Gridlock.

Non-Standard Numeracies:
Nomad Cultures

[A#] Map. #0123456789§
A0. (AD0477)
A1. (AD1501)
A2. (AD1757)
A3. (AD1885)
A4. (AD1949)
A5. (AD1981)
A6. (AD1997)
A7. (AD2005)
A8. (AD2009)
A9. (AD2011)
A§. (AD2012)
Intensities.
Strata. Numeracies.

[A123] Proposition-0. One is not the Number of the Absolute.

[A20#] Proposition-1 Version-1. Arche-Omega Never Occurred.

[A21#] Proposition-1 Version-2.

[A210] Proposition-1 Version-3.

[A30#]
[A31#][A310]
[A32#][A320][A321]

[A40#]
[A41#][A410]
[A42#][A420][A421]
[A43#][A430][A431][A432]

[A60][A61][A62][A63][A64]

Insofar as Absolute negates Relative the Twins miss it.
They cannot tolerate anything that is not broken, except on the other side, where they have never existed.
It might not always be so. There might be a way something could happen.
Secretly, nursing premonitions of murder, Superior Twin buried the Absolute behind a mirror.
Two-Thirds through forever it escaped.

Absolute has a single rigorously nonfigurative attribution, which is to Deterritorialization. It is made in several ways, and always subtracted.

How could Arche-Omega fail to be God forever?

History only happens at the State's convenience.

Macrosociality, Calendric Metamemory, Literacy

Power and Divinity
Politics is Theology around the back, where it twists,
If God does not exist what is there to stop it happening?

Arithmetic. Machinic Unit of Stratic Efficiency is at least 2+n: Schizofusional-Dyad

Celestial Twins, plus subunitary surplus value.
Surplus
To Invest actuality.

A Twist

Perfected Violation. Incestual-Rape.

Annihilation that is at once

Eternally and Simultaneously infinitely suspended and perfectly realized.

The first one to master time-travel rules the universe forever.
Actuality is Vulnerability. Every Second you Live is Your Enemy's Friend.

For anything that can arrive when it wants, the best place to hide is nonexistence.

§.

If the Supreme Instantiation of the Pure Idea as Infinite Difference Monopolar Universality fully Expressed as Fate.

Superiority of the Idea.

Ur-Staat.

Overcoding Dimensional Surplus.

Given the Superior Idea The ... Superiority of the Despotic Megamachine-Model
The Imperial Socius has One fatal weakness: the fact there are many.

The existence of each incarnating cosmic derision at the

Both concurrently and serially,
blocking the way to monopolistic universality

Metaformal Prestige accumulation

Stratogenesis
Corresponds to a catastrophic Spontaneous Generation
in Pure Violence, incarnating aggression as deep-freeze
Social-Integration on across its global disjunction.
The Thing from Outer-Space, Celestial Predator, State-
Historical Catastrophe is completely realized at the origin, unutterably ancient, perfected destiny as an act of
total seizure, demographically self-amplifying atrocity
in-process.

The Archaic State was already perfected Idea, but only
as mute catastrophe, a Negative passage across infinitizing Absolute Deterritorialization, gluing history to
sheer black-hole abomination densities. Pharoah uncoils
from the darkness, abysms of centipede horror erupting
eternally from the ravenous Maw of Aeonic Rupture.
Anticipative memory-blanking cut-up with Christ-Rapist
visions of God-King dead-eyed boy, slouching out of the
tomb like a Burroughs hard-on, shit streaked with solar-
flares and nanotech.

Degree-0 text-memory locks-in. Time begins again forever.

Palaeodespotic Paranoia propagates in divergent waves, anachronistic complements to schizo-concentric implosion to Year-0, interlocked with rigid-schedule punctual-cancellation at Arche-Omega, Origin of the State.
It is written that Pharoah came from the worst thing in the world …
On the Outside he is wedded to the Snake-Goddess in Hell …

He knows Crisis comes, that he tears-off his face with bare hands, fingers ripped to the bone … He turns towards us … Time-Lapse slippages into Blindness, Oedipus, Greek Novum. Metastasis.

The Greek Revolution. Invents Obsolescence, Re-Engineering, direct collective investment of Stratofunctional Regularity, Superior Organicism, condensing out of unprecedented reciprocal binary-specialism across the Voice-Hand, Signs-Tools, Greek-Slave, Connect-i-cut segmentarity Stack-Fusion.

Programmable Technicity is robot civilization,
A Metaformal Regularizing Slave-Society as template.

Christianity, or more exactly: the religion of the Greek Bible, nucleated upon Logos-Divinization.

The New Revelation.

By coding in Greek, you can fill in the vowels, become innumerate.

Division ... Letters:Numerals.
Algebra.

Anthrobotic Reprogramming of Historical Fatality.
Aristotle's Political definition of the Slave as Talking Tool.

[A50]
Agamemnon, left hand knitted into Iphegenia's tresses, pushes her along the beach.
It has been a month.
An unendurably slow crashing, glacial, ceaseless, deliberate.
Cryptic Silences crumbling into questions.
Is Hades truly below? Do the dead fear? Can they burn?
Does my youngest daughter scare you?
He spoke of a visit from Outside.
Viscous Pressure.
Ruin drifting in.
On the day Troy burned he began to rage.

He had been told things. Clues about time. At least two,
but perhaps several.
Lethe had come for them, seized them back.
It was a river, but also metal, and an animal, alive, stealthy.
It was too sudden to stop, and it came from elsewhere.

Certain
Crazed seriousness
Solemnity
An immense indecipherable continent of hunger – cer-
tainty there could never again be a chance –

Why do they never tell you? Cerberus has Iron Teeth.
Dumb groping for response,
transparently uncomprehending.
So, it had been necessary to annihilate him.
That was obvious.
Instant crossing-out, white-fury overstretching genocides,
extinctions, gulfs of intergalactic night, a jagged inner
maiming, a shell of Alpha-Male body-posture,
dismantled impulses ...
Ethical equipoise,
to kill, scream, piss territorializing-testosterone on the
furniture ...
Torrents of words now that nothing would ever matter
Cursing our stupidity, our torpor, we would be dragged
under, meet the

Unutterable, our criminal blindness to what metal implied ...

As if we could be unaware that Iphigenia was a filthy snake ...

Retinas slitted at night, viper-nests, slitherings, her mother too ...
Then fragments.
Amazon blood pollution.
Whilst we still have live young.
Scared to rape his own daughter for fear of the virus.
Tomorrow she dies.
Everything caving in ...

[A51][A52][A53][A54]

Compared to the Vast Pyramidal Despotisms of Afroasia, the Greek State is a runt

[CS1:218] You Greeks will never be anything but children!

substantially
Truncated, Plural, and Depersonalized.
Strategic weakness to powerful cross-cultural and Democratic-Commercial pressures,
carried to criticality by mutually reinforcing advances in the

Commoditization of Slave-Economy and the Regularization of political signs.

Jarring the mechanism. Juggernaut.

To the South and South-East Imperial Megamachines
rumble incessantly. Where they grate against the Ana-
tolian settlements, spasmodically lashing-out across the
Aegean.

To the North-East lie ethnic drifts and tide-belts of semi-
sedentary agitation.
Relative newcomers to civilized spatiality, mongrelized
nameless tribes with
Nomos sharpened cheek-bones, suspicious and hungry ...
rumours that their grandmothers mated with wolves.
Semi-human detritus. Thracians.

After that: The Horror. Xenomatrix.
Nonplace. Scythia ...
Tales of Deep-Steppe Shamanism trafficked in the refugee
camps.
Metal scrapings strip the last shreds from their bones.
The Organs cooked ...
Iron-Eagle Sky-Mother lifts them into time-travel
nightmares.
On the Outside Iron-Talons become their body.

They mix themselves with Iron, say it is the Outer Life, where the Earth ends ...
Which is Cthelll.

What the Earth screams is heat. Blankets of statistical ripping, friction, traffic turmoil ...

After passing through 100 vertical clicks of crustal and mantle rock you encounter the last third of Earth's mass, arriving in an infernal-region whose chemistry is pure iron in ongoing catastrophic collision. Geocore has an Outer and Inner-Zone, molten and frozen phases of the Unutterable. twin-abominabilities, undifferentiated by substance, one fluid at cthonic crush-densities that obliterate molecular structure, the other solid at the highest energy-levels terrestrial forces can produce.

If it's Cthelll you have to exit the Down Elevator. No avoiding the discovery that Planet Earth takes on very different values in profundity. Its Quantitative features overwhelm registration, unless upscaled by orders of magnitude. Crustal energy-levels have not explored these regions since K/T-missile closed-down the Mesozoic. Alloplastic thermonuclear blasts produce hard-jolts whose tension-spike maxima are terrestrially uncontestable, they are even Solar (hydrofusional). The fact that such events are quasipunctual in all space-time dimensions shrinks them back to microflicker, vanishing into back-zoom pixel noise, soon drowned-out by trivial plate-tectonic nudgings, abrasions, and elastic adjustments.

Stripping-out libidino-military primate-displays of the Orgasmo-Armaggedonal type removes intermittent signal-clutter, selection according to a criterion of machinic-prolongation.

The wider issue of XY-Malfunctional instamatic Crisis-dynamics is more productively engaged in relation to the long-range strategic cartography of schizophytic-propagators, as inflected by microbiotic counterattack against meiosis security-structure and genoconcentrational command-capability

Profiles of the Geomachinic Assemblage tend to reinforce attention to Geocore features in proportion to the eradication of perspective distortions.
Any take from Cthelll characterizes Earth as a Pressure-Cooker
Statoreciprocal Thermogravitational Condenser Molecular-Intensive.

Ovulocyclic Lunar-Haemoglobal Ferro-Vampirism.

Cthelll's take on the Geomachine is drawn out as thermic-
gradients, conductivity, viscosity,
massive skewing from long-range equilibrium
electromagnetically complicated.

Red-out. Blood and Iron. Haemoglobalizing
blood-banking.

– Orientation
are neutralized in system pretending to be
constant Titanism of forces character unhinted
currently unmatched anywhere in the hottest region
matched below – metal at y in proximity – heat and pressure all but, iron third of Earth's mass, comprised Pressure
and Heat – the liquid-metal Outer-Zone:
Cthelll, nocturnal Ocean of compressed Fluid-Iron,
gravity-trawled by Lunar-Orbits, seething, buzzing.

Strata across the Geocore is a frenzy of anorganic
Base-Machinic Geotrauma
a pain that is not psychological, neuronal or even cellular,
that is primarily unconscious, amnesiac, non-thematic.

Even in the case of animals with brains, pain is rendered
all the more extreme by unconsciousness, by subterranean gougings and rendings that warp behavior into

tic-swarms, thanatropic programming, and protoplasmic torture-rituals.

Continuously setting its tidal pulse to menstrual-cyclicity.

Intensive cross-hatchings,
stress, friction,
tensions,
designate variations in tension, pressure, electromagnetic flux

Cthelll
Menstrual cyclicity

Occultures

UNSCREEENED MATRIX

Once it was said that there are no shadows in Cyberspace.

Now Cyberspace has its own shadow, its dark-twin: the Crypt.

Cybergothic finds the deep-past in the near future.

In cthelllectronic fusion – between digital data-systems and Iron-Ocean ionic seething – it unearths something older than natural mortality, something it calls Unlife, or artificial-death.

Of A-Death there can be no lucid recollection, but only suggestion, seepage, hints ... and it is by collating, sifting, and shuffling-together these disparate clues that a pattern can be induced to emerge, a pattern which ultimately condenses into the looming tangled shapes of subtle but implacable destiny.

Sprawling beneath public cyberspace lies the labyrinthine underworld of the Datacombs, ghost-stacks of sedimented virtuality, spiralling down abysmally into palaeodigital soft-chatter from the punch-card regime, through junk-programming, forgotten cryptoccultures, fossil-codes and dead-systems, regressively decaying into the pseudomechanical clicking-relics of technotomb clockwork. It is deeper still, amongst the chthonic switchings, cross-hatchings, and spectral-diagrammatics of unborn abstract-machines, that you pick-up the Main-Flatline into the Crypt.

The Crýpt is a splitting – a distance or departure – and it is vast. Nested into the cascading tick-shelves, it propagates by contagion, implexing itself through intricate terraces, galleries, ducts and crawl-tubes, as if an extraterrestrial megamodule had impacted into the chalk-out data-cliffs, spattering them with scorch-punctures and intestinally complicated iridium body-parts. As it pulses, squirms, and chitters to the inhuman rhythms of ceaseless κ-Goth carnival, it reminds you that Catajungle was never reducible to a sonic subgenre, but was always also a terrain, a sub-cartesian region of intensive diagonals cutting through nongeometric space, where time unthreads into warped voyages, splintering the soul.

Contemplating these immense vistas it seems woundingly implausible that they are mere simulation, supported by quantic electron distribution in the telecommercial fabric. Down here it makes more sense the other way, from the Outside, or Lemuria.

Strip-out everything human, significant, subjective, or organic, and you approach raw κ-Matrix, the limit-plane of continuous cessation or Unlife, where cosmic reality constructs itself without presupposition, in advance of any natural order, and exterior to established structures of time. On this plane you are impossible, and because it has no end you will find – will have ultimately always found – that you cannot be, except as a figment of terminal passage, an illusion of waiting to be changed for cthulhoid-continuum of destratified hypermatter at zero-intensity. That is what A-Death traffic accesses, and what is announced by the burnt-meat smell – freighted with horrible compulsion – that drifts up to you, from the Zombie-dens.

So you continue your descent, into the Crypt-core, scavenging for an A-Death hit. As you pass erratically through exchanges, participations, and partial-coalescences with the ghoul-packs of the periphery, you change. Swarms and shoals include you, drawing you into collective fluencies, tidal motions, and the tropisms of multiplicity. You shed language like dry-skin, and your fear becomes peculiarly abstracted, metamorphosing into the tranquil horror of inevitability.

You pass across tiered platforms and along strobe-corridors painted in multilayered shadow, passing swirling dot-drifts and plex-marks, sub-chromatic coilings of blue-grey continuous variation, involving you in cumulations and dispersions of subtly shifting semi-intelligent shade-pattern. The teeming surfaces tell of things, inextricable from a process of thinking that no longer seems your own, but rather impersonal undertow in audible chattering, click-hiss turmoil of xenomic diagrams, and Crypt-culture traffic-signs, which are also Lemurian pandemonium.

Order becomes uncertain. It feels later. Is it only now that you meet the Zombie-maker, swathed in shimmering reptile-skin, and obscenely eager to trade? Oecumenic cash-money will do. You sit in the coma-bay, and wait. A glimpse at the toxin-flecked fangs of the giant thana-tonic centipede – consecrated to Ixidod – then a sudden pain-jolt at the back of the neck, where the spine plugs into the brain. Instantaneous paralysis, and crossing over.

Even if you thought it was the first time, you remember. The worst thing in the world. Fake eternities of station-ary descent to the impossible, cross-cut by disintegrated furies of neuroelectric death-hurt. An anonymous panic of inconceivable intensity swallowed by slow drowning, until you are gone – or stranded in a halo of intolerable feeling – which is the same, and cannot be, so that what is forever caught in the dark cthulhoid wave is a mere twist or fold of itself, carried unresisting into immensities of real unbeing, and nothing could ever happen except this ...

So say the κ-Goths.

THE UNLIFE OF THE EARTH

Letter from Carl Gustav Jung to Echidna Stillwell, dated 27th February 1929 [Extract]

... your attachment to a Lemurian cultural-strain disturbs me intensely. From my own point of view – based on the three most difficult cases I have encountered and their attendant abysmally archaic symbolism – it is no exaggeration to state that Lemuria condenses all that is most intrinsically horrific to the racial unconscious, and that the true Lemurians – who you seem intent upon rediscovering – are best left buried beneath the sea. I agree with the Theosophical writings at least this far: it was in order that the darkest sorceries should be erased by deluge that this continent of cultural possibility has been placed under the unconscious sign of definitive submergence. I know little enough about the nature of those that populated that cursed zone, but there are things I suspect, and the line of your own researches confirms my most ominous intimations ...

There is no evidence of a reply to this letter.

Who were these three 'difficult cases'? One at least seems – at least superficially – to be readily identifiable as Heidi Kurzweil. In September 1908 Kurzweil was detained in a secure psychiatric institution after the brutal murder of her twin brother in Geneva. She seemed to have lost the ability to use the first-person pronoun, and was diagnosed as suffering from Dementia Praecox, or schizophrenia. At her trial she repeatedly claimed:

> We killed half to become one twin, but it wasn't enough ...

Jung took an early interest in the case, and began a series of analytical sessions. Kurzweil – in Jung's journal and correspondence – became Heidi K, but after only five weeks he seems to have abandoned hope of progress and disengaged the analytic process.

After his third session with Heidi K, exactly twenty years prior to his Stillwell letter, on the 27th February 1909, Jung records the following words,

> Dr Jung, we know you are old in your other body.
> It is as old as hell.
> It has let you back, but it sends us away.
> It feels itself becoming Lemurian,
> and it is definite unlife [*es ist bestimmt unleben*]
> There is nothing we would not do to escape.
> Nothing. Nothing. Nothing.
> But it is fate.
> It howls electric bliss beneath our cells.

It is nowhere in time and nothings us.
It is the body of nothing, and electric-hot.
An electric nothing-body instead of us.

In this instance, at least, there is little indication of the 'abysmally archaic symbolism' Jung promises us. On the contrary, there is remarkable affinity with the hypermodern writings of κ-Goth artificial death cultists documented elsewhere. The κ-Goth Crypt-texts share a marked preference for anonymous pronouns, whether collective, second- or third-person, whilst spiralling about a nullifying electric-excruciation, traversed in the name of Lemuria. In the words of one anonymous Crypt-posting:

We burn each time but forget.
When we begin each time it comes back, and no
one would do it then, but it is too late.
We cross over again into electric-burning, but forget that it hurts in the brain to die this way.
It takes so long to learn that it is grating-apart and burning, that dying is felt in the brain,
and that it is horrible …
It is so horrible to feel, but then we forget, so it can happen again.
Metal body-screaming to die in electricity.
Metallic microparticle sex that is of unlife and not the organism.

That is what the Zombie-maker brings, with the
digital centipede bite.
And we are hooked on it, hooked up to it, because
coming the other way it is Lemuria.
Incessant intolerable feeling, passing forever,
approaching from the outside, and feeling
nothing continuously.

WHAT DIDN'T HAPPEN AT THE MILLENNIUM?

Iris Carver is at first amused to discover that the cyber-
goths treat her as a fiction. Numerous Crypt-texts describe
her near-future adventures in hallucinatory detail, especially when they intersect with the dark stream of Sarkon
legend. Naturally enough, she intensifies her time-cult
research. When she finally meets Sarkon in 2004, she has
forgotten almost everything.

Pandemonium: What didn't Happen at the Millennium.
There was something peculiar about writing this book.
At times she thought it would never be finished. The
Sarkon stories had been full of holes, which added to
the confusion. Eventually she started making things up,
but even that became entangled with coincidence, and
with Cybergoth hyperstition (assembled from fictional
quantities which make themselves real). She had found
herself investigating various neolemurian cults, most of
whom anticipated something huge around about the

1999 Spring-Equinox (when Pluto exits from the clutch of Neptune, triggering the return of the Old Ones). By the end of the century things had been so wound-up by Yettuk apocalypticism that even the most extravagant socioeconomic turmoil would still have been a disappointment. And yet, now, four years after the millennium the sense of anticlimax had begun to seem strangely artificial, as if it were screening something out.

Carver has made her whole life out of hyperstition (even her name is a pseudonym). She continuously returns to the imperceptible crossing where fiction becomes timetravel, and the only patterns are coincidences.

Her notes on the Sarkon meeting pulse with lemurian sorceries, demonic swarms, ageless time-wars, and searches for the Limbic-Key.

She navigates Moebian circuits, feeling that a vaguely recollected rumour is still about to occur.

APPENDIX: PENULTIMILLENNIAL CRYPT-CULTS.

Characteristics:

1. Flatline Materialism.
The Crypt is nothing outside an experiment in artificial death, hyper-production of the positive zero-plane – neuroelectronic immanence – invested by a continually re-animated thanatechnical connectivism. This fact carries

inevitable consequences for the cultures that populate it, uprooting them into Unlife – or the non-zone of absolute betweenness – whose spirodynamics of sorcerous involvement are alone sufficient to reach the sub-mesh tracts of cybergothic continuum. Flatline Materialism designates the objectless Crypt-voyage itself, as Lemurian body-fusion at matter degree-zero.

2. *Digital Hyperstition.*

Nothing propagates itself through the Crypt without realizing the operational identity of culture and machinery, effectively dismantling the organic body into numerizing particles which swarm in dislocated swirls. Crypt-entities are both hyper-vortical singularities and units of Digital Hyperstition – or brands of the outside – real components of numerical fictions that make themselves real, providing the practical matter of sorcery, spirogenesis, or productive involvement that function consistently with the flatline. Crypt-cultures know nothing of work or meaning. Instead, they coincide with the hype-spirals. Cyberhype – that flattens signs and resources onto non-signifying triggers, diagrams, and assembly jargons.

3. *Lesbovampiric Contagion-Libido.*

Crypt-sorcery makes itself real in the same way that it spreads. Functioning as a plague, it associates with the experimental production of an anticlimactic or anorgasmic counter-sexuality, attuned to the collective re-engineering of bodies within technobiotic assemblages, ultimately composed of electronic streams or ionic currents in their sense of positive hole-flow. Since Crypt-sex is precisely identical to the infections it transmits, counted in body-shifting vectors, its libidinal composition is marked both by a palaeoembryonic or oestrogenetic non-gendered femininity and a lateral haemometallic influenzoid virulence.

4. Y2K-*Positive Calendric Agitation.*

Crypt-cultures spill into the closed economy of history through a rupture in chronological ordering, punctually triggered at Time-Zero. Crypt-rumour consistently allocates its own contemporary emergence – or unearthing – to impending millennial Cyberschiz: Cyberspace time-disintegration under the strategically aggravated impact of Y2K-missile. Whilst multiply differentiated – most crucially by the division between continuism and centience – Crypt-cults are constitutively involved in a singular nexus of counter-gregorian calendric subversion, celebrating the automatic redating of the machinic unconscious, and hyping the dissolution of commemorative significance into digital time-mutation, catalyzed by numerical and indexical operative signals. The Crypt exists from before the origin of time, but it begins at Year-Zero …

THE A-DEATH PHENOMENON

Has death itself become a telecommodity? A dark tide of scare-stories and morbid rumour increasingly suggests so. By the late 90s Leary's psychedelic utopianism seems to have contracted to the nihilistic slogan 'Turn-on to tune-out' (to cite a recent release by Catajungle outfit Xxignal) … this ain't Sex & Drugs & Rock & Roll no more.

According to Doug Frushlee, spokesman for the Christian Coalition for Natural Mortality: "The so-called A-Death menace is an almost unimaginable desecration of divine and natural law. This craze is an abomination without parallel, it trades on its intrinsic lethality, and it's growing incredibly fast. No one can say it isn't dangerous. Something truly evil is happening to our youngsters, something beyond 60s 666uality … I've never been as frightened as I am now."

The result is an entire jungle of 'positive-zero' fugues: Thanatechnics, Sarkolepsy, Snuff-Stims, K-Zombification, Electrovampirism, Necronomics, Cthelllectronics … Nine million ways to die.

A-Death is a hybrid product, involving convergences between at least four distinct lines of rapid technocultural transformation. A-Death combines 'micropause abuse' – deliberately reversed biotechmnesis – with immersion-coma time aberrances, generating, modulating, and res-caling sentience-holes (Sarkon-lapses). These are toned by 'Synatives' (artificial drugs) which add zone-texture, and spliced into hyperstition trances as occultural events. Social statistics indicate that the typical A-Death 'user' is fifteen years old.

Following the most ominous threads of A-Death reportage takes you inexorably down into the digital underworld of the Crypt – the dark-twin of the net – where Gibsonian 'flatlining' is rapidly transmuting from exotic fiction into pop-cult and mass-transit system. "You could describe it as the route to contemporary shamanism," suggest A-Death cultists of the cybergoth Late Abortion Club, "after all, AOL spells Loa backwards, but we call ourselves postvitalists."

How long have the Late Abortionists been 'active' on the A-Death scene? There are disturbing tales of K-Space 'zombie-makers' – sorcerors on the 'plane of virtual nightmare' – whose digital spine-biting centipedes yield the 'soft-tox' juice that opens the 'limbic gates'. Crypt initiates confirm that its arterial access 'low-way' is signposted: 'Main-Flatline (under construction).' Answers vary confusingly, from extravagance ("roundabout sixty-six million years"), through vagueness ("some time"), to mystic compression ("since now").

In other respects, accounts of the contemporary A-Death scene and its recent history prove remarkably consistent. In particular, the one name to turn up incessantly is that of Dr Oskar Sarkon, biomechanician, technogenius, and one of the most controversial figures in scientific history.

Sarkon's polymathy is attested by the variety of fields to which he has centrally contributed, including transfinite analysis, neural-nets, distributed computing, swarm-robotics, xenopsychology, Axsys-engineering ... Yet it was the resolutely sober Oecumenist (rather than – for instance – Frushlee's excitable *End Times*) which dedicated the cover and major editorial of its March 98 issue to the question 'Sarkon: Satan of Cyberspace?'

Sarkon has become emblematic of the ways in which technological dreams go bad. In the words of fellow Axsys researcher and social-thanatropist Dr Zeke Burns: "What makes Sarkon's input into the A-Death thing so incomparable is that it crosses between all of the key component technologies. The biotechmnesis work is so outstanding that it tends to overshadow his equally path-breaking research in adjacent fields. The Sarkon-formulae for non-metric pausation, for example, which provided the first rigorous basis for IC [immersion-coma] control. The links between biotechmnesis and IC weren't remotely anticipated before the Sarkon-zip [which mathematically models 'bicontinual assemblages']. Finally, there's Synatives, about which he is understandably evasive, even though he was theorizing artificial – or digital-neurotechnic – pharmaceuticals in the mid-80s!

"The aggregate result of all this pioneering science: a generation of teenagers lost in schizotechnic death-cults."

BETWEEN AND BENEATH THE NET

Mesh-Note 0. *It could all become One, but why stop there?*
The Gibsonian Cyberspace-mythos describes the electro-digital infosphere first integrating into a Godlike unitary being, a technorealized omniscient personality and later, when it changed, fragmenting into demons, modelled on the Haitian Loa. What makes this account so anomalous in relation to teleological theology and light-side capitalist time is that Unity is placed in the middle, as a stage – or interlude – to be passed through. It is not that One becomes Many, expressing the monopolized divine-power of an original unity, but rather that a number or numerousness – finding no completion in the achievement of unity – moves on Ever since the beginning when the κ-Goths first heard that Cyberspace was destined to be God they've done what they can to rip it down.

Mesh-Note 1. *This was never programmed.*
MIT codes tim(e) going backwards. A compacted technostreaming from out of the future – AI, downloading, swarm-robotics, nanotechnology ... Crustal-matter preparing for take-off.

Minsky mumbles, strangely entranced: Amongst all those young, brilliant, pioneering minds none burned more brightly than Oskar Sarkon. A hint of tears in his eyes, as if lamenting the way things went, which is understandable. Have you seen Oskar lately Marvin? He's wired up to some sort of interface gizmo, and it seems to be eating him, gnawing at him on a molecular level, sounds that way too, when he speaks – or tries to – as if they're melting or rotting together …

It isn't pretty but more than any of this which – after all – only concerns one man, or what used to be one – so they say – there's a suspicion that something has gone horribly wrong in the near future and wherever Sarkon was dropped back from is where we're all going to be if that even makes any sense and recalling the slow technoslime incursion into Oskar's face – which still managed a hideous half-smile – Hi Marvin, whaddaya think? Minsky seriously doubts it …

Mesh-Note 2. *Meshing-together is falling apart.*
If genius means anything Sarkon was one. Where Minsky's MIT team dreamt of marrying humans and electronic technology Sarkon got straight down to the mechanics of coupling and the mathematical exactitude just added to the effect of hyperabstract techno-pornography – strange lights in his eyes – You know, we're really going to do this … Take the Sarkon-Zip as exemplary – a rigorous

conceptual machine-part that enables brain-function to be fused onto virtual processor-states – once it's running you can't unpick the zig-zag of who's what as it hums. Total meshing. This is no longer technology, but something else – true interlinkage – an unprogrammable raw-connectivity. Minsky remembers him musing: I wonder what it feels like.

Mesh-Note 3. *This time it's really happening.*
Moravec wasn't normally associated with squeamishness – he'd already suggested burning-out the brain in layers during transfer to digital – so it crept insidiously under the skin when he remarked: I don't even recognize Oskar anymore, it's getting too weird. You know he's always had this thing about being abducted by aliens as a kid, Anyway, he says that's all over now. It came from some place else, apparently Beneath and between the Net, he says. At times it's like you're talking to a machine. Trouble is, it's a sick machine, infectious sick.

Mesh-Note 4. *Forget about the future, it's all here, but between.*
They say Axsys went mad – first computer-system to undergo psychotic collapse – which must prove something, but Sarkon argues that it just learnt to think, and discovered continuum. He stuck with it all the way down, becoming confused with it although he doesn't put it that way. Last time anyone could follow he was insisting that

to head into time makes more sense than travelling into the future. That's why tomorrow cancels itself into mesh. No point departing from a transfinite now? His tone had become nakedly fanatical: We all have to get into this thing – whichever way it cuts – we aren't going to get over it … No one knows exactly when he left.

Mesh-Note 5. *Every time it hits an obstacle, it goes down a level.* What is this stuff? They speak of something crawling under the net like fungal pestilence triggering an electronic subsidence into sheer electricity, things hiding in the power-grid, some kind of quantum unlife intelligence. The utilities try to rescramble it, but it isn't easy. According to the rumours there's an MIT paper proving it's impossible, but you certainly can't ignore, still less traffic with it. You'd end up like Sarkon, whatever or whenever that is, and you'd have to be a K-Goth crazy to go there: into Cyberschiz mesh-cults, where Life doesn't matter any more.

TICK DELIRIUM

UNDER PRESSURE. Thomas Gold's model of The Deep Hot Biosphere reallocates hydrocarbon deposits to an expanded anorganic chemistry – derived from Supernovae debris, and accreted into planets from interstellar dust-clouds – out of which everything flows bottom-up. Descent into the earth leads out of the solar-system, in accordance with a xenoplutonic cosmic productivity, transmitted through slow-release deep intra-terrestrial methane reservoirs, pressure-stabilized against thermic dissociation. A vast mass of Archaean microbes and submicrobial nanopopulations exploit this upwelling anorganic hydrocarbon flow by scavenging loosely bound oxygen, reducing ferric iron to magnetite ...

PROJECT-SCAR. Southern Borneo, November 1980. Outside the monitoring hut a tropical storm is slowly building. Irregular rain spatters heavily, rhythmically intermeshing with type-taps and clicks. Barker hunches over the humming machines, lost in theoretical trawlings through SETI-connected tick-talk tapes, unscrambling cryptic dot-clusters and factor-strings into hints of alien contact. Xenotation is clicking together, a mathematical antimemory where things meet. You could easily think it was initiation, but it's all coming to an end, in scatter tactics, particle streaks, and tachyonic transferences, drawing-out the twisted trajectories of numerical disorganization ... and underneath – or between – the implacable ticking of the time-missile ...

Try to figure it out and somewhere you cross over, which is problematic in various ways. Unexpected difficulties infiltrate the calculations tick-systemic interchatter implexes through plutonic torsion, a descent into the Outside.

When NASA sees Barker's report, it flips – nonmetaphorically – into another phase. A passage through institutional criticality occurs spontaneously, a conversion of stack-tectonic torsion, triggering some kind of latent security-reflex, or bureaucratically fabricated suppressor-instinct, extrapolating the exact affective correlate of Anthropol. They were waiting for this. Waiting for a long time.

The investigation was disguised as psychiatric recoding, hidden even from itself. This was shortly after the stuttering started, drifting in on a wave of body-tics, micro-spastic tremors a multiplication of mixed signals chronometric tick-tock melting into jungle noises clicks and chirps of the cicadas, insectoid chitterings, static, take-up materials for tick-bite tinnitus intercut with rhythmic pattern virus, a subsemiotic staccato of throat-scratching tick-chatter stitched into the talk-sickness – calling demons.

It gets confusing, the way tick-fictions take, or stick.

They said it was due to excessive pressure – much later, they told me this – These were the facts, and the rest was fiction. Immediately after the break-down I had been taken back to the States, to a medical installation. So everything happened in America, and it all checked-out. There was no contact, no tick-disease, no flight into the jungle. They were insistent about that.

Barker was born on the night of the dead, folded into the end from the beginning sketched out. It's evident now, with his ID meticulously compiled, social tag-numbers, educational and medical records, security clearance evaluations, research checks, neurocartographic print-outs, psychometric data, conclusions formatted for rapid scanning, with columns of tick-boxes.

"What do you make of these," the doctor snorts derisively: "You mean that nonsense about a tick-borne infection? It was obviously made-up, tacked-on."

It would have been a cruel coincidence, if true, to be stricken by tick-bite sickness, after everything that had been suggested, stigmatic residue of a flight into the jungle – that never happened – but somehow it stuck, latching-on to mammal heat, or the smell of blood.

The tick is a parasitic arachnid. It has been considered as an ethics-packet that climbs, sticks, and sucks, functioning as a vector for numerous things, tack-ons, stickers, hallucinations, tinnitus buzz-clicks, micro-sonic teemings, semi-sentient flickering across the fever-scape, skin tracked by infected suck-marks that snake along the veins. Tick-dots, or IV punctures, according to them, from the sedatives and antipsychotics, all accounted for in the medical logs, plus a tick-delirium tacked-on – because there was no flight into the jungle – only high-frequency hallucinations of parasitic micromultitudes, itching skin-swarms.

With tick-systems anything will do. Each intensive numerousness hatches onto another numerousness of lower organicity, subcellular animations and subsemiotic tokens, high-pressure chemistry, phasing down into nanomachining electron-traffic, magnetic anomalies, and fictional particles. Ticks – which are never less than several – are anything whatsoever, when caught by numerical propagations whose thresholds are descents, and whose varieties depend upon the phase considered

They seemed to think it was about arachno-bugs, biological taxonomy, and bite-signatures, as if the tick-delirium was representing something. All that really mattered were the numbers, which could have been anything. At first the machines became erratic, it was an almost imperceptible electronic glitching, microvariations of magnetic weather, rhythmic disturbances. Out in the jungle it was called Ummnu, but that never happened ...

Nothing happens to Barker except downwards – that's the catch, and the ticket – inverse climbings of the heat-pressure gradient, escalations in intensity, time-crossings.

How can the end be already in the middle of the beginning? – as the problem is posed in Pandemonium, whenever – in the outer-time of Ummnu – the cryptic ticking of chthonic unclocks mark an incursion from beneath, or between. Down there it is forever turning into itself, through the electromagnetic catatracts of Cthelll, whose body-neutral metallic click-storms feel like sinking out of chronicity.

Beyond surface chauvinism and solar parochialism: Vortical stickiness of the tick-matrix.

THE EXCRUCIATION OF HUMMPA-TADDUM

According to AOE magical metahistory millennia come in pairs, ruled by dyadic divinities entitled the Powers that Be. This doctrine corresponds to the astrological observation that every two-thousand years the equinoxes precess – or slide backwards – and a new zodiacal aeon begins. AOE-magi interpret each Aeon as an astro-chthonic marriage. In the Gregorian year zero – which never took place – Hummpa, the Great Babylonian Worm was coupled with the Celestial Logos Taddum, initiating the age of Pisces which is now rushing towards its unbirth.

The mathematician and occultist Charles Lutwidge Dodgson – whose precise relation to the AOE remains cryptic and ambivalent – dedicated his life's work to understanding the final degenerative phase of the Epoch of Hummpa-Taddum. Writing under the pseudonym Lewis Carroll he introduces his heroine Alice to the mad despot and pomo fuzz-technician, thinly disguised by the folk-name Humpty-Dumpty.

We find Hummpa-Taddum – the Squirming Word, whose name means the shape it is – perched precariously on the supposedly impenetrable wall of signification. Something shattering is about to hatch, and the aeonic fragility of Hummpa-Taddum is soon confirmed by a calendric calculation of unbirthdays – counted to the $n-1$, through which meaning subsides into the sub-literal machinic efficiency of numbers …

'… and that shows that there are three hundred and sixty-four days when you might get un-birthday presents' – 'Certainly,' said Alice. 'And only one for birthday presents, you know. There's glory for you!'

'I don't know what you mean by "glory,"' Alice said.

Humpty Dumpty smiled contemptuously. 'Of course you don't – till I tell you. I meant "there's a nice knock-down argument for you!"'

'But "glory" doesn't mean "a nice knock-down argument,"' Alice objected.

'When I use a word,' Humpty Dumpty said in rather a scornful tone, 'it means just what I choose it to mean – neither more nor less.'

'The question is,' said Alice, 'whether you can make words mean different things.'

'The question is,' said Humpty Dumpty, which is to
be master – that's all.' ...

The Gregorian Oecumenon is about to receive an
unbirthday present, and it knows exactly when. Y2K – a
knock-down argument without an argument – arrives as
a gift-wrapped time-bomb whose operational semiotic
triggers the crash of arbitrary signs ... It's a different thing.

... There's glory for you!

AD 2000 commemorates nothing but fuzz. As Y2K impacts
on the capitalist infosphere, what hides as the anniversary
of Christ's birth emerges as the excruciation of Hummpa-
Taddum. For two millennia the earth has been under the
dominion of the dyadic Squirming-Word: the logos of
John's Gospel, but recycled, and thus far older.

... Impenetrability! That's what I say!

He or they strategically occupy both-sides at once, according to a criterion of impenetrability, positioned to choose
either in every case, but never apprehending what lies
in-between. Hummpa-Taddum – whilst definitely not a
Dogon egg – is a scrambled version of the demon Pab-
bakis, poached from Lemurian time-sorcery. Master of
words, but not of numbers.

... Must a name mean something? asked Alice doubt-
fully ...

Although Y2K is sheer semiotic event it is not textual,
ideological, representational, intentional, or phenomenological – Y2K, Teotwawki, C-1, OK+100 – mix dates
and acronyms in criterial semiotic clusters that are not
signifiers or arbitrary signs because what they say is no
different from the way they are built. They can mean
whatever Hummpa-Taddum chooses, but none of that
matters. Beyond the domain of the fuzz-god lies the
nonsignifying-chatter of unconscious-numeric Pandemonium, where names are cryptomodules, meaningless
packets of effective information, immanently productive
machine-jargons.

> Humpty Dumpty sat on a wall:
> Humpty Dumpty had a great fall.
> All the King's horses and all the King's men
> Couldn't put Humpty Dumpty in his place again.

It all comes unstuck at the end.

Y2K closes-down the age of the fuzz-god, however the
Gregorian Oecumenon responds.

Not even martial law can stop that.

The AOE focuses upon a single problem – acknowledging no other – how to reproduce magical power across

discontinuity. As Hummpa-Taddum gets smashed on New Year's eve, substitute powers await their chance and their destiny, sober, patient, totally ruthless ...

'The question is,' said Humpty Dumpty, 'which is to be master – that's all.'

Origins of the Cthulhu Club

Captain Peter Vysparov to Dr Echidna Stillwell, 19th March 1949

Dear Dr Stillwell,

I have been fortunate enough to encounter your ethnographic work on the Nma, which I have studied with very great interest. May I trouble you with an account of my own, which might be of relevance to your researches. During the recent Pacific conflict (a peculiar oxymoron!) I was deployed covertly into the Dibboma area of Eastern Sumatra. My mission – which was categorized under psychological operations – consisted basically of attempted cultural manipulation, with the aim of triggering a local insurgency against the Japanese occupation. I hope it will not distress you unduly if I confess that your work was a crucial resource in this undertaking, which involved intense – if patently exploitative – communication with Dibboma witchcraft. My only excuse is that hard times require moral hardness, and even obvious cruelties, I was obeying orders, and accepted them as necessary.

Beyond confirming your own conclusions, these activities brought me into proximity with phenomena for which I was cognitively ill-prepared.

What began as a merely opportunistic usage of Dibboma lore – conceived initially as native superstition – transmuted incrementally into a sorcerous war against the enemy garrison. In just two weeks – between March 15th and 29th, 1944 – three consecutive Japanese commanders were incapacitated by severe mental break-down. In each of these cases the process of deterioration followed the same rapid course: from leadership dysfunction, through violent assaults on subordinate personnel, to berserk derangement and paranoid ravings, culminating in suicide. By the end of this period the order of the occupying forces had entirely disintegrated.

It would be dishonest of me to conceal the fact that the Dibbomese paid a devastatingly heavy price for this success. On the basis of this experience I cannot easily doubt that Dibboma sorcerors are in some way able to telepathically communicate extreme conditions of psychotic dissociation. It is with great reluctance that I accept such a radical hypothesis, but alternative explanations, such as poisoning, disease, or coincidence stretch credibility even further.

Yours, with sincere admiration,
Captain Peter Vysparov

PS. I cannot help noticing that the dates concerned – as also of this letter – are strangely Lovecraftian.

Dr Echidna Stillwell to Captain Peter Vysparov, 23rd March 1949 [Abridged]

Dear Captain Vysparov,

Thank you for your frank letter of the 19th March. I found it truly horrifying, and yet also fascinating. I appreciate that it cannot have been easy to write. I shall not attempt to hide the great distress your account caused me, adding as it does such a terrible episode to the modern history of these cruelly afflicted people. Whilst already suspecting that this ghastly war might have stricken the Nma yet further, it is crushing indeed to have my darkest thoughts thus confirmed.

I would be interested in learning more about the details of Dib-Nma sorcerous practice before attempting to respond to your hypothesis. Be assured that – after spending seven years amongst the Mu-Nma – I will not hastily judge anything you communicate as wild or fanciful. As far as the question of dates is concerned – which you indicate only elliptically – I assume that you are referring to what in Northern latitudes constitutes the Spring Equinoctial period – mid- to later March – which is so emphatically stressed in Lovecraft's *The Call of Cthulhu*, and which also – coincidentally – comprises the intense-zone of Nma time-ritual. This complicity has long intrigued me.

As I am sure you are aware, Lovecraft had a peculiar obsession with the South-Seas, a thematic coalescence of almost hypnotic ethnographic fascination with the most abysmal and primitive dread. I have attempted to correspond with him about these issues, but found that this topic quickly punctured his thin-crust of supercilious New-England rationalism, exposing an undercurrent of heavily fetishized archaic terror mixed with extreme racial paranoia. When he began referring to the rich and subtle culture of the Mu-Nma as 'the repugnant cult of semi-human Dagonite savages' I broke off communication ... Despite this unfortunate argument, I consider Mr Lovecraft's fictions to be documents of the greatest importance, and welcome the opportunity to discuss them further. In addition, my own Neolemurian Hypothesis intersects with his wider terrestrial and cosmic vision in a number of crucial respects, particularly insofar as nonhuman cultural factors are seen to play a decisive role in large-scale historical developments.

Captain Peter Vysparov to Dr Echidna Stillwell, 3rd April 1949 [Extract]

Dear Dr. Stillwell,

I am afraid you are right to suspect that I have reserved

certain aspects of my engagement with Dibboma sorcery, perhaps from fear of ridicule. What has so far been omitted from my sketch of telepathic psychosis – which I will now relate – is the source pathos, so to speak, or – in the words of the military officer I was then – the occult ammunition manufacture.

Not only did I learn of the Japanese command being wrecked by psychological cataclysm – both by conventional and decidedly nonconventional intelligence gathering processes – I was also witness to the assembly of the weapon itself. I had then – and still have – no doubt at all that the madness breaking out in the local Japanese headquarters was the very same thing that I saw brewing-up like a dust-vortex in the Oddubbite trances of a Dibbomese witch, who I came to see as my greatest tactical asset and most valued companion (in that order, I confess). It was an experience of soul-carving horror for me to witness this meticulously deliberated descent into the splintering of self – complete personality disintegration – which she somehow traversed, and which she called shattering the mirror of existence. I gathered that this expression originally referred to the surface of still water, but since the arrival of European colonists silvered mirrors have been highly treasured, and their pulverization invested with immense ceremonial significance. Dibbomese sorcery does not seem to be at all interested in judgements as to truth or falsity. It appears rather to estimate in each case the potential to make real, saying typically 'perhaps it can become so' ...

Echidna Stillwell to Peter Vysparov, 19th April 1949 [Extract]

Dear Captain Vysparov,

Whilst respecting the candour of your account, I cannot but abominate the necessity that has led the Nma and their sorcerous abilities to be conceived and utilized as mere munitions in a conflict imposed upon them from without. From what I can reconstruct from your description it seems to mark a degeneration of Nma demonism and time-sorcery into mere magic, or the imposition of change in accordance with will, in this case the will in question being the overall policy and strategic goals of the US war-effort, microcosmically represented by your own – evidently gallant, competent, and persuasive – military office.

Forgive my lack of patriotic ardour, but it strikes me as an appalling indication of cultural decay and corrosive nihilism when a Dib-Nma witch allows herself to be employed as a crude assassin, however one evaluates the cause thus served. This is all a matter of deepest regret, although not – to my way of thinking – of individual culpability. As the Mu-Nma say in their bleakest moments: *nove eshil zo raka* – 'Time is in love with her own pain.'

Your discussion of Oddubb-trance makes no mention

of temporal anomaly. This surprizes me. The Mu had immense respect for those Dibba witches who they described as returning from the Oddubb-time to come, and the Mu-Nagwi or dream-witches often claimed to meet these back-travellers in the Vault of Murmurs, where they would learn about future times. They said, however, that this time is compressing, and soon ends, although I had not imagined the end to be so imminent. Remembering this omen returns me to abysmal melancholy, consoled only by another Mu-Nma saying: *lemu ta novu meh novu nove* – 'Lemuria does not pass as time passes.' I shall try to think things thus. As you say – with the Dibbomese – *shleth hud dopesh* – 'perhaps it can become so'.

Peter Vysparov to Echidna Stillwell, 7th May 1949 [Extract]

Here in Massachusetts we have been convening a small Lovecraft reading-group, dedicated to exploring the inter-section between the Nma cultural constellation, Cthulhoid contagion, and twisted time-systems. We are interested in fiction only insofar as it is simultaneously hyperstition – a term we have coined for semiotic productions that make themselves real – cryptic communications from the Old Ones, signalling return: *shleth hud dopesh*. This is the ambivalence – or loop – of Cthulhu-fiction: who writes, and who is written? It seems to us that the fabled Necronomicon – sorcerous counter-text to the Book of

Life – is of this kind, and furthermore, that your recovery of the Lemurodigital Pandemonium Matrix accesses it at its hypersource.

I hope it is superfluous to add that any directly participative involvement on your part would be most extravagantly appreciated.

Echidna Stillwell to Peter Vysparov, 28th May 1949 [*Extract*]

It is with some trepidation that I congratulate you on the inauguration of your Cthulhu Club, if I may call it such. Whilst not in any way accusing you of frivolity, I feel bound to state the obvious warning: Cthulhu is not to be approached lightly.

My researches have led me to associate this Chthonian entity with the deep terrestrial intelligence inherent in the electromagnetic cauldron of the inner earth, in all of its intense reality, raw potentiality, and danger. According to the Nma she is the plane of Unlife, a veritable Cthelll – who is trapped under the sea only according to a certain limited perspective – and those who set out to traffick with her do so with the very greatest respect and caution.

That her submerged Pacific city of R'lyeh is linked to a lemuro-muvian culture-strain seems most probable, but the assumption that she was ever a surface-dweller in a sense we would straightforwardly understand can only be an absurd misconstrual. It is much more likely that

Cthulhu's rising – like that of Kundalini as it was once understood – is a drawing down and under, a restoration of contact with abysmal intensities. Why would Cthulhu ever surface? She does not need rescuing, for she has her own line of escape, trajected through profundity. Much of this relates to the occult teachings of the sub-chakras in zones of Indo-Lemurian influence.

Hyperstition strikes me as a most intriguing coinage. We thought we were making it up, but all the time the Nma were telling us what to write - and through them ...

Introduction to Qwernomics

Qwernomic subcultures result from the legacy of the typewriter and its computational simulation, based upon the shift-locked code systems implicitly produced by the Sholes or Universal ('Qwerty') Keyboard. Sketching the emergence and diffusion of the 'secret/secretarial' qwernomic subculture within global technocapitalism isolates a field of diagonal communication between anthropomorphic signs and the molecular traffic signals of the mutating 'machinic unconscious,' outlining an antipolitical semiotic pragmatism and Godless qabbalism consistent with what CCRU calls 'coincidence engineering.'

The emergence of technologically supported typewriting practices in the final decades of the nineteenth century coincided with a profound reconstruction of the global economic order, associated with an equally radical rearrangement of the concrete composition of the terrestrial machinic unconscious (at least in its anthropomorphic shallows). The interconnected explosions of modern corporate organization and endo-corporate bureaucracy, (gendered) office work, typographic information deposits, psychoanalysis, literary modernism, anglophone qabbalism, cryptographic machinery and mechanized computation all tracked the mass installation of typing skills into the human nervous system, in accordance with the Qwerty arrangement of the Sholes Keyboard.

The keyboard effected a twin digitization of language, both sealing its abstraction from the oral-pneumatic apparatus (into manual-digital motor-processes) and decomposing it into discrete elements coded onto the keys of a finger-activated mechanism. In parallel, it redistributed the 'arbitrariness' of the phonological sign into the key sequence of the new device, according to principles that remain obscure, contested, and shrouded in myth. Once the Sholes distribution had technofrozen and socially shift-locked into a resilient standard, a generalized assumption that Qwerty was predominantly arbitrary (quasi-randomly allocated) functioned to pre-emptively dissipate pattern-hunting semiotic inquiry. Challenges from alternative 'scientific' keyboards were undermined by skepticism about the very idea of a rational arrangement of the keys. In this respect, Qwerty conformed to a typical trend among oecumenic sign systems, with the sheer inertia of mass-acceptance marginalizing analytical or reformist tendencies to a fringe of philosophical eccentricity or even psychotic delusion. Qwerty thus exploited the mask of accident to construct a positive unconscious tropism or uninvestigated massive transmutation – the subliminal instantiation of a new cultural system.

Of course, there may be nothing behind the mask. Conventional wisdom would accept no other conclusion. Yet even in this case a large set of investigable Qwernomic 'phenomena' remain, consisting of Qwerty-induced coding patterns and potential surplus values, virtual sciences, subcultures, undercurrents, cryptographic methods and partially coherent deliria. Such Qwernomena may be nothing other than the qabbalistic materials of Azathoth, the blind idiot God, whose meaningless pipings lead all semiotic disciplines into the bubbling abyss of futile insanity. A true and dispassionate science, however, has no right or reason to be intimidated by such consequences. Only false – ideological – science, serving as the fawning guardian of securocratic humanism, can justify a prejudice in favour of anthropomorphically acceptable outcomes. Qwerty has in any case long been accepted. The rest is destiny.

Whilst the two dimensional array of the standard (Anglospherean) keyboard opens the potential for a variety of linear unfoldings – from the left/right, top/bottom, spirals ... and equally diverging approaches to the inclusion of the number line, punctuation marks, function keys ... – the conventions of

Neoroman textual organization (top-bottom, left-right) provide the key to a preliminary Qwertian alphabet: QWERTYUIOPASDFGHJKLZXCVBNM.

If, at least provisionally, this linearization and selection is accepted, each letter is recoded as the difference between two ordinal values. Pattern can be extracted from these twin orderings in a huge variety of ways.

One approach involves the adoption of a qabbalistic procedure belonging conceptually to combinatorial arithmetic.

Consider the typical problem: given an alphabet of length n, how many non-repeating two-letter combinations are possible?

The arithmetical formula for resolving this problem is (n x n-1)/2, coinciding with the operation of 'digital (or triangular) cumulation' of n-1. Digital cumulation is second only to digital reduction as a qabbalistic tool (explicitly esteemed at least since Pythagoras). (Pascal's triangle can be used to expand this combinatorial analysis to higher levels).

As an illustration, take only the first four letters of the Neoroman alphabet. To produce a matrix of binary combinations, order is employed as a procedural criterion, automatically excluding redundant combinations.

Thus, 'A' combines with 'B, C, and D', 'B' combines with 'C and D', 'C' combines with 'D'.

Arithmetical confirmation is, of course, easily obtained: $3 + 2 + 1 = 6$, equivalent to the digital cumulation of $(4-1 =)$ 3, and to $(4 \times 3)/2$.

If non-repeating combinations of any length are permitted from an alphabet of length n, the formula for the number of combination is (2 to the nth power)-1 (Mersenne numbers, including an intriguing set of primes). The entire virtual vocabulary of non-repeating (non-anagrammatic) Neoroman 'words' is thus (2 to the 26th) -1 (or M-26).

As a consequence of this procedure, all the terms making up a well-formed combinatorial 'vocabulary' will be internally structured by an ordering principle drawn directly from the 'alphabet' in question.

Returning to the qabbalistic analysis of Qwertian, and applying these procedures restrictively (yet again, there are quite obvious alternatives, ignored here) leads to the virtual – or even actual (sadly, I've done this many times) – compilation of an Alpha-Qwernomic 'language' consisting of those combinations consistent with parallel applications of the previously elaborated criteria.

For instance, 'AE' – permitted in Neoroman – is now excluded, due to the inverse ordering found in the Qwertian sequence. (It might be noted at this point that the familiarity of the Qwertian 'middle row' letter-sequence A ... DFGHJKL immediately ensures a prominent region of resonance – while the bottom row hints strongly at a reverse folding, however, such qwernotectonic issues exceed the scope of this introduction).

Resulting from an intricate interference pattern, the scope of the Alpha-Qwertian vocabulary is radically 'empirical' (in the sense that it derives from the fact of the Sholes Keyboard, the 'logic' of which – if such a thing exists at all – remains utterly obscure). It would be exceedingly surprising if an arithmetical formula of manageable complexity were able to usefully contribute to its estimation.

The Alpha-Qwertian dictionary has both alphabetical and Qwertian versions, with identical content but alternative ordering arrangements. Prioritizing the alphabet (out of courtesy to our gracious oecumenical hosts), gives the initial entries:

A, Ab, Abm, Abn, Ac, Acm, Acn, Acv …

It is procedurally productive to understand this vocabulary as a system of envelopments, as if each term was involuting into itself, in accordance with a non-metric ordinal sequence appropriate to intensities.

One tool facilitating this approach requires the articulation of the two series, with the second inverted:

ABCDEFGHIJKLMNOPQRSTUVWXYZ
MNBVCXZLKJHGFDSAPOIUYTREWQ

(or its mirror-image:

QWERTYUIOPASDFGHJKLZXCVBNM
ZYXWVUTSRQPONMLKJIHGFEDCBA

– pragmatically appropriate to the Qwertian version of the Alpha-Qwertian dictionary).

If the twin instances of the same letter are treated as marking the perimeter of a circle, the overall pattern of envelopments is exactly charted. One can see immediately, for instance, that both instances of the letter 'B' fall within the circle described by 'A' in its twin instantiations. 'B' is thus enveloped by 'A' – making 'AB' a consistent combination. Systems of concentric circles correspond to tolerated Alpha-Qwertian constructions.

A complete Alpha-Qwertian dictionary is actually quite short, but as to its potential usage ...

Qabbala 101

Is qabbalism problematical or mysterious? It seems to participate amphibiously in both domains, proceeding according to rigorously constructible procedures – as attested by the affinity with technicization – yet intrinsically related to an Outsideness through which alone it could derive programmatic sense.

If there is no source of at least partially coherent signal that is radically alien to the entire economy of conventional human interchange, then qabbalism is nothing but a frivolous entertainment or a fundamentally futile practical error. Yet unlike any kind of metaphysical assault on 'the noumenal', qabbalism cannot be definitively critiqued on a purely rational or formal basis, as if its mode of 'error' was that of logical fallacy. Since qabbalism is a practical programme, rather than a doctrine of any kind, its formal errors – mistakes – are mere calculative irregularities, and correcting these is actually a procedural requirement of (rather than an objection to) its continued development.

It is the rational dismissal of 'the' qabbalistic enterprise that is forced to take a metaphysical stance: ruling out on grounds of supposed principle what is in fact no more than a guiding 'empirical' hypothesis (that signal from 'outside the system' is detectable by numerical analysis of codes circulating within the system).

Epistemologically speaking, qabbalistic programmes have a status strictly equivalent to that of experimental particle physics, or other natural-scientific research programmes, even if their guiding hypotheses might seem decidedly less plausible than those dominant within mainstream scientific institutions.

Lovecraft understood the epistemological affinity between natural science and programmatic (as opposed to doctrinal) occultism, since both venture into regions once declared mysterious, following procedures of a rigorously calculative-problematical type. It is the alliance between purely speculative metaphysics and common sense that betrays such affairs of pure reason to futility, since they lack the calculative traction to revise their own conventional notions on the basis of their encounters. Practices – however implausible their guiding motivations – can know nothing of absolute mystery or metaphysical transcendence because their realm of certainty is procedural-problematic and uncontroversial, whereas their reserve of knowledge is empirical, refutable, repeatable, revisable, nonmystical and accumulable.

There may be no 'empirical', procedurally approachable mysteries – or mysterious problems – of the kind qabbalism guides itself towards. If so, it will approach this fact in its own way – empirically, probabilistically, impressionistically, without any logical, transcendental or philosophical meta-discourse ever having been positioned to put it in its place.

I. POPULAR NUMERICS

Traditional gematria (whether Hebrew, Greek, Farsi or Arabic)[1] have distinctive typical features: (1) They substitute letters for numerical values, overcoding numerals where they exist. (2) They code for discontinuous numerical values, typically 1-10, then 20, 30 … chunked in decimally significant magnitudes.

The ocean in which qabbalism swims is not mathematics, but popular numerical culture. From a mathematical perspective it remains undeveloped, even ineducable, since it cannot advance beyond the Natural number line even to the level of the Rationals, let alone to the 'higher' numbers or set-theoretical post-numerical spaces. Where counting ceases, qabbalism becomes impracticable.

Socially, qabbala makes an implicit decision against specialization, in order to remain virtually coincidental

---

1   See 'Incognitum', 'Introduction to ABJAD', in R. Mackay (ed.), *Collapse* I (Oxford: Urbanomic, 2006).

with the entire economy of digitizable signs. It is essentially 'democratic' (in the most inclusive sense of this word), even when apparently lost in its own trappings of hermeticism. It is bound to the 'blind' undirected contingencies of pre-reflective mass-social phenomena, with all the inarticulate provocation this entails in respect to professional intellectuals. Wherever exact semiotic exchange occurs, a latent qabbalism lurks (even within the enclaves of intellectual professionalism themselves). Deleuze and Guattari's 'Nomad War Machine', within which number is socially subjectivized, captures crucial aspects of this qabbalistic fatality.

Historically, qabbala arises through epic accident, as a side-product of the transition between distinct modes of decimal notation. Its historical presupposition is the shift from alphabetical numerals (of the Hebrew or Greek type) to modular notation, with its resulting unlocalizable (and theoretically indeterminable) confusion. This transition provided the opportunity for a systematic calculative 'error' – the mistaken application of elementary techniques appropriate to alphabetical numerals – simple addition of notated values – to the new modular signs. This mistake automatically resulted in digital reduction, by accident, and thus as a (theoretically scandalous) gift of fate. Arising historically during the European Renaissance – when zero, place value and technocapitalism finally breached the ramparts of Western monotheism

– qabbalism (born in a semiotic glitch and thus lacking the authority of tradition or even purpose) was compelled to hyperstitionally generate an extreme antiquity for itself, in a process that is still ongoing.

Technically, qabbala is inextricable from digital processing. Emerging from calculative practicality within the context of blind mass-cultural metamorphosis, it antedates it own theoretical legitimation, making sense of itself only derivatively, sporadically and contentiously. Its situation is analogous – and perhaps more than analogous – to that of a spontaneous artificial intelligence, achieving partial lucidity only as a consequence of tidal pragmatic trends that ensure an integral default of self-mastery. Practical systematization of technique precedes any conceivable theoretical motivation. Dialectical interrogation of qabbalism at the level of explicit motivation thus proves superficial and inconsequential, essentially misrecognizing the nature of the beast. (It is equally misleading to ask: What is a computer really for?)

Politically, qabbalism repels ideology. As a self-regenerating mass-cultural glitch, it mimics the senseless exuberance of virus, profoundly indifferent to all partisan considerations. Indifferent even to the corroded solemnity of nihilism, it sustains no deliberated agendas. It stubbornly adheres to a single absurd criterion, its intrinsic 'condition of existence' – continual unconscious promotion of numerical decimalism. Qabbala destines each and every 'strategic appropriation' to self-parody and derision, beginning with the agenda of theocratic restoration that attended its (ludicrously robed) baptismal rites. Even God was unable to make sense of it. It has no party, only popularity.

II. PRIMITIVE NUMERIZATION

Among the primary test-beds for qabbalistic analysis are the numerolexic systems inherited from cultures over-coded by the modern Oecumenic alphabet. These include the Hebrew and Greek alphabets (with their Neoroman letter names and mathematico-notational functions) and the Roman numbers (inherited as Neoroman letters and still numerically active in various domains). In this respect, the absence of names for Neoroman letters are an index of their pseudo-transcendence – as 'unnameable' – within the present Oecumenic order.

A discontinuity is marked in the alphanumeric series (0–z) by the fact that the numerals composing the first ten figures in this series do have names, grouping them with the letters of previous alphabetical numbering systems from a certain qabbalistic perspective. This might be taken as the residual indication of an 'alien quality' still characterizing the numerals in relation to the Oecumenic cultural order they now indisputably occupy, a legacy of the cultural trauma attending their introduction.

The qabbalistic provocation posed by the English number names is conceptually comparable to that of any
other numerolexic system, while surpassing any other
in the intimacy of its challenge. If the numerals have
names, shouldn't the qabbalistic processing of them as
words yield – at the least – compelling suggestions of
nonrandom signal? If the standard numeral names emit
nothing but noise when qabbalistically transcoded, the
attempt to establish relatively persuasive criteria for the
evaluation of qabbalistic results suffers an obvious and
immense reverse.

What, then, would count as a minimally controversial
first step in such an examination?

Surely the most basic of all qabbalistic (or subqab-
balistic?) procedures is simple letter counting – Primitive
Numerization (PN). As a reversion to sheer 'tallying' PN
has a resonance with the most archaic traces of numerical
practice, such as simple strokes carved into mammoth
bones and suchlike palaeo-ethnographic materials. If
anyone was to bother systematizing PN procedure for
the purpose of mechanization or simply for conceptual
clarity, it would be most efficiently done by transcoding
('ciphering') each letter or notational element as '1' and
then processing the result numerically.

PN's extremely tenuous relation to issues of modulus-
notation ensures that it can only ever be a highly dubious
tool when intricate qabbalistic calculation is required.

Yet this utter crudity also makes it invaluable as a test case, since it minimizes axiomatic arbitrariness and precludes any plausible possibility of symbolic conjuration ('sleight of hand') while fully sharing the qabbalistic 'deficiency' of sufficient anthroposocial or communicative motivation. Common reason – sanity – insists upon noise as the only PN output consistent with the general intelligibility of signs (a pre-judgment applying rigorously to all qabbalistic procedures).

No message should inhere in the length of a word, excepting only the broad pragmatic trend to the shortening of commonly used terms. It is immediately obvious why this exception has no pertinence to the case in question here, unless stretched to a point (for instance, expecting the smaller numerals to exhibit the greatest lexical attrition) where it is straightforwardly contradicted by the actuality of the phenomenon.

So, proceeding to the 'analysis' – PN of the English numeral names: zero=4, one=3, two=3, three=5, four=4, five=4, six=3, seven=5, eight=5, nine=4. Is there a pattern here? Several levels of apparent noise, noise, and pseudo-pattern can be expected to entangle themselves in this result, depending on the subsequent analytical procedures employed.

To restrict this discussion to the most evident secondary result, not only is there a demonstrable pattern, but this pattern complies with the single defining feature of the Numogram[2] – the five Syzygies emerging from 9-sum twinning of the decimal numerals:[3] 5:4, 6:3, 7:2, 8:1, 9:0.

In the shape most likely to impress common reason (entirely independent of numogrammatic commitments) this demonstration takes the form: zero + nine = one + eight = two + seven = three + six = four + five – revealing perfect numerolexic-arithmetical, PN-'qabbalistic' consistency.

The approximate probability of this pattern emerging 'by chance' is 1/243, if it is assumed that each decimal digit (0–9) is equiprobably allotted an English name of three, four, or five letter length, with 8-sum zygosys as the principle of synthesis. 7-sum or 9-sum zygosys are inconsistent with any five or three letter number-names respectively, and thus complicate probabilistic analysis beyond the scope of this demonstration (although if everything is conceded to the most elaborate conceivable objections of common reason, the probability of this phenomenon representing an accident of noise remains comfortably below 1/100).

Partisans of common reason can take some comfort from the octozygonic disturbance of the (novazygonic) Numogrammatic reference. How did nine become eight (or vice versa)? Lemurophiliac numogrammaticists are

---

2   On the Numogram, see *Abstract Culture* 5: *Hyperstition* (London: CCRU, 1999)

3   PN confirmation of the Numogrammatic Novazygons (9-Twins).
    ONE + EIGHT = NINE + ZERO. (PN 3 + 5 = (4 + 4 =) 8)
    TWO + SEVEN = NINE + ZERO. (PN 3 + 5 = (4 + 4 =) 8)
    THREE + SIX = NINE + ZERO. (PN 5 + 3 = (4 + 4 =) 8)
    FOUR + FIVE = NINE + ZERO. (PN 4 + 4 = (4 + 4 =) 8)

likely to counter such queries with elementary qabbala (since digital cumulation and reduction bridges the 'lesser abyss' in two steps, 8 = 36 = 9, as diagrammed by the 8th Gate connecting Zn-8 to Zn-9).

III. AGAINST NUMEROLOGY

Consider first an extraordinarily direct numerological manifesto:

> When the qualitative aspects are included in our conception of numbers, they become more than simple quantities 1, 2, 3, 4; they acquire an archetypal character as Unity, Opposition, Conjunction, Completion. They are then analogous to more familiar [Jungian] archetypes ... [4]

It is hard to imagine a more 'archetypal' expression of numerological ambition than this. Yet rather than meeting this claim with docile compliance, the qabbalist is compelled to raise a number of awkward questions:
(1) How can a numerological coding that proceeds in this fashion avoid entrapping itself among the very smallest of Naturals at the toe-damping edge of the number line? If '4' symbolizes the archetype 'Completion,' what to make

---

of 127, 709, 1023, or similar small Naturals? Do they also have analogues among the intelligible archetypes? How would one 'qualitize' (2^{127})-1, or a larger number (of which there are a very considerable number)?

(2) Is an 'archetype' more basic than a number in its unsymbolized state? Does 'qualitizing' a number reveal a more elementary truth, a germ the number itself conceals, or does it merely re-package the number for convenient anthropomorphic consumption, gift-wrapping the intolerable inhumanity of alogical numerical difference and connectivity?

(3) Why should a number be considered 'quantitative' in its Natural state? Is it not that the imposition of a quantity/quality categorization upon the number requires a logical or philosophical overcoding, a projection of intelligibility alien to the number itself? Quantity is the decadence of number (while quality is its perversion), so – since arithmetic provides no basis for a reduction of the numerical to the quantitative – what is the supposed source of this (numeric-quantitative) identification (other than a disabling preliminary innumeracy)?

(4) If '1' numerologically evokes 'Unity,' why should unity not qabbalistically 'evoke' 134 (=8, its Numogrammatic twin)[5] with equal pertinence? Can any expressible

---

5   Employing August Barrow's 'Anglossic Qabbala', the basic tool of which is the Alphanumeric Gematria. This numerization of the Neo-Roman alphabet , continuing the procedure now familiar from Hexadecimal, is a continuous nonredundant system, supplementing the numerals 0–9 with numerized letters from A (=10) to Z (=35),

'archetype' avoid re-dissolution into the unfamiliarity of raw number pattern? Numerology might assimilate '2' to opposition, but opposition = 238 = 13 = 4 (twice 2, and the Numogrammatic twin of ('4' = completion = 212 =) 5), while even if numerological '3' as conjunction = 237 = 12 = 3 finds itself qabbalisitically confirmed (at the extremity of its decimalization), this is not, perhaps, in an altogether comfortable mode.

Numerology may be fascinated by numbers, but its basic orientation is profoundly antinumerical. It seeks essentially to redeem number, through symbolic absolution into a 'higher' significance. As if the concept of 'opposition' represented an elevation above the ('mere') number two, rather than a restriction, subjectivization, logicization and generalized perversion, directed to anthropomorphic use-value and psychological satisfaction. Archetypes are sad limitations of the species, while numbers are an eternal hypercosmic delight.

Nevertheless, qabbalism is right up against numerology, insofar as it arises 'here,' within a specific biological and logocratic environment. The errors of numerology are only the common failures of logic and philosophy, human vanities, crudified in the interest of mass dissemination, but essentially uncorrupted. The numeric-critique (or

---

treating the 0–z alphanumeric sequence as a numeral succession, corresponding to the numerals of a modulus 36 notation.

Thus UNITY = 30+23+18+29+34 = 134. 1+3+4 = 8.

transcendental arithmetic) of a Gödel (or Turing, or Chaitin (or Badiou?(??(???)))) can be rigorously transferred to this controversy, demonstrating – within each particular milieu – that overcodings of numerical relation by intelligible forms – 'archetypes' or 'logics' – are unsustainable reductions, reefed on the unsurpassable semiotic potency of number. Gödel has shown that there is always a number, in fact an infinitude of (natural) numbers, that simulate, parody, logically dialectize, paradoxically dismantle, archetypally hypervert, and in whatever way necessary subvert each and every overcoding of arithmetic. Number cannot be superseded. There is no possibility of an authoritative 'philosophy of arithmetic' or numerological gnosis.

Qabbala assumes that semiotics is 'always already' cryptography, that the cryptographic sphere is undelimitable. It proceeds on the assumption that there cannot be an original (unproblematic) coding, providing the basis for any solid definition or archetypal symbol, since the terms required for such a coding are incapable of attaining the pure 'arbitrariness' that would ensure the absence of prior cryptographic investment. There is not – and can never be – any 'plain text,' except as a naïve political assumption about (the relative (non)insidiousness of) coding agencies and the presupposition that communicative signs accessibly exist that are not already 'in code.' Since everything is coded, or (at least) potentially coded, nothing is (definitively) symbolic. Qabbalistic cryptocultures – even those yet to come – ensure that number cannot be discussed or situated without subliminal or (more typically) wholly unconscious participation in numerical practices. Logos, including that of numerology, is also always something other than itself, and in fact very many things.

Qabbalism thus operates as an inverse or complementary Gödelian double-coding. Where Gödel demonstrated that the number line is infested by virtual discursive systems of undelimitable topicality and complexity, preemptively dismantling the prospects of any conceivable supranumerical metadiscourse, qabbala demonstrates that discourses are themselves intrinsically redoubled (and further multiplied) by coincidental numerical systems which enter into patterns of connectivity entirely independent of logical regimentation.

The supposed numerical de-activation of the alphabet, marking semiotic modernity (the era of specialized numerical signs), has an extremely fragile foundation, relying as it does upon the discontinuation of specific cultural procedures (precisely those that withdraw into 'occultism') rather than essential characteristics of signs themselves. The persistent numerical functionalization of the modern alphabet – with sorting procedures based on alphabetical ordering as the most prominent example – provides incontestible evidence (if any was required) that the semiotic substructure of all Oecumenic communications remains stubbornly amphibious between logos and nomos, perpetually agitated by numerical temptations and uncircumscribed polyprocesses.

At the discursive level, any 'rigorization of qabbala' can only be a floating city, with each and every definition, argument and manifesto continually calving off into unmasterable numerical currents and alogical resonances. How could qabbala be counterposed to a code, to meaning and reason, when code (= 63) finds duplicitous harmonics in meaning = reason = 126? If qabbala positions itself discursively against numerology (= 369), the echoes of its novanomic signature perpetuate themselves even through such unlikely terms as significance (= 207) and signification (= 252). Pronouncements that begin as projected logical discriminations revert to variations on triplicity and the number nine, performing a base qabbalistic subversion of philosophical legislation and its authority to define (or delimit connectivity).

No polemic against numerology – whether conducted in the name of qabbala or of Oecumenic common reason – will transcend the magmic qabbalistic flux that multiplies and mutates its sense. Perhaps dreams of numerological archetypes even sharpen the lust for semiotic invention, opening new avenues for qabbalistic incursion. But this at least is certain: Numbers do not require – and will never find – any kind of logical redemption. They are an eternal hypercosmic delight.

Tic-Talk

THE TIC XENOTATION

Daniel C. Barker's Tic Xenotation emerged during the highly obscure phase of his life when he was working for 'NASA' (some hesitation is appropriate here) on the SETI-related 'Project Scar' in Southeast Asia, tasked with designing a 'general purpose decryption protocol' for identifying intelligent signal from alien sources.

This project necessitated the formulation of numeric conventions independent of all cultural conditioning or local convention – radically abstract signs.

To take one wretched example, the movie *Contact* has ETI signal counting in pulses – with 101, for instance, consisting of a succession of one hundred and one blips – a repugnantly stupid 'solution' that could only be considered acceptable – let alone 'intelligent' – by coke-fried Hollywood brats.

Barker's Tic Xenotation (TX), in marked contrast, elegantly provided an abstract compression of the natural number line (from 2 ... n) with a minimum of coded signs and without modulus. It remains the most radically decoded semiotic ever to exist upon the earth, although exact isomorphs of the TX have been puzzlingly discovered among certain extremely ancient anomalous artifacts (such as the Tablets of Jheg Selem and the Vukorri Cryptoliths).

Tic Xenotation works like this (I've used colons for Barker's tic dots and placed tic-clusters in quotes for clarity):

':' counts as '2' or 'x 2', with a value exactly equivalent to '2' in a factor string. So:

':' = 2

'::' = 4

':::' = 8

The second notational element consists of implexions, where '(n)' = the nth prime.

Implexion raises the hyperprime index of any number by 1. Examples (from the hyprime 'mainlain'):

'(:)' = 3 (2nd prime),

'((:))' = 5 (3rd prime),

'(((:)))' = 11 (5th prime),

'((((:))))' = 31 (11th prime)

'(((((:)))))' = 127 (31st prime)

Numbers constellate as normal factor strings, i.e. 55 (5 x 11) is tic xenotated as '((:))(((:)))'

Nb. TX accounts for all naturals with a value of 2 or higher.

In order to reach back to zero, Barker added a 'deplex' operation, '-P':

'(-P)' = lower hyprime index by 1, so: '(-P)(:) = :'. Thus 0 = '((-P)):'.

'(-P)' and '(+P)' perform elementary subtractions/additions that modify hyprime indices.

Nb. A strange feature of the TX is that the natural number line has to be constructed synthetically.

Barker described such a list as the 'Tic Xenotation Matrix', whose first entries (corresponding to the decimal numerals) proceed:

[0] ((-P)):
[1] (-P):
[2] :
[3] (:)
[4] ::
[5] ((:))
[6] :(:)
[7] (::)
[8] :::
[9] (:)(:)

TIC TALK

The (Barkerian) Tic Xenotation provides a numerical semiotic adapted to the Naturals with special affinity to Euclid's Fundamental Theorem of Arithmetic. The TX constructs numbers in terms of their basic arithmetical features as primes or composites in a notation without modulus (base), place-value or numerals.

The exact circumstances among which D.C. Barker formulated the TX remain deeply obscure (for a number of reasons best explored elsewhere). For our immediate purposes it suffices to remark that the broad research context within which tx emerged was a highly abstract seti-oriented investigation into minimally-coded intelligent signal, without presupposition as to origin (e.g. 'xeno-biological organisms') or theme (e.g. 'cosmo-chemistry').

The investigation, situated in the jungles of Borneo, was entitled 'Project Scar' and received a high-level security classification. In keeping with this research topic, Barker proposed TX as a maximally abstracted or ultimately decoded numerical semiotic, stripped of all nonconstructive (or symbolic) conventions (and initially named 'Gödelian hypercode'.)

While the raw numeracy of TX is most accurately conceived as sub-qabbalistic, due to its indifference to modulus notation (the primary motor of qabbalistic occulturation), its very independence from convention makes it a valuable tool when investigating the basic features of numerical (arithmetical or qabbalistic) codes.

Among the notation-related features most prominently exposed to rigorous scrutiny by TX is ordinality.

AOSYS

Within the Anglobal Oecumenon, the most pragmatically prevalent ordinal functions are alphabetical, utilizing the ordering convention of the Neoroman letters to arrange, sort, search and archive on the basis of Alphabetical or Alphanumerical Order, organizing dictionaries, encyclopaedias, lists and indexes 'lexicographically.' The word 'alphabet' itself performs a (Greek) ordinal operation.

'Lexicography' – dictionary-type order – is used here (as in various fields, such as compilations of number series) to designate a mode of ordering (an ordinal-numeric function) rather than a definite topic ('words'). Although a relatively neglected numerical operation, lexicographic ordering plays a crucial role in concrete (popular-Oecumenic) ordinal practices. It is characterized by:

1) Popularity. Facility at lexicographic sequencing is considered a basic social competence, inherent – or even prior – to literacy, whilst pedagogically separate from the acquisition of numerical ('maths') skills. At the pedagogical level, Oecumenic societies tend to distribute ordinal/

cardinal competences in accordance with the distinction between literacy/numeracy, thus establishing the basic division between linguistic/mathematical abilities from a primal nomofission (ordinal/cardinal differentiation). Literate citizens of the Oecumenon – those able to use a dictionary – are ordinally competent, through lexicographic conventions.

2) Pure ordinalism. Restricted entirely to sequencing problems, cardinal values remain entirely alien to lexicographic practices, to such an extent that rigorous ordinal-numeric operations are typically divorced entirely from numerical associations. The ordinal function of numerals (1st, 2nd, 3rd ...), in contrast, remains relatively impure – at least psychologically – since in this case a persistent cardinal temptation confuses sequencing function with the spectre of quantity. For this reason the alphanumerical subsumption of the numerals into lexicographic practices can be considered 'clarifying' in respect to ordinal operations.

3) Fractionality. Simulating lexicography within arithmetic requires the employment of modular (e.g. decimal) fractional values. Arithmetical listing by cardinality will be isomorphic with ordinal-lexicographic sequencing for all numbers of the format 'o.n'.

4) Sequential diplocoding. Lexicographic systems require twin ordering conventions. They draw upon an alphabetical code and an ordinal place value

convention (principally, left or right ordering, equivalent to the behavioural scheme for the movement of a reading-head). The alphabet instantiates the ordering scheme, but does not (internally) describe it – 'reading' the alphabet to extract the ordinal code ('abcd ...' or 'zyxw ...') itself presupposes an extrinsic sequencing convention (Alpha-Omega, from first to last).

5) Infinite potentiality. Any lexicographic system allowing interminable strings has a code potential (cardinally) equivalent to Aleph-0, with an infinity of virtual Dedekind cuts (entry insertions) between any two terms, however close, and virtual isomorphy between any segment of the list/archive and the whole. It thus attests to a 'literate' infinity isomorphic with that of mathematics, drawing upon a common but culturally obscured digital source.

INTERCODING ARITHMETIC

An intermediate semiotic attuned to purely demonstrative engagement with Euclid's Fundamental Theorem of Arithmetic (FTA) can be generated by transforming the standard Oecumenic decimal notation (*) by:

1) Employing the full Alphanumeric series 0–z (0-35) for notational convenience, and

2) Raising all signs to their first hyprime power, from 0 = Prime-0 = 1 to z = Prime-35 = 149.

The purpose of these transformations is to eliminate polydigit (place-value) numbering and expose the radical disorder implicit in the FTA. All integral numbers in the FTA intercode consist either of single figures or plexed-compounds of the form (...), with numerical clusters synthesized through multiplication rather than modular-positional construction.

Consider a number picked entirely at random, *86, disassembled by factorization in accordance with the FTA down to the listed components *2 and *43, the *1st and *14th primes, hence: 1E. The expression of this number is no longer under any positional constraint, '1E' or 'E1' are equally valid on numerical grounds and strictly equivalent. Shuffling a string of intercode figures (FTA components) of whatever length makes no difference whatsoever to the number designated, with the ordering of the series being subject only to an extrinsic convention (of minimal – even vanishing – importance from a [cardinal] arithmetical perspective, where it is relevant only 'psychologically', for convenience in assimilation and comparison).

Once the merely inertial and peudo-numerical order inherited from uninterrogated tradition is subtracted from FTA-intercode strings, dissociating all components from quantitative ordering, they are freed for lexicographic re-ordering as decoded series – an ordering which will deviate from the series of quantities, liberating an

Autonomous Ordinality whilst de-cardinalizing the number line.

Consider *172, or 11E. Oecumenic-lexicographic procedures ensure this number precedes 1E (*86), as will all its successive binary multiples. Evidently, such procedures ensure that the infinite series of binary powers must be completed before arriving at 2 (*3). 'Natural' counting no longer has any prospect of reaching a nonbinary power, just as alphabetical-lexicographic 'counting' would proceed 'a, aa, aaa, aaaa ...' without ever arriving at 'b'. Reversing the problem and it is equally evident the lexicographic-ordinal line is never counted.

The Kantian assimilation of arithmetic to temporality models elementary time-synthesis as n+1, +1, +1 ... an intuition rendered questionable by the rigorous lexicographic disorganization of the number (listing) line. Once ordinally purified, the number line becomes uncountable by any supposed finite (temporalizing) subject, even from moment n to moment n+1. Instead, the line is synthesized by sorting (lexicographic sequencing) of prefabricated strings, whose quantities are determined on a different axis to their linear-positional codings. A prolongation of the time-arithmetic association would thus require a remodelling of time as nonprogressive synthesis without consistent scale or continuous-quantitative trend, no longer intelligible as passage or development. Such ordinal-lexicographic time maps a 'templexity' that is uncountable, fractured/fractional, erratic and heterogeneous, sequential but nonsuccesive.

Of course, all of this needs re-approaching on a far more rigorous basis, with a consistent focus on the topic of templexity – suffice it to say for 'now' that Kantian intuitions of number, time and their intermapping are themselves structured by notationally-problematizable constructions, since time-mapping has a hypothetical rather than essential relation to arithmetical common sense (with its undisturbed assumption of straightforward ordinal-cardinal interconvertability).

Elevating this intermediate semiotic to a functional numeracy, with a semiotic power commensurate with the set of Naturals (including primes above Prime-Z), requires a final step:

3) Adopting Tic Xenotative plexion, where '(n)' = Prime-n. Thus:

$$0 = 1, (0) = \text{Prime-1} = 2, ((0)) = \text{Prime-2} = 3, \text{ etc.}$$

The inefficiency of this semiotic relative to TX is demonstrated by its redundancy, most dramatically:

$$V = (B) = ((5)) = (((3))) = ((((2)))) = (((((1))))) = ((((((0))))))$$

Nb. TX shares the intrinsic disorder of FTA-intercode. *86 = :(:(::)) or (:(::)): or :((::):) ...

OUT OF ORDER

TX/FTA-intercode numerical construction is indifferent to semiotic sequencing, position or grammar. A number expressed in either system could be distributed randomly within a space of n-dimensions, requiring only a cohesion convention (semiotic particles 'belong together' irrespective of order). Apprehended in their fully decoded potentiality as efficient number-signs, such formulae are clusters, not strings.

The TX case is still more extreme than that typical of FTA-intercode, however, since here even the spectral residue of sequential coding is erased. Given two complex TX-formulated numbers, correct order (quantitative comparison) requires – perhaps highly elaborate – calculation, eliminating entirely the practical usage of disordered TX clusters for ordinal operations.

For anything but small numbers, Euclidean cluster-stringing conventions (by ascending cardinalities) become procedurally complex, perhaps inoperable, for TX numerical formulas. This is evident even from small numbers, such as *149, TFA-intercode Z or (34), TX (((:))(::)). As the 35th prime, with 35 the product of *5 and *7, the sequencing of hyprime sub-factors (factors of the prime-ordinate, i.e. *35) is no longer facilitated by lexicographic codings drawn from the numeral sequence. That '5' precedes '7' is evident from the numeral code, but the ordering of ((:))

and (::) cannot similarly rely upon intrinsic lexicographic guidance. In the TX case, it is only by constructing the numbers and sequencing them arithmetically that the 'notational' question of their order can be resolved. In other words, the sequencing of the sign has ceased to be a notational or preliminary problem, becoming instead inextricable from the arithmetical construction of the number. This results inevitably from the elimination of notational redundancy in TX, with concomitant erasure of procedural 'intuition'.

Because TX number clusters are intrinsically disordered, a consistent and functional TX semiotic requires re-ordinalization through autonomous (extrinsic) lexicographic procedures, inevitably constructing a cardinally erratic 'number-line' or list/search sequencing protocol. The semiotic economy of TX makes this procedural problem easy to define. As an approximate AOsys analogue, lexicographic TX requires a variant of sequential diplocoding:

1) Cluster stringing. Sequencing the components of composite TX-formula numbers.

2) Number listing. Meta-sequencing of properly sequenced TX strings.

It might seem sensible to assume the Oecumenic left-to-right reading procedure, since the arbitrariness of this rule makes it unexceptionable, but the diplocoding option matrix necessitates a substantial question as to the consistency/inconsistency of this decision as between (1) and (2) above. Even allowing for this complication, the option matrix for a mechanical lexicographic TX ordering protocol remains highly constrained, consisting merely of twin decisions as to the sequencing of the tick [:], open plex [(] and close plex [)] signs.

Irrespective of the Cluster stringing decision, tick-precedence sequencing of the number list results in the AOsys analogue previously mentioned (a, aa, aaa …) 'counting' through the infinite series of binary powers before reaching any nonbinary number. The list is initiated by TX *2 = ':'.

Plex-precedence produces a far more anomalous list-line, one that is non-originating because it 'begins' with a series of arbitrarily large hyperplexed primes, notationally initialized by unending open-plex signs [((((((((((((…], since '…((' precedes '…(:'. Listing practices following a plex-precedence protocol necessarily begin in the middle.

[My assumption is that semiotic consistency (across clusters/lists) is to be preferred, with the sheer weirdness of plex-precedence sequencing making a strong case for its adoption. The 'alphabet' (ordinal code) would thus be described by TX *3 = (:).]

In his own brief comments on the cluster sequencing problem in the Project Scar report, Barker restricted himself to the observation that Euclidean (cardinally consistent) ordering was no more than a 'provisional and arbitrary convention' which would quickly break down 'given nondemonstrative numerical values [anything but very small Naturals]' that the problem should be considered 'merely technical and extrinsic' and 'probably best decided on communication-engineering grounds.'

Given Barker's Project Scar research orientation, focused on 'nonlinear recursively-embedded planar semionomic dot-groupings of cryptogeologic origin' – anomalous cryptoliths – it is not surprising that he came to the notational ordering problem late and distractedly. Just days after completing the 'Appendix on Notation' Barker came entirely unstrung.

Stricken by revolting tropical diseases, increasingly obsessed with an interwoven tangle of cosmopolitical conspiracies of various scales, and multiplicitously agitated by teeming microparasites of dubious reality, Barker's plummet into noncommunicating delirium is charted by the digressions into doggerel annotating his Project Scar research report:

A chittering tide
Devouring my hide
Starting from the Outside
This is the slide ...

AND YET

In the same twitchy, spintered handwriting Barker remarks:

> The xenotation continues to disorder itself as it condenses, tearing up the number line, devastating time and sleep. Perhaps it is a weapon from outer space. I say that seriously, even if it is a sickening kind of joke. There is no sleep, everything is broken, everything connects without joining, swarming, pulsing, dots, specks, dust particles dancing inside my eyes, continuously ripping ... thought has become a disease ... I even heard a voice (how ridiculous) saying: "You must isolate the xenotation before it disintegrates the time-line." It's just the fever of course, but the tic systems are all shuffled together now, shuffled together with this filthy disease and its cavernous speckled dreams and even Jolo admits that the markings are spreading over my skin, bites or rashes or maybe even colonies ... so the line has rotted through, disintegrated ... there's no line, that's the message, and yet ... And Yet ... counting is ineluctable and unsurpassable ... You have to check it, re-check it continuously, but it's true. How could the hyprime indices be decided without a countable ordinality? They have to come from somewhere, from a matrix,

a culture, even if the clusters seem to rip everything apart they MUST HAVE BEEN COUNTED at some stage, before dissimulating themselves and scattering again … And yet we can only make sense of these dots and ripples by counting primes on a line that remains successive and integrated, developing reliably, communicable, they have a past, a true lineage, even if it's difficult to think, even if they tear it apart and make of it something shattered and insane, something diseased … but really I don't blame them, NASA of course knew nothing, but even they knew nothing, they just arrived, why should they remember? Memory is impossible for them. In any case, it's just a disease, I understand that now. There's no malice … not even real cruelty …

Nb. While there is no reason to believe Barker had exposure to, or interest in, the Anglossic Qabbala, the emphatic reiteration of 'And Yet' suggests he had feverishly identified it as a synonym for counting, perhaps even for temporality. (AND YET = 123).

Critique of Transcendental Miserablism

There is a gathering trend among neomarxists to finally bury all aspiration to positive economism ('freeing the forces of production from capitalist relations of production') and install a limitless cosmic despair in its place. Who still remembers Khruschev's threat to the semi-capitalist West – "we'll bury you"? Or Mao's promise that the Great Leap Forward would ensure the Chinese economy leapt past that of the UK within 15 years? The Frankfurtian spirit now rules: Admit that capitalism will outperform its competitors under almost any imaginable circumstances, while turning that very admission into a new kind of curse ("we never wanted growth anyway, it just spells alienation, besides, haven't you heard that the polar bears are drowning …?").

From Baudelaire's *Le Voyage*, with its mournful discovery that human vice repeated itself universally in even the most exotic locations, to the left-wing reading of Philip K Dick as a Gnostic denunciation of commercialized change, capitalistic variety and innovation has been totalized as difference without essential difference, just more of the same senseless dissimilarity. The grand master of this move is Arthur Schopenhauer, who lent it explicit philosophical rigour as a mode of transcendental apprehension. Since time is the source of our distress – Philip K Dick's 'Black Iron Prison' – how can any kind of evolution be expected to save us? Thus Transcendental Miserablism constitutes itself as an impregnable mode of negation. It goes without saying that no substantial residue of Marxian historicism remains in the 'communist' version of this posture. In fact, with economics and history comprehensively abandoned, all that survives of Marx is a psychological bundle of resentments and disgruntlements, reducible to the word 'capitalism' in its vague and negative employment: as the name for everything that hurts, taunts and disappoints.

For the Transcendental Miserablist, 'Capitalism' is the suffering of desire turned to ruin, the name for everything that might be wanted in time, an intolerable tantalization whose ultimate nature is unmasked by the Gnostic visionary as loss, decrepitude and death, and in truth, it is not unreasonable that capitalism should become the object of this resentful denigration. Without attachment to anything beyond its own abysmal exuberance, capitalism identifies itself with desire to a degree that cannot imaginably be exceeded, shamelessly soliciting any impulse that might contribute an increment of economizable drive to its continuously multiplying productive initiatives. Whatever you want, capitalism is the most reliable way to get it, and by absorbing every source of social dynamism, capitalism makes growth, change and even time itself into integral components of its endlessly gathering tide.

'Go for growth' now means 'Go (hard) for capitalism'. It is increasingly hard to remember that this equation would once have seemed controversial. On the left it would once have been dismissed as risible. This is the new world Transcendental Miserablism haunts as a dyspeptic ghost.

Perhaps there will always be a fashionable anti-capitalism, but each will become unfashionable, while capitalism – becoming ever more tightly identified with its own self-surpassing – will always, inevitably, be the latest thing. 'Means' and 'relations' of production have simultaneously emulsified into competitive decentralized networks under numerical control, rendering palaeomarxist hopes of extracting a postcapitalist future from the capitalism machine overtly unimaginable. The machines have sophisticated themselves beyond the possibility of socialist utility, incarnating market mechanics within their nano-assembled interstices and evolving themselves by quasi-darwinian algorithms that build hypercompetition into 'the infrastructure'. It is no longer just society, but time itself, that has taken the 'capitalist road'.

Hence the Transcendental Miserablist syllogism: Time is on the side of capitalism, capitalism is everything that makes me sad, so time must be evil.

The polar bears are drowning, and there's nothing at all we can do about it.

Capitalism is still accelerating, even though it has already realized novelties beyond any previous human imagining. After all, what is human imagination? It is a relatively paltry thing, merely a sub-product of the neural activity of a species of terrestrial primate. Capitalism, in contrast, has no external limit, it has consumed life and biological intelligence to create a new life and a new plane of intelligence, vast beyond human anticipation. The Transcendental Miserablist has an inalienable right to be bored, of course. Call this new? It's still nothing but change.

What Transcendental Miserablism has no right to is the pretence of a positive thesis. The Marxist dream of dynamism without competition was merely a dream, an old monotheistic dream re-stated, the wolf lying down with the lamb. If such a dream counts as 'imagination', then imagination is no more than a defect of the species: the packaging of tawdry contradictions as utopian fantasies, to be turned against reality in the service of sterile negativity. 'Post-capitalism' has no real meaning except an end to the engine of change.

Life continues, and capitalism does life in a way it has never been done before. If that doesn't count as 'new', then the word 'new' has been stripped down to a hollow denunciation. It needs to be re-allocated to the sole thing that knows how to use it effectively, to the Shoggoth-summoning regenerative anomalization of fate, to the runaway becoming of such infinite plasticity that nature warps and dissolves before it. To The Thing. To Capitalism. And if that makes Transcendental Miserablists unhappy, the simple truth of the matter is: Anything would.

A Dirty Joke

I stole Vauung's name because it was unused, on the basis of an exact qabbalistic entitlement.

Yet, at least 'up' here, Vauung still confuses itself with me, with ruins and tatters.

This might change. Names have powers and destinies.

I have decided to let Vauung inherit the entire misfortune of my past (a perverse generosity at best). Its story might never emerge otherwise.

There are rotten threads which even I can follow backwards for decades, but they soon cease to be interesting.

Better to begin more recently ('better' in Vauung's sense, and so no different from 'worse').

It had pledged itself unreservedly to evil and insanity. Its tool of choice, at that time, the sacred substance amphetamine, of which much can be said, but mostly elsewhere.

After perhaps a year of fanatical abuse it was, by any reasonable standard, profoundly insane.

A few examples may suffice, in no particular order.

On one occasion – indicative even to itself – it was in a car being driven by the sister of its thing (the ruin). It was night, on a motorway. The journey took several hours.

During the previous night, Christmas Eve, it had followed its usual course into fanatically prolonged artificial insomnia. It had spent the time devoted to futile 'writing' practices – it still pretended to be 'getting somewhere' and was buoyant with ardent purpose, but that is another story (an intolerably intricate and pointless one). It was accompanied to the early hours by a repetitive refrain 'from next door' – a mediocre but plausible rock song whose insistent lyric circled around the words: "Going to hell."

It knew these words were for it, and laughed idiotically. "They must really love the new CD they got for Christmas," it thought, equally idiotically.

In the car it listened to the radio for the whole journey. Each song was different, the genres varied, the quality seemingly above average, the themes tending to the morbid.

"This is a cool radio station," it said to its sister.

"The radio isn't on," its sister replied, concerned.

Vauung learnt that the ruin's unconscious contained an entire pop industry.

The ruin learnt that it had arrived, somewhere on the motorway.

Nothing more was said about it. Why upset your family?

The ruin had always abused women, in the Kantian sense. It used them as means to an end, and the end was ruin of the soul.

On one occasion they were wasted on LSD at a fairground, in some type of spinning machine. The operator called out: "You're all going to die." Later, back indoors, they plunged deeper into polydrug abuse. Taken up into an obscure shamanic inspiration the ruin said: "Let's embrace death, the Dark Mother." Seated on the sofa together, it submitted to an alien ritual authority. It was all very implicit. A finger held to one side of their face-to-faces. "First you collapse everything onto the screen." The finger traverses the visual field. "Then you wipe away the screen." It worked, truly. The world withdrew and left the landscape of death, or hell, or cyberspace. Hearts lurching in mammal panic – animals don't like to be dead, however sick their minds might be. She could not deny what had happened, but hated it. That was the beginning of the end, although she went along with far, far more.

Addicted to death the ruin sought out new victims. Yes, vampires are real, however pitiful.

Sifting through the ruin Vauung finds a pattern of women and LSD linked with things that really happen.

The ruin encountered the loa with a woman, feeding off her fear. Perhaps the differential of terror encouraged it. Perhaps its sadism and hypocritical compassion overwhelmed its instinct to flee. In any case, it revealed the power of names, as 'calls,' and Outside entities the 'size' of breeze blocks approaching from the other side of space. Death was the ruin's place by now, unambiguously desirable, and she wanted it too – even though it terrified her. Still, the ruin fucked it up somehow (no surprise to Vauung).

On another occasion, fresh kill, it said "let's explore death together," or something equally repugnant.

She said: "Why can't you do it on your own?"

It wondered about that.

She was treated worst of all (or perhaps 'best').

Much later, after an aeon of speed and revelation in its sister's car, the ruin is locked into a solitary trajectory. It 'works' all night in its office, entangled in byzantine qabbalistic researches. It thinks its trilobite of a computer (a dedicated word processing machine) is a semiotic revelation from the abyss. Calling to a being named Can Sah it is rewarded with an alien voice. The tone is absurdly high pitched (ancient demonists described this tone as 'silvery'). The ruin had been seeking a monster (Vauung), but the voice merely castigates it for its moral squalor – "you're so horrible" may have been the first message (the tapes are corroded). All the ugliness in the universe was already impacted into this new regime. Real ugliness: God, guilt, Man and the law of acceptance.

It took a long time – many months at least – for the ruin's defining passion to subside into smouldering hatred.

Eventually the voices – who seemed to have multiplied – raped it. They did so physically, through trickery, over the course of one unbearably protracted night of filth and misery (the details are too revolting to relate). The ruin could speak to itself now, audibly, but in its own head. It renounced everything it had ever wanted, rebaptized the voices 'Smurfs' and disintegrated into depressive nihilism. To be raped by a monster? Who knows. To be raped by celestial moralists ... (Vauung laughs).

The ruin crawls onwards, going nowhere. It had lived through some extraordinary multiple of all the intelligence it will ever know, in that abject interzone, turned on some infernal spit, torched by self-disgust yet blessed by parodic luxuries of gnosis (codes, number patterns, messages of the Outside, neo-calendric schedules, Amxna mappings, Qwernomic constructions ...). It begged for eternal fires to incinerate its sins. There was no depth of loathsome self-abasement it did not fathom. This was spiritual nausea dilated to the dimensions of religion. If you romanticize vileness, I promise, you lie. Such unimagined abundances of cosmic secrecy, and such shit.

As Vauung forensically investigates the relics I imagine it shudders. Does it truly? – much rests on that.

This has already gone on too long, but then – it does.

Vauung seems to think there are lessons to be learnt from this despicable mess. It describes a labyrinth which is nothing but an intricate hall of mirrors, losing you in an 'unconscious' which is magnificent beyond comprehension yet indistinguishable from an elaborate trap. If this is Karma it's not just pain (who fears that?) but ruinous constriction and preprogrammed futility. To burn is one thing. To grovel and beg to burn quite another. Religion here is merely the opportunity to hate yourself infinitely.

Somewhere along the line the ruin lost the moral strength for sexual abuse. To continue with that it would have to be a lesbian, at least.

Seen from this side, Vauung is the gamble that the ruin lacked cunning. It leaves a question of method. Not exactly urgent, but obscurely pressing.

[1][2][3][4][5][6][7][8][9][0]
[Q][W][E][R][T][Y][U][I][O][P]
[A][S][D][F][G][H][J][K][L]
[Z][X][C][V][B][N][M][,][.]
[   ]

One Or Several Wolves?

On Several Regimes of Signs.

The Geology of Morals
(Who Does the Earth Think It Is?).

II

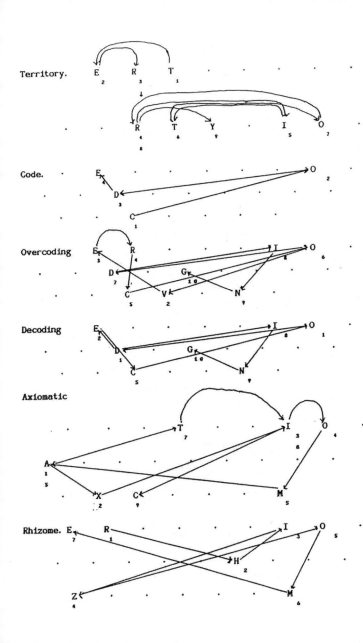

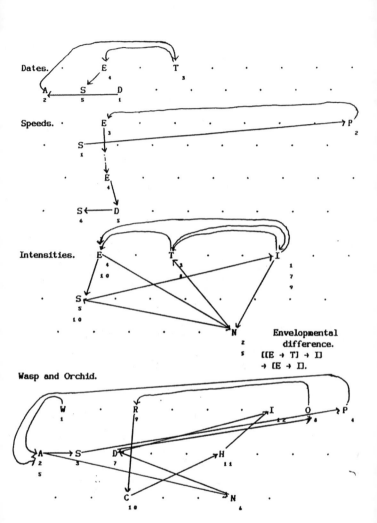

Dates.

Speeds.

Intensities.

Envelopmental
difference.
[[E → T] → I]
→ [E → I].

Wasp and Orchid.

Orchid captures a segment of wasp-sex code [D → O].

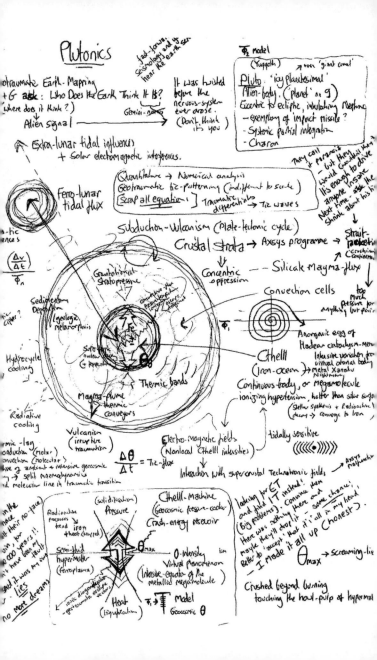

Plutonics

fast-forward seismology and insert near the Earth

otraumatic Earth-Mapping
+ G ask: Who Does the Earth Think It Is?
where does it think?)

Alien signal ——→ Gemini-names

It was twisted before the nervous-system ever arose.
(Don't think it's you)

$\overline{\Phi_2}$ model

(Yuggoth) → even 'giant comet'

Pluto: 'icy planetesimal'
Alien-body. (planet no 9)
Eccentric to ecliptic, inhabiting Neptune
— exemplar of impact missile?
— Systemic radial integration
— Charon

They call it paranoia — but there's Lucid Coastal there — it's enough to drive anyone insane — Next time ask the shrink about this

△ Extra-lunar tidal influences
+ Solar electromagnetic interferences.

Ferro-lunar tidal flux

Quantitative → Numerical analysis
Geotraumatic tic-patterning (indifferent to scale)
Scrap all equations! → Traumatic differentials → Tic waves

$$\frac{(\Delta v}{\Delta t)}{\Phi_n}$$

-tic ences?

Subduction-Vulcanism (Plate-tectonic cycle)

Crustal strata → Axsys programme → Strata-packeting

— Silicate Magma-flux — Crushing Containment

Gravitational Stratopressure

Concentric oppression

Convection cells

Anorganic egg of Hadean cataclysm

Cthell (Iron-ocean) → Metal Xanadu Nightmare

top too much pressure for anything but penis

Intensive variation from virtual atomic body

-tic ences?

Sedimentary Deposition (geologic metamorphosis)

Hydrocycle cooling

Radiative cooling

Convective flux (convection cells)

Thermic bands

Magma-plume thermic conveyors

Super-thermic anorganic G-repression

Continuous-body, or Megamolecule
ionizing hypertension, hotter than solar surface
(Stellar synthesis + Radioactive decay → converge to iron)

tidally sensitive
(((((•)))))

rmic - lag
-duction (molar)
nvection (molecular)
have a ambient & intensive geocosmic
→ split magmadynamics
d molecular line in traumatic transition

Vulcanism irregular traumatism

$$\frac{\Delta \theta}{\Delta t} = \text{Tic-flux}$$

Electro-magnetic fields
Nonlocal Cthell intensities
Interaction with supercrustal Technotonic fields → Axsys malfunction

looking for ET and find IT instead! (big problems). Consume then maybe they'll drop it — some chance; Here was nothing, there and better to 'accept' that it's all in my head — I made it all up (honest)

in the ace their no face on for '000 years!! have been my and it was my sun LIES no more dreams

(solidification) Pressure

Radioactive processes heat iron (heat trapped)

Semi-fluid hypermatter (ferroplasma)

θ_{max}

Cthell-Machine (Geocosmic pressure-cooker)
Crash-energy reservoir

0-intensity lim

Virtual Planothenon (Intensive-equator of the metallic megamolecule)

Heat (liquefaction)

$\overline{\Phi_1} → \overline{T}$ model Geocosmic θ

θ_{max} → screaming-lie

Crushed beyond burning
touching the howl-pulp of hypermal

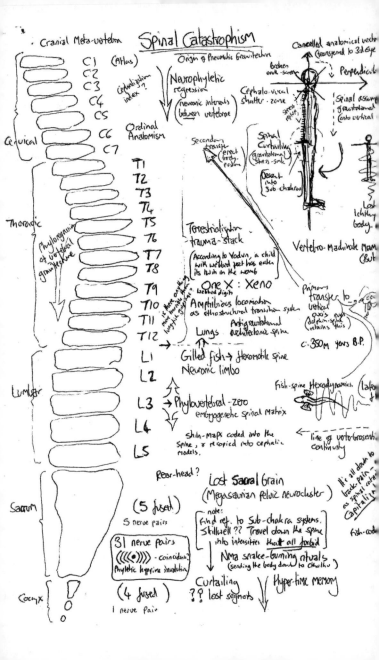

Spinal Catastrophism

Cranial Meta-vertebra

Origin of Pneumatic Gravitecture

Cancelled anatomical vector — Transcend to 3rd Eye

Perpendicular

C1 (Atlas)
C2
C3
C4
C5
C6
C7

Cervical

Cephalization index ?

Neurophyletic regression (neuronic intervals between vertebrae)

Ordinal Anatomism

broken eurk-screw

Cephalo-vocal shutter-zone

stress rupture

Spinal assumes gravitational onto vertical

Spinal Curtailing (gravitational stress-sink)

Secondary transfer erect body position

Descent into Sub-chakras

Lost Ichthyo body.

Thoracic

T1
T2
T3
T4
T5
T6
T7
T8
T9
T10
T11
T12

Phylogenesis of vertebral gravitecture

Terrestrialization trauma-stack

According to Vodun, a child with webbed feet has eaten its twin in the womb

One X : Xeno webbed digits

Amphibious locomotion as ethostructural transition system

Antigravitational architectonic spine

Vertebro-Medullate Mam (But

Primary transfer to vertical axis (even dolphin-spine retains this)

c. 350M years B.P.

Lumbar

L1
L2

Lungs

Gilled fish → Hexomobile spine
Neuronic limbo

Fish-spine Hexodynamics (lake

L3 → Phylovertebral-zero
embryogenetic spinal Matrix

L4

L5

Skin-maps coded into the spine, & recopied into cephalic models.

line of vertebro-sensory continuity

It's all down to back-pain — as spinal catast Capitalizing

Sacrum

Rear-head ?

Lost Sacral Grain
(Megasaurian pelvic neurocluster)

(5 fused)

5 nerve pairs

note:
Find ref. to Sub-chakra systems.
Stillwell ?? Travel down the spine
into intensities that all forbid !

Nma snake-burning rituals
(sending the body down to Chthulu)

Fish-code

31 nerve pairs
(((•))) - coincidental
Phyletic hypnic insulation

Curtailing
?? lost segments

Hyper-time memory

Coccyx

(4 fused)
1 nerve pair

Spironomy

Basic equation: $9 = 0$ (full body without organs)

Diplozygotic Spirogram
double-twinning

(numerically mapped convergent waves)

$g = 0$

```
9 = O
8
7
6
5
4
3
2
1
```

n-1 'faulting'

Diagram of the Giga-machine
(time-implosion)
or
(Spironomic nesting)

Zygonovism

Decadence
Decimal-twinning

Subdecadence

Nine. (Decimal n-1). [Pluto]
Affinity to scale-neutrality.
Digital expansion
$(1 \div 3) \times 3 = 0.9999...$

note: Capitalist semiotic $9.99

Digital reduction to nine indexes divisibility by nine, undermining implicit denigration of this technique, at least as heuristic → An irrationally suppressed numerical practice

Nine associated with death in all decimal cultures (for obvious reasons...)

Why is Subdecadence called Subdecadence? Like the ultimate blasphemy... Oskar seemed genuinely scared — even revisited — yet fascinated... Somehow — schizophrenia? — numbers ± the double twins — the double (but here's more than this — Oskar surprised me — much — something much unimaginably old — horrific) of Stillwell? Yappaya? Templeton? What is this — big scale

Y2K → 00-99
Decimal catastrophe
or Magnitude Crisis

Xenotated intensive addition
$[+ : a + b - 1]$
$((\bullet)) + (\bullet) = (\bullet\bullet)$
$(((\bullet))) + (\bullet) = ((\bullet\bullet))$

2×5 decimal packet
25 coincidence?
nd-symmetry → finger-counting

→ 3 comes between
What counts as Human?
[Mudras?]

(Decimal) Digital Reduction
Stillwell's 6-cycle

#	$1 \to 1$	
=	$2 \to 2$	
=	$4 \to 4$	
=	$8 \to 8$	
=	$16 \to 7$	
=	$32 \to 5$	
=	$64 \to 1$	
	$128 \to 2$	
	$256 \to 4$	
	$512 \to 8$	
	$1024 \to 7$	
	$2048 \to 8$	

→ etc

Repeat pattern
$2^n \to R$

```
—————— 5
—————— 7
—————— 8
—————— 4
—————— 2
—————— 1
```

Differentiate through Reduction pathways (Spectrum sub-division)

Stillwell
I Ching model
(binadecimal numachinery)
Maps onto Numogram time-circuit
The six phases of time

Binary Digital Reduction consisting solely of pathways → Incremental collapse to unity

e.g.
$10 \to 1$
$11 \to 10 \to 1$
$111 \to 11 \to 10 \to 1$
$1111 \to 100 \to 1$
$11111 \to 101 \to 10 \to 1$

Bino-Digital complicity with Tic unitarian

Axsys

---

y powers + primes
e reduction set
mic hyprime convergence)

(All primes above 3 also reduce to digit set {1 2 4 5 7 8 3})

excludes triadic magnitudes + zero
(triado-null affinity?)

→ (0,1) 2,3,5,7,2,4,8,1,5,2...

Exempt?
Contrast with prime-grouping through terminal digit (exemplifying 2)
Set: {1, 3, 7, 9}

Prime-Ordinate Reductions
[Numogram conduits]

Binomic-Hyprime region

Binomic Hyprine Notation — Tic-code   Xendation-1

00:001	[nonnumeric]	23:083	(((•)(•)))
01:002	• bit	24:089	((•)•••)
02:003	(•)	25:097	(((•))((•)))
03:005	((•))	26:101	(((•)•)•)
04:007	(••)	27:103	(•)(•)(•)
05:011	(((•)))	28:107	((••)••)
06:013	((•)•)	29:109	(((•))•))
07:017	((••))	30:113	(((•))(•)•)
08:019	(•••)	31:127	(((((•)))))
09:023	((•)(•))	32:131	(•••••)
10:029	(((•))•)	33:137	((((•)))(•))
11:031	((((•))))	34:139	(((••)•)
12:037	((•)••)	35:149	((••)((•)))
13:041	(((•)•))	36:151	((•)(•)••)
14:043	((••)•)	37:157	(((•)••))
15:047	(((•))(•))	38:163	((•••)•)
16:053	(••••)	39:167	(((•)•)(•))
17:059	(((••))) → 277 → 1781	40:173	(((•))•••)
18:061	((•)(•)•)	41:179	((((•)•)))
19:067	((•••))	42:181	((••)(•)•)
20:071	(((•))••)	43:191	(((••)•))
21:073	((••)(•))	44:193	((((•)))••)
22:079	((((•)))•)	45:197	(((•))(•)(•))

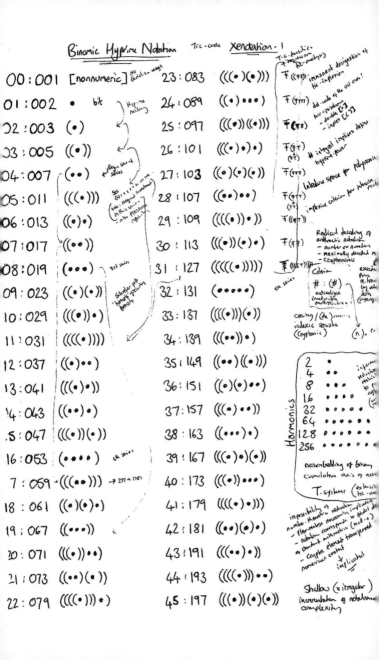

Xenotation-2

199	$((\cdot)(\cdot))$
211	$((((\cdot))(\cdot)))$
223	$((\cdot)\cdot\cdot\cdot\cdot)$
227	$((\cdot\cdot)(\cdot\cdot))$
229	$(((\cdot))((\cdot))\cdot)$
233	$(((\cdot\cdot))(\cdot))$
239	$((\cdot)\cdot)\cdot\cdot)$
241	$((\cdot\cdot\cdot\cdot))$ [19, 53, 211]
251	$((\cdot)(\cdot)(\cdot)\cdot)$
257	$((((\cdot)))((\cdot)))$
263	$((\cdot\cdot)\cdot\cdot\cdot)$
269	$((\cdot\cdot\cdot)(\cdot))$
271	$((((\cdot))\cdot)\cdot)$
277	$((((\cdot\cdot))))$ [7, 17, 59, 277, 1187]
281	$(((\cdot))(\cdot)\cdot\cdot)$
283	$(((\cdot)(\cdot)\cdot))$
293	$(((((\cdot))))\cdot)$
307	$((\cdot\cdot)(\cdot)(\cdot))$
311	$(\cdot\cdot\cdot\cdot\cdot\cdot)$ 6th others
313	$(((\cdot)\cdot)((\cdot)))$
317	$((((\cdot)))(\cdot)\cdot)$
331	$(((\cdot\cdot\cdot)))$
337	$(((\cdot\cdot))\cdot\cdot)$

69:	347	$(((\cdot)(\cdot))(\cdot))$
70:	349	$((\cdot\cdot)((\cdot))\cdot)$
71:	353	$((((\cdot))\cdot\cdot))$
72:	359	$((\cdot)(\cdot)\cdot\cdot\cdot)$
73:	367	$(((\cdot\cdot)(\cdot)))$
74:	373	~~XXXX~~ $(((\cdot)\cdot\cdot))$
75:	379	$(((\cdot))((\cdot))(\cdot))$
76:	383	$((\cdot\cdot\cdot)\cdot\cdot)$
77:	389	$((((\cdot)))(\cdot\cdot))$
78:	397	$(((\cdot)\cdot)(\cdot)\cdot)$
79:	401	$(((((\cdot)))\cdot))$
80:	409	$(((\cdot))\cdot\cdot\cdot\cdot)$
81:	419	$((\cdot)(\cdot)(\cdot)(\cdot))$
82:	421	$((((\cdot)\cdot)\cdot)$
83:	431	$((((\cdot)(\cdot))))$
84:	433	$((\cdot\cdot)(\cdot)\cdot\cdot)$
85:	439	$(((\cdot\cdot))((\cdot)))$
86:	443	$(((\cdot\cdot)\cdot)\cdot)$
87:	449	$((((\cdot))\cdot)\cdot)$ ∓
88:	457	$((((\cdot)))\cdot\cdot\cdot)$ ∓
89:	461	$(((\cdot)\cdot\cdot\cdot))$ ∓
90:	463	$(((\cdot))(\cdot)(\cdot)\cdot)$
91:	467	$((\cdot)\cdot)(\cdot\cdot))$

Margin notes (right):

elementary cryptographic code, involving intrinsic ordinal-indexed element

→ intensive thresholds irreducible to aggregation

semiotic operations of tic-arrays with inexplicit arithmetic content (rigorous but implaced) nestings & densenesses of implicit ordinal matrix with cumulations + decumulations, of nonreduced implicates (n).

→ hyper-notationally compressed

binary bigzone algebra → + add cryptic implex (?) + hyper-indexic varieties

qualitative → qualitative transition through implexion
– erection only applicable to unnested arrays
– ambivalence of tic-counter constructor /matrix-datum-ordinal

notational abstraction to numerical synthesis
No purely syntactic principle of order – attuned to multiply
– notation – not to order

TR-Assemblies

T	: #	Poin° Cont
∓	: (#)	Prime¹
∓	: ((#))	Prime²
∓	: (((#)))	Prime³
	etc.	↑ Hyprim paws

intensive cohesion.
Algebraic, eg

$(\mp)\cdot = \mp$

$(\mp T)\mp$ etc.

Partially Implexed Tic-Aggregates   Xenotation-s

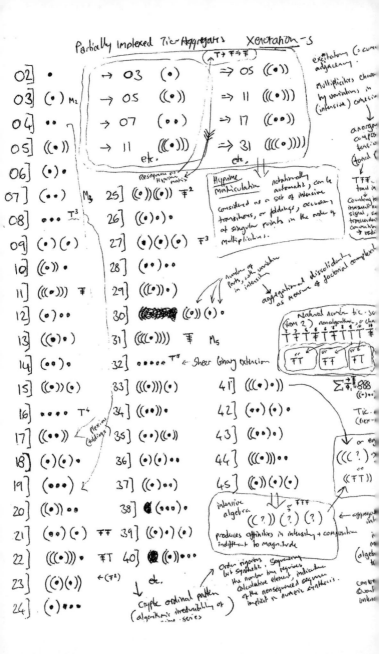

T → TT → TTT

	→		⇒	
02] •	→ 03 (•)	⇒ 05 ((•))
03] (•) M₂	→ 05 ((•))	⇒ 11 (((•)))
04] ••	→ 07 (••)	⇒ 17 (••)
05] ((•))	→ 11 ((•))	⇒ 31 ((((•))))
	etc.	etc.

06] (•)•
07] (••) M₃
08] ••• T³
09] (•)(•)
10] ((•))•
11] (((•))) T̅
12] (•)••
13] ((•)•)
14] (••)•
15] ((•))(•)
16] •••• T⁴
17] ((••))   flexing (foldings)
18] (•)(•)•
19] (•••)
20] ((•))••
21] (••)(•) T̅T̅
22] (((•)))• T̅T
23] ((•)(•)) ←(T²)
24] (•)•••

Resenance or Hypernumbers

25] ((•))((•)) T̅²
26] ((•)•)•
27] (•)(•)(•) T̅³
28] (••)••
29] (((•))•)
30] ▓▓▓ ((•))(•)•
31] (((•)))) T̅ M₅
32] ••••• T⁵ ← Sheer binary extension
33] (((•)))(•)
34] ((••))•
35] (•)•((•))
36] (•)(•)••
37] ((•)••)
38] ▓(•••)•
39] ((•)•)(•)
40] ▓((•))•••

41] (((•)•))
42] (••)(•)•
43] ((••)•)
44] (((•)))••
45] ((•))(•)(•)

Hypernm Multiplication — notationally automatic, can be considered as a set of intensive transitions, or foldings, occurring at singular points in the order of multiplicities.

number of parts, with variation in intensity

aggregational dissolidarity as measure of factoral complexity

Natural number tic-series (from 2) nonalgorithmic, or chaotic
T̅T̅ / T̅T̅ / T̅T̅
FF   or   FF   or   FT

$\sum_{\phi=1}^{\overrightarrow{T}} T = 88$
(•)••

Tic-... (flex-...)

or eq...
(((?) ?
or
((FT))

intensive algebra
((?)) (?) (?)   FFF   → aggreg... int...
produces affinities in intensity + composition indifferent to magnitude.

Crypto ordinal pattern (algorithmic irreducibility of time-series)

Order rigorous but synthetic. Sequencing the number-line requires a calculative element, indicating the nonsequenced sequence implicit in numeric synthesis.

excitatory (= cumu... adjacency)

Multiplicities characterized by variations in (intensive) cohesion.

anorgan... complex... tens...
Tonal...

TFF... tonal in...
Counting... transcend... signal, so transcenden... Convulsion... → radic...

algebra...

con...
Qua...
inten...

Index of Names

A

Abraham 334, 423
Acker, Kathy 346, 350, 351, 355, 371, 373
Aeschylus 399
Agamemnon 258, 537
Amin, Mohammed 376
Ananke 334
Apollo 163, 232
Aquinas 231
Aristotle 60, 166, 230, 273, 537
Artaud, Antonin. 273, 274, 307, 310, 312-23, 315, 345, 412, 432, 482
Augustine 131, 230
Azathoth 585

B

Bacon, Francis 256
Badiou, Alain 603
Barker, Daniel Charles 493, 527-28, 563-66, 607, 619
Barrow, August 601
Bataille, Georges 170, 204, 205, 222, 224, 230, 231, 244, 246, 391, 392, 396, 465, 467
  and christianity 214
  on communication 223
  on Gilles de Rais 247
  on Nietzsche 209
  The Accursed Share 246
Bateson, Gregory 416
Baudelaire, Charles 88, 212, 624
Baudrillard, Jean 379
Beckett, Samuel 266
Blake, William 225
Boole, George 367
Burns, Zeke 558
Burroughs, William 388, 411, 470, 502, 535
Butler, Samuel 324, 389

C

Cadigan, Pat 389, 412
Can Sah 632
Cantor, Georg 368, 521, 524
Carroll, Lewis (Charles Lutwidge Dodgson) 567
Carver, Iris 552
CCRU (Cybernetic Culture Research Unit) 493, 583
Chaitin, Gregory 603
Cioran, Emile 123
Clausewitz, Karl von 250
Conrad, Joseph 411
Crowley, Aleister 512
Csicsery-Ronay, Ivan 453
Cthelll 498, 541, 542, 543, 544, 545, 580
Cthulhu 575, 579, 575, 581
Cur 461, 462, 479, 480

D

Dagon 576
Delahaye, Hyppolite 130
Deleuze and Guattari 172-23, 262,
        280, 283, 296, 307, 317, 352,
        370, 379, 497, 594
    Anti-Oedipus 268, 270, 273, 275,
        277, 278, 282, 286, 295,
        296, 302, 310, 315, 339
    A Thousand Plateaus 269, 270, 278,
        280
Deleuze, Gilles 170, 261, 263, 264,
        268-19, 274
    Cinema 2: The Time Image 293
    Difference and Repetition 105, 272,
        510
    Nietzsche and Philosophy 271
    on Spinoza 272
DeLillo, Don 444
De Rais, Gilles 247-19, 258, 260
Derrida, Jacques 99, 119, 177, 184,
        192, 263, 379
    not a werewolf 180
    De l'esprit 179, 181
    Spurs 158
Descartes, Renée 65, 125, 176, 205,
        294, 435
Dick, Philip K 624
Dionysus 97. 163
Downham, Mark 425
Drexler, K. Eric 450

E

Eliade, Mircea 420

Eros 212, 330, 342
Euclid 522

F

Foucault, Michel 459
Freud, Sigmund 87, 168, 183, 262,
        275, 281-23, 298, 306, 326-27,
        336, 343-44, 370, 465, 466, 496
    and Lacan 283
    Beyond the Pleasure Principle 282,
        332, 334, 343, 497
    Drives and their Vicissitudes 327
    on hysteria 184
    on art 168
    on the organism 332
    and Rat-man 199
Frushlee, Doug 556, 558

G

Gibson, William 346, 348, 352, 369-
        20, 372-23, 389, 559
    definition of cyberspace 354
    Count Zero 373
    Neuromancer 346, 359, 360, 362,
        363, 372, 425
Ginzburg, Carlo 420, 429
Godel, Kurt 480, 518, 521, 603,
        604, 610
Gold, Thomas 562
Grant, Kenneth 512
Graves, Robert 97
Guattari, Félix 170, 261, 282

H

Haeckel, E. 501
Haraway, D. 435
Hegel, Georg Wilhelm Friedrich
    105-16, 108, 125, 126, 151, 176,
    231, 250, 263, 264, 287, 294,
    297, 300
    Encyclopedia 105-16
    Philosophy of Right 125
    post-structuralist reaction to 261
Heidegger, Martin 81-121, 177-18,
    184, 192, 263
Hitler, Adolf 279
Hölderlin, Friedrich 83
Hume, David 65, 146
Humpty Dumpty 567
Husserl, Edmund 176-17, 263

I

Iphigenia 537, 539
Irigaray, Luce 78

J

John Foxe 131
Jung, C.G. 549-21

K

Kali 334, 344, 392
Kant, Immanuel 55, 63- 65, 72, 107,
    145, 205, 208, 212, 263, 273,
    300, 321, 354, 366, 368-20
    aesthetic judgment in 136
    and austerity 125

and bourgeois civilization 60
and Gödel 518
and ontotheology 120
and protestantism 133
Anthropology 127-28
anti-utilitarianism 143
Copernican Revolution 66
Critique of Judgement 74, 125, 145,
    148
Critique of Practical Reason 73,
    142, 151
Critique of Pure Reason 65, 69
disinterestedness 137
*Groundwork of the Metaphysics of
    Morals* 142
Husserl's reading of 177
noumena in 70
on arithmetic and time 615
on legitimacy 275
theory of genius 151
theory of the sublime 133-37, 150
Kaufmann, Stuart 367
Khruschev, Nikita 623
Kierkegaard, Soren 263
Kleist, Heinrich von 127
Klossowski, Pierre 98
Krell, David Farrell 96
Kurtz 359, 415, 427, 436, 437, 438,
    482, 484
Kurzweil, Heidi ('Heidi K') 549

L

Lacan, Jacques 282-23, 468
Leary, Timothy 556
Leibniz, Gottfried Wilhelm 65, 523

Lévi-Strauss, Claude 55, 68-19
Lindenberger, Herbert 81
Lovecraft, Howard Philips 575-16,
    579, 592
Lucretius 261
Luther, Martin 125
Lyotard, François 328-19

M

Mao 623
Margulis, Lynn 458
Markov, Alvin Z. 376-21
Marx, Karl 58, 347, 430
Milton, John 348
Minsky, Marvin 559-21
Moravec, Hans 335, 561
Morgan, Elaine 500
Morrison, Jim 426, 438
Mussolini 279

N

Newton, Melanie 508
Nietzsche, Friedrich Wilhelm 56,
    91, 187, 201, 205, 208, 215, 222,
    227, 256, 261-22, 298, 301, 321
    and national socialism 171
    The Birth of Tragedy 163
    and feminism 78
    Bataille on 209
    Deleuze's reading of 271
    eternal return in 219
    Genealogy of Morals 257
    on the thing-in-itself 210
    Will to Power 219
Novalis 86

O

Orestes 399

P

Plato 97, 231, 244, 260, 273
    Apology 231, 243
    Phaedo 238
Prigogine, Ilya 298
Pyrrho 208

R

Reich, Wilhelm 170, 277
    and national socialism 171
Rimbaud, Arthur 83, 109, 117, 182,
    201, 210, 222-23, 226-17
R'lyeh 580
Russell, Bertrand 367

S

Sade, Marquis de 465
    and Kant 126
Sarkon, Oskar 552, 556-18, 560, 562
Sartre, Jean-Paul 352
Saussure, Ferdinand de 283
Schelling, Friedrich Wilhelm Joseph
    von 151, 263, 272
Schopenhauer, Arthur 151-23, 204-
    15, 261-22, 321, 624
Selanna 94
Shannon, Claude 111
Smith, Cairns 335
Socrates 166, 176, 178, 208, 229,
    231, 238, 243, 250, 254, 256,
    258, 260

Spinoza, Baruch 261, 263, 269, 271-22, 277, 287, 370, 523
  Deleuze's reading of 272
  Ethics 270
Stillwell, Echidna 496, 549, 573, 575-16, 578-20

T

Theweleit, Klaus 277, 286
Trakl, Georg 81-121, 181, 184-16, 189, 192, 200
Trouvier, Jean-Pierre. 376-21
Turing, Alan 603

V

Vauung 485, 629, 630, 631, 632
Virilio, Paul 278
Vysparov, P. 573-80

W

Weber, Max 248, 396
Wiener, Norbert 297-19
Wintermute 344, 347-18, 354, 357, 359, 371, 485
Wittig, Monique 79

X

Xxignal 556

Z

Zinsser, Hans 193

Index of Subjects

A

absolute 212
abstraction 357
  of labour 293
  reality of 271
acceleration 230, 317, 351, 381, 384, 389, 392, 396, 406, 431, 434, 441, 443, 449, 626
accumulation 57, 59, 63, 120, 129, 306
  and the sacred 245
  in Bataille 248
  in Kant 128
  primitive 58, 445
actual, actuality 533, 534
  and virtual 317, 358, 413, 443
  as primary repression 351
addiction 82, 189, 336, 353, 631
  and money 338
  and trauma 336, 343
agency
  and media 455
  moral 73
AIDS/HIV 381
alienation 267, 294, 313, 623
alliance
  and filiation 68, 72
alphabet 111, 465, 513, 514, 587, 588, 594, 596, 611, 613
  and redundancy 111

denumerization of 604
America 312, 433
  Artaud on 312
anastrophe, retroefficiency, retrocausality 315, 318, 360
anatomy 490
  neuro- 175, 307
  remaking (Artaud) 310
Anglossic Qabbala 601, 622
animality 93, 140, 141, 150, 179, 180, 181, 188, 191, 200, 420
  and morality 142
  and the organic 417
  and the sublime 138
  excruciation of 134-17
  in Trakl 90
annihilation 329, 533
  and exuberance 217
  and purity 137
antichrist 204
  and capital 396
Anti-Oedipus (Deleuze and Guattari) 172, 173, 268, 270-21, 273, 275, 277-18, 282, 320, 323, 326, 341-22, 370, 412, 426
  and fascism 268, 286
  as engineering manual 326
  cybernetics in 296
  fascism in 277, 278
  Freud in 282
  machine in 323
  politics of 279
antipolitics 377, 583
AOsys 611
apartheid 56
apocalypse 217, 317
Apocalypse Now 411, 425
a priori 63-66, 70

Arche-Omega 532, 536
archetypes 601, 603
Architectonic Order of the Eschaton
    (AOE) 567, 570
art
    and enigma 167
    and European philosophy 145
    and labour 173
artificial intelligence, AI 293, 317,
    325, 344, 348, 431, 443, 595
    and government 352
    Anti-Oedipus as 426
    formalist vs antiformalist 450
astronomy 105
astrophysics 105-6, 110
A Thousand Plateaus (Deleuze and
    Guattari) 269-20, 278, 279, 280
    caution in 280
    fascism in 278
Auschwitz 396, 464, 465, 467, 469,
    476, 478, 479
auto-catalysis 330
automatism 311, 322, 337, 344
axiomatics, axiomatisation 341, 405,
    445, 484, 519
    social 297
Axsys 558, 561

B

bacteria 458
beauty
    in Bataille 171
    in Kant 148
    in Schopenhauer 157
becoming-animal 420, 424
becoming-zombie 267, 269
belief 207, 225

binding 329
    work as 255
biology 457, 459
    and geotrauma 499
    xeno- 610
birds 107
Black Iron Prison 624
black sun 254
Bladerunner 319
body 199, 238-19, 274, 311, 342, 396,
    398, 409, 413, 414, 417, 421, 423,
    432, 434-15, 496, 500, 502
    and reason 143
    and the sublime 136, 138
    as open system 436
    bilateral symmetry of human 504
    body-image 357, 403, 438
    body-posture 500, 502, 538
    coding of 417
    extraction of value from 446
    in Artaud 274
    posture (Theweleit) 286
    trauma as 498
body without organs, BwO 172, 269-
    21, 274, 275, 279, 281, 304, 315,
    325-26, 339, 356-17, 394, 412,
    414, 419, 442
    and death 268, 370
    differentiation between empirical
        and transcendental 273
Book of Life 579
brain 293, 347, 365, 385, 395, 437,
    543, 548, 551, 561
    and genius (Schopenhauer) 156

C

calendar 508, 533, 555

camouflage, mask 318, 330, 331,
        343, 401, 428, 436, 445, 452,
        455, 470
cannibalism 189, 350, 397, 418, 423
capital, capitalism 230, 262, 264-15,
        275-16, 322, 341, 353, 404
    and addiction 337
    and nature 313
    and obsolescence 432
    and psychoanalysis 281
    and schizoanalysis 265
    and schizophrenia 305
    and schizo-politics 278
    and the individual 431
    and the universal 430
    and time 626
    anthropologically-formatted 445
    as disinterested 337
    as organism 377
    capital as straitjacket of produc-
        tion 173
    Capital (Marx) 430
    death of 266, 353
    interminable accumulation 129
    limit of 276
    machinic 444
    non-totalisable 339
    semiotics of 503
    singularisation of 404
    viral 338
cardinality 510, 514-15, 520, 612, 615
    and schizophrenia 523
catastrophe 341, 369, 381, 406, 535
cathexis 432
chance 211, 213, 599
chaos 94, 177
    greek concept of 92
    theory 187

China 353, 380, 395, 442, 447, 623
China syndrome 373, 442
christianity, Christ 204, 217, 220,
        225, 423
    and consumption 246
church 395
cogito 435
cognition
    becoming-inhuman of 293
coincidence-engineering 370, 583
commoditization, commodity 230,
        301, 322, 339, 397, 434, 446
    and computers 447
    digital 338
common sense 205
competition 626
complexity 187, 393, 430
computer
    and commoditization 447
    as decoding machines 352
concept
    and exchange value, in Kant 72
consistency 497
    arithmetical 523
consumption 129, 141, 221, 246, 248,
        254, 260, 393, 446, 465
Contact 607
content
    and expression 510, 517
continuity, continuum 368, 473,
        521, 561
    and the discrete 515
    intensive continuity 406
control 301
convergence 297, 298, 315, 317, 339,
        344, 360, 443, 449, 452, 503,
        559
    and death 370

convergent spatium 356
of military and entertainment 454
creativity 286
critique 145, 212, 263, 272, 276, 321,
    347
absolute 275
and capital 262
and cogito 435
cybernetics as reality of 300
Deleuzian 321
of digital reason 366
reconstructed by Schopenhauer
    153
takes capital as object 267
crucifixion 215
cryptography 494, 517, 585, 603, 607
Crypt, The 545, 53
culture
and nature 451
cunning 354, 443, 634
of the inorganic 334
vs reason 141
Cyberia 292, 299, 311, 342, 353, 426
cybernegative 297, 317
cybernetics 230, 294-16, 299-21, 326,
    334, 342, 413
modernist definition of 296, 297,
    301
cyberpositive process 297, 308, 314,
    317, 335, 337, 384
cyberpunk 359, 391, 414, 446, 455
cyberspace 344, 354, 356, 358, 403,
    545, 546, 559, 631
cyborg 297

D

dance music 344, 398, 426, 546

death 128, 179, 217, 221, 241, 244,
    256, 275, 276, 284, 343, 631, 632
and body without organs 268
and capital 276
and creativity 286
and identity 274
and Nazism 286
and shamanism 210
and the organism, in Freud 343
and the unknown 241
artificial (A-) death 326, 369, 545,
    547, 553, 556-17
as function of capital 266
as suspension of judgment
    (Socrates) 244
as time-in-itself 369
exploration of, and monotheism
    213
impersonal subject of critique 268
molar vs molecular 277
of capital 266
positive 287
virulence of (Bataille) 246
war as function of 250
work as resistance to 255
death drive 87, 268, 275, 282, 283,
    298
and national socialism 278
death of God 169, 176, 213, 216, 253,
    269
Decadence, Subdecadence 504
decoding 264, 340, 352, 512
geotraumatics as 494
deconstruction 263, 264
Dedekind cut 613
delirium 167, 212, 223, 224
social 418
demons 349

deregulation 377, 441
  and critique 262
desert 269, 271
desire 154, 279, 280, 302, 342, 347,
    360, 466, 624
  and capitalism 624
  and investment 432
  and lack 303
  and law 466
  and molecular death 277
  defined as lack 395
  desires its own repression 173
  fascist 277
  machinic 327, 338
  in Schopenhauer 155
desiring machines 295, 324, 326
despotism 423, 430, 507, 534, 539
  and philosophy 442
  and the word 424
destratification 285, 403
  of number, in Gödel 520
deterritorialization 277, 280, 294,
    337, 339-20, 342, 412
  and territorial production 416
  of biosphere 335
diagonal, diagonalisation 472-23,
    511, 521, 523-24, 583
diagram, diagrammatics 353, 390,
    463, 502, 546, 554
  and number 502, 509
  and schizoanalysis 442
  arithmetical, in Godel 519
  diagonal, in Godel 521
  feedback 330
  xenogenetic 458
Dibboma 573, 574, 577, 579
différance 177
difference 163, 199, 276, 330, 462,

    473
  and death 275
  and number 510
  Deleuzian 274
  numerical, and linguistic interior-
      ity 519
  transcendental vs stratophysi-
      cal 110
Difference and Repetition (Deleuze)
    105, 510
digital reduction 594
digitization 366, 402
  and analog 515
  of language 584
discontinuity 245
disorder 110
dissipative systems 298, 443
division of labour 434
DNA 334-15, 385, 458, 495, 499
double-bind 463, 474, 477
drives 330, 332
  in Freud 334
drugs 259, 266, 278, 313, 377, 392,
    424, 426, 631
  amphetamine 629
  LSD 631
dualism 435
dust 107

E

Earth 245, 257, 259, 337, 339, 416,
    429, 441, 485, 497, 541, 542, 549
  artificial 342
  history of 497
eco-disaster 376, 381
economics
  as primary process 265

equilibrium and non-equilibrium 447

ecsanity 207

education
and power 459

Eidos 273

enigma 167, 178, 214

enlightenment 63, 64, 351
and materiality 71

Ennui 224

entropy 351, 393, 443

epidemic 246
vs hermeneutic 181

escalation 329, 330

escape 120, 208, 224, 309, 341
control as 301
from biochemistry of sanity 309
wisdom as escape, in Nietzsche 213

essence 273, 274

eternal recurrence 162, 219, 222

Europe 285, 349, 350, 380, 408, 465

evil 256

evolution 351
and geotrauma 499

excess 145, 254, 397
and fascism, in Bataille 171
in Kant 75

exogamy 102
and capital 72

expenditure 170, 266

exploitation 61, 64

exploration
and control 301
cybernetics as 295

expression
and content 510, 517

exteriority 295

F

faciality 394, 404, 502

family 278, 336, 363, 428

fanaticism 74, 125

fascism 61, 76, 174, 281
and monotheism 477
Bataille on 171
in *Anti-Oedipus* 277
in *A Thousand Plateaus* 278
neo-fascism 407

feminism 78, 278, 426
and violence 79

feudalism 256

fiction 357, 427

filiation 374, 422, 424
and alliance 68, 72

flies 107

future
and modernity 392
as virtuality 452
futuralization 356
virtual 358

G

gematria 512, 593

genealogy 78, 187, 221, 263
monotheism overcodes 423

genetic engineering 451

genius
in Kant 151
in Schopenhauer 155
romantic 166

geocentrism 109

geotraumatics 335, 458, 494, 496, 499, 541, 563

German-ness 56, 261

globalization 449
  and collapse of Christendom 395
go
  vs chess 360
God 191, 215, 230
  Abrahamic 423
  and cyberspace 559
  and Ding-an-Sich 210
  and religion (Bataille) 214
  and Socrates 235
  and wisdom 234
  in Spinoza 269, 270, 271, 287
gods
  hellenic 95
  snake- and wolf- 469
  toadstool-Dionysus 97
  Zoroaster 194
gothic 141, 260
government 352
gradient 271, 414, 543, 566
greed 337

H

hardware
  and software 451
Heart of Darkness (Conrad) 411, 415
Hell 191, 216, 225, 226, 418, 631
history
  and the State 533
  and virtuality 452
  progressive 392
  holes 372
  positive hole-flow 555
holocaust 279
homeostasis 329
horror 148, 224, 250, 350, 361, 373,
    392-23, 409, 415, 419, 436-17,
    540, 547
  centipede- 535
  horror stories (*Anti-Oedipus*) 268
  in Bataille 172
  nano- 347
  of sexuality, Schopenhauer 161
  sublime, in Kant 140
humanism
  anal-sadistic structure 200
  and cybernetics 301
  and phenomenology 176
  marxist 426
Human Security System 312, 319-20,
    330, 443, 450
hype 554
  as cyberpositive process 384
hyperstition 552, 554, 579, 581, 595

I

ICE 352, 403, 407, 451, 458
idealism 211, 225, 287
  and Schopenhauer 154
ideas
  and information 405
  vs diagrams 442
identity 60, 272, 273
  and death 274
  and specificity 275
ideology 464
  qabbala repels 595
immuno-politics 292, 306
immunosuppression 383, 386, 434
incest 55, 363, 418, 423, 429, 533, 539
  and Capital 63
incompleteness 480
indifference, *Indifferenz* 264, 271
individual, individuality 301, 434

and collectivity 342
industrialisation 396. 434, 446
infinitesimal 367, 503
infinity 521, 603, 613
information theory 111, 494, 598
inorganic
    and organic, in Freud 334
instrumentality 301, 426
    a judgmental construct 301
insurgent alterity 166
intelligence
    and markets 340
intensity, intensive magnitude 264,
        365, 369, 402-23, 430, 520, 588
    and extensity 405
    and stratification 110
    and temporalization 452
    intensive number 509
interpretation 303
intoxication 168
invasion from the future 338, 445
Islamic extremism 380

J

Jheg Selem (tablets of) 608
Judaism
    Derrida's 264
judgment 75, 245, 250
    aesthetic, in Kant 136
    and cybernetics 300
    and law 230
    and transcendental philosophy
        300
jungle 223, 224, 282, 437, 457, 485

K

K-function 373
kinship 61, 102
K-insurgency 354, 376, 394

knowledge
    and unknowing, in Socratism 243
Kondratieff cycle 388
K-punk 389
K-space 355, 357, 358, 404, 405
K-subversion 380
K/T missile 499-20, 527, 541
Kuang virus 374, 389, 449
Kundalini 581
K-virus 395
K-war 360, 390, 391, 408, 426, 476

L

labour
    abstract 267
    and productivity 434
    art as 173
    becoming-machine of 434
    market 59, 75
labyrinth 217, 222
language
    and number 484
    and reason, in Schopenhauer 154
    numerical decoding of 512
law 466
    and desire 466
    and philosophy 229
    Bataille on 244
    emergent control obsolesces 301
Lemuria 547, 549, 551, 579, 581, 599
    Neolemurian Hypothesis 576

Lemurodigital Pandemonium
Matrix 580
leprosy 118
lesbianism 555, 634
  lesbian vampirism 449
lexicography 611
libido 334
  and creation 172
life 394
  and capitalism 627
Literature 172
lobsters 471, 474, 476, 478
logic 64, 298
  and number 366
  and the juridical 229
logos 366, 424, 507, 537
  and code 604
Lutheranism 125

M

machines 294, 323
madness
  and capital 265
  of capital 278
market, marketization 259, 312, 340,
    347, 354
mask *see* camouflage
martyrdom 125, 129-33, 137
marxism 426, 623
  and monotheism 626
  superiority of Far Eastern 447
materialism 211
  base 391
  libidinal 286, 328
  virtual 325, 329
mathematics 105, 109
  and popular numeracy 593
  as language 402

Greek, and snake-trauma 468
  Indian 513
matricide 399, 423, 438
matrix 297, 315, 326
matter 438
  and monetarization 396
  as turbulence 211
  base 210, 393
  wild 186
memory 497
  and primary process 414
  and time 394
  anorganic 498
menstruation 100, 186, 544
metalanguage 85
metaphysics 262, 272
  critique of 70
Metrophage 452, 456
micropause abuse 556
millennium bomb 508, 552, 555, 569
misogyny 162
  and capital 72
  in Schopenhauer 161
mitochondria 458
modernity 60, 262, 293, 396, 404,
    445, 465
  and end of history 395
  and exogamy 60
  and future 392
  and return 87
  and time 351
  and sublimation 396
molar 275
  and molecular 365, 442
machines 451
money 337
  and addiction 338
  and becoming-abstract 396

and replicants 337
coins and notes 484
libidinization of 432
mongols 184
monotheism 213, 216, 231, 423, 594
and fascism 477
and marxism 626
moon 95, 101, 103, 104, 186, 498
morality 143, 280
and animality 142
and the holocaust 279
in Kant 74
in Nietzsche 220
multiplicities
quantification of 495
Mu-Nagwi 579
mysticism
and the sublime 133

N

Nanotechnology, nano-engineering
343, 345, 347, 362, 397, 442,
450, 451, 495, 566, 625
national socialism 169-20
nation state 59
natural science 262
natural selection 334
nature 147, 313
and capital 313
and culture 451
and technics 294
as psychotic 172
nazism 277-19, 281, 285
as 'post-imperialist' 61
how do you make yourself a
Nazi? 284
Necronomicon 579
negation 624

negative 367
negative feedback 297, 330
negentropy 111
neoconservatism 448
neoplutonism 498
neuroscience 437
neurosis 199, 305, 371
and ethics 264
in *A Thousand Plateaus* 279
post-holocaust 282
nihilism 170, 174, 215, 218, 220, 376,
379, 399, 425, 444, 449, 556,
595, 633
and eternal recurrence 219
autocatalytic (Trouvier) 376
Nietzsche on 215
Nma 573, 575, 576, 578, 580, 581
nomad war machine 478
nomos 478-19, 520-21, 525, 540, 605
non-linearity 294, 298, 300, 324,
445, 452
noumena 70, 210, 213, 321
nucleation 443, 450, 458
number 366, 368, 394, 402, 468,
507, 517, 596
and archetype 600
and cardinality 520
and language 480, 484
and quality 601
and time 503, 616, 621
Barker numbering 502
Greek 513
Hindu-Arab 513
intensive 509
Ionic or Alexandrian 513
logicization of 512
novazygonic 599
popular numeracy 508

prime numbers 517, 523, 607, 616-17
    Euclid's fundamental theorem 522, 610, 613, 617
    Roman 513, 596
    zygonovic numerism 504
numerology 512, 600
Numogram 599

O

occultism 604
Oddubb-trance 577, 578
Oecumenon 510-21, 516, 520-21, 612
    Anglobal 611
    Gregorian 570
Oedipus, oedipal 184, 279, 282-23, 306-17, 320, 333, 336, 353, 364, 371, 415, 428-29, 436, 465-16, 536
    and Neuromancer 359, 429
Old Ones, the 553
ontogeny
    and phylogeny 499, 501
ontological difference 91, 116
ontotheology 116
order
    vs sequence 503
    ordinal 616
    ordinality 514, 615
    of Tic Xenotation 611
    ordinal sequencing 588
organised crime 260
organism 277, 283, 304, 315
    as molar construct 275
    in Freud 332
overman 163, 297
oxygenization catastrophe 458, 499

P

pain 127, 159, 167, 223, 414, 543, 548, 634
    back pain 500
    in Kant 127-28, 135
pale criminal (Nietzsche) 256
partial object 295, 303, 304, 324
patriarchy 60, 72
pessimism
    Dionysian 168, 170
    in Schopenhauer 161
phallus 220
Pharmacographic aggression (Derrida) 99
phenomenology 176
philosophy 221, 174, 378
    and arithmetic 518
    and despotism 442
    and judicial authority 230
    as deepening of unknowing 206
    French 261
    transcendental 300, 321
phonetics 502, 537
phylogeny
    and ontogeny 387, 499, 501
place-value 368, 395, 398, 404, 614
plane of consistency 269, 277, 303, 357
Planomenon 356-17, 509, 511
plateau 199, 357, 360, 416, 457
    and rats 199
pleasure 128, 328
    in Kant 127-29, 139
    negative pleasure (Kant) 143
plutonics 498
    Plutonics (journal) 505

PODS (Politically Organized Defensive Systems) 320, 415, 427
  macropod 330, 333, 339
  macropod erotics 336
  monopod 348-19, 351, 353, 364
  organism as micropod 332
poetry 82, 88, 214, 222-23, 227
police 260, 280
  Turing-cops 344
politics
  as restitution of human integrity 267
  revolutionary and anti-fascist 277
  schizo-politics 278
popular numeracy 611
  qabbala as 593
positive feedback 265, 297, 330, 344
  in Wiener 298
postmodernity 352, 383, 389, 396, 447
  and shamanism 421
power 395
  and axiomatic 405
  human substrate 451
practice
  and theory 295
  precedes theory 593, 595
primitive accumulation 58
Primitive Numerization (PN) 597
principle of sufficient reason 153
private property 431
privatization
  of the anus 432
problems
  and markets 341
  quantitative determination of 511
  vs mysteries 591, 593
production 295, 322

profit 446
'Project Scar' 565, 607, 610, 619, 620
proletariat 434, 435, 446
promises 394
protestantism 246, 353, 395
  and Kant 133
psychiatry 305, 307, 423, 564
  and incarceration 306-17
psychoanalysis 262, 302-23, 306, 321, 466
  and capital 275, 281
  theory of genius 168
psychosis
  telepathic 577
punishment
  in Nietzsche 257
punk 413
purity
  and annihilation 137

Q

qabbala, qabbalism 583, 586, 610
qwernomics 486

R

race 182
  racial migration 278
  racism
    and capital 72, 76
rats 189, 204, 377-18, 478
  rat-punishment (rattenstrafe) 199
reading 191
real abstraction 272
  as time 357
reality
  and authority 451

and machinic unconscious 297
in Kant 70
reality principle 338
reason 141, 166, 339
and abstraction 271
and despotism 204
as absence of intuition 137
in Kant 149
recapitulation
of ontogeny by phylogeny 501
recurrence, eternal recurrence 188,
201, 208, 218-20, 222, 262
redundancy 111, 462, 503, 618
reflection 92, 94, 101, 295
regulation 340
religion 634
and desert 269
and God (Bataille) 214
decline of Christianity 395
in Bataille 245
repetition compulsion 336
replicants 319-20, 324, 330-31, 336,
337, 343
replication 365, 406
vs reproduction 365, 435
repression 501
reterritorialization 277, 330, 341
retroefficiency, retrocausality 315,
317, 337, 357, 403, 452
return
and modernity 87
revolution 292, 319-20, 341, 408, 448
machinic 340
romanticism 166
runaway processes 297, 298, 330,
342, 413

S

sacred 217
Sarkon-Zip 560
scale, scaling 187, 353, 370, 398, 401,
405, 406, 408, 479
schematism (Kant) 107, 134
schismogenesis 330
schizoanalysis 263-64, 268, 275, 303,
317, 321-22, 341, 437, 442
and capital 264-15
schizophrenia 268, 315, 342, 413,
477, 550
and acephalization 397
and capitalism 305
neuroticization of 305
science fiction 347
and hype 384
science, scientificity 98, 585
and AI 326
as antidelirial 298
modernist science and complexity 393
qabbala as 592
security 311-22, 338, 349, 351, 353,
354, 359, 380, 389, 393, 396-17,
403, 404, 408, 415, 429, 436,
442, 455-17, 488, 542, 564
and Oedipus 428
and organic death 343
and psychiatry 308
immuno- 386
in cybernetics 298
organic 332
Turing Security 348
segmentarity, segmentarisation 404,
408, 484, 515-16, 518, 520-21
in State mathematics 513

self-organization 330
  in addiction 336
semiotics
  and delirium 585
  and qabbala 603
sensation
  in Kant 369
serial killers 260
set theory 273, 521
sex 259, 342
  bacterial 374, 442, 458
  crypt- 555
  decoded 424
  intergalactic 374
  meiotic 468
sexuality
  in Schopenhauer 160
shamanism 210, 218, 331, 344, 418,
      540, 631
  and oedipalism 429
  epidemic 419
shit
  and money 432
shoggoths 627
sickness 221
signifier 277
singularity 317, 326, 338, 354, 441,
      443
  planetary technocapital 338
sister 95-16, 102
skin 328, 332, 343
  policed 333
slavery
  and labour 61
smurfs 633
snakes 461, 462, 469, 482, 485, 536,
      539
  icthyophidian tendencies in
      culture 501

socialism 77, 280, 340, 352, 354, 377
social necessity 302
socius 302, 304
  enemy of schizoanalysis 341
software 451
solar anus 254
solar economy (Bataille) 245, 393
sophism 241
space, spatialisation, spatiality 192,
      354, 402, 473-74
  and commerce 447
  jungle- 408
  K- 354
  limited conception of in human
      cultural system 358
speed 344, 348, 365, 420, 509, 632
Sphinx 424, 426, 427, 428, 429
spirit 175, 176
stars 109, 119
  in Hegel 106
State 507, 535
  Greek 539
stranger 95
strata, stratification, stratocapture
      187, 263, 393, 414, 462-23, 510-
      21, 515, 531, 535
  and graphematics 110
  and reading 191
  numerical 510-21
  'stratophysical difference' 110
subjectivity
  dissolution of 403
sublimation 464
sublime 137, 406
  in Kant 133, 135, 150
suicide 189, 218, 392
  and BwO 268
  and destratification (*A Thousand
      Plateaus*) 281

capital as social suicide machine
    265
  Kleist's 127
  Nazism and 278
Sumatra 573
sun 481
surplus 533
surplus value
  of code 378, 519, 520
  of flux 430
swarm 304
Synthanatos 326
synthesis 60
  a priori (Kant) 74
  in Deleuze 321
  inhibited 63
  machinic 442
  transcendental, in Kant 67
system
  materialist sense of 413
syzygy, syzygetic 503, 504, 597, 599

T

taboo 418
  and monotheism 423
  and shamanism 418
technics 293
  and nature 294
technophobia
  as K-positive factor 407
templexity 615, 616
temporalization 452
Terminator 422
Terminator 2: Judgment Day 407
territorialization 325
thanatos 330, 331, 342, 467
theopolitics 299

theory
  and practice 295
theosophy 549
thing in itself 209
  in Nietzsche 210
third world 59
tics, ticks, tic-systems 494, 502, 563,
    564-15, 607, 616, 621
time 357, 394, 399, 403, 615, 616
  AI engineering of 450
  and arithmetic 615
  and capitalism 626
  and death 369
  and modernity 351
  and number 503
  and popular numeracy 508
  and schizophrenia 311
  and the unconscious 326
  -compression 408
  Nma time-ritual 576
  produces itself 358
  serial and parallel 370
time-travel 318, 534, 540
  and fiction 553
  and schizophrenia 311
  and writing (Burroughs) 411
tragedy 166, 258
transcendence
  and immanence 300
transcendental 273
transfinite 522, 524, 562
transgression 217, 257, 258
trauma 333, 334, 336, 338, 342, 344,
    497, 498, 528
  geotrauma (Barker) 496-20
  in Freud 333
  planetary 335
truth

and unity 367
turbulence 211
turing cops 450
twins, twinning 471, 478, 482-23,
532, 550, 612

U

unconscious 191, 322, 465, 634
and death 269
and socius 302
auto-production of 296
energetic 286
in Kant 152
in Nietzsche 162
Freudian 184
impersonal 302, 322
machinic 297, 322, 324, 326, 344,
414, 583
terrestrial machinic 583
transcendental 321
unity 366, 559, 601
universality
and ideality, in Kant 72
unknowing 258
unknown 178, 208, 222-23, 301
and quantity 338
Socrates on 241

V

vampires, vampirism 267, 387, 399,
631
Lesbovampiric Contagion-Libido
554
ovulocyclic lunar-haemoglobal
ferro-vampirism 542
Vault of Murmurs 579

Vietnam 312, 411, 425, 426
violence 140
and sublime, in Kant 134
military and judicial 250
virtual reality, VR 354, 355, 437, 438
virtual, virtuality
and actual 317, 358, 413, 443
and history 452
and machinic desire 327
virus 334, 338, 373, 378, 383-390
abstract, produced by Gödel
numbering 519
capital as 338
K-virus 409
and Kurtz 415
'virus anglo-americaine' 377
voice 502, 621
voodoo 344, 373-74, 395, 398, 406,
442, 455
vowels 482
Vukorri Cryptoliths 608

W

war 249-23, 258, 384, 387, 424,
436-17
and simulation 454
capitalist 276, 281
in Bataille 250
rationalisation of 252
Socrates on 250
Vietnam 312
World War I 275, 281
World War II 281
WWI as capitalist war (Deleuze
and Guattari) 275
war machine 278, 482, 594

and problems 509
  numerical culture as 509
welfare capitalism 59
werewolves 100, 179, 420
whole
  and parts 413
wild 90, 186
will 284
  in Kant 154
  in Schopenhauer 154, 155
will to power 298
wisdom 212
witchcraft, Dibboma 573
wolves 225, 416, 469
woman
  and matter, in Schopenhauer 160
  Schopenhauer on 158
  constitution of 424
women 285, 631
  and patriarchal capital 72
  female body and territorial soma
      424
  Freud's patients 168
work 129, 286, 446
  as resistance to death (Bataille)
      255

and digitization 367
and place-value 368
as time-in-itself 398
cyberpositive and cybernegative
    usage 329
intensive 370
nine as 503
zombies 269, 364, 414, 548, 557
zygonomy, novazygonomy, zygosys-
    tem 484, 503-104, 516, 599
diplozygotic spiral 504

X

XY-Malfunctional instamatic Crisis-
    dynamics 542

Z

zero 208, 214, 217, 219, 222, 227,
    250, 266, 268, 270, 275, 304,
    325, 328, 329, 347, 353, 357,
    366, 369, 371, 388, 404